THE WORKS
AND CORRESPONDENCE OF
DAVID RICARDO

VOLUME IX

PLAN OF THE EDITION

THE WORKS

AND CORRESPONDENCE OF

David Ricardo

Edited by Piero Sraffa

with the Collaboration of M. H. Dobb

VOLUME IX

Letters

July 1821–1823

LIBERTY FUND

INDIANAPOLIS

First published by Cambridge University Press in 1951.
© 1951, 1952, 1955, 1973 by the Royal Economic Society
Typographical design © 2004 by Liberty Fund, Inc.

This edition of *The Works and Correspondence of David Ricardo* is published by Liberty Fund, Inc., under license from the Royal Economic Society.

10 09 08 07 06 05 04 P 5 4 3 2 1

Library of Congress Cataloging-in-Publication Data

Ricardo, David, 1772–1823.
[Works. 2004]
The works and correspondence of David Ricardo / edited
by Piero Sraffa; with the collaboration of M. H. Dobb.
p.   cm.
Originally published: Cambridge: At the University Press
for the Royal Economic Society, 1951–1973.
Includes bibliographical references and index.
Contents: v. 1. On the principles of political economy and taxation—
ISBN 0-86597-965-0 (pbk.: alk. paper)
1. Economics.   2. Taxation.   I. Sraffa, Piero.
II. Dobb, M. H.   III. Title.

HB161.R4812 2004
330.15′13′092—dc21   2002016222
ISBN 0-86597-973-1 (vol. 9: pbk.: alk. paper)
ISBN 0-86597-976-6 (set: pbk.: alk. paper)

Liberty Fund, Inc.
8335 Allison Pointe Trail, Suite 300
Indianapolis, IN 46250-1684

Text and cover design by Erin Kirk New, Watkinsville, Georgia
Typography by Impressions Book and Journal Services, Inc.,
Madison, Wisconsin
Printed and bound by Edwards Brothers, Inc., Ann Arbor, Michigan

CONTENTS OF VOLUME IX

PLATES

CALENDARS for 1821 (July–Dec.), 1822, 1823

1821

	JULY	AUG.	SEPT.	OCT.	NOV.	DEC.
S	1 8 15 22 29	- 5 12 19 26	- 2 9 16 23 30	- 7 14 21 28	- 4 11 18 25	- 2 9 16 23 30
M	2 9 16 23 30	- 6 13 20 27	- 3 10 17 24	1 8 15 22 29	- 5 12 19 26	- 3 10 17 24 31
Tu	3 10 17 24 31	- 7 14 21 28	- 4 11 18 25	2 9 16 23 30	- 6 13 20 27	- 4 11 18 25
W	4 11 18 25	1 8 15 22 29	- 5 12 19 26	3 10 17 24 31	- 7 14 21 28	- 5 12 19 26
Th	5 12 19 26	2 9 16 23 30	- 6 13 20 27	4 11 18 25	- 1 8 15 22 29	- 6 13 20 27
F	6 13 20 27	3 10 17 24 31	- 7 14 21 28	- 5 12 19 26	- 2 9 16 23 30	- 7 14 21 28
S	7 14 21 28	- 4 11 18 25	- 1 8 15 22 29	- 6 13 20 27	- 3 10 17 24	- 1 8 15 22 29

1822

	JAN.	FEB.	MAR.	APRIL	MAY	JUNE
S	- 6 13 20 27	- 3 10 17 24	- 3 10 17 24 31	- 7 14 21 28	- 5 12 19 26	- 2 9 16 23 30
M	- 7 14 21 28	- 4 11 18 25	- 4 11 18 25	1 8 15 22 29	- 6 13 20 27	- 3 10 17 24
Tu	1 8 15 22 29	- 5 12 19 26	- 5 12 19 26	2 9 16 23 30	- 7 14 21 28	- 4 11 18 25
W	2 9 16 23 30	- 6 13 20 27	- 6 13 20 27	3 10 17 24	1 8 15 22 29	- 5 12 19 26
Th	3 10 17 24 31	- 7 14 21 28	- 7 14 21 28	4 11 18 25	2 9 16 23 30	- 6 13 20 27
F	4 11 18 25	1 8 15 22	1 8 15 22 29	5 12 19 26	3 10 17 24 31	- 7 14 21 28
S	5 12 19 26	2 9 16 23	2 9 16 23 30	6 13 20 27	4 11 18 25	1 8 15 22 29

	JULY	AUG.	SEPT.	OCT.	NOV.	DEC.
S	- 7 14 21 28	- 4 11 18 25	1 8 15 22 29	- 6 13 20 27	- 3 10 17 24	1 8 15 22 29
M	1 8 15 22 29	- 5 12 19 26	2 9 16 23 30	- 7 14 21 28	- 4 11 18 25	2 9 16 23 30
Tu	2 9 16 23 30	- 6 13 20 27	3 10 17 24	1 8 15 22 29	- 5 12 19 26	3 10 17 24 31
W	3 10 17 24 31	- 7 14 21 28	4 11 18 25	2 9 16 23 30	- 6 13 20 27	4 11 18 25
Th	4 11 18 25	1 8 15 22 29	5 12 19 26	3 10 17 24 31	- 7 14 21 28	5 12 19 26
F	5 12 19 26	2 9 16 23 30	6 13 20 27	4 11 18 25	1 8 15 22 29	6 13 20 27
S	6 13 20 27	3 10 17 24 31	7 14 21 28	5 12 19 26	2 9 16 23 30	7 14 21 28

1823

	JAN.	FEB.	MAR.	APRIL	MAY	JUNE
S	- 5 12 19 26	- 2 9 16 23	- 2 9 16 23 30	- 6 13 20 27	- 4 11 18 25	1 8 15 22 29
M	- 6 13 20 27	- 3 10 17 24	- 3 10 17 24 31	- 7 14 21 28	- 5 12 19 26	2 9 16 23 30
Tu	- 7 14 21 28	- 4 11 18 25	- 4 11 18 25	1 8 15 22 29	- 6 13 20 27	3 10 17 24
W	1 8 15 22 29	- 5 12 19 26	- 5 12 19 26	2 9 16 23 30	- 7 14 21 28	4 11 18 25
Th	2 9 16 23 30	- 6 13 20 27	- 6 13 20 27	3 10 17 24	1 8 15 22 29	5 12 19 26
F	3 10 17 24 31	- 7 14 21 28	- 7 14 21 28	4 11 18 25	2 9 16 23 30	6 13 20 27
S	4 11 18 25	1 8 15 22	1 8 15 22 29	5 12 19 26	3 10 17 24 31	7 14 21 28

	JULY	AUG.	SEPT.	OCT.	NOV.	DEC.
S	- 6 13 20 27	- 3 10 17 24 31	- 7 14 21 28	- 5 12 19 26	- 2 9 16 23 30	- 7 14 21 28
M	- 7 14 21 28	- 4 11 18 25	1 8 15 22 29	- 6 13 20 27	- 3 10 17 24	1 8 15 22 29
Tu	1 8 15 22 29	- 5 12 19 26	2 9 16 23 30	- 7 14 21 28	- 4 11 18 25	2 9 16 23 30
W	2 9 16 23 30	- 6 13 20 27	3 10 17 24	1 8 15 22 29	- 5 12 19 26	3 10 17 24 31
Th	3 10 17 24 31	- 7 14 21 28	4 11 18 25	2 9 16 23 30	- 6 13 20 27	4 11 18 25
F	4 11 18 25	1 8 15 22 29	5 12 19 26	3 10 17 24 31	- 7 14 21 28	5 12 19 26
S	5 12 19 26	2 9 16 23 30	6 13 20 27	4 11 18 25	1 8 15 22 29	6 13 20 27

ABBREVIATIONS

R.P.	Ricardo Papers (consisting of letters received by Ricardo, and other of his papers, in the possession of Mr Frank Ricardo).
Mill-Ricardo papers	The letters and papers of Ricardo that belonged to James Mill, and which passed into the possession of the Cairnes family and Mr C. K. Mill.
'at Albury'	Papers in the possession of Mr Robert Malthus, of The Cottage, Albury, Surrey.

The following abbreviations are used by Malthus, Mill and Bentham, respectively, in their letters:

E.I. Coll., for East India College, Haileybury.
E.I. House, for East India House, London.
Q.S.P., for Queen Square Place, Westminster.

David Ricardo c.1821
from the painting by Thomas Phillips, R.A.
Emery Walker Ltd. phot.

437. RICARDO TO TROWER [1]
[Reply to 435.—Answered by 445]

Gatcomb Park Minchinhampton
4 July 1821

My Dear Trower

Before I left London I gave directions to Mr. Mitchell, at the Vote Office, to send you a copy of the printed minutes of Evidence of the Agricultural Committee as soon as it should be obtainable, which I have no doubt he will do. I hope that you are satisfied with a great part of the Report, there are some absurdities and contradictions in it, but considering how the committee was formed, and the opposition which was given to sound principles by the landed gentlemen, I think it on the whole creditable to the Committee.

I am glad that you think I have vindicated my book against Malthus's attacks, in my notes:—if I have not, it is owing to my weakness, and not to his strength, for I am quite sure that his book abounds with inconsistencies and contradictions. I am not surprised that you should not agree with me in my definition of exchangeable value, but when you say that "the labour expended upon a commodity is the measure by which the accuracy of its exchangeable value is ascertained and constantly[2] regulated" you admit all I contend for. I do not, I think, say that the labour expended on a commodity is a measure of its exchangeable value, but of its positive value. I then add that exchangeable value is regu-

---

[1] Addressed: 'Hutches Trower Esq.ʳ / Unsted Wood / Godalming / Surry'.

MS at University College, London.—*Letters to Trower,* XLVII.

[2] Trower had said 'eventually'.

lated by positive value, and therefore is regulated by the quantity of labour expended.

You say if there were no exchange of commodities they could have no value, and I agree with you, if you mean exchangeable value, but if I am obliged to devote one month's labour to make me a coat, and only one weeks labour to make a hat, although I should never exchange either of them, the coat would be four times the value of the hat; and if a robber were to break into my house and take part of my property, I would rather that he took 3 hats than one coat. It is in the early stages of society, when few exchanges are made, that the value of commodities is[1] most peculiarly estimated by the quantity of labour necessary to produce them, as stated by Adam Smith.

I confess I do not rightly understand what meaning you attach to the words "exchangeable value," when you say that "the labour which a commodity can command is what actually constitutes its exchangeable value." A yard of superfine cloth we will suppose can command a month's labour of one man, but in the course of a year, from some cause, it commands only a fortnight's labour of one man, you are bound to say that the exchangeable value of cloth has fallen one half. You are bound to say this whether the cloth be produced with a great deal less labour in consequence of the discovery of improved machinery, or the food and some of the other necessaries of the labourer be produced with so much difficulty that wages rise and therefore labour rises as compared with cloth and many other things. You would say then cloth has fallen one half in exchangeable value although it should exchange for precisely the same quantity of gold, silver, iron, lead, hats, tea, sugar and a thousand other things and you would use precisely the same language if by the

---

[1] 'the value of commodities is' replaces 'the commodities are'.

discovery of machinery cloth was produced with great additional facility and consequently would exchange for only one
half the same quantity of gold, silver, iron, lead, hats, tea,
sugar and a thousand other things. Now the difference
between you and me is this: in the latter case I should say
with you that cloth had fallen to half its former exchangeable
value and my proof would be that it would exchange for
only half the former quantity of labour and of *all other things,*
but in the other case I should say cloth has not altered in
exchangeable value because it will exchange for precisely the
same quantity of all other things. It is true it will exchange
for more labour, and why? because labour has fallen in
exchangeable value, and the proof is it will exchange for only
half the quantity of gold, silver, lead, iron and all other things,
excepting perhaps corn and some other necessaries, which
have also fallen in value. I cannot approve of your saying
that cloth has fallen in exchangeable value merely because it
will exchange for less labour, no more than I can approve of
the same terms being applied to the fact of its exchanging for
less salt, or for less sugar. Surely such a use of the words
exchangeable value tends to perplex and mislead. Labour
rising in value is one thing, commodities falling in value is
another, but once admit your language and these 2 different
things are confounded. It would be quite accurate to say in
both cases that cloth had fallen in exchangeable value estimated in labour, as it would be to say it had fallen in value
estimated in salt if such should be the fact, but then the
medium by which you measure exchangeable value is named
and you only express a fact—this is very different however
from saying that cloth has fallen in exchangeable value without mentioning the medium in which its alteration in value
is specifically confined.

In what I have said respecting natural and market price

I have obviated your objections in regard to the difference between cost and value. Cost is an ambiguous word and sometimes includes the profit of stock, and sometimes excludes it. In the way you use it, and I think properly use it, there is no ambiguity, you include in it the profits of stock.

I cannot but flatter myself with the hopes of a continuance of peace in Europe—the agitations which at present exist will I think subside, and we shall witness a general course of prosperity. When our purses are again filled indeed, we may as usual become quarrelsome, but I hope nations are becoming wiser, and are every day more convinced that the prosperity of one country is not promoted by the distress of another— that restrictions on commerce are not favorable to wealth, and that the[1] particular welfare of each country, as well as the general welfare of all, is best encouraged by unbounded freedom of trade, and the establishment of the most liberal policy. I must do our ministers the justice to say that I believe they view these questions in their true light and would make great improvements in our commercial code if they were not thwarted and opposed by the narrow and selfish policy of the particular interests which are so powerfully exerted in the H. of Commons to check improvement and support monopolies.—

Mrs. Ricardo unites with me in best regards to Mrs. Trower and yourself.

Ever Truly Y^rs
DAVID RICARDO

[1] 'individual' is del. here.

438. MILL TO RICARDO [1]
[*Answered by* 441]

East India House July 5th 1821

My dear Sir

I am extremely sorry to announce to you what respecting myself is very bad news; my inability to visit you along
with Mr. Tooke. It would have been difficult to arrange
matters in this office in such a manner as to get away for at
least another week; but I am called upon in another way,
which fixes the inability upon other grounds. I am bound
to Napier, for an article "Liberty of the Press", for his
Encyclopedia. This I expected not to have any demand upon
me for, during several months, because the N.? to which
"Jurisprudence" belongs is not yet published, and I knew
"Liberty of the Press" could only be included in the next.
I had, however, a letter from Napier the other day in which
he tells me that the present N.? has only been delayed on
account of Dugald Stewart's Preliminary Dissertation; that
in the mean time he has begun the printing of the subsequent
N.?; that considerable progress has been made in it, and that
my article will be wanted in a month. It would be impossible
for me to have it ready in a month, if I had nothing else to do.
But I cannot think of an excursion of pleasure, when I should
be interrupting so many people by my delay. I must get
relieved from my duties here, as quickly as possible, and bury
myself at Marlow, [2] where my family now are, till I have
completed my task. It will be of no small importance to put
the subject upon a good foundation, and I am anxious to
treat it as well as I am able. I am still not without hopes of
stealing a week in which I can make a run down to you; but
it must be somewhat late in the season. We shall hear from
one another in the mean time, and may perhaps find a time

[1] MS in *R.P.*   [2] Great Marlow, Bucks.

that will be convenient for both. I hope the Ladies will not forget me in the mean time. My hopes of pleasure from their society, in the old scenes and occupations, were such that I do not easily submit even to postpone the realizing of them.[1]

The news of the death of Bonaparte will have reached you. The only effect it will have here is that of relieving us from some expense. In France it will have some portion of the effect which the death of the Pretender has had here: to make the Government pursue despotism with somewhat less fear, and more effrontery.

I hear various accounts about the "august ceremony".[2] There are rumours about the King's head. The agitating of the question about the queen, too, is exciting apprehension, more, I am persuaded, than there is any ground for. In fact the people seem to understand the nature of the "imposing spectacle"; and in spite of the Marquess and Nicky Van,[3] can see nothing in it but a subject of laughter and contempt. The thing might be endured, because it is old; but to attempt in the present day to puff it up into a matter of importance, and instead of performing it with the utmost simplicity, as a thing the day for which had gone by, to make it a draw for the public money, is only to compel people to consider how little it accords with the spirit of the times, how unworthy it is of the people of a civilised age, and how much more properly it would have been extinguished with the

---

[1] On 10 July 1821 Mill, from the East India House, wrote to Napier: 'I have been hard at work upon the article Liberty of the Press, and for that purpose suspended the printing of my book on Political Economy...I have refused to pay my annual visit to Ricardo, that I may work for you, so that you must not blame me if there is a little delay.' (See *Selections from the Correspondence of M. Napier,* p. 27; Bain, *James Mill,* p. 194.)

[2] The coronation of George IV, on 19 July 1821.

[3] The Marquess of Londonderry (Lord Castlereagh) and Nicholas Vansittart.

barbarous ages which gave it birth. The folly of it, by the 5 July 1821
ostentation of the present performance, will become so
apparent, as probably to prevent a repetition. The effect of
it seems likely to be, according to all I see and hear, to render
monarchy more contemptible; by making it appear the
principal piece of a harliquinade.

I hope I shall hear from you soon, and am as at all times,

Most truly Yours

J. MILL

439. RICARDO TO McCULLOCH [1]
[*Answered by* 474]

Gatcomb Park 8 July 1821

My Dear Sir

At Mr. Mushet's request I write these 2 lines to say that 8 July 1821
he is busily employed in correcting his tables so as to render
them correct in principle. You may expect he says to receive
a copy of his New Edition in a fortnight or 3 weeks.— [2]

Your observations on the Report of the Agricultural
Committee are excellent. [3] I am much flattered by knowing
that I fought hard against the principle of the first passage
which you quote, [4] but without success. Mr. Huskisson did

---

[1] Addressed: 'J. R. M'Culloch / Buccleugh Place / Edinburgh'.
   MS in British Museum.—*Letters to M*c*Culloch,* XXVII.
[2] It was this ed. that M*c*Culloch reviewed; see above, VIII, 392.
[3] 'Report of the Agricultural Committee', leading article in the *Scotsman,* 30 June 1821.
[4] In this passage the Committee suggest for the consideration of Parliament 'whether a trade in corn, constantly open to all nations of the world, and subject

only to such a fixed duty as might *compensate to the grower the loss of that encouragement which he received during the late war from the obstacles thrown in the way of free importation,* and thereby protect the capitals now vested in agriculture from an unequal competition in the home market,—is not, as a permanent system, preferable to that state of law by which the corn trade is now regulated. It would be indispensable, for the just execution of

not himself quite agree with its correctness but the difference between him and me is this, he would uphold agriculture permanently up to its present height—I would reduce it gradually to the level at which it would have been if the trade had been free, for I should call the trade free if wheat was subject to a permanent duty of 8/- p^r q^r to countervail the peculiar taxes to which Land is subject. You have not noticed the passage in Page 16 beginning with "Assuming, therefore," nor in page 17—"They can however have no difficulty in stating" which are both very objectionable. There is a great inconsistency in Page 11 with the former part of the Report. We say "Taking therefore as the basis" &c^a, here we say that steady prices are advantageous to the landlord, and we have before said that steady prices can only be obtained by permitting them to be low, and on a level with the prices of other countries—the conclusion then is that low prices are beneficial to landlords—to this I cannot agree—but I have not time now to write another word.

Y^{rs} truly

DAVID RICARDO

this principle, that such duty should be calculated fairly to countervail the difference of expense, including the ordinary rate of profit, at which corn, in the present state of this country, can be grown and brought to market within the United Kingdom, compared with the expense, including also the ordinary rate of profit, of producing it in any of those countries from whence our principal supplies of foreign corn have usually been drawn, joined to the ordinary charges of conveying it from thence to our markets.' ('Report from Committee on the Agriculture of the U.K.,' 1821, p. 16.)—*Scotsman's* italics.

440. MALTHUS TO RICARDO [1]
[Answered by 442]

St Catherine's July [7th, 1821] [2]

My dear Ricardo

Your letter [3] did not reach me so soon as it ought, from the irregularity of the post or the servants, here, where the family is but just settled.

7 July 1821

Mrs. Malthus and I are much obliged to you for your very kind invitation which it would give us great pleasure to accept, if we could; but having come here later than we intended, and being obliged to return the 24th or 25th of this month we shall not be permitted still further to shorten our visit to the Eckersalls, as I hinted to you in Town. We must therefore defer our visit to Gatcomb till a better opportunity.

Pray has Maculloch specifically objected to your new doctrine relating to Machinery? From the manner in which you proposed the question to the Club I conclude he has. [4] I thought he would at all events be much disappointed to see your new chapter, after having written the article on machinery in the last Edinburgh. [5]

I fear I must have expressed myself very clumsily throughout the whole of my long final chapter in my last work, [6] as both in your notes and conversation you appear quite to have

---

[1] Addressed: 'D. Ricardo Esqr MP. / Gatcomb / Minchinhampton / Glostershire'. Postmark, Bath 7 July 1821.

MS in *R.P.*

[2] Omitted in MS.

[3] Ricardo's letter is wanting.

[4] At the meeting of the Political Economy Club on 25 June (when Malthus's question 'Can there be a Glut of commodities?' was discussed) Ricardo had proposed for consideration at the next meeting the query 'Whether Machinery has a tendency to diminish the demand for labour?' Owing to Ricardo's absence from the next two meetings, the discussion was deferred till 4 Feb. 1822. (See *Political Economy Club, Minutes of Proceedings, 1821–1881*, pp. 43–6.)

[5] See above, VIII, 366, n. 2.

[6] Ch. VII, 'On the Immediate Causes of the Progress of Wealth.'

misunderstood me. You constantly say that it is not a question about the motives to produce. Now I have certainly intended to make it almost entirely a question about motives. We see in almost every part of the world vast powers of production which are not put into action, and I explain this phenomenon by saying that from the want of a proper distribution of the actual produce adequate motives are not furnished to continued production. By inquiring into the immediate causes of the progress of wealth I clearly mean to inquire mainly into motives. I dont at all wish to deny that some persons or others are entitled to consume all that is produced; but the grand question is whether it is distributed in such a manner between the different parties concerned as to occasion the most effective demand for future produce: and I distinctly maintain that an attempt to accumulate very rapidly which necessarily implies a considerable diminution of unproductive consumption, by greatly impairing the usual motives to production must prematurely check the progress of wealth. This surely is the great *practical* question, and not whether we ought to call the sort of stagnation which would be thus occasioned a glut. That I hold to be a matter of very subordinate importance.

But if it be true that an attempt to accumulate very rapidly will occasion such a division between labour and profits as almost to destroy both the motive and the power of future accumulation and consequently the power of maintaining and employing an increasing population, must it not be acknowledged that such an attempt to accumulate, or that saving too much, may be really prejudicial to a country. Do look at my chapter again after this explanation.

With regard to the question you put to me at the club, I should distinctly answer that under all common circumstances, if an increased power of production be not accompanied by

an increase of *unproductive* expenditure, it will inevitably 7 July 1821
lower profits and throw labourers out of employment. But
on the other hand if it be accompanied by a proper proportion of *unproductive* expenditure it will certainly raise both
profits and wages and greatly advance the wealth of the
country. On the former supposition I should expect that the
result would be great indolence among the labouring classes,
and a diminished instead of increased gross produce. This
indolence would contribute to the low profits.

Mrs. M. joins with me in kind regards to Mrs. Ricardo,
and all your pleasant family circle.

We are in a very pretty and Romantic valley, and should
enjoy it much if the weather were finer.

Ever truly Yours
T R MALTHUS

441. RICARDO TO MILL [1]
[*Reply to 438.—Answered by* 448]

Gatcomb Park
9 July 1821

My Dear Sir

Your letter, in which you announce to us that you must 9 July 1821
give up your intended visit to Gatcomb, has disappointed us
all, as we had made sure of seeing you either this or the
following month. We cannot exactly see the cogency of the
reasons which you give for absenting yourself. We do not
think that the Article on the Liberty of the Press should not
be written, but think so well of our Glostershire air, that we
are of opinion it would not have suffered although you had
worked upon it at Gatcomb instead of Marlow. We would
have allowed you an ample measure of time for this important

---

[1] MS in Mill-Ricardo papers.

duty, and yet enough would have remained to permit our enjoying the country together. I do not know how you can reconcile it to your conscience, to induce me to make walks, and otherwise improve my grounds, and then desert me in the way you do. I beg that you will take all these matters into your serious consideration, and make me such amends as may be in your power, by presenting yourself at Gatcomb at the very earliest moment that your engagements will permit.

Bonaparte was I think too distant from France, and his confinement too certain, to have produced much influence on the councils of that country; his death therefore will add nothing to the chance of the progress of despotism, but may rather have a beneficial influence on the government, as his son may be considered in the light of a Pretender to the crown, of whom the disaffected may make more use than they could of his incarcerated father.

I see by Denman's speech[1] that he does not attach so little importance to the "August ceremony" as you do. He says I think a great deal too much of the importance of adhering to old customs. According to him Institutions are not to be preserved or given up as they may be really beneficial or otherwise, but we must enquire what have been their date, and how long they have had the sanction of custom and usage, and in proportion to their antiquity they are entitled to our respect and veneration. I think there is some respect due to old customs; as much as to induce one to preserve them until their inutility is most manifest, but that once established, I can see no reason for adhering to them merely because they were venerable in the eyes of our fathers.—

[1] A speech before the Privy Council on 6 July 1821 in support of the Queen's claim to be crowned.

9 July 1821

I have had a letter from M Culloch[1] in which he appears to me to allow that the effect of the use of machinery may be to diminish the annual gross produce of the country—this I conceive is giving up the question, for with a diminished gross produce, there must be less ability to employ labour.—

Malthus is at Bath, and I had hopes of seeing him here, but the time for his absence from London is necessarily so limited, that he cannot afford the time necessary to pay me a visit. I have received a long letter from him[2] in which he says I have misunderstood his book, as the principal object of his enquiry was as to the motives for producing, and to account why with such vast powers of production adequate motives were not afforded to produce. I think he has not understood himself, for what are all his attacks on Say and on me, surely not because we have said that in all cases there would be motives sufficient to push production to its utmost extent, but because we have said, that, when produced, commodities would always find a market, and some consumers would be found for them who had an equivalent to give for them.

The country here is looking very beautiful—our hay-making is now in full vigor, and no superabundance of agricultural labour in the market. The barley and oats I am told do not look well, but the wheat is promising. The manufacturers have full employment for their men; Osman told me yesterday that Mr. Hicks was employing his men extra hours, and of course giving them extra pay. If the labouring class, in Agriculture, and Manufactures, are doing well, we must console ourselves for the misfortunes of land-lords and tenants—they form but a small proportion of the whole population, and it is no small comfort to reflect that the losses they sustain are more than made up by the prosperity of other capitalists.

---

[1] Letter 434.　　　　　[2] Letter 440.

9 July 1821   Mr. and Mrs. Clutterbuck are staying with us. Mrs. Clutterbuck is in better health, and stronger, than I have known her for some time. Osman and his wife only got home on wednesday. On friday they came here, and we have insisted on detaining them here the whole of this week. They and all the rest of our circle desire to be kindly remembered to you.

Ever Y.^{rs}

DAVID RICARDO

442. RICARDO TO MALTHUS [1]
[*Reply to* 440.—*Answered by* 443]

Gatcomb Park Minchinhampton
9 July 1821

My Dear Malthus

9 July 1821   I am sorry that you will not spare me a few days before you return to London. Pray reconsider your determination, and if you can alter it, do. On Saturday I expect Mr. Tooke —it is a long time since he fixed on that day to come to me, and I am sure the pleasure of his visit will be much increased, both to him and to me, if you also formed one of our party.

M Culloch has specifically, and strongly, objected to my chapter on Machinery—he thinks I have ruined my book by admitting it, and have done a serious injury to the science, both by the opinions which I avow, and by the manner I have avowed them. Two or three letters have passed between us on this subject;—in his last, he appears to me to acknowledge that the effect of the use of machinery may be to diminish the annual quantity and value of gross produce. In yielding this, he gives up the question, for it is impossible

---

[1] Addressed: 'The Revd T. R. Malthus / —Eckersell's Esqre / St. Catherine's / Bath'. Franked by Ricardo 'July Ten 1821'.   MS in the possession of Dr Bonar to whom it was given by Col. Malthus.—*Letters to Malthus*, LXXVI.

to contend that with a diminished quantity of gross produce there would be the same means of employing labour. The truth of my propositions on this subject appear to me absolutely demonstrable.

M'Culloch is lamenting over the departure from my plan of currency, and means to make it the subject of an article in the Edin. Review, as he has already done in the Scotsman.[1] I very much regret that in the great change we have made, from an unregulated currency, to one regulated by a fixed standard, we had not more able men to manage it than the present Bank Directors. If their object had been to make the revulsion as oppressive as possible, they could not have pursued measures more calculated to make it so than those which they have actually pursued. Almost the whole of the pressure has arisen from the increased value which their operations have given to the standard itself. They are indeed a very ignorant set.

You are right in supposing that I have understood you in your book not to profess to enquire into the motives for producing, but into the effects which would result from abundant production. You say in your letter "We see in almost every part of the world vast powers of production which are not put into action and I explain this phenomenon by saying that from the want of the proper distribution of the actual produce adequate motives are not furnished to continued production." If this had been what I conceived you to have said I should not have a word to say against you, but I have rather understood you to say that vast powers of production are put into action and the result is unfavourable to the interests of mankind, and you have suggested as a remedy either that less should be produced, or more should be unproductively consumed. If you had said, "after arriving

---

[1] See above, VIII, 378, n. 5 and 392, n. 2.

at a certain limit there will in the actual circumstances be no use to try to produce more—the end cannot be accomplished, and if it could instead of more less would belong to the class which provided the capital", I should have agreed with you —yet in that case I should say the real cause of this faulty distribution would be to be found in the inadequate quantity of labour in the market, and would be effectually cured by an additional supply of it. But I say with you, there could be no adequate motive to push production to this length, and therefore it would never go so far. I do not know whether I am correct in my observation, that "I say so with you," for you often appear to me to contend not only that production can go on so far without an adequate motive, but that it actually has done so lately, and that we are now suffering the consequences of it in stagnation of trade, in a want of employment for our labourers &c. &c., and the remedy you propose is an increase of consumption. It is against this latter doctrine that I protest and give my decided opposition. I acknowledge there may not be adequate motives for production, and therefore things will not be produced, but I cannot allow, first that with these inadequate motives commodities will be produced, and secondly that, if their production is attended with loss to the producer, it is for any other reason than because too great a proportion is given to the labourers employed. Increase their number, and the evil is remedied. Let the employer consume more himself, and there will be no diminution of demand for labour, but the pay of the labourer, which was before extravagantly high, will be reduced. You say in your letter "If an increased power of production be not accompanied by an increase of unproductive expenditure it will inevitably lower profits and throw labourers out of employment." In this proposition I do not wholly[1] agree.

---

[1] 'wholly' is ins.

9 July 1821

First I say it must be accompanied with an increase either of productive or of unproductive expenditure. If the labourer receives a large proportion of the produce as wages, all that he receives more than is sufficient to prompt him to the necessary exertions of his powers, is as much unproductive consumption as if it were consumed by his master, or by the state—there is no difference whatever. A master manufacturer might be so extravagant in his expenditure, or might pay so much in taxes, that his capital might be deteriorated for many years together—his situation would be the same, if, from his own will, or from the inadequacy of the population, he paid so much to his labourers as to leave himself without adequate profits, or without any profits whatever. From taxation he might not be able to escape, but from this last most unnecessary UNPRODUCTIVE[1] expenditure, he could, and would escape, for he could have the same quantity of labour, with less pay, if he only saved less;—his saving would be without an end and would therefore be absurd. You perceive then I fully admit more than you ask for—I say that under these circumstances without an increase of unproductive expenditure on the part of the masters, profits will fall; but I say this further, that even with an increased unproductive consumption and expenditure by the labouring classes profits will fall. Diminish this latter unproductive expenditure, and profits will again rise;—this may be done two ways, either by an increase of hands which will lower wages, and therefore the unproductive expenditure of the labouring class;—or by an increase of the unproductive expenditure of the employing class, which will also lower wages by reducing the demand for labour.[2]

---

[1] Underlined twice in MS.
[2] For a similar discussion of the effects of unproductive expenditure, see above, I, 150–1, especially the additions in ed. 3.

9 July 1821   I fear I have been guilty of needless repetition but I have really a great wish to shew you what the points are on which our difference really exists. I am glad to hear that you are in a pleasant country. Mrs. Ricardo, my sons, and daughters all unite with me in kind remembrances to Mrs. Malthus and yourself.

Ever Y^{rs}

DAVID RICARDO

443. MALTHUS TO RICARDO [1]
[*Reply to* 442.—*Answered by* 444]

St Catherine's Bath
July 16th 1821

My dear Ricardo,

16 July 1821   It would have given me, I assure you, very great pleasure to join your party while Mr. Tooke was with you, but we are expecting Mrs. Taunton [2] tomorrow to join the family circle here, and I should not be forgiven if I were to secede, particularly as we shall be returning to Town early in next week.

I thought Maculloch would be very much vexed at your chapter on machinery, coming so immediately, as it did, upon his review. I quite agree with you in the theory of your proposition, but practically I think that the cases are very rare in which for any length of time the gross produce is deminished by machinery. You have used one expression [3] which is liable to be taken fast hold of by the labouring classes; and perhaps you have not fully considered all the

[1] Addressed: 'D. Ricardo Esqr M.P. / Gatcomb Park / Minchin-hampton / Gloucestershire'.
  MS in *R.P.*
[2] Mrs. Malthus' sister.
[3] 'That the opinion entertained by the labouring class, that the employment of machinery is frequently detrimental to their interests, is not founded on prejudice and error, but is conformable to the correct principles of political economy.' (Above, I, 392.)

bearings of your concession on the other parts of your work. You have said for instance in your letter [to]¹ me that an increased power of production must be accompanied with an increase of productive or unproductive expenditure, which could not be the case if the gross produce were diminished. *I,* indeed, was alluding to a temporary *increase* of produce, and therefore the observation was perfectly just as applied to me. I only mention it to shew how the concession may bear unexpectedly on other opinions and expressions.

With regard to our present subject of discussion it seems as if we should never thoroughly understand each other, and I almost despair of being ever able to explain myself, if you could read the two first paragraphs of the first section of my last chapter, and yet "understand me to say that vast powers of production are put into action, and the result is unfavourable to the interests of mankind".

I expressly say that it is my object to shew what are the causes which call forth the powers of production; and if I recommend a certain proportion of unproductive consumption, it is obviously and expressly with the sole view of furnishing the necessary motive to the greatest continued production. And I think still that this certain proportion of unproductive consumption varying according to the fertility of the soil &c: is absolutely and indispensably necessary to call forth the resources of a country. Is it not almost a contradiction, to quote with approbation that passage of Adam Smith which says that the demand for food is limited by the narrow capacity of the human stomach, but that the demand for luxuries and conveniences has no limits, and yet to say that parsimony, or the saving of expenditure in luxuries and conveniences and increasing the production of necessaries cannot be unfavourable to wealth.

¹ Omitted in MS.

Surely I have no where said, as you seem to intimate, that people will continue to produce without a motive; because I expressly give as the reason for the scanty produce of the world, the want of sufficient motives to produce. Now among the motives to produce, one of the most essential certainly is that an adequate share of what is produced should belong to those who set all industry in motion. But you yourself allow that a great temporary saving, commencing when profits were sufficient to encourage it, might occasion such a division of the produce as would leave no motive to a further increase of production. And if a state of things in which for a time there is no motive to a further increase of production be not properly denominated a stagnation, I do not know what can be so called; particularly as this stagnation must inevitably throw the rising generation out of employment. We know from repeated experience that the money price of labour never falls till many workmen have been for some time out of work. And the question is, whether this stagnation of capital, and subsequent stagnation in the demand for labour arising from increased production without an adequate proportion of unproductive consumption on the part of the landlords and capitalists, could take place without prejudice to the country, without occasioning a less degree both of happiness and wealth than would have occurred if the unproductive consumption of the landlords and capitalists had been so proportioned to the natural surplus of the society as to have continued uninterrupted the motives to production, and prevented first an unnatural demand for labour, and then a necessary and sudden diminiution of such demand. But if this be so, how can it be said with truth that parsimony, though it may be prejudicial to the producers cannot be prejudicial to the state; or that an increase of unproductive consumption among landlords and capitalists may not sometimes be the proper remedy for a state of things in which the motives to production fail.

You yourself indeed say the same thing in your letter. In speaking of the low profits occasioned by excessive saving, you intimate that the great proportion of the produce awarded to the labourer may be remedied in two ways, either by the increase of hands, or by an increase of the unproductive expenditure of the employing class. Now the first remedy, to the extent you require we have not at our disposal. Consequently the second remedy or an increase of unproductive consumption on the part of the landlords and capitalists is the one which according to you we must resort to, to restore and continue the motives to production. But this conclusion which I think quite just, appears to me hardly consistent with the *strong protest* which you make in another part of your letter against an increase of consumption as a remedy to the stagnation of trade in this country. We may however consistently differ in the application of a principle in which we *agree;* for I think we may now be said to agree that a certain amount of unproductive expenditure on the part of those who have the means of setting industry in motion is necessary in order that they may be awarded a proper share of the produce; but you think that in the case of this country the evils we complain of do not in any degree arise from a partial approach to the kind of stagnation above described. On the propriety of applying our principles respecting profits to the case of this country I will not now enter into a discussion, but will only say that the symptoms appear to me exactly to resemble those which would arise from the sudden conversion of unproductive labour into productive, and the diminution of unproductive consumption; and that as a matter of opinion I am inclined to believe that if the Stockholders in their new situation saved less and spent more profits would be higher and the stagnation of trade diminished. But our question is now more about general principles; and if on general principles a certain proportion of unproductive consumption on the part of landlords and capitalists is absolutely necessary to maintain a fair rate of profits, surely it is a part of the theory of profits and demand which ought to receive a full discussion.

The unproductive consumption of the labouring classes themselves, beyond what is necessary, not only to their powers, but to their increase, is so far different from the unproductive consumption of their employers, as to occasion exactly the opposite effect on profits. Indeed, though it may fairly, in one sense, be called unproductive expenditure, it comes under that division of the whole produce which is destined to replace a capital, and not that which is destined for immediate consumption (according to Adam Smith).

It is justly to be lamented that the Bank directors have managed the matter of the currency so ill. This is shewn by the state of the exchanges. But besides the fall of prices and rise of money occasioned in this way I cannot help thinking that there is a further effect of the same kind both here and in America occasioned by the diminution of demand and relative excess of supply, and that more is attributed both to the paper and the Bank directors than belongs to them.

Pray remember me to Mr. Took. Mrs. M. joins with me in kind regards to Mrs. Ricardo and the family.

Ever truly Y^{rs}

T R MALTHUS

444. RICARDO TO MALTHUS [1]
[Reply to 443.—Answered by 455]

Gatcomb Park
21 July 1821

My Dear Malthus

I think that the concession which I have made will not
bear the construction you have put upon it. "An increased
power of production, must be accompanied with an increase
of productive or unproductive expenditure"[.] This is the
sentence on which you have remarked, and you say could
not be true if the gross produce were diminished. Certainly
not; but I have never said that with an increased power of
production the gross produce would be diminished—I have
never said that machinery enables you to get a greater
quantity of gross produce, my sole complaint against it is
that it sometimes [2] actually diminishes the gross produce.

With respect to the particular subject of discussion between us you seem to be surprised that I should understand
you to say in your book "that vast powers of production
are put into action, and the result is unfavorable to the interests of mankind." Have you not said so? Is it not your
objection to machinery that it often produces a quantity of
commodities for which there is no demand, and that it is the
glut which is the consequence of quantity which is unfavorable to the interests of mankind. Even as you state your proposition in your present letter, I have a right to conclude that
you see great evils in great powers of production, from the
quantity of commodities which will be the result, and the
low price to which they will fall. Saving, you would say,
would first lead to great production—then to low prices,

---

[1] Addressed: 'The Revd T. R. Malthus / —Eckersall's Esqre / St. Catherine's / Bath'. Franked by Ricardo 'July Twenty two 1821'.

MS at Albury.—*Letters to Malthus,* LXXVII.
[2] 'sometimes' is ins.

which would necessarily be followed by low profits. With very low profits the motives for saving would cease, and therefore the motives for increased production would also cease. Do you not then say that increased production is often attended with evil consequences to mankind, because it destroys the motives to industry, and to the keeping up of the increased production? Now in much of this I cannot agree with you. I indeed allow that the case is possible to conceive of saving being so universal that no profit will arise from the employment of capital, but then I contend that the specific reason is, because all that fund which should, and in ordinary cases, does, constitute profit, goes to wages, and immoderately swells that fund which is destined to the support of labour. The labourers are immoderately paid for their labour, and they necessarily become the unproductive consumers of the country. I agree too that the capitalists being in such a case without a sufficient motive for saving from revenue, to add to capital, will cease doing so—will, if you please, even expend a part of their capital; but I ask what evil will result from this? none to the capitalist, you will allow, for his enjoyments and his profits will be thereby increased, or he would continue to save. None to the labourers, for which we should repine; because their situation was so exceedingly favorable that they could bear a deduction from their wages and yet be in a most prosperous condition. Here it is where we most differ. You think that the capitalist could not cease saving, on account of the lowness of his profits, without a cessation, in some degree, of employment to the people. I on the contrary think that with all the abatements from the fund destined to the payment of labour, which I acknowledge would be the consequence of the new course of the capitalists, enough would remain to employ all the labour that could be obtained, and to pay it liberally, so that in fact there would be little diminution in the quantity of commodities produced,—the distribution only would be different; more would go [to][1] the capitalists, and less to the labourers.

I do not think that stagnation is a proper term to apply to a state of things in which for a time there is no motive to a further increase of production. When in the course of things profits shall be so low, from a great accumulation of capital, and a want of means of providing food for an increasing population, all motive for further savings will cease, but there will be no stagnation—all that is produced will be at its fair relative price and will be freely exchanged.—Surely the word stagnation is improperly applied to such a state of things, for there will not be a general glut, nor will any particular commodity be necessarily produced in greater abundance than the demand shall warrant.

You say "we know from repeated experience that the money price of labour never falls till many workmen have been for some time out of work." I know no such thing, and if wages were previously high, I can see no reason whatever why they should not fall before many labourers are thrown out of work. All general reasoning I apprehend is in favor of my view of this question, for why should some agree to go without any wages while others were most liberally re-warded. Once more I must say that a sudden and diminished demand for labour in this case must mean a diminished re-ward to the labourer, and not a diminished employment of him—he will work at least as much as before, but will have a less proportion of the produce of his work, and this will be so in order that his employer may have an adequate motive for employing him at all, which he certainly would not have if his share of the produce were reduced so low as to make

[1] Omitted in MS.

increased production an evil rather than a benefit to him. "It is" (never) "said that[1] an increase of unproductive consumption among landlords and capitalists may not sometimes be the proper remedy for a state of things in which the motives for production fail"—I know of no one who has recommended a perseverance in parsimony even after the profits of capital have vanished. I have never done so, and I should be amongst the first to reprobate the folly of the capitalist in not indulging himself in unproductive consumption. I have indeed said that nothing can be produced for which there will not be a demand, unless, from miscalculation, while the employment of stock affords even moderate profits, but I have not said that production may not in theory be pushed so far as to destroy the motive on the part of the capitalist to continue producing to the same extent. I believe it might possibly be pushed so far, but we have never witnessed it in our days, and I feel quite confident that however injurious such a state of things may be to the capitalist, it is so only because it is attended with disproportionate and unusual benefits to the labourers. The remedy therefore, and the sole remedy, is a more just distribution of the produce; and this can be brought about only, as I said in my last letter, by an increase of workmen, or by a more liberal unproductive expenditure on the part of the capitalist. I should not make a protest against an increase of consumption, as a remedy to the stagnation of trade, if I thought, as you do, that we were now suffering from too great savings. As I have already said I do not see how stagnation of trade can arise from such a cause.

We appear then not to differ *very* widely in our general principles, but more so respecting the applications of them.[2] Such and such evils may exist, but the question is, do they

---

[1] Malthus asked 'how can it be said with truth that', etc.; above, p.20.

[2] Cp. Trower, above, VIII, 393.

exist now? I think not, none of the symptoms indicate that they do, and in my opinion increased savings would alleviate rather than aggravate the sufferings of which we have lately had to complain. Stagnation is a derangement of the system, and not too much general production, arising from too great an accumulation of capital.

Mr. Tooke has been here since saturday last.—I am going with him to-morrow to Bromesberrow from whence he will go to Ross and down the Wye to Chepstow. We have had plenty of talk on subjects of Political Economy, and have found out points on which there is partial difference of opinion between us. He brought with him two pamphlets in which you are often mentioned as well as myself; perhaps you have seen them—their titles are An Inquiry into those Principles advocated by Mr. Malthus relative to the nature of Demand, and the necessity of consumption[1]—the other Observations on certain Verbal disputes in Political Economy.[2]—

Mrs. Ricardo unites with me in kind regards to Mrs. Malthus and yourself. Mr. Tooke also desires to be kindly remembered.

Ever truly Y.^r

DAVID RICARDO

[1] This is the half-title; the full title runs, *An Inquiry into those Principles respecting the Nature of Demand and the Necessity of Consumption, lately advocated by Mr. Malthus, from which it is concluded, that Taxation and the Maintenance of Unproductive Consumers can be conducive to the Progress of Wealth* [Anon.], London, R. Hunter, 1821. The writer attacks Malthus for advocating taxation and unproductive consumption; but the ambiguous title seems to have misled some of its readers (cp. E. R. A. Seligman

'On Some Neglected British Economists' in *Economic Journal*, Sept. 1903, p. 351).
[2] *Observations on Certain Verbal Disputes in Political Economy, particularly relating to Value, and to Demand and Supply* [Anon.], London, R. Hunter, 1821. Marx notices (*Theorien über den Mehrwert*, 1905, vol. III, p. 146) a striking similarity between this pamphlet and Samuel Bailey's *Critical Dissertation on Value*, 1825, also published anonymously and by the same bookseller.

445. TROWER TO RICARDO [1]
[Reply to 437.—Answered by 447]

Unsted Wood. July 22. 1821.

My Dear Ricardo

22 July 1821   I returned yesterday from Muntham, where I have been passing a week with my Brother. He has a pleasant residence in an agreeable Country, where he enjoys his retirement very much.—He is almost as little of a Country Gentleman as you are, and passes his time, principally among his Books, and in exercise—His eldest Son [2] is a young man of very considerable promise, who in about a year, or so, will be going to Oxford; and who naturally forms a subject of great interest to his father. He has a great taste for poetry, and is continually composing pieces of great merit.—

Many thanks for the Report which you were kind enough to send me. I approve it very much; and have no doubt its circulation will do much good. The great desideratum is to propagate sound notions upon the subject. Such notions the Report, upon the whole, contains. I judge from its doctrines, that *you* have had a considerable share in its construction; and I also hear from many quarters that such is the fact. I hope they mean to publish the *evidence,* as, no doubt, it must contain many important facts, interesting to an agriculturist.—

I entirely agree in what you say in your last letter on the subject of exchangeable value: The difference between us, if any, is merely in the mode of stating the question. When I say "that the labor, which a Commodity can *command* is what actually constitutes its exchangeable value"—I do not

---

[1] Addressed: 'To / David Ricardo Esqr / M.P. / Gatcomb Park / Minchinhampton'.
MS in *R.P.*

[2] Walter John Trower (*ca.* 1805–1877) afterwards Fellow of Oriel College and later a bishop. (J. Foster, *Alumni Oxonienses.*)

22 July 1821

mean to *confine* the term *labor,* so as to *exclude commodities;* but to express, that the labor, or *other commodities,* which a given commodity can *command* is what actually constitutes its exchangeable value, *as,* the labor which a Commodity *contains* (if I may so express myself) is what actually constitutes its *cost.*

You say, "I do not, I think, say, that the labor expended upon a commodity is a measure of its *exchangeable value,* but of its *positive value.* I then add, that exchangeable value is regulated by positive value and therefore is regulated by the quantity of labor expended." But if you will refer to your Chapter on value, I think you will find, that the *inference* from what you say is, that you consider the labor expended as the measure of exchangeable value— for you observe page 3/4[1]. "In the early stages of society the exchangeable value of these commodities, or *the rule, which determines how much of one shall be given in exchange for another, depends solely* on the comparative quantity of labor *expended on each.*" Again page 12.[2] "In speaking however of labor as being the foundation of all value, and the relative quantity of labor *as determining the relative value of commodities*" &.

I know very well, that in laying down the *principle,* you intend to exclude the consideration of the temporary fluctuations of the market; but, then, the question is, whether, in so doing, you have properly employed the term *exchangeable value; this is in fact the sole question; you* consider *exchangeable value* as synonimous with *natural price,* whereas I confess it appears to me, that *exchangeable value* should be applied to the *market price,* to the value you *can actually obtain* in exchange for the commodity you part from. No doubt, the foundation of *that value* is the *natural value* of the commodity

[1] Above I, 12.   [2] Above, I, 20.

exchanged—but then, the natural and the exchangeable value are rarely ever alike; and require to be distinguished by different terms.

This is almost the only point in which I think Malthus is in the right in his controversy with you; and it relates merely to the employment of a term, although he endeavours to magnify it into a question of principle, and of considerable importance. I confess I think, that ambiguity and confusion are avoided by expressing by the term *cost* the labor expended upon a commodity, and by expressing by the term *exchangeable value* the amount of labor, or of other commodities, which that commodity can command—

Well! so the mighty Corronation's over; and without the turbulence some persons apprehended. The Queen, I think, has acted in this matter with bad judgment;[1] and has shewn, beyond dispute, how much she has sunk in public estimation—Her law officers made out but a poor case as to her right of Corronation; and after that, prudence required she should remain quiet. However, as I am one of those, who think as *ill of her as possible;* the more she puts herself in the wrong the better I am pleased, for the more will the eyes of the public be opened to her real character. Ministers, in the first instance, put *themselves* as much in the wrong as possible, and now Her Majesty is following their wise example.

How have you found matters in your part of the Country? Are rents, tithes, poor rates, wages and tradesmen's Bills coming down? These are the points to attend to—but the grumbling stupid farmer is looking only for increased prices.—

[1] Her claim to be crowned with the King on 19 July having been disallowed by the Privy Council, Queen Caroline drove to Westminster Abbey on Coronation day and was refused admission by the officers at the doors.

How should you value *Tithes;* in reference to value of money or *land.* I say the *former*—I have been offered *mine* at 28 years purchase and I think I ought to purchase them at 26—

22 July 1821

Mrs. Trower begs to join with me in kind remembrances to Mrs. Ricardo and family and believe me

Yrs ever truly

HUTCHES TROWER

446. SAY TO RICARDO [1]
[*Reply to 430.—Answered by 488*]

Mon cher Monsieur

J'ai reçu avec votre lettre du 8 mai, un exemplaire de la 3.ᵉ edition de votre important ouvrage. Agréez-en tous mes remerciemens. J'y vois de nouvelles preuves que les matieres d'Economie politique sont prodigieusement compliquées, puisque, tout en cherchant la verité de bonne foi, et après que nous avons, les uns et les autres, consacré des années entieres à approfondir les questions que presente cette science, il est encore plusieurs points sur lesquels M. Malthus, vous, et moi ne pouvons entierement nous mettre d'accord.

19 July 1821

Au milieu de ces dissentimens, c'est néanmoins un bien bon signe que nous soyons d'accord sur l'essentiel; je veux dire sur la possibilité qu'ont les hommes de multiplier leurs richesses.

[1] MS in *R.P.—Minor Papers,* pp. 185–90. The text given in *Mélanges,* pp. 112–22 and *Œuvres diverses,* pp. 418–22 differs considerably from that of the original printed above and is probably a new version prepared by Say in 1825 with a view to publication; it contains notably several additional jibes at Ricardo's 'abstractions'.

Vous m'exhortez à soumettre à de nouvelles meditations la doctrine qui fonde les richesses sur la valeur echangeable des choses. Je l'avais deja fait à l'epoque où je fus critiqué par vous dans votre premiere edition; j'ai recommencé le même examen en publiant la quatrieme edition de mon Traité d'Economie politique; je viens de remettre ce même sujet sur le metier en travaillant à un ouvrage[1] bien plus considerable que tout ce que j'ai fait jusqu'à present; et je vous avoue que cette doctrine me semble toujours conforme aux faits (qui sont nos maitres à tous) et qu'à mes yeux elle ne laisse sans explication aucun des phenomènes de l'Economie politique.

Elle a de plus l'avantage de raisonner sur des quantités appréciables, caractere essentiel de toute doctrine scientifique, caractere qui peut seul assurer la marche des investigateurs. Car enfin pour savoir ce qui fait grandir ou diminuer nos biens, il faut savoir ce qui les constitue *grands* ou *petits.* C'est, permettez-moi de vous le dire, ce que ne peut enseigner la considération de la *valeur en utilité* (*value in use*) mots qui me paraissent incompatibles, parce que l'idée de *valeur* ne peut etre séparée de celle de comparaison et d'échange.

Je persiste donc à croire que créer de l'utilité c'est créer de la richesse, mais que nous n'avons d'autre mesure de cette utilité créée, que la plus ou moins grande quantité d'un autre produit quelconque; quantité qui forme la *valeur echangeable* du premier, son *prix-courant.*

L'utilité qui est naturellement dans une chose, et qui ne lui a pas été donnée, comme celle de l'eau, fait partie de nos *richesses naturelles;* mais n'ayant aucune valeur echangeable, elle ne peut être l'objet des recherches de la science econo-

---

[1] *Cours complet d'Economie politique pratique,* 6 vols., published in 1828–1829.

mique. Et pourquoi l'eau n'a t'elle point de valeur echangeable? Parce qu'elle n'est pas un sujet d'échange, parce que,
pour en avoir, personne n'etant obligé d'en acquérir, elle
n'est l'objet d'aucune demande.

Une grande utilité qui peut se donner à peu de frais,
rapproche la chose à laquelle elle est conferée, d'une
richesse naturelle, d'une chose qui a son utilité par elle même
et sans frais; mais en Economie politique, nous ne pouvons
nous occuper que de la portion d'utilité qui a été donnée
avec des frais.

Les circonstances qui occasionnent des frais sans production d'utilité, comme les impôts, ne produisent pas de la
richesse; et lorsqu'on les fait payer au consommateur, on lui
fait payer un prix pour lequel on ne lui donne rien en
échange.

En d'autres termes, les seules richesses nouvelles sont des
services productifs, premiers fruits de notre industrie, de nos
capitaux, et de nos terres. On les echange entr'eux, ou bien
on echange leurs produits; et la quantité que l'on donne des
uns pour avoir les autres, est l'indication de la *valeur* qu'on
y attache, valeur qui seule fait le sujet de notre etude.

Il me semble, Monsieur, qu'il n'y a rien dans toute cette
doctrine que de parfaitement conforme à la verité, et je vous
engage à mon tour à la soumettre à de nouvelles méditations
de votre part, avec toute la profondeur dont vous etes
capable. Vous allez voir qu'elle explique les principales
difficultés que vous m'opposez.

Vous dites (pag. 332. 4th ed.)[1] "When I give 2000 times
more cloth for a pound of gold than I give for a pound of
iron, does it prove that I attach 2000 times more utility
to gold than I do to iron? etc." Non; mais en supposant
pour un moment qu'une livre d'or et une livre de fer rendent

---

[1] Should be '3rd ed.' Above, I, 283.

à l'homme un service parfaitement égal malgré l'inégalité de leur valeur, je dis qu'il y a dans une livre de fer:

>1999 degrés d'utilité naturelle fesant partie des richesses que la nature ne nous fait pas payer, et qui ne concernent pas l'Economie politique;

>et 1 degré d'utilité créée par l'industrie, les capitaux et les terres, utilité que nous payons et qui est la seule qui fasse partie des richesses echangeables, ____ unique objet de nos recherches.

2000—degrés d'utilité en tout, residans dans une livre de fer. Tandis que dans une livre d'or il y a:

2000—degrés d'utilité tout entiere echangeable parce qu'elle est tout entiere le fruit de notre industrie, de nos capitaux et de nos terres; utilité qui fait partie, non de nos richesses naturelles, mais de nos richesses sociales, les seules dont l'Economie politique puisse s'occuper.

Voila ce qui m'attire le reproche que vous me faites (pag. 336)[1] lorsque vous dites: "Mr. Say constantly overlooks the essential difference that there is between value in use, and value in exchange." Certainement je néglige ce qui n'a qu'une *valeur d'utilité,* ou plutot de l'utilité sans valeur, car je regarde ces mots: *valeur d'utilité* (*value in use*) comme un contre sens; et que je prétends que l'utilité sans valeur n'entre pas dans les considerations de l'Economie politique.

A l'egard de l'exemple ingénieux que vous me citez dans votre derniere lettre, de deux pains d'égale valeur, provenus de deux terrains d'inégale fertilité, je vous demande la permission de l'expliquer selon ma doctrine, comme j'ai fait pour l'exemple de la livre d'or et de la livre de fer. La nature fait present au proprietaire du terrain, d'un service productif qu'il peut faire payer au consommateur, parce qu'il a le monopole de ce service indispensable. Ce present que lui

---

[1] Above, I, 286.

fait la nature, est plus grand lorsque le terrain est fertile; il est plus petit lorsque le terrain est ingrat. Si le service du terrain etait sans bornes, inepuisable, à la portée de tout le monde, ce serait un present fait à tout le monde et dont nous jouirions sans le payer, comme du vent qui enfle nos voiles, chaque fois que nous voulons nous en servir. Le consommateur serait infiniment riche s'il pouvait acquerir au même prix toutes les portions d'utilité qu'il voudrait consacrer à la satisfaction de ses besoins; mais toutes ses richesses seraient naturelles: elles n'auraient plus de valeur echangeable; il n'y aurait plus d'Economie politique; mais l'on n'en aurait plus besoin.

Je ne comprends pas pourquoi vous me dites dans votre lettre en parlant de cette doctrine: "The information is not useful and can lead to no inference whatever that may guide our future practice." Il me semble au contraire que nous en pouvons tirer cette induction que les grands progrès de la production consistent dans la substitution des services gratuits de la nature à la place des services dispendieux de l'industrie, des capitaux et des terres.

Vous ajoutez: "What we wish to know is what the general law is that regulates the value of bread as compared with the value of other things." C'est ce qu'enseigne la doctrine de l'offre et de la demande (want and supply). Le besoin qu'on a d'une chose en fait naître la demande; la necessité de produire la chose en restreint la demande. Lorsqu'aux yeux du consommateur, une chose vaut autant que les frais de production qu'elle coûte, on la produit. Lorsque la valeur qu'on y attache n'egale pas la valeur des services productifs nécessaires pour qu'elle existe, on ne la produit pas. Cette derniere circonstance est une preuve que la même quantité de services productifs peut former un produit qu'on estime valoir plus que cette chose.

Je ne crains pas de me tromper en affirmant que ces doctrines, (avec tous leurs dévelopemens) enseignent tout ce qu'on peut etre desireux de savoir sur ce sujet.

C'est avec beaucoup de plaisir que j'apprends que vous avez formé en Angleterre, un Club d'Economistes politiques; et je ne doute pas qu'il ne contribue puissamment à repandre les principes de cette science. Je m'estimerais heureux d'y être associé. En attendant si vous croyez que nos controverses puissent interesser ses membres, je vous engage à leur communiquer cette lettre.[1]

Agréez, Mon cher Monsieur, l'assurance de ma haute consideration et de mon très sincère dévouement

J. B. SAY

Paris [19][2] Juillet 1821.

David Ricardo, Esqr à Londres

P.S. J'ai vu avec peine que plusieurs des ecrivains Anglais qui ont fait mention de mes Lettres à Malthus, outre qu'ils n'ont pas toujours rendu fidelement mon sens, ont interpreté ironiquement les eloges que je donne à l'illustre auteur de l'Essai sur la population. Comme vous le voyez quelquefois, ayez la bonté de lui dire que les temoignages de mon admiration pour son premier ouvrage[3], sont la fidele expression des sentimens que je professe et qui ne peuvent etre alterés par les discussions où nous sommes entrés sur des questions d'Economie politique. J'ai lu les principaux ecrits où l'on a attaqué sa doctrine de la population, et je serais bien aise qu'il sût qu'ils n'ont ebranlé en rien l'estime que je fais et de la doctrine, et du livre, et de son respectable auteur.

---

[1] Ricardo did so at the next meeting of the Club which he attended, on 4 Feb. 1822. See below, p. 172, n. 2.

[2] Omitted in MS, but given in *Mélanges* and *Œuvres diverses*.

[3] *Essay on Population*.

447. RICARDO TO TROWER [1]
[*Reply to 445.—Answered by 456*]

Gatcomb Park
22 Aug 1821

My Dear Trower

It is nearly a month since your letter to me was written, and it ought long before this to have been answered, but the fact is that in proportion to my time being unoccupied by business, I become more and more idle, and feel more and more disposed to indulge in excursions of pleasure and amusement. Since I have been here I have always had some friend with me, and a great deal of my time has been passed in visits to my son, who lives in a beautiful country, which I always shew to my friends,[2] and to other places within a moderate distance of my own habitation.

I am glad you approve on the whole of the Report of the Agricultural Committee. I had no other hand in its construction than using the best arguments I could in support of those doctrines which I thought correct, and never sparing the doctrines of my opponents when I thought they were unsound and could be shewn to be so. When the Committee broke up there were very few points on which Mr. Huskisson and I differed.

The Committee has done, and will, I think, do good, by giving information to the House itself. The agricultural gentlemen will soon have enough of committees. I feel quite sure that if we had a committee every year, the restrictions on the trade of corn, instead of being increased, would be after a very few years wholly abolished. Mr. Huskisson justly observed to me that the landed gentlemen entered the committee as plaintiffs and left it defendants. I am quite

22 Aug. 1821

---

[1] Addressed: 'Hutches Trower Esq[r] / Unsted Wood / Godalming / Surrey'. MS at University College, London.—*Letters to Trower,* XLVIII.
[2] See above, p. 27; cp. VIII, 231.

astonished that the evidence is not yet published—it must appear soon, and when it does a copy of it shall be sent to you.

With respect to our difference of opinion on the subject of exchangeable value it is more an apparent difference than a real one. In speaking of exchangeable value you have not any idea of real value in your mind—I invariably have. Your criticisms on passages in my book are I have little doubt correct, because they are also the criticisms of others on the same passages. A pamphlet has appeared "On certain verbal disputes in Polit. Econ."[1] where the same ground of objection is taken as you take; the fault lies not in the doctrine itself, but in my faulty manner of explaining it. The exchangeable value of a commodity cannot alter, I say, unless either its real value, or the real value of the things it is exchanged for alter. This cannot be disputed. If a coat would purchase 4 hats and will afterwards purchase 5, I admit that both the coat and the hats have varied in exchangeable value, but they have done so in consequence of one or other of them varying in real value, and therefore if I use the word value without prefixing the word exchangeable to it, it will be correct for me to say that the coat has risen in value whilst hats have not varied, or that hats have fallen in value while coats have remained stationary. With this explanation look at the passage (Pages 3/4 and 12) which you quote and tell me why they are objectionable.

The troubles of the poor Queen are now at an end, and if ministers had not grossly mismanaged the business she might have been carried to her grave, with the sympathy of the people indeed, but without any increased odium to the Government. Her will, directing where her body should be buried, had removed all difficulty from the question of her interment—why then should not ministers have humored

---

[1] See above, p. 27, n. 2.

the people in any wish they might have formed respecting the course of the procession? Can there be the least doubt that the public tranquility would not have been disturbed if the strongly expressed opinion that the Queen's remains should go through the city had been complied with.[1]

From the high price of the English and French funds we are I suppose to conclude that the peace of Europe is not to be disturbed by the disputes between Turkey and her greek subjects. I hope that peace will be maintained, but considering the great effect which war would have at the present moment on the price of the public securities, I think it quite astonishing that with such appearances of angry discussions being likely to take place between Turkey and Russia they keep at their present elevation.

Mushet has published a curious set of tables,[2] to prove that the Stockholder has, on the whole, derived no advantage, first from the depreciation, and then from the restoration in the value of money. He has in his methodical manner, and with great labour calculated the advantage or disadvantage from year to year, has considered each loan separately, and shewn what ought to have been, and what actually has been paid to the public creditor. The result is, and I believe it is a correct one, that the Stockholders as a body if they had received uniformly what was really due to them, might now have been entitled to £72,704 pr. ann^{m} more than they actually receive, in money of the standard value.

You ask me how I should value tithes—whether I should value them in reference to monied or landed capital. I differ with you, and think in reference to the latter. I think Tithes at 28 years purchase is a much cheaper purchase than Land

---

[1] Queen Caroline died on 7 Aug. 1821. Her will directed that she should be buried at Brunswick. The Government's attempt to keep the funeral procession out of the City occasioned a riot in which two men were killed by the military.

[2] See above, VIII, 390 n. 1.

at 28 years purchase particularly if you contemplate the increasing prosperity and population of the country. In an improving country Tithes always increase in a greater proportion than rent, because they are always the same proportion of the gross produce of the land; rent, even when it increases, is probably always a diminished proportion of the gross produce. Should the rent of your land in 50 or a hundred years rise 50 pc, I have no doubt whatever that the Tithes on the same land will rise very considerably more than 50 pc. If your Tithes are at a fair valuation, and not unusually high you would do well I think to purchase them at 28 years purchase.

Matters are bad enough in this part of the country. Rents are falling, and tenants much distressed. Poor rates, wages and tradesmen's bills also fall, but tithes I believe keep up. Labourers appear to be well off, no scarcity of work, and wages fully adequate to obtain for them more than the usual quantity of necessaries and comforts. Manufacturing labour is also fully employed, but the masters say they do not get their usual profits—by usual I suppose they mean unusual and exorbitant profits.—

I did not know that your brother was a country gentleman, or rather that he resided in the country. I should not expect that he could enter much into country amusements but what enjoyment can be greater to a man fond of Books than a good library in a beautiful and healthy retirement—particularly if it be varied with the pleasures of society in London for 2 or 3 months in the year. I hope your brothers eldest son will realise the expectations which he has raised—it will be very gratifying to his father.

Mrs. Ricardo joins with me in kind remembrances to Mrs. Trower.

Ever truly Y^{rs}

DAVID RICARDO

448. MILL TO RICARDO [1]
[*Reply to* 441.—*Answered by* 449]

E.I. House 23ᵈ August 1821

My Dear Sir

I have had my hands so full during the last month, that
I have only now found time to answer your kind letter; at
least I have always found an excuse to myself for deferring it
till now. My family have been at Marlow; and going back-
wards and forwards, to spend as much time with them as I
could, has much broken in upon any liesure I might have had.

And now that I have taken pen in hand, I know not that
I have any thing to say, except that I wish much to have
a letter from you, to hear how every body fares, that is at, or
connected with Gatcomb. I heard something of you, in a
minutes' conversation the other day with Mr. Tooke, who
seems to have been highly delighted with his excursion—
was at Bromesbarrow, down the Wye, &.c. I envied him
while he told me.

For me, beside my official occupations, I have been chiefly
engrossed with my article Liberty of the Press, which after
all does not please me. I was too much hurried for it; and
Napier having omitted to give me any information, as to his
wish for quantity, I exceeded what he had left room for, and
was obliged to spoil the thing more by curtailment.

I hear that the great men of Whiggery are very much
alarmed at the success of the mob, in resisting the constituted
authorities, on the day of the queens funeral. The folly of the
ministers, they say, is very great; the barefaced obstructions
of the jury, in conducting their inquiry, are very bad; but
nothing like the calamity of the people thinking that they
may in time successfully resist the organs of misrule. I met
Douglas Kinnaird yesterday at a great dinner given by the
court of Directors, who told me Hume is quite downcast,

23 Aug. 1821

[1] MS in *R.P.*

that he had seen him the day before; that Hume said, despotism was in his opinion unavoidable; that the aristocracy were almost to a man the friends of it in their heart; that the people were to a great degree indifferent; and that it was perfectly useless for a few individuals to torment themselves by vain efforts.—What do you say to all this? Are you in the hopeful way of despondency too?—I laughed, and Kinnaird asked me what I thought. If Hume, I said, had been looking to the aristocracy for aid against the progress of misrule, he ought to have despaired from the beginning. The despotism was theirs; and it was not likely they would be soon dissatisfied with it. That with the people, however, the case was different. True, they were as yet impotent, from knowing imperfectly what they want, and the means they possess of commanding it—that this ignorance was however fast passing away—and the passing events were powerfully contributing to enlighten them. It is very curious that almost every body you meet with—whig and tory—agree in declaring their opinion of one thing—that a great struggle between the two orders, the rich and the poor, is in this country commenced—and that the people must in the end prevail;—and yet that the class of the rich act as if they were perfectly sure of the contrary—for if the people must gain the victory, but are made to suffer intensely in the gaining of it, what can these people mean who would enrage the victors to the utmost? The old adage seems to be true; that when God wants to destroy a set of men, he first makes them mad. The aristocracy might at least imitate the Spanish Don, on his death bed, who, when his confessor was telling him what the Devil would do to him, if he did not first make his peace with God, said, "I hope, my lord the Devil will not be so cruel." Upon being upbraided by the priest for talking of the devil so respectfully, he replied, that as it was doubtful into what hands he might fall, good words would at any rate do no harm.—But enough of the aristocracy who will be, 23 Aug. 1821 what they are, and always have been.

I desire exceedingly to know what you have been about, and what you are still to be about—in short, your history, past, present, and to come; as much of it as I know not, and you do. I have given you mine, all of it that is worth giving. I was much delighted with the country about Marlow, and enjoyed as much of it as I could; and had I got done with my article a week sooner, I would have proposed to make a run over, and spend it with you. John has been at home for some weeks:[1] very much grown; looking almost a man; in other respects not much different from what he went. He has got the French language—but almost forgot his own—and is nearly as shy and awkward as before. His love of study, however, remains; and he shews tractability and good sense. If he do not make what the French call an *aimable* man, I have no doubt he will make what the English call an amiable and a useful one.

I have been for several days suffering severely with the tooth-ache—and at this moment the pain is so great that I can hardly see the paper—and therefore good bye

Yours ever
J. MILL

449. RICARDO TO MILL[2]
[*Reply to* 448.—*Answered by* 450]

Gatcomb Park 28 Aug 1821

My Dear Sir

When I saw your hand writing on the direction of a 28 Aug. 1821 letter to me, I expected it was to announce that your labors were at an end, and that you were preparing to leave London to pass a short time with me. I was much disappointed at the intelligence which it actually gave me, and must request of

---

[1] After his residence in France; see above, VIII, 293. [2] MS in Mill-Ricardo papers.

you to make an effort to come here, if not immediately, at any rate during the time we shall stay here previous to the next parliamentary campaign. I wish too you would bring John with you, I desire much to see him after his long visit to foreign parts, and to hear the history of his adventures from his own mouth. It would give me pleasure to see him although it should happen that you cannot find time to come: he will have his time for reading and study nearly as much undisturbed here as at home and will benefit a little by mixing with strangers—it may tend to remove the shyness which you say still adheres to him.

I am sorry that you were obliged to curtail your article on the Liberty of the Press. As for its not pleasing you, that is of little consequence:—you are not a good judge of your own performances, and I have no doubt that it will add to your reputation.

My information respecting Gatcomb, its inhabitants, and those connected with Gatcomb, is soon given—we are obliged to you for feeling an interest about us. Mr. and Mrs. Clutterbuck, and their children, have been with us ever since we have been here—they leave us this week for Bromesberrow. Osman and his wife have been occasionally here, and I have been sometimes with them;—we all continue to love each other and to enjoy each other's company. Clutterbuck is thinking of changing his residence, and our party have had two or three pleasant excursions to parts of the country, within 20 miles of us, to see places that were either for sale, or to be had on lease—they have however not yet fixed on the spot to which they will go. David is much as usual, obliging but not so studious as I could wish him to be. Mortimer and his two youngest sisters enjoy themselves very much with their horses, a day seldom passes without their riding. There have [been][1] some important changes in this

[1] Omitted in MS.

part of our stud since you were here; Mary is promoted to a large horse—Birtha has succeeded to Mary's, and Mortimer has a pretty pony which his uncle Frank gave to him.

My occupations are nearly the same as usual—Books always afford me amusement and as I forget their contents very soon after reading them, a small library is an inexhaustible resource to me. I have been drawn away from my library oftener than I could wish, sometimes by occasional visitors, sometimes by my family—often by my active companion Clutterbuck, but I have passed my time happily and agreeably. I have been reading Clarendon's history of the Rebellion, and have looked with some interest at a work on Polit. Econ. by Mr. Piercy Ravenstone which though full of the greatest errors has some good things in it—he is a strenuous and an able advocate for Reform.[1]

The Whigs are an inconsistent set of people—they are the loudest in their complaints of the bad measures which are pursued by Government, and yet the opposers of every scheme which shall afford us a chance of obliging the Government to pursue none but good measures. The only prospect we have of putting aside the struggle which they say has commenced between the rich and the other classes, is for the rich to yield what is justly due to the other classes, but this is the last measure which they are willing to have recourse to. I cannot help flattering myself that justice will prevail at last, without a recurrence to actual violence; but if it does, it will only be because the event of the struggle will be so obvious to all eyes that expediency, the expediency of the rich, will make it necessary even in their view. As for Hume, he will always talk of despairing of seeing things mend, but his energy in acting will not be diminished. He

[1] *A few Doubts as to the Correctness of some Opinions generally entertained on the subjects of Population and Political Economy,* by Piercy Ravenstone, London, Andrews, 1821.

gave a just account of himself at Mr. Coke's annual feast— he said that he had as much pleasure in the pursuit in which he had engaged as those he was addressing had in their pursuits connected with Agriculture.[1] If Humes efforts were never to be attended with more success than in the last session, and they have been attended with some, he would persevere —he is very much alive to public opinion, and he has been sufficiently praised by the public to ensure the continuance of his exertions.

Mr. Ellwin, a gentleman who resides at Bath, and whom you have met at my house in Brook Street, is now staying with me—he leaves me to-morrow. On tuesday next I expect Sydney Smith and his family at Gatcomb. They will be on their way from Taunton to York—He and I will have plenty of conversation on Reform.

I have not seen Torrens book[2]—he promised to send me a copy of it but he has not done it. When he made the promise I told him I should send him a copy of my 3^{d} edition, but I could not do it because I did not know his residence. Have you read it? Tooke is not very much delighted with it. I have received a letter from Say[3] with a defence of the passages in his book which I have criticized in my last edition. It is I think very bad. It gives up the whole question, and yet pretends that it is consistent with the book, and with itself, in every part.

You will see by the manner in which this sheet is written that I forgot the high dignity to which I had attained, and was really calculating on not putting you to 9 pence addi-

---

[1] See Hume's speech at Coke's 'Sheep Shearing' at Holkham in *Morning Chronicle,* 11 July 1821.
[2] *An Essay on the Production of Wealth,* by Robert Torrens, London, Longman, 1821 (advertised as 'published this day' in the *Scotsman* of 28 July).
[3] Letter 446.

tional expence.[1] Mrs. Ricardo and the rest of the circle here desire their kind remembrances to you.

Y.^{rs} very truly

DAVID RICARDO

450. MILL TO RICARDO[2]
[*Reply to 449.—Answered by 453*]

E. I. House 31st Aug. 1821.

My Dear Sir

This is not an answer to your kind letter received the other day. I comply with Place's request to write to you about his reply to Godwin.

He is speculating about a publisher—and after being in two or three minds, has come to think, that Murray would be the best, provided he would undertake it—and that nothing is so likely to make him favourable, as information that you think well of the production. In all this I saw good reason to concur. I was then asked, if I thought you would give any thing in the shape of a recommendation to Murray. I replied, that I thought it very likely you would be willing to read the manuscript, and if so, that you would have no objection to state to Murray what you thought of it.

I have read, or heard read, a considerable part of it. There is in it pertinent matter, sufficient to establish the conclusions though not always displayed to the best advantage.

If I do not hear from you, on monday,[3] to forbid the sending it—you will probably receive it in a few days.

---

[1] The ending, written crosswise, fills the space which had been left for the address on the back of the sheet. The custom of using the same sheet as cover was due to a lower postage being charged, to the recipient, on single-sheet let-ters; but members of parliament had the privilege of 'franking' letters, so there was no charge anyway.

[2] MS in *R.P.*

[3] 3 September.

Many thanks for your kind invitation to John. I am not yet without hopes of spending a week with you, when my colleagues have all finished their holidays—in which case we shall come together. If I find that is impossible, I shall be very happy to send him alone.

I beg my best regards to Mrs. Ricardo—the young ladies &.c. You seem to be all very happy—at which I rejoice.

Yours &.c.

J. MILL

450A. PLACE TO RICARDO [1]
[*Answered by* 451]

[London, ca. 3 Sept. 1821]

To David Ricardo Esq.

My Dear Sir

I have sent you the M.S. reply to Godwin on the Principle of Population and request you will have the goodness to look it over. I should not have thought of imposing such a task upon you had I not been requested to do so by our common friend Mill. He has read nearly the whole of it carefully at his own house the remainder we read together at Marlow. He is of opinion that Mr Murray should be requested to print and publish it, he supposes he will be willing to do so at his own expence on condition of dividing the profits should there be any to divide. He therefore proposes that I should send the M.S. to you that you may look at it and that should you be of opinion that it ought to be published you should speak to Mr Murray on the subject as that might be an inducement to him to do so.

Mr Mill will write to you on the subject.

Yours very truly

FRANCIS PLACE

[1] MS copy in Seligman Library of Columbia University.

451. RICARDO TO PLACE [1]
[*Reply to* 450A]

Gatcomb Park, Minchinhampton
9 Sept 1821

Dear Sir

I have gone through the whole of your MS[2] with the greatest attention, and have great pleasure in saying that in my humble judgment it is a complete and satisfactory answer to all Mr. Godwins objections to the theory of Population, as explained by Mr. Malthus. I have no doubt but that its publication will bring you great credit and fame, and will be deemed a proof of your being possessed of a good stock of industry and talents. I hope you will be able to make such arrangements as that it may speedily appear in print. To take off a little of the value of my praise I must candidly confess that I am not very familiar with calculations concerning births, marriages and deaths, and therefore am entitled to be considered only in the light of an ordinary reader, paying great attention to the subject before him.

In looking over the paper of my notes, made during the time I was perusing your MS, I observe that there are some parts in which I do not quite agree with you and which I shall now, without any apology, submit for your re-consideration. First, in the latter part of the first chapter it is I think *inferred that under a system of equality population would*

9 Sept. 1821

---

[1] Addressed: 'Mr. Place / Charing Cross / London'. On the cover, in another hand: 'Returning the M.S.'

MS in Seligman Library of Columbia University (where are also Place's comments on this letter, 6 pp., unpublished). I am indebted to Mr G. W. Zinke for acquainting me with its existence and for obtaining a photostat.

[2] Published under the title *Illustrations and Proofs of the Principle of Population: including An Examination of the Proposed Remedies of Mr. Malthus, and a Reply to the Objections of Mr. Godwin and Others,* by Francis Place, London, Longman, 1822. For Godwin's attack on Malthus, to which it replies, see above, VIII, 291, n. 3.

press with more force against the means of subsistence than it now does. This I do not think is true. I believe, that under such a system, mankind would increase much faster than it now does, but so would food also. A larger proportion of the whole capital of the country would be employed in the production of food-necessaries, and a less proportion in the production of luxuries, and thus we might go on, even with an increase of capital, without any increased difficulty, till that distant time, which because of its distance, Mr. Malthus says should not damp our ardour. Whether this would be a more happy state of society is another question which it is not now necessary to discuss. It should always be remembered that we are not forcing the production of food to the extent of our power. Without one shilling more capital, without any additional labour being employed in the country, we might probably increase the quantity of food 25 pc. On this foundation are raised all Mr. Owen's speculations.—

2. Chap. 3 Section 1 Page 4.[1] Is the passage I have marked quite fair towards Mr. Godwin. "I have proved by general reasoning" says Mr. Godwin "that so and so cannot be true. I will now shew you by an appeal to facts that I am correct, but if my facts do not afford the evidence which I think they do my general reasoning will still be conclusive." You have shewn, and may shew, that his general reasoning is defective, but I do not see the justice of the charge of his pretending to be thought right "whether he is so or not—whether the thing he asserts be possible or impossible".

3. Page 28[2] Your table supposes the increase of population to be the same the last year that it is the first—surely this cannot be right. Population does not indeed increase in the same steady geometrical ratio that money does, which accu-

[1] p. 41 of the published book.   [2] p. 70.

mulates at compound interest, but still it increases at some rate which may be called geometrical. Your table is constructed on a principle of arithmetical increase.

4 Page 29[1] For the same reason as that just given I object to halving the increase in the 10 years to find out the population of 1795.

5 Chap. 3 Section 2 Page 4[2] If a population of 3 millions increases to 4,500,000 in 55 years, by the addition of one child to every 8 marriages, it will increase to 6,750,000 in 110 years and consequently will double in a smaller period than 110 years.

"If $\frac{1}{8}$ of child to a marriage &c. &c. &c." the answer 37 cannot be correct, for population increases in a geometrical ratio. If £1 p^r Ann^m at 5 pc. accumulates at compound interest for 20 years it will amount to £33, but we should be wrong therefore to infer that if £2 p^r Ann^m accumulated for half the period that would also amount to £33, it would in fact only amount to £25.

6. Chap 3 Sec^n 3 Page 3[3] You remark the absurdity of Mr. Godwins thinking it necessary that there should be 8 births to a marriage in America in order to double the population in 25 years, and that it is inconsistent with his own data, but I do not think you dwell enough on this important part of the difference between you.

7 Chap 6 Sec^n 1 Page 2[4] Your remarks on the word "right" as used by Mr. Malthus[5] is strictly correct perhaps,

[1] p. 71.
[2] pp. 75–6.
[3] p. 86.
[4] p. 137.
[5] 'There is one right which man has generally been thought to possess, which I am confident he neither does nor can possess—a right to subsistence when his labour will not fairly purchase it. Our laws indeed say that he has this right, and bind the society to furnish employment and food to those who cannot get them in the regular market; but in so doing they attempt to reverse the laws of nature; and it is in consequence to be expected, not only that they

but you should in fairness recollect in what sense he meant to use it. "The law professes" Mr. Malthus might say "to give every man a right to the enjoyment of his own property, but in effect the right is withholden from him if at the same time it gives a contrary and inconsistent right to another man to be maintained out of that property["]. The labour of a poor man is his property and therefore by analogy he has a right to all that it will procure him, but it is inconsistent and inexpedient to give him a right to any part of my property if he do not obtain it, by my freely giving it to him in exchange for his labour. By "right" and "law of nature" Mr. Malthus clearly means, "moral right" "utility" "the good of the whole" or some equivalent expression. I am not defending the accuracy of Mr. Malthus's language on this occasion—I know it is not strictly correct, I as well as you am a disciple of the Bentham and Mill school, but his meaning cannot be mistaken.

8. Page 5[1] same Chap. I am not satisfied with the reply here given to Mr. Malthus's proposal.[2] If men depended wholly on their own exertions for support, a state of society might and I think would exist, in which *it could not be* [*"*]*successfully shewn* that no labourer and very few artizans have a prospect of being able to maintain a family.["][3]

9. Page 8[4] You agree with Mr. Malthus that his plan if adopted would lower the poor rates, but you say it would

should fail in that object, but that the poor, who were intended to be benefitted, should suffer most cruelly from the inhuman deceit thus practised upon them.' (*Essay on Population,* 5th ed., 1817, vol. III, p. 154.)
[1] pp. 139–40.
[2] 'I should propose a regulation to be made, declaring, that no child born from any marriage, taking place after the expiration of a year from the date of the law, and no illegitimate child born two years from the same date, should ever be entitled to parish assistance.' (*Essay on Population,* vol. III, p. 179.)
[3] 'Mr. Godwin, in reply to this [*i.e.* Malthus's proposal], has successfully shown that no labourer' etc. (Place, p. 140.)
[4] pp. 143–4.

reduce the poor to the very lowest state possible. Why? not if it raised wages, and this is what Mr. Malthus expects from it. You are bound to shew, that wages will not be raised, when a portion of the money now paid for labour, under another name, is withdrawn, and transferred to the employers of labour. You say that private benevolence would degrade the poor man more than the aid he receives, from the poor rates. I believe otherwise. Mr. Malthus be it remembered does not propose the abolition of the poor laws as a measure of relief to the rich, but as one of relief to the poor them-selves. Is it not a little inconsistent to say, as you appear to me to say, that the poor laws have degraded the poor of this country, and yet warn us against their gradual abolition for fear of degrading our people to the level of the degradation of the poor in countries where there are no poor laws.

Chap. 6 Sect. 2 Page 4[1] If it be a general though erroneous belief in a country that to increase the population be a meritorious act, is it not likely that fewer will be restrained from marriage in such a country, than in another where more just notions of what is really meritorious, and what is really pernicious, prevail? To say that "God never sends mouths but he sends meat" is not so different, as at first sight appears, to saying "that to raise up subjects for his king and country is a meritorious act.["]

The accusations you bring against the rich are many of them just, but those concerning "the law of settlement" "the payment of wages from the poor rates" "the heavy taxes laid on the necessaries of life" are I think all unjust—the last has not the effect which the poor think they have, and the two former are the effects of a bad system which the rich do not, on account of any benefit to themselves, uphold. I cannot doubt that the original establishment of the poor laws proceeded from benevolent but mistaken views, and I

[1] p. 152.

think it hurts the cause which you so well support to cast blame where it is not deserved. As a matter of fact it may be true that the poor make these complaints, but you appear to me too much to countenance them.

Chap. 6. Sec. 2 Page 3.[1] You quote from Malthus and afterwards say "Thus he[2] is held out as a seditious grumbler if not a blasphemer without any sufficient cause for his grumbling." This accusation is made against Mr. Malthus, and is wholly unfounded. Does he say he has no cause for grumbling? quite the contrary he says he has, but that he mistakes the cause of his distress. This is not fair criticism. That which follows in this page &c. is excellent. I have read your defence of the working class with great interest. I believe you have done them but justice, and that they are often cruelly calumniated. This part of your work will do much good, if you abate a little of the asperity with which the rich are handled. I find no fault with the severity of the passages. I complain of their injustice. You say that the object of the rich is to keep down the recompence to the labourer to the lowest rate at which they can be supported, and your proof is that their allottment from the rates is regulated by such lowest rate. It is idle to complain of those who employ labourers endeavoring to get them to do their work at low wages—this is true of all employers of labourers, not of the rich particularly; and as for the niggardly allowance from the rates what would you have them do? Would it not be worse if every man wanting work could be sure of being liberally relieved. The sincerest friends of the poor think, perhaps erroneously, that the situation of the poor would be improved if the pittance of which you complain were withdrawn from them altogether. Is it just to say (Page 12[3]) "Having got him in that state, the next thing was to reduce him as low as possible". Magistrates &c. are often

---

[1] p. 154.   [2] The labouring man.   [3] p. 167.

ignorant—the consequences of their acts may have been injurious to the working classes, but that they designed their misery without any prospect of benefit to themselves is inconceivable. Point out if you can what they gained by it. Accuse the individual judge who uttered the words which you quote,[1] he deserves to be held up to public odium, but do not charge such offences too indiscriminately. Indeed in candor you ought to mention the judge's name and the case to which you allude.

Page 14[2] I agree that the two things you recommend should be done, but these would be very insufficient as measures of relief to the labouring classes. They are as injurious to the rich as to the poor.

Page 15[3] You acknowledge, that to delay marriage, and to prevent too many being born, are the only efficient remedies for the evils which the poor suffer. Mr. Malthus proposes the gradual abolition of the poor laws as a means to accelerate this desirable end,—you no where I think shew that the means would not be efficacious.

Chap. 8. Page 8 last section.[4] May we not say that the exertions of the middling rank in this country, of which you speak with just praise, have been in part the effect of their having a better government than other countries. The liberty of the press—the public discussion of all measures of importance in Parliament, may have produced some effects on the minds and dispositions of the middling class.

[1] 'If he [the labouring man] congregated, or made an attempt to congregate, for the purpose of preventing his own degradation, he was prosecuted as a felon, and told from the seat of justice, by the mouth of an English judge, that "*his crime was worse than felony, and as bad as murder*", and sentenced to two years solitary confinement' (p. 168).

[2] pp. 171–2. Place recommends the repeal of the combination laws, of the laws restraining emigration, and of all laws in restriction of trade, particularly the corn laws.

[3] pp. 173–4.

[4] p. 256.

Chap 9 p 1[1] Mill does not shew the effect that would be produced by spade husbandry, but the effect that would follow from an increasing people, which should constantly require an additional proportion of the population to be employed in husbandry. He would recommend spade husbandry, if it could be shewn that the capital and labour employed in it, yielded more than an equal capital and the same quantity of labour in plough or machinery husbandry.

If in Ireland the people raised corn with their spades, and could do it economically, no complaint could be justly made against spade husbandry. The term is unfortunately chosen. The evil of which the Irish ought to complain is the small value of the food of the people compared with the value of the other objects of their consumption, and the small desire they have of possessing those other objects. Cheap food is not an evil, but a good, if it be not accompanied with an insensibility to the comforts and decencies of life. Of what consequence is it that I give the value of a years food for a coat if I can with great facility obtain the food? Another great evil is the uncertainty to which the crops of their cheap food is liable, and the bad quality of it as a nutritious food. If it could be easily saved from year to year, or if the nutritious part could be economically extracted and put by for scarce years, the greatest objection against the cheap food of the Irish would fall to the ground.

Page 3.[2] Ireland is in fact rather in the situation of a new than an old country.

You say[3] some think that it is in consequence of there being an increase of people that there is an increase of food.

---

[1] p. 260. Mill's article 'Colony', in *Supplement to the Encyclopaedia Britannica,* is quoted.
[2] pp. 261–2.
[3] p. 262.

I am one of those. There may be an increase of people without an increase of food, because the same quantity of food may be divided amongst a larger number of people, but there can be no motive for increasing the quantity of food, till there is an effective demand for it, and that can never arise without a previous increase of people. I should say that capital increases first—then the demand for more labourers—then a better condition of the labourer. If the labourer had previously been improvident, and his family was scantily provided with food, there will at once arise an increased demand for food, if otherwise, the people must actually increase before such increased demand. In the one case the people had increased before the increase of capital; and were in wretchedness and poverty—in the other, they increased after the capital, and were always prosperous and happy.

Page 4.[1] You here very properly admit that the misery of the people proceeds from the quantity of food being insufficient for their wants, without any reference to its being raised by the spade, or of its inferior value.

I have now gone through all my remarks and it is for you to deal with them as you think they may deserve.

I can have no hesitation in expressing my opinion of your MS to Mr. Murray, which I will do to day or to-morrow. That opinion will not have probably, because it ought not to have, much weight with him. In a day or two you will perhaps call upon him yourself and I shall be happy to hear that it is to come forth under his auspices.

I am Dr Sir

Yours faithfully

DAVID RICARDO.

I send the MS by the Coach which passes through M Hampton this day.

---

[1] p. 264.

452. RICARDO TO MURRAY [1]

Dear Sir

9 Sept. 1821
        Mr. Place of Charing Cross has been writing a Reply
to Mr. Godwins book on Population, in which he defends
Mr. Malthus's doctrines from Mr. Godwin's attacks. A few
days ago Mr. Place wrote to me, communicating his wish to
have an introduction through my means to you, that he
might confer with you respecting the publication of his
book:—he, at the same time sent me his MS, with a request
that I would read it, and after reading it give my opinion
to you of its merits. I am sorry that he selected me for this
latter task—not that the reading of it was disagreeable to me,
quite the contrary, but because I am sure he fixed on a judge
very ill qualified to pronounce judgment on such a work.
Having said thus much I must proceed to fulfil the remainder
of the obligation which I have taken on myself, and give
you my opinion, leaving you to estimate it at its just value.

        I think then that Mr. Place's Reply is a triumphant one;
he appears to me to grapple with all Mr. Godwins strongest
arguments, and completely to overturn them. Mr. Malthus's
views are shewn to be, in all essential particulars, correct,
and on the whole I think Mr. Place has shewn himself to be
possessed of a great deal of industry and talents.

        Mr. Place may probably call on you in a few days—you
will dispose of him as you think proper. [2]

                              I am Dear Sir
                                 Yours very truly
                                    DAVID RICARDO

Gatcomb Park, Minchinhampton
    9 Sept: 1821

---

[1] Addressed: 'John Murray Esq' / Albermale Street / London'.
    MS in the possession of Sir John Murray.
[2] On 21 Sept. 1821 Place writes to Ricardo: 'Mr. Murray has my M.S. to shew to some friend of his. I am to hear from him in two or three days' (postscript to a letter relating to the accounts of the Chrestomathic School; unpublished, MS in *R.P*). See further, below, p. 115–16.

453. RICARDO TO MILL [1]
[Reply to 450]

Gatcomb Park
9 Sep.[r] 1821

My Dear Sir

I have read Mr. Place's MS with great attention, and 9 Sept. 1821
with great pleasure. I am much more impressed than ever
I was before with an idea of his talents,—he has shewn more
of patient investigation in this work than I ever knew him
to shew before. His success against Godwin appears to me
to be complete—not one objection of the least importance
remains unanswered. I hope it will be published. I have
written to Murray my opinion of it,—and have told him that
Mr. Place would probably call upon him in a few days to
confer with him on the subject of its publication.—I am not
very familiar with calculations respecting births, deaths and
marriages and therefore am a little afraid of the correctness
of my opinion of Mr. Place's book, but his refutation is so
complete in more views than one of Mr. Godwins speculations that I have no hesitation in saying that I am quite
satisfied with it. Mr. Place will probably shew you my letter
to him;[2] in it I have freely animadverted on those parts which
I do not quite like. You will agree with me in some of my
objections, in others I suspect you will not. I think his
charges against the rich are many of them unjust, and are
therefore likely to hurt rather than benefit the good cause.
He is a friend to the poor laws, and appears not to see that
their abolition will tend to raise the wages of labour. I forgot
to say to Mr. Place that in the book which I believe I mentioned to you, before, "Ravenstone on Population and
Political Economy" the same view or nearly the same as

---

[1] Addressed: 'James Mill Esq[r] /   MS in Mill-Ricardo papers.
East India House / London'.   [2] Letter 451.

Godwin's is taken—there may be something in that book worth his attention—it is published by Andrews 167 New Bond Street.

I hope you will be able to pay us a visit soon—I shall depend on seeing John at all events—he must always be a welcome visitor, for he knows how to find amusement for himself, and never depends wholly on others.

Sydney Smith has been staying 2 days with me—he came very near on his way from Taunton to York, at the former of which places his father resides, and near to the latter his living is situated. He was as usual full of laugh and joke. In his serious conversation he is always on the liberal side, but has a strong propensity to halt half way—he is for tolerating all religions, but is inclined to be intolerant to those whom he supposes to have no religion. I contended for Dr. Lindsay's principle, that even the Atheist should be heard, but Sydney Smith condemns him without hearing him, and then makes the sentence which he has pronounced upon him the excuse for hearing him. In Politics too he is in his heart a reformer but he does not fairly avow it—he is afraid of offending those with whom he usually associates by too openly avowing opinions which they do not favour. He is much inclined in favor of the ballot—has not heard any arguments against it that preponderate over those in favor of it, but yet he will not unequivocally say that he is in favor of it. He condemns the whigs however for not speaking out on the subject of reform, indeed I do not know how their equivocation on this question can be defended.—

Mrs. Ricardo,—my girls and boys desire to be kindly remembered to you.

Ever truly Y^{rs}

DAVID RICARDO

454. RICARDO TO MALTHUS [1]
[*Answered by* 455]

Gatcomb Park
10 Sep 1821

My Dear Malthus

I do not know whether you received the last letter   10 Sept. 1821
which I addressed to you at S.ᵗ Catherines,[2] as it must have
arrived there just about the time you were leaving that place
for Haileybury. Perhaps you may be this way again at
Christmas, if so we shall hope to see you.

Mr. Place's reply to Godwin is finished—he wishes much
that Murray should publish it, and for the purpose of con-
ferring with him on the subject, asked me for an introduction
to Murray. To enable me to speak my sentiments of the
merits of his book he sent me the MS copy, which I have
read, and returned to him. Nothing that I have ever seen
from Place's pen ever appeared to me to have half the merit
of this Reply—he meets Godwin on all his grounds, and
every where triumphantly answers him. On the question of
the American population he is quite successful, and shews by
official documents what the amount was of emigrants from
these kingdoms to America, and how utterly inadequate im-
migration has been to the actual increase of population in that
country. He has stated the case of the poor with great force,
and I think in many respects with great justice. He tells you
what their complaints are against the rich, the chief of which
are a want of sympathy with their distress, and oppressive
laws—such as combination laws, corn laws, restraints on

---

[1] Addressed: 'The Revᵈ T. R. Malthus / East India College / Hertford'.

MS in the University of Chicago Library, which purchased it in December 1932 from a London bookseller, R. Atkinson (Cata- logue 94, item 154).—Printed in *Journal of Political Economy*, Feb. 1933, p. 117 ff., with notes by Professor Jacob Viner (who has kindly supplied a photostat for collation).

[2] Letter 444.

commerce and many others. In some of his charges he
is I think most unjust to the rich, and the only injustice
which he does to you is in charging you with giving countenance to the calumnious accusations which are so generally
brought against the poor. From the representations I
have made to him[1] I trust that he will alter this part of his
work.

He does not wish to take any measures at present to get rid
even gradually of the poor laws; he thinks that the situation
of the poor would be made worse by their abolition. He
would rely entirely on appeals judiciously made to the understandings of the people—on their being instructed that their
happiness or misery depends mainly on their number compared with the demand for their labour, and therefore on
themselves. I think his arguments are popular, and will
be easily understood. If you had answered Godwin you
would have dwelt very much, and very properly, on the arguments which you have before advanced in Chap.[rs] 11 and 12
—Book 2[d] of your own work[2]—Place has said little on that
source of error in our conclusions from Registers. Place
speaks of one of Owens preventives to an excessive population[3]—he does not dwell upon it, but I have a little doubt
whether it is right even to mention it.

Have you seen a work on Population and Polit. Econ. by
Mr. Ravenstone.[4] I have read it. I think it is full of errors and
shews that the author has a very limited knowledge of the

---

[1] Above, p. 53–4.
[2] *Essay on Population,* 5th ed.,
1817, Book 11, Chap. xi 'On the
Fruitfulness of Marriages', Chap.
xii 'Effects of Epidemics on
Registers of Births, Deaths and
Marriages'.
[3] Cp. above, VIII, 71, n. 1 and
see Place's *Illustrations and Proofs*

of the Principle of Population,
Chap. vi, Section iii, 'Ideas of the
Author, relative to the Means of
preventing the People from increasing faster than food', where
however Owen's name is not
mentioned.
[4] See above, p. 45, n.

subject, yet I felt great interest in perusing it. The cause of 10 Sept. 1821 the distress of the la[bour]ing[1] class is well stated, but he appears not to be aware of the diffi[cul]ty of providing a remedy.

I have received a long letter from Say[2] in vindication of his doctrine of value, utility &c.ª—I send it to you by this day's post for your perusal—when you have read it return it to me in two parcels—it is too heavy for one frank.

Tell me your opinion of it. It appears to me to be a poor piece of reasoning.

Sydney Smith has been at Gatcomb with his family— they staid 2 nights here, on their way from Taunton to their own house. He was as agreeable as usual and we were all much pleased with his society.

Pray make our kind regards to Mrs. Malthus and believe me

Ever truly Yours
DAVID RICARDO

455. MALTHUS TO RICARDO[3]
[Reply to 444 & 454.—Answered by 458]

E I Coll Sepr 13th 1821.

My dear Ricardo,

I was just thinking of writing to you on a knotty point 13 Sept. 1821 when your letter arrived. I received your former letter just as we were getting into the carriage on our way home, but partly from a good deal of business of various kinds which I found on my arrival, and partly from despair of approaching you much nearer on the question we were then discussing, I did not rejoin.

---

[1] Covered by seal.
[2] Letter 446.

[3] Addressed: 'D. Ricardo Esqr MP. / Gatcomb Park / Minchinhampton'.—MS in *R.P.*

I am glad to hear your account of Place's work, and hope it will be of use. I should think Murray would have no objection to publish it. If it is written, as you say in a popular manner, it may perhaps have a good sale. I am much obliged to you for the representation you have made in my defence. I am not conscious of ever having said anything to countenance calumnious reports against the poor, and most certainly I never intended to do so. The principal accusations which you say he has brought against the rich seem rather to have originated in ignorance than want of sympathy.

I have only had an opportunity of looking a little at Mr. Ravenstone's book. It is certainly as you say full of errors, but I believe he is a well meaning man and I shall look at it again.

I think Say's argument may be considered rather as an artificial and ingenious mode of avoiding the consequences of his doctrine than as a satisfactory explanation. I have always thought his doctrine of utility an abuse of the natural meaning of the term, and even according to his present mode of explanation, much contradiction is involved in it. At the same time I should say, that as there is certainly no measure of utility, taken in the common acceptation of the term, and as a part of the same article, how usefulsoever, may become quite useless if it be in excess above the demand, there is no other way of approximating towards an estimate of relative wealth, than by an estimate of relative value, formed by a comparison with the objects *least liable to variations.* (but *not,* as Mr. Say says,[1] merely with the "la plus ou moins grande quantité d'un autre produit *quelconque*["]). By the by I may say, en passant, relative to this subject, that I now incline more to that explanation of value which your views would dictate, but that I am more than ever convinced

[1] Above, p. 32.

that I am right in the approximating measure of it which I have proposed.

The knotty question I wanted to lay before you is a case in point. I wish to ask whether any commodity can with propriety be considered as of a fixed value independently of money, which while it continues to require the same advances of labour and capital for its production, is obtained at different periods, at a very different rate of profits. The natural price of a commodity according to Adam Smith consists of the necessary advances, together with the ordinary rate of profits upon them; and this I think you would allow. Now of two commodities, which, I would ask, is likely to remain the most fixed? that, in which, while the advances in labour increase, the rate of profits diminishes; or that, in which while the advances in labour remain the same the profits of stock diminish. The latter article must it appears to me, be considered as falling in value estimated in any steady commodity, that is either in money obtained by a given quantity of labour without capital, or in money obtained by a given quantity of labour, a given quantity of capital, and a given rate of profits. If this be so, supposing at an early period of society (owing to the small quantity of labour necessary to produce corn) profits were 100 per cent, and money were produced in the same country at the same rate of profits, then upon the increase of the quantity of labour on the land, and fall of profits, when corn and labour estimated in such money might appear to have doubled; would it not be more correct to say that money and those commodities which had continued to require the same quantity of labour, had fallen to half their value. They would certainly appear to have done so estimated in any common *external* commodity which had all along been produced by the same quantity of labour, and at the same rate of profits. In the same country, where profits are the same, the prices of commodities may vary according to the quantity of labour, but this is only a *relative* variation, and may arise from a high value of one, as well as a low value of the other. We cannot surely assume that the cost of producing the necessaries of the labourer is low *absolutely* when the land is productive, if what is gained by the small quantity of labour employed is counterbalanced by the very high rate of profits.

I fear I have not explained myself tolerably, but you will see that the question involves most important consequences. Let me hear from you on the subject; and by the by tell me what you think of Torrens.[1] Kind regards to Mrs. R.

Ever truly Yours

T R MALTHUS

In the two extreme cases of the highest profits and the lowest profits on the land, may not corn and labour remain of the same value estimated in some external steady commodity, although in the interval considerable variations may have taken place from supply and demand.

456. TROWER TO RICARDO[2]
[*Reply to* 447.—*Answered by* 461]

Unsted Wood. Sept 13. 1821

My Dear Ricardo

I have received, and *read through,* the bulky volume of evidence[3], which you have had the kindness to order to be sent to me.—It is a most valuable body of interesting and

---

[1] Torrens's *Essay on the Production of Wealth.*
[2] Addressed: 'To / David Ricardo / M.P. / Gatcomb Park / Minchinhampton'.
    MS in *R.P.*

[3] 'Minutes of Evidence before the Select Committee on Petitions complaining of the Depressed State of Agriculture', *Parliamentary Papers,* 1821, vol. IX.

13 Sept. 1821

important information; and is well worth all the time and labor, it has cost the Committee. I have risen from the perusal of it, with a stronger conviction, (*if possible,*) than I had before, of the inexhaustible resources of this active, intelligent, and enterprising people. It is glorious to see how the Vessel of the State has righted itself, and You, my good friend, have the gratification of reflecting, that it is mainly owing to your able and judicious suggestions, that She has been steered safely through the shoals and quicksands by which she was surrounded—Every opinion I have entertained upon the subject is fully confirmed by the evidence before the Committee, and I have no doubt, not only that the Corn trade ought to be thrown open for the benefit even of the Agriculturists themselves; but, that no long period will elapse before the mischievous Corn Act will be repealed. The evidence of your friend Mr. Tooke is excellent, and proves him to be a very able man, and thoroughly master of the subject. Mr. Wakefields evidence is also good, and that of Mr. Jacob contains some interesting and important information relating to foreign agriculture. It is impossible to turn over these pages without being struck how inferior an animal, in point of intelligence, and information, the Farmer is to the manufacturer or the agent. They have afforded as little information to the Committee as possible; and have exhibited very exagerated pictures of their distresses. Take for Instance, the evidence of the Elmans, and the statement of account produced by the younger[1]—No account is taken of *live stock* on the Farm, whereas it is well known, that every farmer looks to his Stock for the payment of his Rent; and that no man, in his senses, would so farm an estate as to keep

[1] 'Statement of Expenses and Produce of 100 Acres of Arable Land in the Weald of Sussex, exclusive of Rent', delivered by John Ellman, junior. ('Minutes of Evidence before the Select Committee on...Agriculture', p. iii ff.)

13 Sept. 1821 no stock; or take a farm, which did not admit of his keeping them.—

From this subject the transition to the *weather* is very natural which, bad as it is, I believe is more conducive to the interests of the farmer, than a fine harvest would have been. Another abundant supply would have visited him severely. Whereas, at present, there is a good deal of old Corn in hand, which will fetch good prices, and we have it in evidence before the Com:, that the variations always exceed the proportions of surplus or deficiency, of which I have no doubt.—

I must now refer to your last letter, and to the observations you make on the subject of exchangeable value. You say, that "in speaking of exchangeable value, you have not any idea of real value in your mind. I invariably have." No doubt, this is the source of the difference between us. But, then, I say you ought not to express by the same term two different ideas. For you will not deny, that there is a *real difference* between exchangeable and real value. They do not always coincide—Exchangeable value is the *market* value of a Commodity—Real value is its *cost*. The *market* value, tho' governed by the real *value,* and constantly gravitating towards it, scarcely ever corresponds with it. Why then should not these two ideas be kept perfectly distinct, and be expressed by different terms. Surely, by so doing the subject is made more intelligible.—I have not seen the pamphlet you mention, nor several others which I observe advertised— vz.ᵗ Lord Stourtons Letters to Lord Liverpool[1]—Torrens' new publication.[2] Are these, or any others, which I have not noticed, worth my reading. I confess I feel, that, now, the

---

[1] *Two Letters to the Rt. Hon. the Earl of Liverpool, First Lord of the Treasury, on the Distresses of Agriculture...*, London, Maw- man, 1821. *A Third Letter* was published in the same year.
[2] *Essay on the Production of Wealth.*

subject, with respect to *Principles,* is set at rest; although, no doubt, there are many minor points still disputed by some writers. But, what I am anxious to see is *an ample application of these Principles to the practical operation of Taxation.* What we now want is a Text Book, to which Statesmen may refer, at once, to regulate their financial operations. Hitherto, Taxes have not been levied upon any settled principle, on the contrary, for the most part, they have been at war with all principle—Convenience has been the only guide. Whatever article seemed capable of bearing the burden of Taxation, and was likely to prove productive has been selected. But it is time to abandon this disgraceful, and ruinous mode of proceeding, and to avail ourselves of the benefits to be derived from the vast body of light, which has been lately thrown upon this important subject. The Time will come when our purse strings must be pulled again; and we ought to be prepared with a knowledge how best to wield our resources. For such a task I know nobody better qualified than *yourself;* indeed, you have already opened up the subject, in your excellent work; and I should rejoice to see you compleat what has been so ably begun.—

When are we to have Mill's Book out. I see no notice of it in the papers.

A great deal of the harvest in this part of the Country, is still out, and of course considerably damaged. The prices are getting up, but as there is so much inferior corn, I think what is *good* will fetch a high price, without any fear of reaching the importation prices. I think the best Wheat might sell for £27 or £28 whilst the average would remain under £20—

The curious proceedings of the Coroners Inquests[1] are no

---

[1] At the inquests on the bodies of the two men killed at the Queen's funeral, the juries had a whole Regiment drawn up in order to identify the guilty.

doubt preparing amusement for you in S.ͭ Stephens after Christmas.

I have purchased my Tithes at 28 years purchase, and they certainly are not set at a rack Rent; so, upon the whole, I am very well satisfied.

What you say about Tithes is very true, but, it is rather too speculative an opinion to *act upon.* In calculations for the investment of ones money, it is, *unfortunately,* necessary to take a much more limited view, than what would include the probable variations of *half a century hence.* It will be very little matter to either *of us* how the case may stand *then. Our* account will be wound up, I imagine, long before *that,* and the Balance struck; and God grant it may be satisfactory.

I think, therefore, that the purchase of Tithes should be considered as the buying off from the land a disagreeable Tax, and should be estimated in reference to the value of money. Land possesses many advantages, which its *produce* in the shape of Tithes does not. Influence, enjoyment, amusement, residence &. &.

Besides, although it is true, that tithes are always the same proportion of gross produce, whilst rent *may* bear a smaller, and a smaller proportion to that produce; still that will depend upon *circumstances.* It is not a *necessary* condition, as far as the purchaser of Tithes on *any particular portion* of Land is concerned—

If in the progress of wealth inferior land should be taken into cultivation, no doubt, on *that land* the Rent would be a diminished proportion of the gross produce, as compared with the land of a better quality—

But, this circumstance would not *necessarily* affect the Rent upon land previously in cultivation. That Rent would not *thereby* become a less proportion of the gross produce. On the contrary the improvements in agriculture, which would be, I may almost say, the inevitable consequence of 13 Sept. 1821 such a progressive state of society, might occasion that Rent to become a larger proportion of the gross produce.

You will say perhaps, that any additional produce drawn from the old land, the result of improvements, might bear a less proportion than the former produce did, to the gross produce, and that upon this additional produce the Tithes would equally operate.

But, supposing this to be the case, I shall derive upon this additional capital so employed the average rate of interest, or I should not so employ it, and if I had invested my money in Tithes I should have received no more.—

But it is time for me to close this long letter. So pray make Mrs. Trower's and my Compliments to Mrs. Ricardo, and believe me My Dear Ricardo—

Yrs very truly
HUTCHES TROWER.

457. RICARDO TO WHEATLEY [1]

Gatcomb Park
Minchinhampton
18 Sept 1821

Sir

I received your letter and the pamphlet which accom- 18 Sept. 1821 panied it yesterday. Although I agree in principle with you,

[1] Addressed: 'John Wheatley Esq.ʳ / Shrewsbury'. Franked by Ricardo 'September Eighteen 1821'.
MS in British Museum, Add. 29,764, fol. 44; it is included in a volume of MSS described as 'Autograph letters, and some other papers, chiefly connected with R. B. Sheridan; 1790–1843'.— *Letters to Trower*, XLIX.

On the life and writings of John Wheatley (1772–1830) see an article by F. W. Fetter in the *Journal of Political Economy,* June 1942, pp. 357–76.
Wheatley's chief work is *An Essay on the Theory of Money and Principles of Commerce,* 2 vols., 4to.; vol. I published by Cadell and Davies, London, 1807; vol. II publ. by Cadell, London, 1822, but

on the evils of a variable currency, and the impolicy of a country's using measures to raise the price of its corn as compared with its manufactures, yet I do not agree with many of the arguments and conclusions in the pamphlet. My opinions on these subjects are before the public, and therefore I shall only now say that I think it an error to suppose that the price of corn is regulated by supply and demand, only, without reference to the cost of producing it. In manufacturing goods and exporting them for corn, the cost of that corn is the cost of the production of the goods, and if by restricting the importation of corn we, instead of making the goods, raise the corn, at home, the only loss we sustain is the greater cost of producing it. From the tenor of your pamphlet I should think you estimated the loss much higher, and attributed the high price of corn to the diminished quantity and not to the greater difficulty of producing it.

On the question of the currency, your calculations would lead us to infer that the nation had been great losers by restoring it to a fixed and increased value:—now I will agree that in some cases such a measure might be very unjust, but I do not see how it can affect the interests of a country as a

printed at Shrewsbury; it was first advertised in the *Monthly Literary Advertiser* of 10 Jan. 1822.

While this letter undoubtedly refers to matters contained in vol. II of the *Essay*, it has hitherto been puzzling that Ricardo should refer to a quarto volume as a 'pamphlet' and also that he should have received it some four months before publication. Professor Viner has now found (and I am indebted to him for the communication) that a section of vol. II was separately printed in advance of publication; a copy

of this (which appears to be the 'pamphlet' commented on in Ricardo's letter) is in the Yale Library. The title-page is as follows: '*A Plan to Relieve the Country from its Difficulties.* Shrewsbury, 1821. Printed at the Chronicle Office'. The verso of the title-page reads: 'The following plan, for the relief of the country, is taken from Mr. Wheatley's Work on the Theory of Money and Principles of Commerce: the Second Volume of which is now in the Press.'

whole. You say that the *farmers and manufacturers* have lost £230,000,000 millions[1] a year by the reduction of prices.[2] I ask, has no one gained these £230,000,000? and if you say some have, I again ask who have, if they be not *farmers and manufacturers?* You will not say that the stockholder has gained this immense sum, for the whole of his annual interest amounts only to £29,000,000,—you will not say that the stockholders and public officers together have gained it, for the whole public[3] revenue of the country from which they are paid amounts only to £54,000,000—the fact is that some manufacturers, and some farmers, have been gainers, and others losers, as always is the case when the currency is tampered with—the only injury which these classes have sustained, as classes, is the real increase of taxation, which may probably amount to 5 or 6 millions p^r Ann^m on the depreciation of 1813.

I perceive that you rather misconceive my opinions on this question—I never should advise a government to restore a currency, which was depreciated 30 pc^t, to par; I should recommend, as you propose, but not in the same manner, that the currency should be fixed at the depreciated value by [lowerin]g[4] the standard, and that no further deviations should [take] place. It was without any legislation that the cu[rrency] from 1813 to[5] 1819, became of an increased value, and within 5 pc^t of the value of gold,—it was in this state of things, and not with a currency depreciated 30 pc^t, that I advised a recurrence to the old standard. The advice might

---

[1] The repetition is in MS.
[2] Wheatley argues that the restrictions on the importation of corn reduce its price in the home market, owing to the increased production and therefore impoverish the landlords and farmers as well as the manufacturers. See *Essay on the Theory of Money,* vol. II, ch. v.
[3] 'public' is ins.
[4] MS torn here and below.
[5] 'from 1813 to' replaces 'in'.

18 Sept. 1821 have been bad, and the measure unwise, but in judging of it, injustice would be done to me, and those who agreed with me, by referring to a state of things which had ceased to exist, for more than 4 years.

I am Sir

Your obed.^t Servt

DAVID RICARDO

458. RICARDO TO MALTHUS [1]

[*Reply to 455.—Answered by 459*]

Gatcomb Park

18 Sep.^t 1821

My Dear Malthus

18 Sept. 1821 Without imputing the least blame to you, I fear that I do not quite understand your "knotty point." You appear to me to compare things together, which cannot, under any supposable circumstances, be made the subject of comparison. You compare a commodity in the production of which the advances in labour remain the same while the profits of stock diminish, to another commodity "obtained by a given quantity of labour, a given quantity of capital, and a given rate of profits". Is not this supposing two rates of profit at the same time? Perhaps this was not meant, and your question was asked on the supposition of profits varying equally in all trades. If so, I have no hesitation in answering that if from an increased quantity of labour on the land, corn should appear to have doubled in money price, and not from any increased facility in the production of money, we ought to say as we always do say that corn had risen 100 pc.^t, and not that money had fallen 50. In differing on this point

[1] Addressed: 'The Revd T. R. Malthus / East India College / Hertford'. Franked by Ricardo 'September Nineteen 1821'.— MS at Albury.—*Letters to Malthus,* LXXVIII.

we in reality come to our old dispute, whether the quantity of labour in a commodity should be the regulator of its value, or whether the value of all things, should, under all circumstances, be estimated by the quantity of corn for which they would exchange. You say "we cannot surely assume that the cost of producing the necessaries of the labourer is low absolutely when the land is productive, if what is gained by the small quantity of labour employed is counterbalanced by the very high rate of profits" I of course should say that the cost of these necessaries was low if they were produced with little labour, but would not you who adopt another measure, and *sometimes* think value is to be estimated by the quantity of things generally which the commodity could command, would not you say, that the cost of these necessaries was small in value agreeing as you would that they would not command an abundance of other things? I do not know what you mean by the low cost of necessaries being counterbalanced by the very high rate of profits. If 100 q^{rs} of corn be to be divided between my labourers and me, its cost being made up of wages and profits, its cost will be the same, whether profits be high or low, and this division will in no degree affect the price of the corn, but if at a subsequent time 80 q^{rs} only can be obtained with the same labour and capital, and in consequence a greater proportion of the 80 be given to the labourers than was before given of the 100, corn will rise absolutely both in my measure and in yours. It is I who am willing to take some one or more of the external commodities, in the production of which, while the advances in labour increase in money value, the profits of stock diminish, as a steady measure, but which you so often reject, and insist that whether the produce of a given quantity of labour be 100 or 80 q^{rs}, in either case, corn has remained a steady measure of value. In the case you have supposed, you say that the commodity in which the same advances for labour were made, while profits diminished, "would not only fall one half relatively to corn, but it would appear to do so estimated in any common external commodity which had all along been produced by the same quantity of labour, *and at the same rate of profits*" I wish you had named this commodity. In the first place I deny that it would be produced at the same rate of profits, for there cannot be two rates of profit at the same time in the same country, and secondly I contend that this commodity would also fall to one half relatively to corn, and therefore would appear invariable when compared with the other commodities.

Perhaps by external commodity, you mean a foreign commodity to be imported from abroad. If so, why should not that commodity vary in reference to corn in the same degree as any home made commodity. If a hogshead of claret, were worth a certain quantity of cloth, of hats, of hardware &c.ᵃ &c.ᵃ would its relative value to these things alter because it was more difficult to raise corn in England, and its price rose because we refused to import it from other countries? To me it appears most clear that claret would not vary as compared with the things which I before enumerated, and that it would vary as compared with corn. Pray think of this and tell me whether I am not right.

In the postscript to your letter you ask "In the two extreme cases of the highest profits, and the lowest profits on the land, may not corn and labour remain of the same value estimated in some external commodity, although in the interval considerable variations may have taken place from supply and demand"? I answer, no, it could not remain of the same value. You would allow it could not remain of the same value estimated in home commodities, and as it is by means of these home commodities that we should purchase

the external commodities, I cannot see the slightest reason 18 Sept. 1821
for supposing that these commodities so exchanged could
alter in relative value. I hope I have made myself understood. I am glad you approach a little towards my views,
I wish you had told me to what extent.—Torrens told me
he should send me his book, he has not done so and I have
not seen it.

Ever Y^{rs}

DAVID RICARDO

459. MALTHUS TO RICARDO [1]
[*Reply to 458.—Answered by 460*]

E I Coll Sepr 25. 1821.

My dear Ricardo,

I am sorry that I did not make myself understood. I 25 Sept. 1821
thought that the term *external* would have prevented you
from supposing that I meant a commodity in the same country,
where of course I am aware that profits would be nearly the
same. I will try an illustration.

Suppose that corn money and commodities, were obtained
in the great mass of nations connected with each other by
commerce, *at a rate of profit of ten per cent;* but that in one
country *half the quantity of labour* only was necessary to produce corn, while other commodities were produced with as
much labour as in the rest of the world: and further let us
suppose that a free trade is established. It is obvious that
under these circumstances, the country with the fertile soil
would purchase nearly all the manufactured commodities it
might want with its corn—that its corn, which might have
been cheap at first from redundant supply, would rise from
exportation nearly to the general level, estimated in the

---

[1] MS in *R.P.*

money of the commercial world, while its manufactured commodities would be high, and those bulky domestic commodities which could not be imported might be very greatly above their level in other countries. In this state of things, if we could suppose the national capital and the demand for labour to be nearly stationary, we might conceive that labour would be the same in money price as elsewhere, while profits might be a hundred per cent, and the price of domestic goods double the price in other countries. Proceeding from this point it is obvious, that in the course of a hundred years (if accumulation were supposed) labour and corn might continue at nearly the same price, while domestic commodities, from the fall of profits to the level of other countries, would fall to half their price estimated in the money of the commercial world, which is all along supposed to be obtained by the same quantity of labour and capital, and at the same rate of profits.

The supposition which I have here made is not likely to be exactly realised; but a striking approximation to it actually exists in the case of America. The only difference is that the demand for labour, as we should naturally expect under such circumstances, has awarded to the labourer a large quantity of corn, the effect of which has been to keep the general rate of profits comparatively low, that is, at 20 per cent perhaps instead of a 100. This has prevented the domestic commodities of America from being so much affected by profits, though, on that account, they have been more affected by wages, which owing to a demand for labour much greater than in Europe, acting upon a price of corn not much less, are considerably higher than in other countries. But altogether it appears to me certain that in the progress of the cultivation of America, the price of her domestic commodities will decidedly fall estimated in hogsheads of French Claret or in the money of Europe, while a mean between her corn and labour will remain nearly the same.

According to my views, whenever money or any other commodity is obtained by double the quantity of labour necessary to produce corn, and also at a very high rate of profits compared with other countries it is an infallible sign that such money or commodity is extremely scarce compared with the demand for it and that consequently it will fall in value in the progress of accumulation and cultivation. A hogshead of claret in a stationary country, may continue for years to exchange for the same quantity of hats in a progressive country; but this is merely because in the latter country the fall in the value of silver counterbalances in price the real diminution in the cost of producing hats occasioned by the fall of profits.

The diminution in the cost of producing hats or money, which arises solely from the fall of corn and labour is quite of a precarious nature and is at all times liable to be completely put an end to by such a demand for corn and labour as is extremely probable, and has often been actually experienced in the commercial world.

No other supposition can render money of the same value at all times than that of supposing it be obtained always by the same quantity of labour without *any capital.* Surely, on the first blush of it, it seems almost a contradiction to suppose money of the same value, which with the same labour, is at one time obtained at profits of 100 per cent and at another of 5 per cent.

My approximation to you on the subject of value only consists in a greater disposition to reject commodities in general, as a *measure,* and refer only to those where the cost of production including profits seems to continue most nearly the same. Torrens's is a cleverly written work,[1] and on

[1] *Essay on the Production of Wealth.*

25 Sept. 1821 the whole I think, almost as much in my favour as yours. But he is still infested with the heresy of attempting to account for prices and profits without reference to demand and supply on which every thing really depends. Tell me if I have made myself understood.

Ever Yours,
T R MALTHUS

460. RICARDO TO MALTHUS [1]
[*Reply to 459.—Answered by 462*]

[Gatcomb Park, 28 Sept. 1821]

My Dear Malthus

28 Sept. 1821   The case you put to me appears to me to be an impossible one. How can all countries produce their commodities with the same quantity of labour; all, except one, produce their corn with the same quantity of labour also; and yet all, the one not excepted, have their profits on capital at the same rate? The one which you suppose to raise its corn with only half the quantity of labour required in the others, would, in all probability, obtain its labour at a much cheaper price, and consequently profits would be higher in that country.

If indeed a free trade should be established between all these countries, then their profits might be all nearly at the same rate, because the price of corn and necessaries, estimated in quantity of labour, would be nearly the same in all. In carrying on this supposed case we must be informed whether the country in which corn is obtained with comparatively little labour, can continue to obtain it on the same terms, after she is called upon to supply the markets of other

[1] Addressed: 'The Revd T. R. Malthus / East India College / Hertford'. Franked by Ricardo 'Minchinhampton September Twenty eight 1821'. MS at Albury.—*Letters to Malthus*, LXXIX.

countries; if she can, then the comparative prices of corn and commodities will be altered in all countries;—in the country producing the cheap corn, money will be rather at a higher level than before, and therefore corn rather dearer, but commodities generally will be at no higher price they will be indeed rather cheaper, because they will be imported from abroad, and from countries where the level of currency will be somewhat reduced, and therefore the cost price of commodities in those countries will be lower, and consequently they can be sold cheaper to the country importing them. Bulky commodities, and the price of labour, will only be raised in this particular country, because the level of currency will be somewhat raised—labour will in the real measure of value be rather lowered, that is to say, the portion of produce paid to the labourer, manufactured and raw produce, together, will probably be rather increased, but in consequence of free trade and a better distribution of capital, the proportion of the whole produce of a given capital[1] which the labourers will receive will be diminished—his proportion will really be obtained with less labour.

The benefit to other countries cannot be doubted—corn and labour will fall very greatly in those countries, and consequently profits will rise, and as part of their exports in return for corn must in the first instance be money—the general level of currency will be reduced and commodities generally will fall, not because they can be produced cheaper, but because they are measured by a more valuable money. This is on the supposition that corn can continue to be produced with little labour in the excepted country, but suppose the increased demand for corn should oblige this country to cultivate poorer land, then the price of corn would rise from another cause besides the higher level of currency, and if

[1] 'of a given capital' is ins.

this difficulty should be nearly as great as in other countries corn would be nearly as high, but while it could afford on any terms to export corn for commodities there would be previously to the importation of commodities an influx of the precious metals, and a higher level of currency. Without such higher level of currency commodities could never be imported from countries where they were before at the same price, and where they required the same quantity of labour to produce them. Your case is an impossible one, 1st because you suppose the profits in two countries to be the same, although the cost of producing necessaries in one of them be only one half of what it is in the other. 2dly you assume as a matter of course that with a free trade the price of corn in the exporting country would rise to the price of corn in the importing country, whereas it would fall in the importing country to the price in the exporting country, if its cost of production was not increased in that country, and if it rose it would rise only in proportion to the increased cost of production. When there is a free trade between countries it is impossible that profits can differ very much—the only cause of difference in such case will be the different modes of living of the labourers; in one country they may be contented with potatoes and a mud hovel, in another they may require a decent house and wheaten bread. You say "Proceeding from this point it is obvious, that in the course of a hundred years (if accumulation were supposed) labour and corn might continue at nearly the same price, while domestic commodities, from the fall of profits to the level of other countries, would fall to half their price estimated in the money of the commercial world" Domestic commodities are to fall because profits fall. If profits fell *I* do not see why domestic commodities should fall; but why should profits fall if corn and labour continued at nearly the same price—I know of no cause of the fall of profits but the fall[1] of labour. You say 'a striking approximation to this case actually exists in America, the only difference" you continue "is that circumstances in America have made labour high" but this is the only important feature in the case. I am however decidedly of opinion that if in America labour was very low and profits consequently much higher than they are, there would be very little fall in the domestic commodities of America.

I agree indeed with you that in the progress of the cultivation of America her corn must rise with the increased difficulty of producing it—this circumstance must have a tendency to reduce the relative[2] quantity, or rather lower the level, of American currency, which will not fail by increasing the value of money to lower the value of those commodities in America which are too bulky to be exported.* The commodities which America exports will not be similarly affected. Nothing is to me so little important as the fall and rise of commodities in money, the great enquiries on which to fix our attention are the rise or fall of corn, labour, and commodities in real value, that is to say the increase or diminution of the quantity of labour necessary to raise corn, and to manufacture commodities. It may be curious to develop the effect of an alteration of real value on money price, but mankind are only really interested in making labour productive, in the enjoyment of abundance, and in a good distribution of the produce obtained by capital and industry. I cannot help thinking that in your speculations you suppose these much too closely connected with money price.

* On reading over my letter I am doubtful whether this opinion respecting exportable commodities is correct.

[1] Should be 'rise'.   [2] 'relative' is ins.

28 Sept. 1821

I have read a very good critique on Godwin in the Edin. Review, and I am quite sure that I know the writer.[1] It is very well done, and most satisfactorily exposes Godwin's ignorance as well as his disingenuousness.

Ever Yours

DAVID RICARDO

I cannot agree with you that in the progress of the cultivation of America a mean between her corn and labour will remain nearly at the same price as it now is, estimated in money or in hogsheads of claret; it will in my opinion rise. Let me take your own supposition. A country produces her corn with half the labour of another country, consequently she employs only half the capital in producing a given quantity[2]. In this country corn will be at only half the price, at which it is in another; 100 q^{rs} will sell for £200, while in another it sells for £400. Suppose profits in both countries to be 20 pc^t, in one a capital of £166 will be employed in the raising of 100 q^{rs} of corn, in the other £333 will be so employed, and 20 pc^t on each of these capitals will be on one £33 and on the other £66. To get £33 the one must have $16\frac{1}{2}$ q^{rs} for his share of the 100 q^{rs}, the other must have precisely the same quantity, and consequently $83\frac{1}{2}$ quarters are paid in both cases for wages and other charges. But the farmer in the fertile country employs only half the labour that the other employs, and consequently with the same money wages each labourer will have the command of double the quantity of corn, he will have what you call double real wages.

Now suppose that in the progress of the fertile country it [does][3] at last arrive at the state in which it is necessary to

---

[1] July 1821, Art. VI, 'Godwin on Malthus'. The author was Malthus; see below, pp. 89–90 and 94.

[2] 'or wages must be enormously high in which case she may employ nearly the same amount of capital' is del. here.

[3] Covered by seal.

[empl]oy £333 instead of £166 to raise 100 q^{rs} of corn, it is indeed possible, under the extravagant supposition with which we have commenced, that labour might continue at the same money price, but it is quite impossible that corn should not be doubled in money price, for twice the quantity of labourers at these uniform money wages would be required to produce it. If Corn doubles in price, and wages remain stationary, the mean between the two must necessarily rise, and consequently estimated in claret or in money, a mean between her corn and labour cannot as you say remain nearly the same. If, (as I had a right to suppose) labour in such a country was at a low money price, when corn could be produced with so much facility, the conclusion, when corn rose, would be much more in my favor.

I cannot allow that hats would fall in a progressive country because of a fall of profits. How can it be said that the cost of producing hats is reduced by a fall of profits, if a fall of profits must be accompanied by a rise of wages. Shew me that a fall of profits may take place without a rise of wages, in any fixed measure of value, and then I will yield this point. But *you* have no right to talk of a fall of profits, your case is that of a progressive country with low profits, and enormous wages. If of every 100 q^{rs} of corn, where it can be produced with little labour, 83 be given to the labourers, while no more is given in countries where double the quantity of labourers are employed to produce 100 q^{rs} of corn, *you* are bound to say that wages are enormously high. In my measure of value they would not be enormously high, but the commodity on which wages were expended would be extravagantly low,—at any rate we should both agree that profits in such a state of things would be very moderate.

It is hardly fair to tax you with so long a letter, and so soon too!

461. RICARDO TO TROWER [1]
[Reply to 456.—Answered by 466]

Bromesberrow Place, Ledbury
4 Oct.! 1821

My Dear Trower

4 Oct. 1821   I was much pleased to find by your last letter, that you thought well of the information, contained in the minutes of Evidence, which accompanied our Report from the Agricultural Committee, and that in your criticisms on the evidence of the different individuals called before the committee, your opinion coincides so nearly with my own. The only part of Mr. Tooke's evidence, in which I cannot agree with him, is that in which he says, that if the trade in Corn were left perfectly free, the growers of corn in the United Kingdom would be able to compete with the corn growers of other countries, meaning thereby, as he explained himself, there would be as much probability of our exporting corn to other countries, on an average of years, as of importing it from those countries.[2] This I do not believe—our manufacturing superiority—our greater riches—our dense population, all have a tendency to make us importers of corn, and although the quantity we should import would be only a few weeks consumption, yet I think we should be habitually and constantly an importing country. In the Committee the great holders of land went to the other extreme of Mr. Tooke's opinion, they thought that with a free trade in Corn we should import almost all our corn, and in that case they asked what was to become of the aristocracy; if they were ruined they wanted to know what class in the community could perform the important services which they rendered as magistrates, grand jurors, &c. &c. If indeed all our land was

---

[1] Addressed: 'Hutches Trower Esq! / Unsted Wood / Godalming / Surrey'.

MS at University College, London.—*Letters to Trower,* L.

[2] Minutes of Evidence, pp. 288–9.

to go out of cultivation, as these alarmists anticipated, then the question of importation would be a serious one indeed, and we should be obliged to give due consideration to the important political consequences which might result from it. Mr. Jacobs facts are interesting, but on the scientific part of the subject I thought him quite wild, and persevered in my questions to him till I believe he thought me rude. I knew by his publications[1] that he had taken a very prejudiced and unskilful view of the subject.

On the subject of "Real value" and "Exchangeable value" you ask why should not these two ideas be kept perfectly distinct, and be expressed by distinct terms? Why indeed should they not? I reply, but I ask in my turn whether they are not kept distinct by prefixing the word "real" to one, and "exchangeable" to the other?

I have neither seen Torrens' publication, nor Lord Stourton's letter to Lord Liverpool. Of the last I have heard nothing, but of Torrens' book I have heard a favorable account from Malthus[2]—he says it is well and clearly written, and on the whole he thinks it makes as much for his (Malthus's) view of the question, as for mine. I do not know why Mill's book does not appear, I believe he has finished it.

I, as well as you, would like to see an application of the Principles of Political Economy, as now understood, to the practical operation of taxation, and I hope it will not be long before such a work appears. Ministers will always look more to the facility with which they can raise money by a tax, and the produce they can obtain from it, than to its consequences on the prosperity and future resources of the country (witness the legacy duty); this however is no argument against the general dissemination of good doctrines, for if a minister was not restrained by an honest legislature, he would receive no

[1] See above, VI, 180, n. 1.   [2] Above, p. 79–80.

inconsiderable check from an enlightened public. You make a great mistake in supposing me capable of producing so important a work.

About Gatcomb we have not lost a great deal of corn from the badness of the weather, though it has suffered some damage, but I hear great complaints made by the farmers in the part of the country where I am now writing—their crops are entirely spoiled.

The proceedings of the Coroner's Inquest on the late Affray at the Queens funeral have a better chance than ever of being made the subject of discussion in parliament, since they have ended in the dismissal of Sir R. Wilson from the army. According to what we at present know, I think he has been very harshly used.[1]

I cannot agree with you that in the investment of one's money it is necessary to take a much more limited view than what would include the probable variation of half a century. Although *we* shall not be alive then, our children or our children's children will, and in investments of money we never fail to estimate a future and contingent benefit at its just value, accordingly as it may be near or distant. In comparing the purchases of land and of tithes it is quite right to estimate the advantages of the former, in the shape of influence, enjoyment and amusement, at its just value; but the objection you make that in buying tithes you only make the common rate of interest and you would have made as much if you had employed the same amount of capital in improving your land, or else you would not so employ

---

[1] Major-General Sir R. Wilson, M.P., had been dismissed for having, when present at the funeral in his private capacity, rebuked the soldiers who fired on the people. The debate on his dismissal took place on 13 Feb. 1822; that on the circumstances of the Queen's funeral on 6 March 1822. (*Hansard,* N.S., VI, 282 ff., 923 ff.)

it, is not a good one, and entirely changes the question in dispute.

What we were discussing was whether it would be more advantageous to buy land, or buy tithes; but the proposition as stated by you would be whether it was more advantageous to employ a capital in improving land, or in buying tithes. I have no doubt that in an improving country the latter would be most advantageous but it is essentially a different question from that which we were before discussing—if you buy land you have no capital with which to improve land, you obtain only the rent and that rent will improve in proportion as it becomes the interest of your tenant to expend a greater capital on that land, even although he should not in the least improve it. By such expenditure he may derive more from it, and of that increased quantity he may be constrained to give you a portion—you will have a larger portion, and each portion will be of a greater value, but I contend the tithe holder will be still better off—his proportion of the whole produce will be as before—he will not only have a larger portion, but the same proportion, the landlords *proportion* of the whole produce will be probably diminished.

Sydney Smith and his family passed a couple of days with me on their way from Taunton to York.[1] He was in his usual good spirits and we were sorry to lose him so soon. His articles in the Edin. Review on Spring Guns, and Prisons,[2] are I think both very good,—he is a good reasoner, and has much the best of the argument with the Judges. I like the article on Godwins book, I have not heard who the writer is, but I have no doubt whatever that it was written by Malthus

[1] He had been at Taunton with his family to see his father, Robert Smith, now 82 years of age; and he was returning to his parsonage at Foston, near York.

(See *A Memoir of the Rev. Sydney Smith,* by Lady Holland, London, 1855, vol. II, pp. 217–19.)
[2] July 1821, Arts. II and VIII.

4 Oct. 1821 himself.[1] His doctrines are very fairly vindicated against the calumny by which they are usually assailed, and I think the principles themselves most successfully established. In Malthus book there is much attackable matter, but he is very unfairly used by his antagonists, and his leading principle is studiously kept out of view.

I am passing a few days with my son, who is living in a fertile and beautiful country. A walk of ten minutes takes one to the summit of the first and lowest of the Malvern Hills from whence there is an extensive prospect, and a good view of Eastnor Castle (Lord Somers's) and Park. I dare say you know the country.

Mrs. Ricardo unites with me in compliments to Mrs. Trower.

Believe me
My dear Trower
Ever truly yours
DAVID RICARDO

Sydney Smith when a youth lived in this very spot.

462. MALTHUS TO RICARDO [2]
[*Reply to 460.—Answered by 463*]

[*ca.* 9 Oct. 1821][3]

My dear Ricardo

9 Oct. 1821 I am either most unfortunate in my explanations, or your mind is so entirely prepossessed with your own views on the subject of our discussion, that you will not give to any statement, which departs from them the degree of attention which is necessary to put you in possession of what is meant.

---

[1] See above, p. 84.
[2] Addressed: 'D. Ricardo Esqr M.P. / Gatcomb Park / Minchinhampton Gloucestershire.'

MS in *R.P.*
[3] Headed by Ricardo 'Received 10ᵗʰ Octʳ 1821'. London postmark, 9 Oct. 1821.

9 Oct. 1821

You say that my case is an impossible one 1st because I suppose profits in two countries to be the same although the cost of producing necessaries in one of them be only one half of what it is in the other, and 2^{nly} because I assume that with a free trade the price of corn in the exporting country would rise to the price of the importing country, whereas it would fall in the importing country to the price of the exporting country.

With regard to your first objection, I would ask you, Where I have made the supposition you impute to me? Surely not in my last letter. Unless by mistake I left out a word. My first supposition was that profits would be 100 per cent in the country where corn was obtained with double the facility, while it was ten per cent in all others. And in my second illustration which had a direct reference to America I supposed that profits were 20 per cent or double what they were in the states of Europe. Do look again at my letter and tell me if I deceive myself.

With regard to your second objection, though it may be your opinion that the price of the corn of all the states of Europe will fall in proportion to the facility of production in America, I am certainly of a different opinion; and as some proof that I have reason on my side I refer to the actual state of things, and ask whether since the colonization of North America, it appears that American corn has more approached the level of European, or European corn sunk to the level of American. Could it indeed have been expected from theory that the small surplus which could be annually exported from America with the greatest quantity of labour which she could obtain from the most rapid possible increase of a small population would be sufficient to lower essentially the prices of corn all over Europe.

You say that you cannot agree with me that in the progress of cultivation in America a mean between corn and labour will remain nearly at the same price as it now is,—estimated in money, or in hogsheads of claret; and then you immediately *suppose* that in America corn will be only at half the price that it is in other countries. But what can possibly entitle you to make this *supposition,* if it be contrary to the fact. My observation, as you quote it, relates *specifically* to America. And if it be an acknowledged truth that in America for above half a century before the termination of the war, the bullion price of corn had been less below the average of Europe than the bullion price of labour had been above it, surely I have pretty strong reasons for concluding that a mean between corn and labour in America, a hundred years hence, is more likely to fall than rise as compared with the corn and claret of Flanders and France, supposing them to continue the same.

You say further that if in such a country labour were at a low money price, *which you have a right to suppose* where corn is obtained with so much facility, the conclusion would be much more in your favour. Now this is the kind of answer to me which I think I may fairly complain of. According to your theory labour ought certainly to be low. But I dispute your theory; and say that with whatever facility the corn was obtained if there were such a *demand* for it at home and abroad as to raise it nearly [to][1] the price of other countries, which might easily happen in a well situated colony for 150 years together, then of necessity, (on account of the demand for labour and the quantity of corn earned by the labourer) the bullion price of labour must be high. And as a proof I refer to the actual state of things in America. Surely in such a case your business is to shew that the fact in no respect invalidates your theory; but to assume a *different* fact, than the one I refer to, in order to refute me seems to be

[1] Omitted in MS.

an odd mode of arguing. I have never heard the *fact* of the high bullion price of labour in the United States, before the late distresses, called in question by a single person, and it was to America *with a high price of labour,* that, as I said before, I *specifically* referred when I expressed the opinion that a mean between corn and labour would not be higher a hundred years hence.

You say that you cannot allow that hats would fall in a progressive country on account of the fall of profits; but that if I can shew that a fall of profits may take place without a rise of wages in any fixed measure of value, you will yield the point. Now it certainly appears to me, that if in every country the same quantity of gold and silver were obtained by the same quantity of labour, without *any capital,* money would be a more fixed measure of value than under any other circumstances. But in this case it is quite certain, that the money prices of commodities in different countries which had cost the same quantity of labour, would vary exactly as the rate of profits, and hats in a progressive country would fall as profits fell. The only stationary commodities would be corn and labour—Labour would be stationary by the hypothesis, and corn would have a constant *tendency* to maintain the same price, because the increasing quantity of labour and capital necessary to produce it would be just counterbalanced by the fall of profits, or the diminished quantity of necessaries given to the labourer. In the same country where the profits may be supposed to be equal (as far as the whole can be made to consist of labour and profits) prices will vary as the quantity of labour employed. In different countries where profits are unequal, the prices of commodities which have cost the same quantity of labour, will vary as profits.

According to your theory—if in a country which had been growing its corn and producing its money at a profit of ten per cent, the facility of production on the land were doubled, corn and labour would sink to one half, and profits would rise perhaps to above a hundred per cent. Now I wish to ask what is to become of the money which was before produced. It is obvious that the corn and labour of the country could absorb at first but little more than the half of what they did before; and yet as the profit of producing money as well as other commodities would be a hundred per cent, there could be little doubt of its continued production. Would not this great plenty of money in an isolated country necessarily keep up the prices of labour and commodities; and if the country were not isolated, the exportation of its corn would prevent any considerable fall. It appears to me I confess most extremely difficult to assimilate a country with an abundant capital, to a country with a scanty capital, merely because you *suppose* them by some sudden change to obtain their corn with the same quantity of labour. Much time and loss of capital must take place before they can be in a similar situation. In the case of the greatest improvements in agriculture, and a fall in the price of corn, it is my opinion that if labour were to fall before an increase of population had taken place, it could only be from glut and want of demand.

I am glad you approve of the Review in the Edinburgh. If you have discovered the author dont betray the secret. I hope Place has met with a favourable reception with Murray and is coming out. I am going to Town tomorrow to Holland House for a couple of days, and on other business. I met the Hollands at Lord Cowpers the other day at Pansanger and Lady H. made me promise to pay this visit. Mrs. M joins with me in kind regards to Mrs. Ricardo who I hope is quite well.

Ever truly Yours
T R Malthus.

463. RICARDO TO MALTHUS [1]
[Reply to 462.—Answered by 467]

Gatcomb Park
11 Oct[r] 1821

My Dear Malthus

It is certainly probable that the fault is with me, in not 11 Oct. 1821
understanding the propositions you submit to me, and it may
arise, as you say, from my being too much prepossessed in
favour of my own views; but I do not plead guilty to the
charge of not giving the requisite degree of attention to the
propositions themselves. You now say "Where have I made
the supposition you impute to me? surely not in my last
letter. My first supposition was that profits would be 100
per cent in the country where corn was obtained with double
the facility, while it was 10 pc[t] in all others." If you had
done so, then indeed I should be justly chargeable with in-
attention, but these were your words in the letter which I
was answering. "I will try an illustration. Suppose that
corn, money and commodities were obtained in the great
mass of nations connected with each other by commerce, at
a rate of ten per cent; but that in one country half the quantity
of labour only was necessary to produce corn, while other
commodities were produced with as much labour as in the
rest of the world:" not one word is said of profits being at
a different rate in this country, and as you had said that in
the great mass of nations profits were at 10 pc[t] I concluded
that in this country also profits were supposed to be at 10 pc[t].
In this instance then you must acknowledge the fault was
yours and not mine. You do indeed afterwards suppose that
this single country exports its corn, and obtains the high

---

[1] Addressed: 'The Rev[d] T. R.   MS at Albury.—*Letters to Mal-*
Malthus / East India College /   *thus*, LXXX.
Hertford'.

price of other countries for it, and by such means raises its profits to 100 pc.ᵗ, but this evidently would depend on the fact whether she would get the price of other countries, or whether domestic competition would lower the price of corn in the countries to which it was exported, to the growing price of the exporting country.

This I now understand to be your case. If the country which raised its corn, with such great facility, were completely insulated from all other countries, you would probably allow that corn, in that country, would be cheap in proportion to the facility of producing it. You would allow this also if all other countries were determined to protect their own agriculture and absolutely refused to import foreign corn. But in the case of a free trade, then you think the price would rise in the exporting country to the level of the price of other countries, and consequently profits would be enormously high. If I could admit the fact of a high price, which I cannot do, I should adopt[1] your conclusion—I should say that general profits would be higher[2] than they had been before the rise in the price of corn. Rents would undoubtedly be higher for the landlord would have at least the same portion of corn as before, and that portion would be greatly enhanced in value. Labour would be higher, because the labourer would require higher money wages when corn was doubled in price. And profits would be higher because the capitalist would have more corn than before at the same time that it bore a higher price. All these classes would be benefited by the high relative value of corn to manufactured commodities, and the capitalist more particularly so, because amongst those manufactured commodities are to be found some of the necessaries of the labourer, and therefore by the payment of a less portion of corn to the labourer he would

---

[1] Replaces 'reject'.   [2] Replaces 'lower'.

still have the command of an increased quantity of food and necessaries for himself and his family. The question then between us is, would the price of corn rise permanently, or would it not, in the country which continued to possess the great facility of producing it?

There is only one case in which I think such a rise possible, and that is on the supposition that the whole capital of the country was employed in producing corn, and yet could not produce it in sufficient quantity to satisfy the demand of other countries. In that case corn would be at a monopoly price, in the same manner as those rare wines which can only be produced in particular districts are at a monopoly price, because competition could not have its full effect. In the article of corn it would be limited by the scarcity of capital, which gave to the growers of corn large profits, in the same way as the East India Company or any other Company might make large profits. In the article of wine the price would be augmented by the scarcity of the land on which the grapes were grown, and would chiefly go to the landlord in form of rent. But supposing no monopoly—supposing capital to be so abundant that all the corn demanded could be supplied, then I hold it to be demonstrable, that the price would sink to the growing price of it in the exporting country.

There is however another point on which we differ—you say a striking approximation to this actually exists in the case of America,—the only difference is that the demand for labour has awarded a larger quantity of corn to the labourer, the effect of which has been to keep the rate of profit comparatively low. But you surely do not mean that the exchangeable value of the commodities exported by America are in the least degree affected by the quantity of corn awarded to the labourer. I do not think you are justified in your expectation that in consequence of the accumulation of capital in America any commodity should fall there until it ceased to possess the character of a monopolized commodity. Corn, and the bulky commodities of America (which latter are always regulated by the price of corn) could not fall until corn was sold at a price depending on the quantity of labour actually expended on its production, and not on the demand of other countries. When that time came it would cease to be a monopolised commodity, and would fall, as well as profits, to the fair competition rates. I deny that America comes at all within your supposed case, and the proof is that if you were to isolate America from all other countries, you would not lower her rate of profits, otherwise than by preventing her from receiving a supply of labour from other countries; but do the same thing to a country, circumstanced as you have supposed, and profits would immediately fall from 100 to perhaps 20 pc^t. Your case in fact is that of a country possessed of a peculiar commodity in very general demand, and on which competition operates most feebly. We have often discussed this peculiar case, and have always agreed in our opinions on it. I confess however I am astonished to hear you say that this is the case of America— you might with as much reason contend that it was also the case of Russia, of Poland, of the Cape of Good Hope, of Botany Bay. If indeed America could send her produce from the interior to Europe without expence, and if the ports of all countries were open freely to receive the corn with which America could under the circumstances I have supposed, supply, then I should say the cases were similar, but with the enormous expences of sending corn from the interior of the country, America can really produce a very inconsiderable supply to Europe at an expence much less than Europe can grow it. You ask what can entitle me to suppose that corn will be at half the price in America that it is in other countries, and then argue on that supposition so contrary to the fact. I answer I did not apply my argument to America, but to your case which supposed a country to produce corn with half the labour which was required to produce it in other countries. If America can do this, then I apply it to America. You complain that I do not reason fairly with you, that my theory requires labour to be low in America, but you dispute my theory and refer to the actual state of things in America where labour is high, and yet I contend that I have a right to suppose labour low. I was dealing with your case, and not with America. With respect to America I am not in possession of the facts of her case, and I cannot admit that my theory requires the price of labour to be low in that country. It requires rent to be low, for without that there cannot be a great surplus produce to divide between the two other classes, after satisfying the landlord. You will always make me say, that profits depend on the low price of corn—I never do say so, I contend that they depend on wages, and although in my opinion wages will be mainly regulated by the facility of obtaining necessaries, they do not entirely depend on such facility. You wish to confine me to that theory, but I reject it,—it is none of mine, and I have often told you so. I think I *do* shew that your fact does not invalidate my theory which you say I am bound to do, and I do not assume a different fact than the one you refer to in order to refute you. Surely it is fair to say "for such and such reasons your conclusion is not correct, but my argument would have been still stronger against you, if, as I have a right to suppose, labour in such a country were cheap, because the necessaries of the labourer are there obtained with facility."

In a country situated as you suppose America to be I do not see what is to make her corn rise; it is already, according to your argument, at a monopoly price, and cannot rise above that price, unless there should be a greater demand, and a higher price in Europe, which you say regulates the price in America; or unless America should become so populous that the price of her corn should be regulated by the expence of growing it, as in other countries, and that expence should exceed the present expence in Europe. If your theory be correct, this may not happen in 150 years, notwithstanding the greatest accumulations of capital; but will not labour fall during all that time? If it does fall, then the mean between corn and labour will fall. But suppose the other case, suppose the COST[1] price of corn in America should rise above the present cost price in Europe, is it conceivable that labour should fall under such circumstances—to me it appears impossible, unless we suppose money to alter in value. In this case then also the mean between corn and labour would vary in value.

If hats were produced under the same circumstances as money they would not fall in price in consequence of a fall of profits. If hats were produced by the employment of capital, and money were produced, as you suppose, without any capital, then I allow, and have said so in my book,[2] hats would fall in price with a fall of profits—but I say again that too much importance is attached to money—facility of production is the great and interesting point. How does that operate on the interests of mankind?

You ask what is to become of the money before produced in a country which should grow its corn with 10 pc.^t profit if it had its facility of producing corn doubled, and profits were to rise to 100 pc.^t: you ask further whether she would not continue to produce money as well as other com-

---

[1] Underlined three times in MS.   [2] Above, I, 44–5; a passage added in ed. 3 of the *Principles*.

modities as the profits of producing it would be also 100 pc^t.
If the facility of producing corn were doubled a great deal of
labour would be employed on other things, and therefore the
corn and commodities of the country would altogether be of
as great a money value as before, and would require the same
quantity of money to circulate them. With respect to the
production of more money, that would depend on the demand for it, and the prices of other things. I think the production of money would continue as before, but it is quite
possible that there might be less encouragement to produce
money than other things, and therefore capital might afford
100 pc^t profit in all employments except that one. I wonder
you should refuse to assent to this obvious conclusion. You
say it is your opinion that if labour were to fall in consequence
of improvements in Agriculture before an increase of population had taken place, it could only be from glut and want of
demand. Is this opinion consistent with another which I
think you hold, and in which I agree, that one of the regu-
lators of the price of labour is the price of the necessaries of
the labourer?

I have mentioned my suspicions respecting the writer of
the article on population in the Edin. Review to several
persons—I will not utter them from this time.—I hear
nothing about Murray and Place. I hope your visit at
Holland House was an agreeable one. Mrs. Ricardo unites
with me in kind regards to Mrs. Malthus—we are all well
and are leading gay lives, one week at Worcester Music
meeting and Bromesberrow, another at Bath &c^a.—

Ever truly Yours

DAVID RICARDO

464. RICARDO TO MILL [1]
[*Answered by* 469]

Gatcomb Park
14 Oct.ʳ 1821

My dear Sir

 I have read your article on the Liberty of the Press[2] with great pleasure, and am very much enlightened by it. It has always appeared to me a subject full of difficulty, but I think you have shewn with great skill that the difficulty is not in defining the offence, but in ascertaining the fact whether the offence has been committed, and for that you must depend on the evidence, as in all other cases of offences complained of. The principles you lay down naturally follow from those which you had before established in your article on Government, and you clearly shew that without a liberty almost unbounded for the Press, one of the most important securities for the peoples interests being attended to by their Governors would fail, and that without this security all others would be unavailing.

I was startled at the extent of your proposition respecting the liberty to be allowed of exhorting the people by means of the Press to resist their Governors, and to overthrow the Government. I understood full well that without great facilities being afforded to a people to resist, there could be no real freedom, but between this, and openly allowing exhortations to resistance, is a great stride, and notwithstanding the good reasons given by you in favor of it, I hesitate in agreeing to it before I have given it more consideration. I fear you would make the overturning of a Government too easy, which would certainly be an evil, as well as the making it too difficult.

[1] Addressed: 'James Mill Esqʳ / East India House / London'.
   MS in Mill-Ricardo papers.

[2] In *Supplement to the Encyclopaedia Britannica.*

I have only one other remark to make. You admit that truth should be a justification for all writings tending to disturb the peace of individuals, but you speak of some exceptions which it might perhaps be wise to allow against the general rule. Of the cases you mention as exceptions you speak I think much too favorably. Why should a vain man be protected in the concealment of the poverty and lowness of his birth, because an undue regard is paid to rank and riches. Why should his foible be excused more than the foibles of all the rest of mankind which you are willing should be made public. I think I could have brought forward a stronger case than yours, and yet I would not on any account exempt it from the general rule. You are too indulgent too to the feelings of a man who privately infringes the religious ordinances of the society of which he is a member. Why throw a veil over him? He has his choice either to be satisfied with his own approbation and that of the few who think like him and openly to profess his principles, or to pay the price for obtaining that of the multitude. It surely would be a dangerous principle to establish that duplicity and deceit should be encouraged and upheld by a positive law. I know that your own conclusion is that truth without any exception should be the sole criterion by which writings hurting the feelings of individuals should be tried, but in your argument you appear to me to lean too favorably to some of the cases which others might wish to except.

I am glad to hear that the printing of your Polit. Econ. is now immediately to commence.

I wish you had told me what Murray has agreed upon respecting the publication of Mr. Place's book.

We have lately been very gay here. We have been down the Wye with the girls and Osman and his wife, and Clutterbuck with his. Since which we have passed a week at

14 Oct. 1821 Bromesberrow, and have been at Malvern and Worcester. Next week we go for a few days to Bath. I do not yet relinquish the hope of seeing you here. Miss Edgeworth has written to me to ask me respecting my engagements—she intends accepting an invitation which I gave her when I met her last year at Mr. Smiths and to pass a few days with her two sisters at Gatcomb. Perhaps you may like to meet her, if so I will let you know the time she fixes upon for her visit. That or any other time will be agreeable to me to receive you. You recollect John is to come with you if you come, and alone if you do not.—We are undertaking further improvements in our grounds, and you will be just in time to give an opinion of them before they are carried into execution if you come soon.

Ever Y^{rs}

DAVID RICARDO

465. TOOKE TO RICARDO [1]

Wimbledon 13th Octr 1821.

My dear Sir

13 Oct. 1821   On my return hither last night I found your few lines of the 11th.—I will speak to Mr. Jno Thornton, who is only *very* distantly related to my partners [2] but with whom I am sufficiently acquainted, in behalf of Mr. Basevi J^r—and I will use my best endeavors to engage in his favor such of my friends as I may find to be embarked in this new Fire and Life insurance Company to which you allude but of which I have hitherto heard few particulars. [3] If Mr. Basevi J^r

---

[1] MS in *R.P.*
[2] Tooke was partner in and 'chiefly conducted' the house of Stephen Thornton, Brothers, & Co., Russia merchants. (See 'First Report from the Lords' Committee on Foreign Trade, Minutes of Evidence', p. 25, in

Parliamentary Papers, 1820, vol. III.)
[3] The Guardian Fire and Life Assurance Company was established about this time, and John Thornton (1783–1861), of Clapham, was one of the directors. At their first meeting on 5 Nov.

would call upon me in the City I should be happy to see him and he might then point out to me more distinctly the channels in which I might be useful to him.—

I have not during the long interval which has elapsed since the interchange of our last letters been unmindful of yourself and my other friends at Gatcomb Park, and I have really been frequently on the point of addressing you a line of chitchat, but have as often been prevented by the pressure of business when in town and by domestic avocations during the short intervals that I have passed here. Of the degree in which I am occupied you may judge when I tell you that this is the first day for the last six weeks (Sundays excepted) that I have been able to stay down here.—It was said by the celebrated Ld Chesterfield of the old Duke of Newcastle, that the Duke having lost half an hour in the morning seemed all the rest of the day as if he was looking after it:—so I may say that having spent a fortnight (a delightful one) in the summer away from business I am obliged to work double tides thro the rest of the season to make up for it.

In the second week of next month I propose striking my tent at this place and pitching it for the following six months in Russell square. I shall then have a little more leisure by the saving at least of my daily journeying from here to town and back and I may probably avail myself of that increased leisure to treat you at greater length with my lucubrations, not worth much at best, than I can now do; for even now I am called off by Mrs. Tooke and our gardener for my opinion and sanction to improvements and other operations with a view to winter work here; this being one of the few oppor-

1821, the directors, out of four candidates for the appointment of surveyor, elected George Basevi, junr. (1794–1845), the architect. (See A. W. Tarn and C. E. Byles, *A Record of the Guardian Assurance Company Ltd. 1821–1921*, London, privately printed, 1921, pp. 64–5, 132.)

tunities which they have of consulting me. I must therefore dispatch your queries in a summary way. Your execration of the Corn laws cannot exceed mine.—The ports will certainly not open in November; and the chances are rather against their opening even in Feb^ry. We must in the meantime submit thro the winter to eat bad bread at a high price.[1] —I received the Copy of the Minutes of Evidence[2] which you were so good as to direct to be sent to me. On a reperusal of my own evidence I perceive too many sins of omission and commission but particularly of the former, to admit of my being fully satisfied.—On one point however passing events confirm the justness of one of the opinions which I expressed and in which I believe that I had the advantage of your concurrence, viz: that low prices arising from superabundance of agricultural produce and a consequently distressed state of the Agricultural interests would not *necessarily* entail a decline in the revenue.—If you continue to take in that blackguard Cobbet you will have seen that he has honored me with a portion of that abuse of which he is so lavish upon you.—Your being deservedly the highest authority on such subjects is quite a sufficient cause for his omitting no opportunity of attacking you. He has let me off as easily as I could expect, and he has left untouched the position that similar distress was complained of in the middle of last Century when the state of the currency could not account for it.[3]

[1] Cp. Tooke's *History of Prices,* vol. II, p. 83.
[2] Before the Agricultural Committee.
[3] See 'Cobbett's Letters to Landlords, on the Agricultural Report and Evidence, Letter III' in *Cobbett's Weekly Register,* 29 Sept. 1821. Cobbett attacks the Committee for their ascribing the distress to 'redundant production', rather than to Peel's Bill, and for amusing themselves 'with the curious conundrums of Mr. Tooke'. 'The ingenious Mr. Tooke has discovered (and the Committee "*entirely concur*" with him;) this ingenious person has

Tomorrow Mr. Mill and his son, Mr. Warburton and one or two other Economical friends pass the day with me here and you may reckon that at 8 oClock in the evening, precisely, *London time,* we shall be drinking your health, not omitting that of Mrs. Ricardo and the rest of your family circle, to whom Mrs. Tooke and our Eyton[1] join in kindest regards with

13 Oct. 1821

Yours most truly

THO.ˢ TOOKE

I dined at my neighbor Murray's two days ago (where by the way I met Belzoni)[2] and he told me that Mr. Malthus explains the improvement in the revenue by ascribing it to an increase of population proceeding from the stimulus of former high prices.

466. TROWER TO RICARDO[3]
[*Reply to 461.—Answered by 471*]

Unsted Wood—Godalming
Nov.ʳ 2—1821

My Dear Ricardo

Your Letter from the neighborhood of Ledbury reminds me of a flying tour I made through that Country,

2 Nov. 1821

discovered that the people do not eat more bread in times of abundance than they do in common times; and that the increased consumption in times of abundance "can amount to little more than *waste*". Nothing so monstruous as this was, surely, ever put upon paper before' (p. 726).

[1] 'William Eyton Tooke [1806–1830], son of the eminent political economist, a young man of singular worth both moral and intellectual, lost to the world by an early death' (J. S. Mill, *Autobiography,* p. 81).

[2] Giovanni Belzoni, the African traveller, was at this time 'one of the fashionable lions of London'. John Murray, his publisher, had recently bought a country house at Wimbledon. (S. Smiles, *A Publisher and His Friends, Memoir and Correspondence of the late John Murray,* London, 1891, vol. II, pp. 82, 97.)

[3] Addressed: 'To / David Ricardo Esqr / M.P. / Gatcomb Park— / Minchinhampton'.

MS in *R.P.*

some years ago; of whose beautiful scenery I have a general recollection—The Malvern hills command an extensive view, over a rich Country; but, I recollect turning my back upon Worcestershire, to look to the glorious Mountains of Wales— A bird's eye view, however extensive, surprises at first, but soon fatigues the sight; whilst the eye delights to range over a bold and broken prospect.—

I remember, that my Uncle,[1] some years ago, resided near Ledbury, and I think he called the name of the place he inhabited, Berrow Court[2]; but I was not aware, that it was the place now belonging to your Son.—

Sydney Smith's performances in the Edingburgh Review are all very well; but, it is a shame, that he should dissipate his powerful understanding in disjointed performances, which cannot cost him any effort, and will never add to his reputation. The fact is, he is a very idle fellow, and will not exert, as he ought to do, the talents with which nature has blessed him. Living in retirement the larger part of the year, with little necessary occupation to fill his time, he might, with due dilligence, have distinguished himself among the litterati of the age—As it is, his bon mots, and his jokes, will perish with the circles they enliven.

Although I dont go quite so far as Mr. Tooke does in thinking that, in the event of the ports being open to Corn, there would be as much probability of our *importing* as of our *exporting* that article—Yet, I believe, that the difference between the cost of production of Corn here and abroad

[1] Apparently Robert Smith (father of Sydney Smith; cp. the postscript to letter 461, written from Bromesberrow Place, above, p. 90), who is said to have spent a great part of his life 'in diminishing his fortune by buying, altering, spoiling, and then selling about nineteen different places in England, till, in his old age, he at last settled at Bishop's Lydiard', near Taunton, where he died in 1827, aged 88. (See Lady Holland, *A Memoir of Sydney Smith*, vol. 1, p. 2.)

[2] Cp. above, VII, 232, n. 2.

would not eventually[1] be considerable. I am satisfied, that the case is the same with respect to the powers of the *soil,* as with the powers of the *mind.* Much more depends upon *cultivation,* than upon natural fertility. And this Country has so infinitely the advantage in its knowledge of the science of agriculture, as greatly to counteract the disadvantages arising from any inferiority of soil.—It is true, that this knowledge will ere long spread to our neighbours; but, is it not equally true, that the causes in full operation, upon the continent, must shortly lead to the cultivation of lands, *there,* of inferior quality.—

In the Article on the Agricultural Report, in the Quarterly Review of the last Month,[2] there appears to me a good exposition of the real nature of Rent: and the effects of an accumulation of capital on Agriculture and Manufactures. But, I cannot agree with the author in thinking, that this view justifies the opinion, "that it is an error to consider these as governed by the *same rules.*"[3] He says, "the price of Manufactures is governed *generally* by the cost of production, and *only as an exception,* by supply and demand; whilst the price of raw produce is governed by supply and demand, and *only as an exception,* by cost of production; and that an increased demand will eventually sink the former, and raise the latter."[4]

The reason of the distinction, here made, appears to be this—that it is only the portion of Corn, grown upon the

---

[1] Might be read 'constantly'.

[2] July 1821 [published in October], Art. IX; reviews the Report and West's *Essay on the Application of Capital to Land.* Whishaw, in a letter to Thomas Smith, 5 Feb. 1822, attributes the review to 'a forward, clever young man from Oxford, named Senior, a fellow of Magdalen' (*The 'Pope' of Holland House,* p. 242).

[3] p. 467. The reviewer justifies his opinion by this 'fundamental distinction', *i.e.* 'every additional capital employed in manufactures produces a greater proportionate net return, while every additional capital employed in agriculture produces a smaller proportionate net return'.

[4] *ib.* pp. 470–71.

land last taken into cultivation, that is actually governed by the cost of production; and that all the other corn sells at a price much above its cost of production; and therefore cannot be said to be governed by it. But, surely, the same remark may be applied to manufactures, although its truth may not be equally obvious. Competition, no doubt, will, eventually, bring manufacturing machinery nearly to a level; but it can only do so, by slow degrees, and *never entirely*. At all times, and under all circumstances, the natural prices of manufactures must, in some degree, be different, although their market price is the same. Competition, in the long run, puts an end to monopoly; but, every inventor of an improved machine enjoys that monopoly for a time, and, during that interval, he is placed precisely in the same situation as the farmer, whose Corn is grown upon land of superior quality. The same rule therefore applies to Manufactures and Raw produce, although the application of that rule is somewhat different—The only difference is, that the machines, which produce Corn are constantly deteriorating, whilst those that produce manufactures are constantly improving.—

The bounty of Sr R. Wilson's political adherents, it seems probable, will prevent his losing in a pecuniary point of view, from his dismissal from the Army, whatever injury he may sustain in other respects. I understand, among the Officers of the Army, who would appear to be as much interested in the question as any part of the public, there is no doubt entertained as to the propriety of his dismissal. The facts of the case are not, as yet, before the public; nevertheless, as usual, this impartial and unprejudiced public, are deciding with all possible violence and obstinacy.—

In a constitutional point of view, I take it, there can be no question, whatever may have been Sr R. Wilson's offence, the King has exercised a power vested in him by his pre-

rogative. He is the sole head of the Army, which is under his
entire control. The Mutiny act provides for the treatment of
military offences, whilst those, of another description, committed by military men, are subject to the decision of the
Crown. I admit, that it is, and must be, at all times, a fair
subject of enquiry on the part of the public, whether the
prerogative has, or has not, been judiciously exercised. But,
upon that point we cannot, and therefore ought not, to
decide, till the facts are before us—In point of *principle* I take
the case of Lord Cochrane to be perfectly analogous, and
most people were of opinion, that the prerogative was then
wholesomely exercised.[1]—

What is your opinion of the probable prices of the Funds.
Should you deem it advisable to invest money in good
mortgages at 5 pC. which is now in the Stocks. I hear that
the rate of interest on mortgage is falling.

Adieu my Dear Ricardo. Mrs. Trower begs to join in
kind remembrances to Mrs. Ricardo and Yourself, and
believe me

Yrs very truly—

HUTCHES TROWER

467. MALTHUS TO RICARDO [2]
[*Reply to 463.—Answered by 468*]

E I Coll. Novr 25th 1821.

My dear Ricardo

I have been afraid of going on with our discussions,
though I have much to say on the subject lest, they should
take up too much of our time. When a difficulty strikes me,

---

[1] Lord Cochrane had been dismissed from the Navy after his
conviction for the fraud on the
Stock Exchange in 1814.

[2] Addressed: 'D. Ricardo Esqr
MP / Gatcomb Park / Minchin-
hampton, / Gloucestershire.'
MS in *R.P.*

25 Nov. 1821

and I propose it to you, I am inclined to be satisfied with hearing your opinion on the subject without rejoinder. If you satisfy me, the matter is settled. If you do not, I hold my opinion, comforting myself with the reflection that having submitted my thoughts to the most ingenious man I know, and he not shewing me that I am wrong, I am entitled to fancy that I am right, forgetting perhaps all along that it may be only owing to my prejudices or stupidity that I am not convinced.

I write now to hope that you will be in Town for the first meeting of the political Econ^y club, which I have just heard is to take place on monday the 3rd of December. It is a busy time generally just at the end of our term, and I must be in College early tuesday morning, but I think I shall be in Town on saturday and stay till that time.

Shall I have any chance of seeing you. It would give me great pleasure.

I conclude you must have met with Torrens work by this time. He has an elaborate chapter on Effectual demand[1]; but I am more firmly than ever convinced that the doctrine "Des Debouchés["] is fundamentally and radically erroneous.

In great haste

Ever most truly Yours

T R MALTHUS

[1] *An Essay on the Production of Wealth*, Ch. VI, Sec. VI, 'On the Principles of Demand and Supply.'

468. RICARDO TO MALTHUS [1]
[*Reply to 467*]

Gatcomb Park
27 Nov.ʳ 1821

My Dear Malthus

Your excuse for not going on with the discussion which   27 Nov. 1821
you commenced is ingenious, and I ought to be satisfied with
it, as it is accompanied with a pretty compliment to me—
indeed as pretty an one as could well be paid to a person who
is so uniformly your adversary. I however agree with you;
—we know each other's sentiments so well that we are not
likely to do each other much good by private discussion.—
If I could manage my pen as well as you do yours, I think
we might do some good to the public by a public discussion.

I am sorry that I shall be obliged to miss 2 of the Political
Economy meetings, as I shall not be in London till towards
the latter end of the month of January.

On the 7ᵗʰ of Dec.ʳ I am to dine at Hereford, by invitation,
with Hume, at a public dinner, which is to be given to him
for the purpose of presenting him a silver tankard, and a
hogshead of Cider, in token of the respect and gratitude of
the inhabitants of Hereford for his public services. Hume
comes from town on the occasion, and is to be met at Ross
at 11 oClock in the forenoon, and escorted with due honor
into Hereford. I hope every thing will be conducted in an
orderly and peacable manner—I have a great aversion to a
row. [2]—

I have not yet seen Torrens book, nor shall I see it in all
probability till I get to London. Torrens has some concern

---

[1] Addressed: 'The Revᵈ T. R. Malthus / East India College / Hertford'. Franked by Ricardo 'November Twenty eight 1821'.

MS at Albury.—*Letters to Malthus*, LXXXI.

[2] Ricardo's speech on this occasion is given above, V, 471 ff.

27 Nov. 1821   in the Champion[1] in which there is a paper weekly on Polit. Economy. I think these essays are well done, but you probably would not agree with me in that opinion

Ever Y^{rs}

D RICARDO

469. MILL TO RICARDO [2]
[*Reply to 464.—Answered by 470*]

East India House 30th Novr 1821

My dear Sir

30 Nov. 1821   I have at last been able to despatch for you a copy of my Elements,[3] though you already know sufficiently what it contains; but I shall be anxious to know, when you have read the whole in print, to what degree you think it calculated to answer the end we design it for, and if any thing, without remaking, which I should hardly submit to, could be done to make it answer it better. We may possibly have in time a call for a second edition, (as 350 copies were subscribed, that is, sold to the booksellers, the first day) unless expectation should unfortunately be disappointed. In some respects I shall value the opinion of the unlearned more than yours. I wish you could make some of the ladies read it. At one time I intended to send, for this purpose, copies to my two friends Mrs. Osman and Miss Ricardo; but I hardly know enough of them to be sure that they would not have thought it imposing an obligation upon them, which they would have

---

[1] A periodical which, from Sunday, 30 Sept. 1821, had adopted the subtitle 'Weekly Review of Politics and Political Economy' and the motto 'The Greatest Happiness of the Greatest Number': at the same time it had begun the publication of a series of articles, numbered progressively, under the general title 'The Economist', in which the Ricardian doctrines of Foreign Trade, Rent, Profits, etc., were popularly expounded. These articles were signed at first 'S. E.', and later in the year 'F.'

[2] MS in *R.P.*

[3] *Elements of Political Economy*, London, Baldwin, 1821.

deemed a *bore,* and so I abstained; but if you give me a hint, it shall immediately be obeyed; and as I think they are both perfectly capable of learning the science, I should like very much to excite them to it.[1]

I have heard nothing of you for a long time, though I confess it is my own fault. I have for five or six weeks been by no means well, and every thing has been a burthen to me. I long adhered to the intention of getting down to you for a few days, but at last, as I shall now have the pleasure of seeing you in a little time in London, I must hope that I shall be able to make up next year for my disappointment in this. Had I sooner decided about my own matters I should have sent John; but now he is engaged with masters, &.c., and must postpone his pleasure, as I do mine.

About public affairs I need not send you my reflections, because you anticipate them. The ministers are chiefly puzzled about Canning. I have it from good authority, that when, since the Kings return from Hanover, Lord Liverpool obtained an audience for the express purpose of stating that his remaining in office must depend upon the admission of Canning into the cabinet, the King said he would speak to him candidly, and like an old friend; that he had indubitable proofs in his possession of an illicit intercourse having subsisted between Mr. Canning and his wife (the queen); he put it therefore to Lord Liverpool himself, whether he would submit to have Mr. Canning in his cabinet.—What think you of this?—For my part I am an unbeliever.—I doubt not it is a lie, made by the King, to save himself from importunity, and that he has no such evidence.

Place's answer to Godwin is unfortunate. Murray kept it

[1] A copy of Mill's *Elements,* 1821, inscribed by him 'To Mrs. Osman Ricardo from her sincere Friend the Author' and much annotated by the recipient, was formerly in the library at Bromesberrow Place.

a shameful length of time, and at last returned it without any answer at all. It has since been proposed to both Longman and Baldwin, but neither will undertake to publish, at their own risk, and Place himself says he cannot afford to lose money by it.[1] I am vexed, both that so much labour should be thrown away, and that the public should lose the benefit of the publication.

I have received from Mr. Caff[2] an invitation to dine with the Gentlemen of the Polit. Econ. Club, on monday next. But I think there is a mistake. It seems to be distinctly in my recollection, that the first meeting was to be, not on the first, but the last monday of Dec.

Adieu. I wish you pleasant festivities at the approaching festive season. I shall be with you in spirit, though not in body. Unless I get rid of this dispepsia, I shall have heart for nothing. I have been refusing all invitations, and fit for nothing of an evening but my own *fauteuil,* with my wife and children, whom I can keep as long as they amuse me, and then send away.

I wish to be most kindly remembered to the Lady of Gatcomb. I have often thought of her in my present languor —she is an excellent Doctoress, and I have a notion that she and Mrs. Cleaver,[3] are the *first* of nurses.

Let me hear from you soon, and believe

Most truly yours

J. MILL

I have heard what leads me to believe (heard since writing the above) that Canning will be Governor General of India.

---

[1] It was published by Longman in 1822. See above, p. 49, n. 2.
[2] Mr Caff, or Cuff, presumably the innkeeper of the Freemasons' Tavern, where the club used to dine. See *Political Economy Club,* *Minutes of Proceedings, 1821–1882,* p. 45; and for the meeting on Monday, 3 Dec. 1821, at which Mill was present, *ib.* p. 43.
[3] Mrs Ricardo's servant.

If you speak of this, do not mention me as your authority—
though it was not given to me as a secret.[1]

470. RICARDO TO MILL[2]
[*Reply to 469*]

Bromesberrow Place
10 Dec.ʳ 1821

My Dear Sir

    I intended to write to you immediately after reading
your book,[3] but I have been so much on the move lately that
I could not find half an hour for the purpose, till now:—but
let me proceed methodically. In the first place, then, I must
express my regret at the account you give of yourself, you
have I suppose some gouty humor flying about you, and
altho this visit is troublesome the complaint will as before
quickly leave you, and I shall hope soon to see you with all
the sprightliness and activity of youth. I am sorry that
neither you and John together, nor John singly, could contrive to pay me a visit this year.
    And now for the book; I thank you much for it. I have
read it with attention, and you must be aware that there are
few things in it from which I can differ. There are, I perceive,
a very few in which we do not quite agree; I have taken notes
of them, and they will either serve for matters of conversation, or I will write them out, and send them to you, whenever you desire it. If I am right in my views, on these very
few points, you will be inclined to make some very trifling
alterations in your next edition. Respecting the clearness
with which your views are expressed, of course they are all
very clear to me, and to my judgment they would be so to

[1] Canning was appointed Governor-General in 1822; but he
did not take up the post, having
returned to the Foreign Office on
the death of Castlereagh.
[2] MS in Mill-Ricardo papers.
[3] *Elements of Political Economy.*

all who paid common attention to the subject they were reading; but of this, as you justly observe, I cannot be so good a judge as the unlearned. There are two young ladies, of the latter class, who wish to become learned, and would be glad to become so through your means, and you must consider this as the hint which you desired me to give you if I found any such disposition existing. Mrs. Osman says, that you promised to give her a copy of your book, and she holds you to that promise. She has been diligently preparing for it, for she has been studying Mrs. Marcet's work with great attention, and I am happy to add with great profit, and appears to understand it well. Your book will confirm the good doctrines in her mind, and will supply her with some new ideas on the subject.

Mary, my daughter, is also eager to receive this present from you, she engages to pay her utmost attention to its contents, and is greatly pleased at your having thought of her. Hume and I, speaking of your book, of which he has not read much, both regretted that you had used the word "procreation" so often in a book you call a school book; it will we fear excite prejudice in the minds of many against it, and the doctrines might have been nearly as well explained without the use of it.

You will see where I am by the beginning of my letter. I came here on wednesday, and went on friday morning with my son to Hereford. We found that town in a great bustle, the streets full of people, and the windows lined with females waiting for the arrival of Hume. More than 180 horsemen, and many carriages went from Hereford to meet him, and in about an hour after my arrival the cavalcade made its appearance. After the horses were properly arranged on each side, the carriages made their appearance, in the first of which was Hume, seated between the chairman and deputy for the day. This carriage and the next which followed containing Price the member for the county, were drawn by the people. When the carriages came opposite to the hotel Hume alighted amidst the waving of banners, the beating of drums, and the acclamations of the people. In a moment he was up in the balcony, and ready to repay them by a speech, which he can make always at a moments notice. He told the people how badly they were governed, and how much he expected from their increasing intelligence. He implored them to be active, and to make their opinions known &c.ᵃ &c.ᵃ.

After dinner the tankard was presented to him, and the hogshead of cider placed at his disposal—he then made another speech, which lasted an hour and a half, and which was very favorably listened to. The company consisted of 250, we had a good deal of speaking, and some very good speaking. Reform was mentioned by all, and acknowledged to be the great object to be looked to. I was obliged to say a few words, and did not fail to say something in favor of the importance of secret suffrage.[1] After spending nearly 6 hours at the dinner table, a large party of us accompanied Hume to Mr. Prices house in the neighbourhood. I staid there 2 nights, and returned here yesterday. Hume was going to day to dine with the Corporation of Monmouth, where he is to receive the freedom of the city, and to morrow he will be with me here. On the next day we shall all go to Gatcomb. Thus have I given you a faithful history of our proceedings.

Hume, as you may suppose, is highly gratified at the reception which he every where meets with—he has struck out in a new line, and will continue to be highly prized, till he has a few more competitors. He has been of essential service in rousing the public feeling to a conviction of the

[1] See above, V, 473–4.

10 Dec. 1821 wasteful expenditure which is going on, and I really believe it is a better class of the people that are now active than that which had been previously operated upon by Cobbett and Hunt.

I am sorry to hear of the fate of Place's MS. I hear that the Polit. Econ Club met on the day appointed, and that 20 were present—I do not know whether you were of the number. Do you see the Champion?[1] There is a paper in it every week on Polit. Economy in which the correct principles are very well explained. I suppose Torrens writes it. It appears as if Canning could not get over the formidable obstacle of the Kings hatred.—

Osman and his wife desire to be kindly remembered to you.

Ever Y^{rs}

DAVID RICARDO

I find I have made a mistake about the promise to Mrs. Osman of your book, the promise on your part was that you would make your book so easy that she could understand it, and on hers that she would read it if you did.

471. RICARDO TO TROWER[2]

[*Reply to 466.—Answered by 478*]

Bromesberrow Place
11 Decr 1821

My Dear Trower

11 Dec. 1821   It appears to be your fate to receive letters from me dated from this place. I intended writing to you before I left home, but I had various things to do which obliged me to defer it till this moment. I came here on Wednesday last on

[1] Cp. above, p. 114, n. 1.
[2] Addressed: 'Hutches Trower Esqr / Unsted Wood / Godalming', and franked by Ricardo 'Gloucester December Twelve'. MS at University College, London.—*Letters to Trower,* LI.

my way to Hereford, to which place I was invited, by the admirers of Mr. Hume, to attend a public dinner, which they meant to give him in that town, on the occasion of presenting him with a hogshead of Cider, and a silver tankard, which had been purchased from a fund created by subscriptions of one shilling. I went to Hereford on friday, and soon after my arrival there, saw my friend Hume arrive in a carriage drawn by the people, and preceded by a great number of horsemen and banners. The whole population of the town appeared to be in the streets, and the windows were crowded with women. He was greeted with that portion of noisy acclamations which is usually bestowed on popular favorites. In a moment he was in the balcony of the Inn, next to a window which I occupied, and from thence made a long speech to the gentlemen in the street which was constantly interrupted with cheering. At 3 oClock we sat down to dinner. Our number was 250 mostly consisting, I should think, of farmers and trades-men; perhaps there were about 50 of the higher class of gentlemen of fortune in the neigh-bourhood. After dinner we had plenty of speaking—Hume performed for an hour and a half, the rest who were called upon, of which number I was one, spoke for a very moderate time.[1] The day went off well and a large party of us went, as was previously agreed on, to Mr. Prices, the member for the County, (whose father is the author of a work on the Picturesque)[2] where we were handsomely entertained for 2 days.

Hume as you may believe is highly gratified. He was to be yesterday at Monmouth and he will to day join me here,[3]

---

[1] See above, V, 471.

[2] Uvedale Price, *An Essay on the Picturesque, as compared with the Sublime and the Beautiful, and, on the use of Studying Pictures for the*

purpose of Improving Real Land-scape, London, 1794.

[3] 'Ledbury, Dec. 12.—Last night Mr. Hume arrived at this place very unexpectedly, on his road

and return with me to Gatcomb. You will call all these proceedings by the name of "Radical," but I believe they are calculated to do much good—to increase the interest of the people in the affairs of government, and to make them better judges of what constitutes good and what bad government— at the same time this will be useful to our governors, and incline them to economy and forbearance.

Your remarks on the article in the Quarterly Review, on the Agricultural Report, appear to me to be very just. I am glad I have got so good an ally, for what I think the correct principles, and you must partake of the pleasure which I feel in observing that they are every day making way. Mrs. Marcet's last edition is a very improved one,—in it she recognizes much of which her former editions did not speak at all, or of which they spoke doubtingly.[1] The Champion has given a series of papers on Rent, Wages, Taxes &c. &c. all of which appear to me sound.[2] Mill has just published his book too in which all the good doctrines are advocated.[3] So that we ought to be satisfied with the progress we are making. In the country I find much error prevailing on the subject of the currency, every ill which befals the country is by some ascribed to Peel's bill, and Peel's bill is as invariably ascribed to me. The whole fall in the value of corn and cattle is by such persons said to be merely nominal, these things they say have not in fact fallen, it is money which has risen—they will not hear of a variation in the value of money of 10 pc. which

---

from Ross, on a visit to Mr. O. Ricardo, at Bramsbury; and, although five minutes did not elapse in the change of post horses, the populace recognised him, took out the horses, and drew the carriage through the town, as a mark of their approbation' (*The Times,* 17 Dec. 1821).

[1] *Conversations on Political Economy; in which the Elements of that Science are Familiarly Explained,* by the Author of 'Conversations on Chemistry', 4th ed., London, Longman, 1821.

[2] See above, p. 114, n. 1.

[3] See above, p. 114, n. 3.

I am very willing to allow them, nor will they listen to my defence of myself against their unjust accusation. I proposed a scheme by the adoption of which there would not have been a demand for one ounce of gold, either on the part of the Bank, or of any one else, and another is adopted by which both the Bank and individuals are obliged to demand a great quantity of gold and I am held responsible for the consequences. If I had been a bank director, and had had the management of this currency question, I maintain that I could have reverted to a metallic standard by raising money (only) 5 pc., I do not say that having a metallic standard I could protect it from the usual fluctuations to which standards have at all times been subject. Cobbet says I am little better than a fool in speaking of gold as a standard, that the only fair standard is corn.[1] He shews his ignorance in saying so, but supposing it true, can he tell me what is to secure us from variations in his standard,—it would perhaps be more variable than any other. But it is useless to say all this to you who know it so well.

Hume says Ministers cannot make out any thing of a case against Sir Rob. Wilson—that they thought they had a case against him, but that they were wholly deceived by false statements.

---

[1] See 'Cobbett's Letters to Landlords, On the Agricultural Report and Evidence, Letter V' in *Cobbett's Weekly Register*, 20 Oct. 1821: 'To refer to the *market price of gold as a standard* is exactly what the Oracle did; the Oracle of the "*Collective Wisdom.*" Gold, says he, being the *standard of all things in the world;* every price *depending on that of gold;* and gold now being within *four and a half per cent.* of its lowest possible price, the prices of *other things* cannot, by this measure, be brought down more than four and a half per cent'. 'This was the ground *upon which Peel's Bill was passed!* This queer, this 'Change-Alley, this Jew-like notion of the price of gold being the standard. However, this was no *new* notion; it had been harped on by *Oracle Horner* and his Bullion Committee; by *Lord King;* and by a great many others, long before *the Oracle by excellence* spouted it forth' (pp. 925–6).

11 Dec. 1821 What think you of the late changes in the Administration?[1]
Is not Peel very much elevated? Do his talents entitle him
to fill so prominent a situation? Will things be arranged
finally without some provision being made for Canning? He
is a formidable opponent, but I suppose he cannot under any
circumstances fairly come over to our side.

There will be many interesting questions brought before
Parliament next Session. Economy and Retrenchment will
be a standing dish. We shall have the question of the Corn
Laws, the disturbance in Ireland—Sir Rob. Wilson's case—
the criminal law and many others—I like business.

Pray give my kind remembrances to Mrs. Trower and
believe me ever my dear Trower

Y^{rs} truly

DAVID RICARDO

472. RICARDO TO M^{c}CULLOCH [2]

Gatcomb Park, Minchinhampton
14 Decr 1821

Dear Sir

14 Dec. 1821 This letter will be delivered to you by Mr. John Austin,
a gentleman with whom I have been acquainted for some
years, and whose brother is married to my daughter[3]. His
visit to your country is for a commercial object, and to
accomplish that object it may be necessary for him to employ
some reputable gentlemen in the law. As he is a stranger in
Scotland, the opinion of one so well able to form a correct
one as yourself, respecting the gentlemen whom he may think

[1] Peel, Home Secretary; Marquis Wellesley, Lord Lieutenant of Ireland; Goulburn, Chief Secretary for Ireland.
[2] Addressed: 'J. R. M'Culloch Esqr / Buccleugh Place / Edinburgh'.
MS in British Museum.—*Letters to McCulloch*, XXVIII.
[3] Priscilla.

it necessary to employ, may be of essential service to him. I am sure you will readily allow him to consult you, and by so doing, or by any otherwise serving him you will greatly oblige

Dear Sir
Yours very truly
DAVID RICARDO

J. R. M'Culloch

473. RICARDO TO MILL [1]

Gatcomb
18 Dec.ʳ 1821

My Dear Sir

The two ladies are very thankful for the books you sent to them and very much pleased with the letters which accompanied them. Whether they will have the courage to write to you, and say so themselves I very much doubt— they have however commenced studying Political Economy, and will I hope be able to overcome all difficulties in the way of fully comprehending it.

I send you a hasty sketch of my remarks—I have, as a friend ought to do, diligently looked out for faults, and have scarcely been able to discover any. After all, those things which I deem faults, may not be such, and they may appear faults to my eyes only because I view them with a pre- judiced mind.

Hume left me on sunday.

Yours truly
DAVID RICARDO

[1] Addressed: 'James Mill Esqʳ / East India House / London'.—MS in Mill-Ricardo papers.

[ENCLOSURE: RICARDO'S NOTES ON MILL'S
ELEMENTS OF POLITICAL ECONOMY]

18 Dec. 1821   Section 2. Chap. 2. The fecundity of the woman would
not be admitted as a conclusive argument, by the objectors
to the theory, that the population of a rich, luxurious and
populous country could under favorable circumstances,
increase in the same proportion as a new and poor country,
because they contend, that in consequence of the prevalence
of luxury, so many women are withdrawn from the office of
childbearing, that there are not a sufficient number left to
augment the population in the same proportion as at an
earlier period. They contend that the demand for nurses, and
female servants of all descriptions, lessen the number of
childbearing women.

Page 48 "In a country in which all were reduced &c^a"[1]
Can there be any such country? In all old states rent will
constitute a fund which will ensure the existence of a comparatively rich class. I do not quite agree with the opinion
expressed in the first part of the paragraph "that considerable
savings may be made from the expenditure of the rich to
mitigate the effects of the deficiency". This result could not
take place for 2 or 3 years, and it would equally take place
in the case supposed if we had not reached the end of our
resources. Whether the land be very much subdivided or
not, there must exist a very large surplus produce in the
shape of rent. Under these circumstances it is impossible
that all should be poor. I do not speak of this ultimate state
as a desirable one, I agree with you that the mass of the
people would be exposed to great misery in it, but I think
you have drawn it too strongly.

[1] 'In a country in which all were   the usual supply would diffuse
reduced to the state of wages,   general, irremediable calamity.'
any considerable diminution of

You say in this chapter that the demand for labour and the power of employing it will be in proportion to the increase of capital—I believe I have said the same, and it may be perhaps right to say so in an elementary book, altho' it is not strictly correct. The power of employing labour depends on the increase of a particular part of capital, not on the increase of the whole capital. (See my Chapter on Machinery). 18 Dec. 1821

Do you not underrate the power and the willingness to save? You do not speak of the two ways by which capital may be increased by saving; of one, the common and usual way, devoting more of the annual production to productive employments, you do speak, but you say nothing of the great increase which sometimes takes place in capital by the discovery of cheaper modes of producing.

Section 2 Chap. 3 I see the same difficulty, in this section, that I have seen in my own, on the same subject, of laying down a general and positive rule with respect to quantity of labour realised in commod^{ts} being the rule and measure of their exchangeable value. The exceptions will be opposed to you as they have been to me. In page 76 there is a passage ending with these words "without in the least affecting the truth of the previous proposition &c^a &c^a. If a watch and a common Jack altered in relative value without any more or less labour being required for the production of either of them, could we say that the proposition "that quantity of labour determines exchangeable value" was universally true? What I call exceptions and modifications of the general rule you appear to me to say come under the general rule itself.

Sec^n Page 89 I cannot agree in the distinction here taken, that the advantage in commerce is derived to all countries from what they receive, and not from what they send out.

They in fact never receive any thing without sending something to pay for it, and it is the exchange which is beneficial. It is no exchange unless a commodity be given as well as received. I do not see how such a transaction can be separated into two parts and how it can be justly said that one part only is beneficial. What we get in exchange for our commodity really constitutes the price or value for which we sell it.

109 "Excepting only that part comparatively small which is fixed in durable machinery" Can this part be called justly comparatively small? It consists not only of durable machinery but of ships, canals, roads, bridges, workshops &c$^{a.}$ &c$^{a.}$.

119 "But in these circumstances" &c^{a}. The latter part of this paragraph is not clear. Why would the bank pay for their notes when they came back £4? Answer. Their stock of gold would inevitably be soon exhausted and they would be obliged to buy in the market at £4– what they sold at £3. 17. 10$\frac{1}{2}$ in order to replace that stock.

120 "If no coins were in circulation &c$^{a.}$" They could derive great profit from it if they took this opportunity of buying gold at £2. 10– then increased their issues, and sold it at £4.–

120 "In the case of a metallic currency &c^{a}" There is a little ambiguity in this passage. Government could not diminish the value of the currency taken as a whole, they could diminish the value of each particular coin of which that currency was composed.

127 I should be very unwilling to allow government to keep the same quantity of paper in circulation under the circumstances supposed. By what criterion should we be able to distinguish a real demand for gold, from a diminished capital and circulation from improvements in the art of economising the use of money &c$^{a.}$ &c$^{a.}$?

18 Dec. 1821

Page 145 "If a balance is due &c.ᵃ &c.ᵃ ["] To the settling of this transaction by bills it is necessary that the Merchant at Amsterdam should owe £1000 to Hamburgh, or that he can receive the bullion which is in £1000 at a less expence from Hamburgh than from England. In selling his demand on England at Hamburgh, Hamburgh becomes his debtor instead of England. [1]

147 "When the currencies &c.ᵃ" This should be qualified a little, for without any alteration in the quantity of metal in either, the relative value of their currencies may undergo a change, within the range of the expences of sending the metal from one to the other. If 10000 guilder were of the same intrinsic value as £1000, and the expence of sending money 2 pcᵗ, £1000 might for a considerable length of time purchase a bill for 10200 guilders at one period, and at another, for a considerable length of time also, it might only purchase a bill for about 9800. This might be usefully put in a note.

153 [2] Whenever two commodities are exchanged between merchants of different countries, it is certain, that, valued in the commodity exported, the commodity imported must exceed the value of the commodity exported, by all the expences attending the conveyance of both commodities. If England in a season of scarcity sends cloth to Poland for corn, the corn when it comes to England must at least be

[1] In MS this remark and the following one are added at the end of the paper.
[2] 'If England in a season of scarcity sends to Poland for corn, the corn in England will not be loaded with the expense both of carrying home the corn and carrying out the cloth, while Poland will bear no part of the cost of carriage but will have her cloth free of the cost of carriage, therefore as cheap as in England. The facts, it is evident, will be these: The corn will be dearer in England than in Poland, by the cost of bringing it from Poland; and the cloth will be dearer in Poland than in England, by the cost of carrying the cloth.'

more valuable than the cloth which was sent, by all the expences attending the conveyance, both of the cloth and corn, or it could not possibly be for the advantage of any body to be engaged in the transaction. The same holds true with respect to money. If I consent to send money from England, to import corn from Poland, when it arrives in England, it must be of a value, not only equal to its cost in Poland, but also equal to the charges of sending the money and conveying the corn. One hundred q^{rs} of corn in Poland are worth we will suppose £200[,] the charge of sending the money £5. If I send the money therefore the corn will cost me £205, but the charge of bringing the corn to England we will suppose to be £10, when therefore it arrives in England it will stand me in £215 and unless I sell it for more than that sum I get no profit. Is not this £215 made up of £200 original cost, £5 for conveying the money, and £10 for conveying the corn? I see your meaning about the exchange in which you are right, but you have not chosen the right words to express it in.

163 "As the man.....[1] so the grower of corn sustains not any the smallest loss or inconvenience" Should not this be qualified by saying that he sustains only the general loss sustained by all other consumers in being forced to pay more for the protected commodity?

167 I object again to the doctrine that all advantage in trade is derived from the commodities received and not by those which are sent.

171 Is not a colony more injured by being obliged to buy of the mother country than by being obliged to sell to it? The produce of the colony though sent to the mother country, and therefore liable to more charges than if sent to

---

[1] 'As the man who has embarked his capital in the trade which is called protected, derives no additional profit from the protection;'.

the country where it is finally to be sold, is nevertheless
diffused generally to all places where it is in demand, and
therefore finally obtains the best price, deduction being
always made for the increased charges. But the colony is
obliged to obtain its commodities from one single market,
and is obliged to buy in that market altho' she might possibly
buy the same goods much cheaper elsewhere. It is evident,
I think, that she not only bears the increased charges, but
also the increased cost, on the commodities she purchases.

Page 181   Whether the producer of cloth can add to his
capital, from that part of his cloth which belongs to him as
profits, depends upon the ability he may have of exchanging
this portion of his cloth for food, raw materials, tools and
labour.

Page 194   "In such a case &c^a" This does not answer
the objection usually made. If every man was intent on
saving, more food and necessaries, (the materials which are
chiefly employed in procuring labour), would be produced
than could be consumed. The supply above the demand
would produce such a glut, that with the increased quantity
you could command no more labour than before. All motive
to save would cease, for it could not be accomplished, but
the precise reason of this is, that capital increases faster than
population, and consequently that the labourers would be in
a condition to command a very great quantity of the net
produce. This could only last till the population was increased,
when labour would again fall, and the net produce be more
advantageously distributed for the capitalist. During the
period of very high wages, food and necessaries would not
be produced in such quantities as to occasion a glut, for it
would be the interest of the producer to produce such things
as were in demand, and suited to the tastes of those who had
high wages to expend.

192 "But to the very same amount &c.ª &c.ª" I cannot agree with this, for the additional quantity of cloth might be made by an additional capital saved from last year's revenue, and not from a capital withdrawn from other employments. I agree with the conclusion, but not with the statement. The clothier who produces the cloth with his saved capital, as I have supposed, and for which there is not an adequate demand, did it as a means to an end, he wished to sell his cloth and purchase some other thing. It is that other thing which he ought to have produced, and then there would not have been a glut of any commodity. There cannot be a glut of any thing but from an accident, almost always from miscalculation.

199 "If a body of people &c.ª &c.ª" There would be a period, more or less long, in which there would be no rent, and consequently there could be no public revenue. An objection may be made against this tax that it would tend to arrest improvement or would finally in some cases fall on the consumer of raw produce; I mean in the case of a landlord expending a great deal of capital on his land for which he receives a return not under the name of profit, but under the name of rent. These expences would not be incurred, unless by a rise in the price of raw produce the capitalist should have reason to think that he should be repaid for the peculiar disadvantage to which he was exposed. Under such a system of taxation great encouragement would be given to gambling. On the approach of war land would fall in proportion to the expectation of the duration of the war, and with every battle or treaty people would speculate according as their hopes or fears predominated. Land would be so uncertain a property that no safe provision could by means of the possession of it be made for children. On the whole I should greatly prefer the present system of taxation. If land is to be peculiarly the

subject of taxation it would be desirable to adopt the Asiatic 18 Dec. 1821 mode, and consider the government at all times, both in war and peace, the sole possessor of the land, and entitled to all the rent.

202. Is it accurate to say that the legislature *does* possess the power of increasing the productions of the state? By good laws it may take away all the impediments in the way of increasing them,—it may secure to industry all the fruits of its labour &c.ᵃ &c.ᵃ, but the legislature does not by these laws actually increase productions.

234 "In neither of these cases &cᵃ &cᵃ"[1] you should I think add "provided an equal tax were laid upon all similar commodities when imported". From what follows it is clear that is your meaning, but the passage would be more clear if you said so.—

The account of the effects of different taxes is I think very concisely and ably stated.

474. McCULLOCH TO RICARDO[2]
[Reply to 436 & 439.—Answered by 476]

Edinburgh 23 Decemʳ 1821

My Dear Sir

It was my intention, as it was my duty, to have written 23 Dec. 1821 you long ere now to thank you for your kindness in favouring me with your opinion of Mr. Mushets Tables—I deferred dooing so at first untill I should have an opportunity of

---

[1] 'In neither of these cases ['that in which any number of commodities are taxed one by one... and that in which all commodities are taxed by an *ad valorem* duty'] has the high price of commodities —in other words, the low purchasing power of money, any tendency to send money out of the country.'

[2] Addressed: 'David Ricardo Esq M.P. / Gatcomb Park / Minchinhampton / Gloucestershire'.
MS in *R.P.*

forwarding you a copy of an article on money I have written
for the Supp to the E Brittannica—But owing to the endless
delays incident to such publications it was only within
these two days that I received spare copies of this Tract—
I shall, by the first conveyance, send a copy of it addressed
to you at your house in London, and I shall be happy to
have your opinion of its execution—The theory is your
own—

You would perhaps perceive from an advertisement
inserted in the Scotsman, that I am again engaged in teaching
a private class of Political Economy[1]—But it is my intention,
and indeed I have already made a commencement, to write
a course of Lectures and to have a public class next session[2]—
Various motives induce me to engage in this undertaking—
If once I had the Lectures written, it would be a comparatively easy task to polish and improve them, and I might
thus be enabled to assist in disseminating the sound principles
of the science and to make a little money without a great deal
of trouble—In compiling a course of Lectures I must have
for my object to be instructive rather than profound; and
must dwell more on the useful and practical parts of the
science than on those that involve in a theoretical discussion—
I shall not, however, omit the latter; but in order to make my
Lectures interesting I must enforce those points chiefly which
will give me some hold of the sympathies of my auditors,
and which they will most readily understand—I gave two
introductory Discourses[3] to my present class, and if it was

[1] 'POLITICAL ECONOMY.—Mr. J. R. McCulloch intends opening a Private Class, for Instruction in Political Economy on Tuesday, 20th November. 10. Buccleugh Place, 29. Oct. 1821.' (Advt., *Scotsman*, 3 Nov. 1821.)—McCul- loch gives an outline of his method of teaching to private classes in *Discourse on the Rise...of Political Economy*, 1824, pp. 109–10.

[2] See below, p. 272, n. 1.

[3] See below, p. 162.

not presuming too much on your goodness to desire you to read manuscript Lectures, I would send them to you when you come to London, and would feel extremely obliged by your opinion and advice respecting them and the conduct of my course in general. This is a matter of the greatest consequence to me: for owing to the fall in the value of land I scarcely get any thing for the little property belonging to me in the south of Scotland[1]—Perhaps you could again spare me for a few weeks your Notes on Mr. Malthus last work; they would be of great use in treating of the laws regulating profits, and many other subjects, and they will be perfectly safe in my custody—You mentioned in one of the letters you have honoured me with that you had got a very able work on the subject of money written by a gentleman of Ilfracombe, but which was not intended for publication— Might I also ask you for a loan of this book[2]—I should also like to know whether you are in possession of any information respecting the history of commerce and finance in Holland—This I am sure is a quarter from which much curious and valuable illustration might be derived—I have not been able to meet with any other works on such subjects in the latin or french languages, for I cannot read the german, except the Richesse de la Hollande and a Memorial presented to the Prince of Orange in 1750[3]—

[1] 'A small freehold estate called Auchengool, in the stewartry of Kirkcudbright', which McCulloch had inherited from his grandfather. (Gentleman's Magazine, Jan. 1865, p. III.)

[2] See above, VIII, 337, n. 2.

[3] La Richesse de la Hollande, 2 vols., Amsterdam, 1778, attributed by McCulloch to Accarias de Serionne. Proposals made by His late Highness the Prince of Orange to their High Mightinesses the States General, and to the States of Holland and West Friezeland, for Redressing and Amending the Trade of the Republic, translated from the Dutch, London, 1751. (See McCulloch's Literature of Political Economy, pp. 47 and 63, and his article 'Rise, Progress, and Decline of Commerce in Holland', Edinburgh Review, July 1830, Art. V.)

23 Dec. 1821   You would be very well pleased to see the scrape into which the enemies of public liberty and of the freedom of the press in Scotland have got—Can you conceive anything more reprehensible than for the Lord Advocate, the person at the head of the government of Scotland and who exercises the functions of the Grand Juries in England, to become a private partner in a paper[1] which carried its abuse of the very persons with whom his Lordship was daily associating to a much farther extent than the John Bull? If the House of Commons were what it ought to be his Lordship would not at present be in a very comfortable situation—There is an Article in the number of the Edinburgh Review just published on Scottish Juries[2] which is deserving of your attention— It is written in a very moderate tone, but it states enough to satisfy every reasonable man that as Jury trial is now conducted in this part of the Empire, it is an engine of the grossest oppression and abuse—The Sheriffs here are not like the Sheriffs in England—they are all lawyers in the interest of the Crown and appointed only for their subserviency—These Sheriffs rake on, just as they think proper, all the persons capable of serving on any particular occasion as Jurymen, and from these persons the Judge PICKS a Jury! When such is the state of the law—when any person may be sent to Botany bay without even a chance of any thing like justice—you must admire our courage, or rather our foolhardiness in daring to oppose ministers in any thing they do—

[1] *The Beacon,* a libellous Tory newspaper begun in January 1821 and discontinued in August of the same year when its secret subscribers, including William Rae (the Lord Advocate) and Walter Scott, withdrew their support after the disclosure of their names. For a Whig account of the affair see H. Cockburn, *Memorials of his Time,* Edinburgh, 1856, pp. 380–3; for a Tory account, J. G. Lockhart, *Life of Scott,* 1837, vol. v, pp. 152–5.
[2] Oct. 1821, Art. IX, 'Nomination of Scottish Juries' (by H. Cockburn; see his *Memorials,* p. 386).

We would be all greatly delighted if when the subject comes to be discussed in the House, you would make a short speech declaring your opinion of this odious system—Perhaps you never took any notice of the articles in the Scotsman respecting the police of this city—It is, however, a very knavish business; and if you will look into the Scotsman[1] before last you will perceive that the Lord President of the Court of Session, the highest Judge in this division of the Empire told a deputation of most respectable citizens, who waited on him by appointment that "he would rather their throats should be cut" than he should alter an opinion he had given!

But I have encroached too long on your valuable time; and shall, therefore, conclude with wishing you many joyous returns of this festive season, and with great respect and esteem I am My Dear Sir

Yours most faithfully

J. R. M^cCULLOCH

475. MARIA EDGEWORTH TO RICARDO [2]

at T W Carr Esqre
Frognel
Hampstead
Decr 27th 1821

My dear Sir

Will you write a line to let me know at what time you and Mrs. Ricardo intend coming to Town

I have a good reason for asking this impertinent question but I will not tell you what it is till I have your answer.

My sisters Fanny and Harriet and I hope that you and yours

[1] No. of 15 December.

[2] Addressed: 'D. Ricardo Esqre / Gatcombe-Park / Minchinhampton'.

MS in *R.P.*

Miss Edgeworth and her sisters had visited Ricardo at Gatcomb in November of this year.

27 Dec. 1821 continue in the kind dispositions towards us in which we left you.—We cannot hope for more.

Yours truly with sincere esteem and grateful regard

MARIA EDGEWORTH

Have you any Spare Rooms in Brook S^t.

476. RICARDO TO M^{c}CULLOCH [1]
[*Reply to* 474.—*Answered by* 479]

Gatcomb Park 3 Jany 1822

My Dear Sir

3 Jan. 1822 I thank you very much for the attention and kindness which you have shewn to Mr. John Austin, the gentleman to whom I lately gave a letter of introduction to you. [2] Mr. Austin has written from Edinburgh, to his brother, who lives in this neighborhood, giving him an account of the kind treatment which he had received from you, and by which he is very deeply impressed: his only regret was that he had engaged too large a portion of your valuable time. In giving a letter to Mr. Austin I by no means wished to call upon you for so great a sacrifice of time as he says you have made to him, and I shall greatly regret, with him, if your kind disposition has in this instance subjected you to inconvenience.

Your letter reached me a few days ago, and as I had a favorable opportunity of sending the notes on Mr. Malthus book, for which you ask, to London on the day that I received your letter, I immediately dispatched them, and I have no doubt that ere this you will have had them. I looked for the pamphlet on money which I formerly mentioned to you, to send with the notes, but without success;—it may possibly

---

[1] Addressed: 'J. R. MCulloch Esqr / Buccleugh Place / Edinburgh'. Franked by Ricardo: 'Tetbury, January Three 1821'; postmark, 1822.—MS in British Museum.—*Letters to McCulloch*, XXIX.

[2] Letter 472.

be in my bookcase in London, in which case you shall have it when I have an opportunity of sending it; or I may have lent it to some friend, and it may not have been returned to me. I remember I thought it clever, but there is nothing in it which can be new to you.

I am sorry to say that I have no book on the subject of the commerce and finance of Holland,—if I had, it should be much at your service. I agree with you that much valuable illustration might be derived from a detailed history of the commerce and finance of that country.

I am glad to hear that your exertions do not relax in teaching the principles of Political Economy, and that you contemplate giving lectures to a public class, instead of a private one, next session. I do not know any man who has been more useful in disseminating the sound principles of the science than yourself. Your writings are so clear, and your illustrations so satisfactory, that they cannot fail to convince. Your contributions to the Supplement of the Encyclopedia, and to the Edin. Review, contain the most valuable instruction. I shall have great pleasure in looking over the manuscript lectures which you have already prepared, or any other you may hereafter send me, but I have not the least hope that I can give you any useful opinion or advice respecting the conduct of your course. On every point of arrangement I am very ignorant, and am sure that in all I do I make the worst possible. I shall look out carefully for any thing that I shall think an error in principle, and shall submit it to your consideration, in order that I may remove your erroneous opinion if it be yours, or have my own corrected by you, if it be mine. It will give me great pleasure to hear that your arrangements respecting the lectures become a source of permanent and considerable emolument to yourself, as besides the interest which I take in your welfare, a proof will thereby be afforded of the service which you are rendering to others. I shall not be in London till the latter end of this month or the beginning of february, and therefore I shall not see your article on money before that time, unless you would be kind enough to enclose it under separate covers directed to me here. If it should be printed before february I wish you would do so. Cobbett and his followers keep up incessant attacks upon me, for having said in my evidence before the Bank Committee, that the restoring the currency to the ancient standard, would only alter its value 5 pc.[1] He forgets that I was speaking of the plan recommended by me for restoring it, which would not have called for the use of any gold, and which would therefore not have occasioned any demand for that metal; and then, I ask, what there was in reverting to a bullion standard to make prices alter more than 5 pc.? Suppose that in 1819, when gold was at £4. 2 – p.ʳ oz, we had had two prices, a paper price and a bullion price; £4. 2 –, in paper, would have purchased no more than £3. 17. $10\frac{1}{2}$ in gold. By raising the value of paper 5 p.ᵗ would not £3. 17. $10\frac{1}{2}$ in paper purchase the same, as the like sum in gold?[2] If indeed during the operation of limiting the amount of paper, I make immense purchases of gold, and lock it up in a chest, or devote it to uses to which it had not before been applied, I raise the value of gold, and thereby lower the prices of goods, both in gold and in paper, which latter must conform to the value of gold; and this is precisely what the Bank have done. They have, from ignorance, made the reverting to a fixed currency as difficult a task to the country as possible.

Cobbett forgets too that Peel's bill absolutely prohibited

[1] See below, p. 141, n. 1, and cp. above, V, 385.
[2] These two sentences, only slightly altered, and the substance of the argument that follows, were embodied by McCulloch in an article in the *Scotsman*, 2 Feb. 1822; see below, p. 149, n. 1.

the Bank from paying in specie till 1823. All the friends of
that bill had a right to expect that the Bank would make no
preparation for specie payments till 1822, one year before the
period fixed, and I for one flattered myself that if from 1819
to 1822 it were found that the system of bullion payments
was a safe and easy one, specie payments would be still
further deferred, but the Bank had strong prejudices against
the plan and immediately commenced purchasing bullion and
coining money, and were absolutely forced to come to the
legislature for permission, last year, to pay in specie, as they
had accumulated a large quantity of coin. After they had
been foolish enough to do so, it became a matter of indifference
whether parliament agreed to their request or refused it—
indeed it was more desirable to comply with it:—the evil
had already been done by the purchase and accumulation of
gold, and no further mischief could arise from the substitution of the coins (in circulation) for the paper which they
were desirous of withdrawing.—Some of Mr. Cobbett's
admirers spoke of my false predictions at Monmouth—the
same men were at Hereford, where I had an opportunity of
speaking for myself, for I was present, and then they said
nothing.[1]

---

[1] Cp. above, p. 121. The following appeared in *Cobbett's Weekly
Register,* 29 Dec. 1821, p. 1596,
under the title 'MESSRS HUME
AND RICARDO': 'That the former
was invited to a dinner in *Herefordshire* I heard and was glad of;
but, what the devil did the *latter*
do there? What merits had *he*,
except those of having asserted,
that it was the *easiest thing in the
world to carry Peel's Bill into
effect,* and that the fall in prices
could be only *four and a half per
cent.?* He is, to be sure, the
Oracle in a certain place; but,
what could the *Herefordshire
farmers* see in him, or have to do
with him? Faith! the Radical
shoe-makers and carpenters and
smiths and labourers know a little
better than this. Their *Oracles*
are a little more correct in their
predictions. At *Monmouth,* to
which place Mr Hume went, there
was a little of good sense in the
proceedings. There the Oracle
got some decent raps on the
fingers; but, there he was not.'

The Lord Advocate's conduct in the affair of the Beacon has been very reprehensible, but I fear it will not be noticed as it ought to be by the House of Commons. From the little you have said in your letter, it is clear that, bad as the chance is of any one who has a contest with government in a court of law here, for any offence given to them through the press, it is infinitely more so in Scotland, from the manner in which Juries are selected. I will read the article in the Edin. Review which you recommend with attention, and will say a few words on the subject in the House if I do not find at the time that the sentiments which I would wish to express should have been already much better expressed by others.

Mr. Austin says something in his letter of an intention half formed in your mind of paying a visit to London in the Spring—I hope you will give every encouragement to the complete formation of so good a resolution: it would give me the greatest pleasure to see you.

Ever Dear Sir,

Yours truly

DAVID RICARDO

Will you have the goodness to order the Scotsman to be sent to London as soon as the month of february commences? I will pay my subscription to the agents in Warwick Lane London as soon as I go to town.

477. MARIA EDGEWORTH TO RICARDO [1]

Mrs. Baillie's
Hampstead
Jan.ʸ 7ᵗʰ [1822] [2]

My dear Sir

I will not keep you in any suspense on a subject so little   7 Jan. 1822
worth your curiosity as what merely concerns my own convenience.—I asked when you were likely to come to Town
because if you had decided to come any time between Monday the 14ᵗʰ and the beginning of Feb.ʸ I should then have
written to Mrs. Ricardo to have told her that during that
time I am disengaged and to ask her whether it could be
convenient and agreeable to her to receive my sisters and
myself for a few days.

I know that this is a strange proposal to make as few people
have either the wish or the power to lodge any but their own
family in a London house—But I cannot come to settle for
any time in Town or to take apartments for ourselves till towards the end of February—I am engaged to spend the beginning of that month and a full fortnight or three weeks with
Lady E Whitbread at Kensington Gore.

Now this brings my time of being in Town to the busy
season and after the meeting of parliament when I know that
we could not have any chance of enjoying your society and
that of your family as quietly and fully and with as selfish a
monopoly as I wish—I had therefore built this castle in the
air as I fear it will turn out—The foundation being wanting—
viz your being in Town and your being able to receive us—

So leaving this among the vast heap of overturned *Chateaux
en Espagne* I will go on to what I trust will not be of that
number.

---

[1] MS in *R.P.*
[2] In MS '1821'; but cp. letter 475
and *Life and Letters of Maria*

Edgeworth, ed. by A. J. C. Hare,
vol. II, p. 51. She was staying
with Joanna Baillie.

Mrs. Edgeworth has just bought into the French funds—and has received the inclosed letter from her Paris banker M. Delessert.[1]—Will you do me the favor to read it and will you write a few lines to me to direct how she must proceed about the *procuration*—She wants to know whether this power of Attorney must be drawn out in London or Dublin and what attesting names must be put to it—

Forgive me for the trouble I give you my dear Sir—Remember us in the kindest manner to Mrs. Ricardo and all your happy family and believe me

very sincerely yours
with much esteem and regard
MARIA EDGEWORTH

I have never seen you since we spent some pleasant days with your amiable daughter Mrs. Clutterbuck and her charming well-educated children—

478. TROWER TO RICARDO[2]
[*Reply to 471.—Answered by 481*]

Unsted Wood—Jan: 10. 1822

My Dear Ricardo

We are just returned home from Sussex, where we have been passing our Christmas with my Brother in Law Mr. Slater, at Newick Park. It is a very nice place, but in rather too wet a Country, at least it appears so to *me,* the character of whose soil is so opposite.

I was amused with the account you gave me of the public Honors paid to our friend Hume, and in which *You* participated. I am fully disposed to give him great credit for his indefatiguable exertions in the House of Commons. No doubt, he has done, and still will do a great deal of good;

---

[1] The enclosure is wanting.   [2] MS in *R.P.*

and is deserving of the applause of his fellow Citizens. An
ample allowance of noisy acclamation is a very convenient
and economical mode of remunerating public services; and
I dare say, it is a species of payment with which our friend
Hume is perfectly satisfied. Unfortunately,—"These little
things are great to little Men."

I rejoice in the appointment of Lord Wellesley to Ireland,
from whose great talents, and stateman like abilities much
may be expected. But, it is not merely the power with which
he is vested as Lord Lieutenant, that will enable him to meet
and overcome the difficulties of Ireland. What I expect from
him is, that the information he will obtain will enable him
to place before Ministers, in such strong colors, the system
that must be adopted, as to induce them to bring that system
before Parliament for their consideration and adoption—The
removing the disabilities from the Catholicks may do something, but not much, I think, towards healing the present
disorders. It appears to me, that no permanent or substantial
good can be done till all *small farms* and small tenancies, are
got rid of. These are the curse of Ireland. They are calculated
to destroy that wholesome dependence of the lower upon
the upper classes, which is one of the master links of society;
and to encourage habits of idleness, which are the bane of all
moral feeling. I am aware, there would be difficulty in
carrying this measure into execution, but the object is most
important. The two great deficiencies in Ireland are *want of
capital,* and *want of Industry.* By destroying small tenancies
you would obtain both. Suppose, for instance, no farms were
let of less extent than 50. Acres. In the first place it would
require a man of some substance to take such a farm; and in
the next, it would require the constant labor of certain
numbers of men to cultivate it. The Cottar would be converted
into a laborer, and would, with regular industry, obtain, not

merely the means of bare existence, as at present, but the comforts of an improved condition. But, where are these tenants to come from? If these small tenancies ceased to exist a great part of the work of those dreadful scourges, the middle men in Ireland, would be destroyed, and they might be converted into farmers. Besides the adoption of a system carrying with it the appearance of security, and fair remuneration, would necessarily draw, in time, the required capital into Ireland.

But how is the present system to be got rid of? Gradually no doubt. Not by interfering with existing engagements, but by making prospective enactments, giving time, and notice for the settlement of all vested interests. Some such system, as this, does appear to me, I confess, calculated to afford rational ground of hope, that the gradual improvement of the condition of the wretched people of Ireland may be accomplished. Let me hear what you have to say to it: and what other plans, in your view of this important subject, are better calculated to produce the desired object.

The question of Tithes is, no doubt, one that cannot be overlooked; but it is beset with difficulties, and dependent, as it seems to me, in some measure, upon the question of Catholick Emancipation—

I agree with You in thinking, Peel is too much elevated. No doubt, he is a very superior man, and calculated to take an upper walk in public life. But, as yet, I hardly know wh^t to think of his *Principles.* I doubt whether they are of a cast sufficiently liberal to satisfy my mind. On the Catholick question they certainly are not. But he has lately manifested a reserve and a caution, that I dont know very well what to think of. Dont flatter yourselves there is any chance of having Canning on *your side.* At all events he will do *better than that;* but, I hope he will not be sent to India; as I think it is the situation, of all others, for which he is least qualified. The Governor of India should be a man of cool judgment, of high rank, of popular yet dignified manners; and I cannot think that Canning, with all his talents, and it is impossible to estimate them too highly, can be said to possess in an eminent degree these qualifications.—

It seems probable, that, in some shape or other, you will have the Agricultural question before Parliament again. The Landlords and Farmers will cry aloud for a delivery from the Malt Tax; the benefit of which reduction would be felt principally by the *consumers*. Surely it would be much wiser to take off taxes, which would give a stimulus to our general trade, and diminish that horrible warfare that is carrying on against the smugglers. As to any immediate relief to the farmers the case does not admit of it; beyond that natural and obvious relief, which ought to be afforded, and which is now in operation all over the Country, in the diminutions of Rents and Tithes. And as to the Landlords, as a body, I do not much sympathise in *their* condition; they are now called upon to make sacrifices, which they are very capable of making, and which it is but justice, that they should make.

I have sent for Mills Book, and am very impatient to see it; as I am not well aware what his object is, in publishing it, agreeing so entirely as he does with the views you have given of the subject. There is a very good Review in the Quarterly of Godwins coarse and vulgar and impotent attack upon Malthus;[1] and a very fair view of the true object of the Essay. I am glad to see, that both the Edingburgh and Quarterly concur in supporting the doctrines of that able work.—

About a month ago, I was passing a few days with Mr. Charles Taylor the Member for Wales,[2] in company with

---

[1] *Quarterly Review,* Oct. 1821 [published in December], Art. VII. [2] C. W. Taylor, M.P. for Wells.

Dr. Wollaston, S.ʳ J. Seabright,[1] and Mr. Warburton, the latter of whom told me, that Mill had been writing a very able article on Government, in one of the Cyclopedias; pray tell me where I can see it. No doubt it is sufficiently *Radical;* but I like to see these Gentlemen spread out the Principles upon which they propose to lay their Democratic Foundation, that we may get a full view of their system, and ascertain the extent of their speculations.

When do you remove to Brook Street, I suppose the period is fast approaching, should circumstances call me to London I shall not fail to beat up your Quarters.—

Mrs. Trower begs to join with me in kind remembrances, to Mrs. Ricardo, Yourself and family and believe me My Dear Ricardo

Yrs very truly

HUTCHES TROWER

479. McCULLOCH TO RICARDO [2]
[*Reply to 476.—Answered by 483*]

Edinburgh 13ᵗʰ January 1822

My Dear Sir

I have safely received the parcel containing your notes on Mr. Malthus, and your letter of the 3ʳᵈ and for both of which I am highly obliged to you—I am sorry it was not in my power to have shewn greater attention to Mr. Austin; both because he is a friend of yours, and because he is himself a very intelligent, unassuming, and agreeable person—Do not suppose that he made any incroachment on my time; far

---

[1] Sir John Sebright, M.P. for Herefordshire.

[2] Addressed: 'David Ricardo Esquire M.P. / Gatcomb Park / Gloucestershire' and marked 'Hand by John Austin Esq.' MS in *R.P.—Letters of McCulloch to Ricardo*, XI.

13 Jan. 1822

from it—The time I spent in his company could not easily have been turned to greater advantage—

I am delighted with what you say in your letter respecting the proceedings in Parliament in 1819 with reference to Mr. Peels bill—Nothing could be more satisfactory; it is indeed quite an unanswerable statement, and I shall take an early opportunity to insert the substance of it in the Scotsman[1]—

I have availed myself of Mr. Austins going to Gloucestershire to send you a copy of my article on Money,[2] and I shall be most happy to know your opinion of it—I regret that I was not fully aware of the circumstances mentioned in your last letter before it was printed—When I began the article I intended to have added to it a history of the paper money of some of the principal countries, but as this would have swelled the article to too great length I was obliged to defer it to some other opportunity—

I am truly obliged to you for the kind manner in which you have spoken of my projected course of Lectures on Political Economy; and when you arrive at London I shall use the liberty which you have given me to send the two introductory discourses to you for your perusal—I am sure I shall derive much instruction from your criticisms—

Nothing would give me so much pleasure as a visit to London when you are there; but I shall be so much occupied during the ensuing spring and summer in preparing for the winters campaign that I must, though with very great reluctance, deny myself the pleasure of visiting the Metropolis till some more favourable opportunity—

Have the goodness to excuse my writing to you on such

---

[1] 'Notice of Mr. Peel's Bill—Reasons for Maintaining it Inviolate', leading article in *Scotsman*, 2 Feb. 1822; see above, p. 140, n. 2.
[2] In *Supplement to the Encyclopaedia Britannica*.

paper. I find my stock of letter paper is exhausted and as it is sunday I cannot replace it. Believe me to be with the greatest regard and esteem

Yours most faithfully

J. R. McCulloch

480. M^cCULLOCH TO RICARDO [1]
[Answered by 483]

[13 January 1822]

My Dear Sir

13 Jan. 1822   Since I wrote the accompanying letter I have obtained from my excellent friend Mr. J. A. Murray Advocate[2] a copy of a reprint of the exceedingly scarce pamphlet of Sir Dudley North[3] which he requests me to forward to you—I also send you the Card which Mr. Murray has sent me with the pamphlet —He had once the pleasure of meeting you, and I am sure that if he should again happen to be in London when you are there you would be much pleased to renew your acquaintance

---

[1] Addressed: 'David Ricardo Esq' —undated and not passed through the post; was no doubt sent by hand with the preceding letter, and Ricardo replies to both together. Sunday, 13 Jan. 1822 is probably the date also of J. A. Murray's letter.

MS in *R.P.*

[2] John Archibald Murray (1779–1859), a writer in the *Edinburgh Review* since its commencement, afterwards M.P., Lord Advocate and, as Lord Murray, a judge.

[3] *Discourses upon Trade; Principally Directed to the Cases of the Interest Coynage Clipping Increase of Money*, 1691. McCulloch reprinted it in *A select collection of Early English Tracts on Commerce*, for the Political Economy Club, London, 1856. In his preface McCulloch says that this pamphlet was supposed to be entirely lost until a copy came to light at the sale of the library of the Rev. Rogers Ruding and was purchased 'by a gentleman of Edinburgh, who printed a few copies for distribution among his friends'. —Mill, who had been 'on the look-out for it for years', was 'exceedingly' gratified by the discovery and asked Napier to secure for him 'a copy of the impression which is to be made by your friend.' (Letter of 14 Jan. 1822, in Bain's *James Mill*, p. 202.)

—Mr. Murray has made great sacrifices for the good cause—   13 Jan. 1822
Had he consented to modify his opinions he might have been
at this moment Lord Advocate of Scotland—But although
a gentleman of exceedingly mild and pleasant manners, he
has too much sturdiness of mind, and too thorough a contempt for every thing that savours of dereliction of principle,
to purchase the highest honours that ministry could bestow
at such a price—

Yours most truly
J. R. McCulloch

[*Enclosure, addressed:* 'J. R. Macculloch Esq / 10 Bucclugh Place']

122 George Street Sunday

Dear Sir
    I send you two copies of North. One for yourself and the other
for Mr. Richard. I intended to have written to him but so many
years have passed since I saw him at the King of Clubs that I can not
hope to retain any place in his recollection. There is no mark of
respect and regard which I should not have great pleasure in paying
to him. Believe me

very truly yours
John A. Murray

481. RICARDO TO TROWER [1]
[Reply to 478]

Gatcomb Park
25 Jany 1822

My Dear Trower
    This day week I shall leave Gatcomb for London, and   25 Jan. 1822
shall soon after enter with all my energies on my parliamentary duties. I expect that the Agricultural question will
occupy a great deal of attention, and I am not without my

---

[1] Addressed: 'Hutches Trower   MS at University College, Lon-
Esqr / Unsted Wood / Godalming /   don.—*Letters to Trower*, LII.
Surry'.

fears that some injudicious measures may be adopted, in consequence of the general prevalence of error on that important subject. I have read with attention all that has been said at the different meetings, and although I think I see a decided improvement in the public mind on the policy of corn laws, yet it appears to me that very few take a rational and scientific view of the origin of the distress, and of the true means of remedying it. They all concur in attributing the want of a remunerating price to enormous taxation, in which opinion I cannot agree; although I am willing to allow that an immediate repeal of some of the taxes which affect agricultural produce, would materially relieve the farmer. There is an interval between the repeal of a tax which falls indirectly on a commodity, and the fall of the price of such commodity, that is favorable to the producer, and the benefit of this interval would be enjoyed by farmers. It might, if the distress is owing to temporary causes, be sufficiently long to enable them to surmount the difficulty which immediately presses upon them, it would however be quite unscientific therefore to say that it was the burthen of taxation which was the cause of the low price of corn. The cause of the low price is nothing else but the supply exceeding the demand. Why it should do so now, and why it should have done so for 2 years back is an interesting enquiry, and many may have their different theories to account for it. When I say the cause of the low price is nothing else than the supply exceeding the demand, I am not quite correct, for I appear to exclude the alteration in the value of the currency as one of the causes, which I am not desirous of doing. To that cause I ascribe an effect of 10 pc. and in so doing I am making a liberal allowance. I perceive that a meeting of your county is called to consider this subject—I hope you will do, what you are so well able to do, express your own correct views on this most important

25 Jan. 1822

question, and not let the reveries of a Webb Hall,[1] and the exaggerated, and often wicked, statements of a Cobbett, pass every where uncontradicted[2]. I shall look to the public papers with great interest for a full and correct account of your speech.

I agree with much of what you say about Ireland, but on some points we differ. I think it desirable that small farms, and small tenancies, should be got rid of, but I do not look upon these, and many other[3] things which might be advantageously corrected in Ireland, as the cause of the evils under which that unfortunate country groans, but as the effect of those evils. If Ireland had a good system of law—if property was secure—if an Englishman lending money to an Irishman could by some easy process oblige him to fulfill his contract, and not be set at defiance by the chicanery of sheriffs agents in Ireland, capital would flow into Ireland, and an accumulation of capital would lead to all the beneficial results which every where follows[4] from it. The most economical processes would be adopted—small farms would be laid into large—there would be an abundant demand for labour, and thus would Ireland take her just rank among nations. The evils of Ireland, I, in my conscience believe, arise from misrule, and I hope that during the administration of Lord Wellesley a commencement will be made in the reformation of the enormous abuses under which that country labours. Hume I believe means to attack the Tithe system of Ireland in the House of Commons.[5] I do not know whether he is sufficiently skilful to meddle with so intricate a subject advantageously,

[1] George Webb Hall, Chairman of the Agricultural Association, was organizing petitions and addressing meetings all over the country in support of extreme measures for the protection of agriculture.

[2] Replaces 'unrefuted'.

[3] 'evils, as the' is del. here.

[4] Replaces 'flows'.

[5] See *Hansard,* N.S., VI, 136 (7 Feb. 1822) and VII, 1147 ff. (19 June 1822).

but he will not fail I think to do some good. The oftener that abuses of all kinds are stated and discussed the better; it sets able heads to work, and the people become informed as to their real interests. This reacts on the Government, and thus abuses, even on our present imperfect system, are often finally redressed.

You will have received Mill's article on Government, which I sent you many days ago.[1]—You will not approve of it, but I think it an excellent article, and well reasoned throughout. Since writing that article he has written two others for the Supplement to the Encyclopedia which are I think both very good—one is on Jurisprudence, the other on the Liberty of the Press.[2] If you cannot conveniently get the Encyclopedia, I can lend you the articles, as I have one copy of each in London, and I think you will like to read them.

I am not a good judge of his book on Political Economy, I have thought so much on the subject myself, that I can form a very inadequate idea of the impression which his work is calculated to make on one who is a learner, but I am told by learners that it is very clear, and fully accomplishes the object which he professes to have in view.

I received some months ago a letter from M Say in answer to my last observations on his book, to which I intend very shortly to send him my reply. You will probably like to see both his letter and my answer[3]—I will shew them to you when I see you in London.

The reviews of Godwin's work both in the Quarterly and Edinburgh were I think very good;—surely in the minds of

[1] *The Article Government, Reprinted from the Supplement to the Encyclopaedia Britannica,* Traveller Office, May 5, 1821. Ricardo's copy of this reprint is in the Goldsmiths' Library of the University of London.

[2] *The Article Liberty of the Press, Reprinted from the Supplement to the Encyclopaedia Britannica,* Innes, printer, London, no date. Ricardo's copy is in the Goldsmiths' Library.

[3] Letters 446 and 488.

all reasonable men the principle for which Malthus contends 25 Jan. 1822
is fully established.

I continue to hear, from time to time, from Mr. MCulloch; he is a zealous advocate for the correct principles of Polit. Economy and is more actively employed in their dissemination than any individual I know. Besides the excellent articles which he writes in the Supp^t to the Encyclopedia, in the Edinburgh Review, and the Scotsman, he gives lectures on Polit. Economy in Edinburgh, and contemplates the extending them next year to a general instead of a private class —this is as it should be, notwithstanding the wise observations of Lord John Russell on the little advantages to be derived from a knowledge of this science, in his letter to the Electors of Huntingdon.[1]

Mrs. Ricardo joins with me in kind remembrances to Mrs. Trower. Believe me My dear Trower

Ever most truly yours

DAVID RICARDO

I hope we shall see you very soon in London.

---

[1] 'There is a party amongst us, however, distinguished in what is called the *Science* of Political Economy, who wish to substitute the corn of Poland and Russia for our own. Their principle is, that you ought always to buy where you can buy cheapest....They care not for the difference between an agricultural and manufacturing population in all that concerns morals, order, national strength and national tranquillity. Wealth is the only object of their speculation; nor do they much consider the two or three millions of people who may be reduced to utter beggary in the course of their operations. This they call diverting capital into another channel. Their reasonings lie so much in abstract terms, their speculations deal so much by the gross, that they have the same insensibility about the sufferings of a people, that a General has respecting the loss of men wearied by his operations....Political economy is now the fashion; and the Farmers of England, are likely, if they do not keep a good look out, to be the victims.' (A cutting of this letter of Lord John Russell, from the *Morning Chronicle* of 18 Jan. 1822, was found in the pocket-book used by Ricardo on his Continental tour, in *R.P.*)

482. RICARDO TO SINCLAIR [1]

Gatcomb Park, Minchin-Hampton, 29th January 1822.

Dear Sir,

You are fully aware that you and I do not agree in our opinion of the causes of the present agricultural distress, nor in our views of the remedies which it would be expedient to apply to it. We agree still less on the disadvantage which you suppose to have resulted to the importer of corn, from the increased value of the currency. The question you put to Mr. Attwood is not a fair one; for the same cause which would elevate the exchange from 18 to 25, would lower corn from 40s. to 28s. 9d. *per* quarter, and it would be a matter of indifference to the foreign exporter of corn to England, if he sold it at 40s., and negociated his bill at 18 francs *per* pound Sterling, or sold it at 28s. 9d., and negociated his bill at 25 francs. Is it not a fallacy to suppose money so to rise in value that gold should appear to fall from £.5, 10s. to £.3:17:10$\frac{1}{2}$, the exchange rise from 18 to 25, and yet suppose wheat to remain steadily at 40s. *per* quarter? I remain, Dear Sir, your faithful and obedient servant,

DAVID RICARDO.

483. RICARDO TO McCULLOCH [2]
[*Reply to 479 & 480.—Answered by 484*]

London 8 Feb[y] 1822

My Dear Sir

I have found the book which I once mentioned to you.[3] The title of it is "Elementary Thoughts on the Bullion

---

[1] *Correspondence of Sir John Sinclair,* vol. 1, p. 375; *Letters to Trower,* LIII.—The letter refers to a pamphlet by Sinclair, *Address to the Owners and Occupiers of Land,* Edinburgh, Constable, 1822, of which there is a copy in *R.P.*
[2] MS in British Museum.—*Letters to M'Culloch,* XXX.
[3] Above, p. 138–9 and VIII, 337.

Question, the Nat.! Debt, the resources of Great Britain, and
the probable duration of the Constitution" and I will send
it to you immediately if you will like to have it. Perhaps you
would prefer to have it sent with the Manuscript lectures,
which I shall have to return to you, when you put me in
possession of them.

I have read your article on money in "the Supp.!" with
great pleasure—it is sound in principle, and full of information respecting the various changes which our money has at
different times undergone.

I have written to Mr. Murray to thank him for the copy of
Sir Dudley North's Discourses on Trade. I had no idea that
any one entertained such correct opinions, as are expressed
in this publication, at so early a period. I have a perfect
recollection of meeting Mr. Murray at the King of Clubs;
indeed I have reason to do so, for he expressed himself very
kindly towards me. I hope I shall soon have an opportunity
of improving my acquaintance with him.

I very much fear that you will not agree with me in the
opinion which I gave in the House of Commons the other
evening that Taxation was not the cause of Agricultural
distress.[1] A relief from taxation would be useful to farmers
and landlords, as well as to all other people, but that is no
proof that the distress is owing to taxation. The question
I conceive is simply this "Could England have been in a
state of great agricultural distress if she had been absolutely
without any taxation?" the answer I think is clear and obvious
that she could, because she might have a redundant quantity
of agricultural produce. If a country has prohibited the
importation of corn, and all at once opens her ports, and
corn can be imported at a cheap price, she will be involved
in Agricultural distress. If a country has a succession of good

---

[1] See above, V, 123.

crops, she will have agricultural distress. If she suddenly and greatly improves in her agricultural processes she will suffer distress. All these causes have combined to produce distress in England, for we have opened our ports to the unlimited importation of cheap corn from Ireland, we have had 2 or 3 good crops, and we have improved our husbandry.

We shall probably not agree in our opinions of the actual state of the country. I think it is on the whole in a flourishing condition, and that our wealth is daily increasing. Every thing indicates that our manufactures are in a progressive state of improvement, and from the produce of the revenue I should conclude that their prosperity more than makes up for the losses and adversity of the agricultural class. I cannot help thinking that the distress in Agriculture will not be of long duration, and cannot help fearing that we may have a reaction which will be very beneficial to farmers and very hurtful to all other classes. I hope we shall escape through this crisis without aggravating the evil by bad legislation— I have no hope of good measures being adopted, the land-lords are too powerful in the House of Commons to give us any hope that they will relinquish the tax which they have in fact contrived to impose on the rest of the community.— They appear very much discontented and out of humor, and I almost doubt whether I should obtain a hearing if I attempted to express views so very opposite to their own.

I attended a meeting of our Political Economy club on monday last,—we had a full attendance, and several knotty points were discussed.[1] There is a note in the last edition of

---

[1] At the meeting on 4 February Ricardo read the letters which he had exchanged with Say (see below, p. 172, n. 2) and 'Mr. Tooke read the copy of a letter, from himself to Mr. Mill relative to the effect of Taxation on Prices. The following questions were discussed: 1.—Has Machinery a tendency to diminish the demand for Labour? D. RICARDO. 2.—What is the effect of Taxation on Prices in a

my book,[1] in which I express an opinion, that if a com-
modity be raised in price, in consequence of being taxed, and
the same quantity as before be consumed, the additional
price will not make it necessary to employ any more money
for its circulation. The same opinion is expressed by Mill in
his book.[2] The correctness of this view was doubted, and it
was accordingly made the subject of conversation:—the
majority of the company were I think convinced that the
proposition was a true one. My opinion of the effects
of machinery on the demand for labour, was also discussed,
but I could hardly satisfy myself of the general opinion on
that disputed point—we are to resume the conversation on
both subjects when Mill and Torrens are with us—they were
both absent on account of ill health.

> With great regard I remain
> Ever truly Yours
> DAVID RICARDO

484. M^cCULLOCH TO RICARDO[3]
[Reply to 483.—Answered by 486]

Edinburgh 12 Feby 1822

My Dear Sir

I am very much pleased by what you say of my article
on Money, though I always suspect that in you I have a very
indulgent critic—You would perceive from last Scotsman[4]
that my opinion respecting the causes of the agricultural
distress entirely coincided with your own—This distress un-

country having no Foreign Trade?
T. TOOKE. The further considera-
tion of the latter was deferred till
the next meeting'. (*Political Eco-
nomy Club, Minutes of Proceedings
1821–1882*, p. 46, and cp. p. 45;
see also Bain, *James Mill*, p. 197.)

[1] Above, I, 213–14.
[2] *Elements of Political Economy*, 1821, pp. 234–5.
[3] MS in *R.P.*—*Letters of McCulloch to Ricardo*, XII.
[4] No. for 9 February; editorial comment on the County meetings.

questionably arises from the low price of the principal articles of farming produce, and it is an utter absurdity to suppose that low price can ever be caused by excessive taxation—I do not know but I should be of your opinion—for I assure you I always differ from you with the greatest pain—respecting the state of the country, if we had got rid of the Corn laws; but so long as they are maintained I do not see how it is possible to escape great fluctuations of price; and when prices are factitiously increased to a high level in a country like this, with so large a manufacturing population, the greatest distress must inevitably be the result—If the price of corn were next year to rise to 100*l* a quarter, which is no improbable supposition, we should certainly have another radical rebellion— Neither do I think that our prosperity can ever rest on a firm basis while our taxation is so oppressive—We should not forget the example of Holland—The greatness of her commerce long concealed the effects of the canker that was preying on her vitals; but low profits ultimately proved too heavy a drawback on her prosperity to be counterpoised— Why should not like causes be in England productive of like effects?

I have promised to write an article for the forthcoming Review on the comparative effects of high and low taxes on the Revenue.[1] In this article I should like to notice as particularly as I could the effects which the different taxes have had on the revenue in Ireland—Sir John Newport made some curious statements on this subject in the course of last session;[2] but as I have no acquaintance with the Hon. Bart. I should be extremely obliged to you, if you would endeavour

[1] See below, p. 185, n. 1.
[2] Sir John Newport, M.P. for Waterford, had stated that in Ireland 'the receipts of the exchequer had diminished in the exact proportion as the burthens of the people had been increased.' (Speech on 15 June 1821, *Hansard*, N.S., V, 1193.)

to procure from him what information he possesses on this subject that I may embody it into the Review—Though you may not know Sir John yourself some of your friends will know him, and I trust that the importance of the subject, and the object which I have in view will apologise for the trouble to which I am putting you—As I must have the article ready in a short time, be so good as [to][1] send me the papers, in the event of your procuring them, by the Mail—

Some of our Police Commissioners leave this for London in a day or two when I shall send one of my manuscript Lectures; I have some more prepared but they are so ill written that I cannot think of asking you to look at them untill I get them rewritten—If the Police bill introduced by the Magistrates of this City be allowed to pass into a law it will be a most shameful act—Out of a population of 130,000 I do not in my conscience believe that it is approved by 130 persons—You have no idea what depredations have been committed by the agents of our Police; and because the Commissioners elected by the inhabitants have detected these frauds, and exposed them, and reduced the expenses of the establishment to about a half of what it formerly was, the one half of their constituents are to be disfranchised, and the whole power vested in the hands of *ex officio* Commissioners appointed by the Town Council—that is, by a body with whom the inhabitants have no more concern than they have with the Congress of Buenos Ayres—I trust to your goodness to excuse me for putting you to all this trouble, and I remain with the greatest respect and esteem and regard

Yours ever faithfully

J. R. M^cCULLOCH

[1] Omitted in MS.

485. M^cCULLOCH TO RICARDO [1]
[*Answered by* 486 & 491]

Edinburgh 13th Feby 1822

My Dear Sir

I send you herewith my second Lecture which contains an outline of my projected course on Political Economy [2]— I hope you will be able to read it without much difficulty, and I shall be most happy to hear what you think of it—The first Lecture is on the nature of the evidence on which conclusions in the Political and Economical sciences are founded, [3] and I shall avail myself of some future opportunity to send it to you when I have rendered it legible—

This will be delivered to you by Mr. Thomas Dick one of the Commissioners of Police for this city—He has gone to London to attend the Committee on the Police bill—If you could give him, or any of the other commissioners, introductions to any of your friends who are members, it might be of considerable service—We are all deeply interested in the fate of this question—If the bill introduced by Mr. William Dundass be passed into a law, it will in effect form the heaviest, the most oppressive, and most degrading law to which any part of the country was ever subjected—

Have the goodness to send me the book on bullion, &c, [4] along with the enclosed Lecture by Mr. Dick when he returns

---

[1] Addressed: 'David Ricardo Esq' —not passed through the post.
   MS in *R.P.*—*Letters of McCulloch to Ricardo*, XIII.
[2] Probably embodied in McCulloch's *A Discourse on the Rise, Progress, Peculiar Objects, and Importance, of Political Economy: containing an Outline of a Course of Lectures on the Principles and Doctrines of that Science*, Edin-burgh, Constable, 1824, p. 72 ff.
[3] Cp. the leading article in the *Scotsman*, 12 May 1821, 'Nature of the Evidence from which Conclusions in Political Economy ought to be Deduced.—Mr Owen's Pretended Experiment shown to be No Experiment at all', partly reproduced in McCulloch's *Discourse*, 1824, p. 10 ff.
[4] See above, pp. 156–7.

to Edinburgh—If however you should not have had time to look over the Lecture previously to Mr. Dicks departure it is of no moment, as I can get it at some future period—I am with great regard

Yours ever faithfully

J. R. McCULLOCH

486. RICARDO TO McCULLOCH [1]
[*Reply to 484 & 485.—Answered by 495*]

London 19 Feb 1822

My Dear Sir

While I was out this morning, taking a short walk with my daughters, your friend Mr. Dick called at my house, and left the parcel with which you had entrusted him. I am very sorry that I did not see him. I shall however take immediate steps to secure a meeting with him, and will do all the service in my power to him, by introducing him to such of my friends as are members of parliament.—

Sir John Newport shewed me the paper which he had prepared for you and as my power of franking was exhausted yesterday,[2] I got him to direct the letter, which inclosed his observations, to you. I hope they will be of use to the object which you have in view.

I shall not fail to oppose, with my vote, the police bill, which you describe as being so little accordant with the wishes of the people of Edinburgh, and shall use my best endeavors to call the attention of my friends to its principle and provisions.

I endeavored last night to express my opinion rather fully, for one so little able to speak as myself, to the House on the

---

[1] MS in British Museum.—*Letters to McCulloch*, XXXI.

[2] As an M.P. he was entitled to send free ten letters a day.

present question which so powerfully interests the country.[1] The House listened to me with attention, and appeared to follow and understand my arguments, but I am sorry to say that the reporter of the Times does not appear to have understood me. I have seen no other paper, but I am sure if you had been one of my auditors you would have given your assent to every one of the propositions which I advanced.

Nothing could be worse than the lectures on Political Economy lately given to the House by Brougham—he is not even perfect in Adam Smith's work, and really appears not to have paid any attention to the works which have been published in our day.—

I will read your lecture with attention, and will return it with my observations, if I have any to make on it, by Mr. Dick. I will also send you by him the book on bullion, which you need not give yourself the trouble to return to me.

I am again appointed one of the Agricultural Committee,[2] but I fear that I shall be able to do little good in it. We have gained something in getting the present law condemned by all parties, and I have very little doubt but that the same reasons which are given for the condemnation of the present law may be employed against the principle of any protecting law which they may be desirous of establishing.

I remain with great esteem

Y^{rs} very truly

DAVID RICARDO

[1] The agricultural distress; see above, V, 129 ff.

[2] All the members of the Agri-cultural Committee of 1821 were reappointed in 1822.

487. RICARDO TO TROWER [1]

20 Feb 1822
London

My dear Trower

I thank you for the account you have given me of your proceedings at the County meeting.[2] I was sorry to find, before I received your letter,[3] that your speech had been cut short by the impatience and clamor of your audience. I wish you had not ventured on the delicate topic of the repeal of taxes having been the cause of Agricultural distress, for if that doctrine be true, which I very much doubt, it was one which could not be successfully handled in such an assembly. They would not perhaps have been more civil to you if you had supported the less unpalatable doctrine of which I profess

20 Feb. 1822

---

[1] Addressed: 'Hutches Trower Esq! / Unsted Wood / Godalming'.
MS at University College, London.—*Letters to Trower,* LIV.
[2] The meeting of the freeholders of Surrey, held at Epsom on 18 Feb. 1822, to petition Parliament for a reduction of taxation and for parliamentary reform. 'Mr. Trower expressed his regret that the important questions of agricultural distress and parliamentary reform had been mixed up together on the present occasion. It was not so much to Mr. Peel's bill, as to that lamentable corn bill which was passed in 1815 that the present low prices of agricultural products were to be attributed. In saying this he did not intend to advocate the fooleries of Mr. Webb Hall. He thought that much of the present agricultural distress was attributable to the late abundant harvests. The hon. gentleman proceeded in this position at some length amidst general outcries from the meeting; in the midst of it he was interrupted by some person asking him whether he thought taxation to be among the probable causes of the distress now existing among the farmers. Upon his answering that the farmers had suffered most from the taxes that had been taken off, so great a confusion was created in the multitude that the speaker found it impossible to proceed. Having made two or three ineffectual attempts to obtain a farther hearing, he gave way to Mr. Grey Bennet, who stated that he was not surprised that the startling proposition of Mr. Trower, that the country was too little taxed, had caused the commotion which had just taken place.' (Report in *The Times,* 19 Feb. 1822.)
[3] Trower's letter is missing.

myself to be the advocate, that taxation is not the cause of Agricultural distress, and that a repeal of taxes will lighten the burthens of all, but will not afford particular relief to the Agricultural class.—This doctrine I was advancing in the H of Commons on the same day you had been speaking at Epsom, and as I had a more polite, and a less numerous audience, the expression of my opinions was listened to with patience and attention.[1] I flatter myself that in the progress of the debates on this subject many will be found to advocate the same doctrines.—I wish that the Table you gave the reporters may be published—if it is not, send it to me, and I will endeavor to get it into some of the papers.[2] Every thing which tends to shew the excessive quantity at market, whether of corn, of cattle, or of sheep, will be highly useful towards the establishing of correct notions on this important subject. Cobbett and his followers contend that the alteration in the value of money has been of inestimable advantage to the working classes,[3] they contend therefore that it has increased the demand for provisions, and yet he as well as others give us constant accounts of the quantities of corn remaining at market unsold, and of cattle and sheep penned at fairs for which there is no adequate demand—can we have a stronger proof of increased supply? An alteration in the value of money is a sufficient reason for an altered price of com-

[1] See above, V, 137.
[2] The Editors of *Letters to Trower* identify this Table with 'Statistics of quantities and prices of grain, etc. after harvest, for 1820–1, and 1821–2', fragments of which they found among Trower's papers. They also give (pp. 178–9) a letter from John Grenside, a Corn Factor, to Trower, 15 Feb. 1822, which contains 'An Account of Corn Imported into the Port of London (including Foreign)' from 1819 to 1821, which may be the Table referred to.—The figures cover part of the same ground as, but do not agree in detail with, those in Appendix B of *Protection to Agriculture*.
[3] 'The labourers are better off than they were, and will get better still' (*Cobbett's Weekly Register,* 16 Feb. 1822, p. 437).

modities, but it can have no effect on quantity. If it plunges 20 Feb. 1822
the farmer and landlord into distress, why are the other
classes of producers exempted from its effects? Is not taxation
from the same cause increased to the merchant, the manufacturer &c., &c.? Never was there a greater fallacy than
that of ascribing the present distress either to taxation, or to
the altered value of money. Cobbett is a mischievous
scoundrel; he ascribes the evils under which the country is
laboring to the altered value of money, and yet recommends
the people to hoard gold, which he knows will increase the
value of money still more.[1] It is confusion he wants, and he
cares not what means he takes to produce it. But in spite of
him the country will get over its difficulties, and when it is
again prosperous he will have the insolence to say that he
foretold it.—

What say you to Brougham's speech? What a falling off
was there! I have not heard for a long time from any man
who pretends to know anything of Political Economy so
many absurd opinions as were delivered by him on Monday
sen'night[2],—they will be a standing dish for the remainder
of the Session.—Believe me ever

Most truly Y^{rs}

DAVID RICARDO

[1] 'Get sovereigns with the money, and lock those sovereigns safely up for a *little while,* at any rate. They will neither eat or drink. They cannot prove a *loss;* and they may be a very great gain' ('To the Money-Hoarders', in *Cobbett's Weekly Register,* 22 Dec. 1821, p. 1531).
[2] 11 February, on his own motion on the Distressed State of the Country; cp. above, V, 124–5.

488. RICARDO TO SAY [1]
[*Reply to 446.*—*Answered by* 496]

London 5[2] March 1822

Dear Sir

I have received the letter which you kindly sent to me in answer to mine of May last. I am much indebted to you for the trouble you have taken in explaining your view of the subject of value, and I am happy to observe that the difference between us is much less than I had hitherto considered it. You speak of two different utilities which commodities possess, one, which they derive from nature, without any of the labour of man, the other, which they derive exclusively from his labour. You say that for the first of these, which you call natural utility, nothing valuable can be obtained in exchange, and it is only for that portion of utility which is given to a commodity by labour or industry, for which any thing valuable can be obtained. You add "mais en Economie Politique nous ne pouvons nous occuper que de la portion d'utilité qui a eté donné *avec des frais.*["] You explain on these principles the case I had put to you of a pound of iron and a pound of gold, which I had supposed had exactly the same utility, though the gold was 2000 times more valuable. If we give 2000 times more for the gold than the iron, you say, it is because that particular utility of which only Political Economy treats, namely that given by labour, is 2000 times greater than that given to

---

[1] MS in the possession of M. Raoul-Duval (with two MS notes by Say).—*Mélanges,* pp. 123–30; *Œuvres diverses,* pp. 423–6 (in French translation).—A copy, identical with Ricardo's original but not in his handwriting and dated 3 March 1822, in *R.P.;* it was printed in *Minor Papers,* pp. 190–94.

Ricardo had written this letter a month before and read it to the Political Economy Club on 4 Feb. 1822; see above, p. 154 and below, p. 172, n. 2.

[2] Replaces '3'.

iron, and you add that the iron has 1999 portions of natural 5 March 1822 utility for which nothing is given; of which the gold has none.

Although I cannot quite approve of the terms used to explain this truth, yet I do now, and always have substantially agreed in the reasoning which proves it, for I have always contended that commodities are valuable in proportion to the quantity of labour bestowed upon them, and when you say that they are valuable in proportion as they are useful, and they are useful in proportion to the quantity of labour or industry bestowed upon them, you are in fact expressing the same opinion in other words.

It follows from your doctrine that if by any[1] process, of the 2000 portions of the utility given to gold by labour, 1000 portions were given to it by nature, and the other 1000 portions by labour, gold would fall to one half of its former exchangeable value. But would a pound of gold form the same portion of riches as before? you would be bound to say it would not, because you say riches do not depend on quantity but on value. I, on the contrary, who do not estimate riches by value, but by the whole quantity of utility which the commodities which constitute riches possess, from whatever source derived, whether from nature or from industry, should say that I was equally rich in the possession of a pound of gold after the discovery of the economical process, although my riches would be of only half their former value. In saying so I should be justified by various passages in your different works. In your last edition of The "Catechisme"[2] you say Page 2 that the riches of a person are in proportion to the value of the commodities which he possesses, and not in proportion to their quantity: so far you repeat the same opinion, but when your

---

[1] 'economical' is ins. here by Say in the MS.

[2] The second edition; see the close of this letter.

pupil calls upon you to explain what is the measure of the value of things, your answer that it is the quantity of all other things that the proprietor is enabled to command by their means, if he consents to exchange them. Now in this I think there is a contradiction, for we are told that riches are in proportion to value, and value in proportion to the quantity of things, therefore riches are in proportion to the quantity of things; and yet you say that riches are in proportion to value, and not in proportion to the quantity of things.[1]

Let us suppose that the same cause, namely, an economical process, which lowers the value of gold one half, lowers at the same time, in the same degree, and by the same means, hats, shoes, cloth, and linen. In this state of things a pound of gold will command just as many hats, shoes, cloth, and linen as before any of the economical processes were discovered. I ask is the man equally rich as before who has a pound of gold? you first answer no, because he has not a commodity of equal value, and you secondly answer yes, because he can command an equal quantity of various other commodities.

In your letter to Mr. Malthus you say, very justly, that if corn and woollen goods be produced with so much facility, that with their former cost in productive services, double the quantity be produced, they will fall one half in value. You consider value as the measure of riches, and yet you say that a person getting in exchange a double *quantity* of

---

[1] Note in Say's handwriting attached to the MS: 'Mr. Ricardo trouve là un paralogisme parce qu'il fait abstraction du possesseur, dont je ne fais jamais abstraction. Je dis que la richesse est en proportion de la valeur de ce que l'on possède, et la valeur de ce que l'on possède en proportion de ce que l'on peut acquérir. Je ne pense pas que l'on puisse parler de la richesse absolument, j'entends de la richesse dont s'occupe l'Economie politique qui est toujours relative.' Cp. below, p. 189.

these woollen goods and corn gets a larger portion of riches.

["] Les produits[1], dans un tel echange, sont mis en opposition de valeur avec les services productifs; or, comme en tout echange, l'un des deux termes vaut d'autant plus qu'il obtient une plus grande quantité de l'autre, il resulte que les services productifs valent d'autant plus que les produits sont plus multipliés, et a plus bas prix. Voila pourquoi la baisse des produits, en augmentant la valeur des fonds productifs d'une nation et des revenus qui en émanent, augmente les richesses nationales. Cette demonstration qui se trouve en detail au chap 3 du liv. 2 de mon Traité d'economie politique (4e edition [)] a rendu ce me semble, quelque service a la science, en expliquant ce que jusque-la avait eté senti sans etre expliqué, c'est que bien que la richesse soit une valeur exchangeable, la richesse generale est accrue par le bas prix des marchandises et de toute espece de produits.["] Double the production of A, B, C and D by economical processes and you do not augment the riches of either, but collectively they are nevertheless doubly as rich as before. Surely in this explanation the words riches and value are not always used in the same sense. According to my view they would be singly and collectively doubly rich, but their riches would not have increased in value: they would not increase in value, because they would have no more of that utility, given exclusively by labour.

On the other point respecting the circumstances which make two loaves raised on land of unequal fertility of equal value, although the rent derived from them will be different, we in many respects agree. Rent is the effect of the monopoly of land of a certain fertility, and must rise with the value of the loaf, and with the difficulty of producing additional

[1] In MS, by a slip of the pen,   the MS to 'produits', as it is in 'services'; corrected by Say on   *Lettres à Malthus*, p. 57.

loaves. But the last loaf produced pays little or no rent, and its value, as well as the value of all other loaves, rises, because a greater quantity of its utility is derived from labour and industry, and a smaller quantity from natural means. You say demand and supply regulates the price of bread; that is true, but what regulates supply? the cost of production,— the quantity of utility imparted to bread by industry. Rent is the effect of high price, not the cause. In some loaves there must necessarily be little rent, I should say no rent at all. You say bread is regulated in value by productive services, true but in some bread of five shillings value the productive services may be divided thus Rent 2/- Profit 1/- and labour 2/- and in another equal quantity of bread of the same value they may be divided as follows Rent nothing, Profit 1/- and labour 4/-. I object to the lumping the productive services altogether, I want to know the part which each performs in giving value to bread.[1]

At the last meeting of our Political Economy Club, I read your letter, for which I was desired to return you the thanks of the meeting.[2]—Our society is a very unpretending one,

---

[1] Note in Say's handwriting attached to the MS: 'Je ne dis pas que les services productifs seuls determinent le prix du pain; ils déterminent l'offre; mais le prix n'est pas le resultat de l'offre seule. Il est le resultat de l'offre combinée avec la demande. Or c'est le besoin qu'on a de pain accompagné de l'offre de le payer au prix où l'on en demande une quantité quelconque, qui est ce que j'appelle la quantité demande ou l'autre element du prix.

'Si le besoin de pain est tel qu'on en demande une quantité de...à 5 Shillings; et que le travail pour créer cette quantité de pain coûte dans un terrain determiné 2 Shillings, l'interet du capital 1^{Sh} le profit de la terre (Rent) sera 2.

'Si le besoin est moins grand ou la societé moins riche au point que l'on ne puisse plus demander la même quantité de pain qu'au prix de 3 Sh. alors il y aura 2^{Sh} pour le travail: 1^{Sh} pour le capital et rien pour la terre.

'Je ne dis pas *Bread is regulated in value by productive services*, je dis: *Supply is regulated by productive services, but supply is only one of the elements of price.*'

[2] At the meeting on 4 Feb. 1822, 'a letter from M. Say to Mr. Ricardo was read on the difference of

and had made no provision for the admission of Honorary 5 March 1822 members—they have now however passed a law to admit foreigners only in that character, and I am happy to inform you that we have elected you unanimously. We hope in good time to elevate ourselves from a "Club" to a more dignified title, and to become a numerous as well as a scientific body.—

I have received from Mr. Place the 2.^{d} Edition of your Catechisme D'Economie Politique[1] for which I am very much obliged to you.—I have not yet had time to look at more than the 2 first chapters,—I promise myself pleasure and instruction from the perusal of the remainder.—

I remain Dear Sir with the greatest esteem

Your faithful servant

DAVID RICARDO

489. RICARDO TO FOSTER [2]

London 5 March 1822

Sir

I am of opinion that without a breach of national faith, 5 March 1822 the Government could not, if it had the means, pay off the 3 pc.^{ts} Stock at a less rate than one hundred pounds money

opinion between them relative to Wealth and Exchangeable Value, as well as the answer of Mr. Ricardo. The thanks of the Club were voted to both gentlemen for their communications'. On the same occasion Swinton Holland proposed Say as an honorary member; he was elected at the next meeting, on 4 March (*Political Economy Club, Minutes of Proceedings, 1821–1882*, pp. 46–7). Apparently

Ricardo kept his letter for a month before despatching it so that he might announce Say's election.

[1] *Catéchisme d'Économie politique* ..., 'Seconde édition entièrement refondue et augmentée de Notes en faveur des personnes qui veulent approfondir davantage les principes de cette science', Paris, Bossange, 1821.

[2] MS in the Baker Library of Harvard University.

5 March 1822

for every one hundred pounds capital stock. In other words the par of the 3 pc^{ts} as well as of the 4 and 5 pc^{ts} is 100.—

        I am Sir

                Your most obed^t Servt

                   DAVID RICARDO

Peter Le Neve Foster Esqr

490. RICARDO TO TROWER [1]

London 5 March 1822

My Dear Trower

5 March 1822

    I have not been able to examine your plan of paying off a considerable portion of debt, by allowing persons to compound for their assessed taxes; but on a cursory view I should conclude that it contained some fallacy which would be detected on a close examination. You propose to allow at the rate of 5 pc^t to those who purchase their life interest in the assessed taxes, and the money obtained is to be employed at 4 pc^t in paying off debt. You do not add to the whole burden of taxation, and yet with the disadvantage I have stated you think the debt will be much more diminished on your plan, than if the present mode be persevered in. I might possibly agree that yours was the safest plan because it left little or nothing in the power of ministers, but it is impossible, I should think, to be so economical as the one now in operation. One error is immediately observable; you suppose that a 5 million sinking fund will only pay off 60 millions in 12 years, but you forget that it operates at compound interest, and therefore that its effect will be very greatly increased. Perhaps I may be wrong, and if I am you will be kind to set me right. [2]

[1] MS at University College, London.—*Letters to Trower*, LV.
[2] Trower's plan is set forth in one of his MSS (now in the possession of Dr Bonar), which is printed in full in *Letters to Trower*, pp. 183–5. In substance, he suggested that individuals should be allowed to

5 March 1822

Sir H. Parnell mentioned a plan to me which would have the effect of making the sinking fund available, and at the same time of placing it out of the grasp of ministers.[1] It is as follows: Employ your 5 millions in making your perpetual annuities terminable ones, and you secure the object of extinguishing a large portion of debt in a period of short duration in the existence of a nation. Long ann^s are at 20 years purchase, and 4 prc^{ts} are at 25 years purchase in the market. Give 5 millions p^r Ann to the holders of 500 millions of 4 pc^{ts} and they will agree to accept 25 million p^r Ann^m (instead of 20 million p^r Ann^m) on the condition that the interest should cease altogether in 1860, the period at which the Long Ann^{ty} terminates. In 1860 then our debt would be reduced to 300 millions, and indeed might be altogether extinguished if in the meantime by a surplus of revenue a larger sum could be diverted to the above purpose. This will explain the principle: it might be desirable to extinguish a smaller sum in fewer years, by devoting the 5 millions to that purpose, or you might extinguish different amounts of debt at differently determinate periods—this you will easily understand.

I am glad you approved of the sentiments I expressed in my speech in Parliament.[2] It is a great disadvantage to me that the reporters not understanding the subject cannot readily follow me—they often represent me as uttering perfect nonsense.

---

purchase a life composition for their assessed taxes, at the rate of interest of 5 per cent., and the proceeds be used to redeem 4 per cent. Stock at par. The deficiency due to the difference between the two rates of interest should be taken out of the sum annually appropriated for the Sinking Fund. It is assumed that the payers of assessed taxes are generally between the ages of 35 and 50, and the average purchase of the life interest about 12 years.

[1] Parnell expounded this plan in the House of Commons in March 1823 (*Hansard*, N.S., VIII, 536, 548); see Ricardo's comments, above, V, 270–1.

[2] Cp. above, p. 166.

The country circulation is I believe very much reduced, and I trust it is issued by bankers of character and property. I have not much fear of their being shaken by a return to specie payments. If Cobbetts recommendation should again endanger the safety of the Bank of England in consequence of an extensive practice of hoarding sovereigns, which I by no means apprehend, it might become necessary to adopt the Ingot plan of payment once more.[1] I should however be very sorry if the present system were not persevered in as long as it was practicable. Cobbett's aim is mischief, but he will not be able to succeed in it, if the Bank manage their affairs with common discretion. The Directors are very ill calculated to regulate a currency situated as ours now is, and if there is anything to fear it is from their incapacity. I shall not fail to repeat my cautions to them from time to time when the subject comes under discussion.—Huskisson must have great influence in the situation which he fills, and he cannot fail to direct it usefully and scientifically.

I do not think that we shall examine evidence in the Agricultural Committee. We have got rid, after a long discussion, of a proposal made by Mr. Banks to devote a million of the public money to the purchase of corn—we negatived it. Some more absurd proposals are before us, but they I trust will meet with the same fate. The present corn law will I think be repealed, and another less objectionable, but still a bad one, will be substituted in its place. I have gained an important and powerful ally, in the Committee, by the nomination of Mr. Whitmore[2], who is a zealous advocate for the correct

[1] See *Cobbett's Weekly Register,* 2 March 1822, 'To the Money Hoarders'. 'It is for you to *hoard away.*...The Bank can, you will remember, stop paying in *sovereigns* whenever it *pleases,* until May 1823. There are persons, indeed, who will go and demand *bars;* but that is not so convenient' (p. 530).

[2] William Wolryche Whitmore (1787–1858), M.P. for Bridg-

doctrines. On the other hand I have lost the assistance of 5 March 1822 Huskisson, who absents himself on the plea that Wodehouse made an attack on him in the House, but I think his real reason is that he cannot approve, and will not oppose, the plan recommended by the Government.[1]

The House broke up early this evening, which has given me an opportunity of scribbling to you. My letter is a strange jumble, compounded much in the same manner as my speeches. You must treat me as the House of Commons does; try to make out what I mean and excuse the manner of my expressing my meaning.—

With kind regards to Mrs. Trower, in which I am joined by Mrs. Ricardo I remain very truly Yours

DAVID RICARDO

491. RICARDO TO McCULLOCH [2]
[*Reply to 485.—Answered by 495*]

London 19th March 1822

My Dear Sir

I have heard from Mr. Dick this day that he has already 19 March 1822 sent you the papers with which I entrusted him, and which I concluded he would himself convey to you. It becomes

---

north; author of *A Letter on the Present State and Future Prospects of Agriculture. Addressed to the Agriculturists of the County of Salop,* published later in 1822 (London, Hatchard).

[1] Huskisson had announced in the House of Commons on 20 Feb. 1822 that, since he was accused of having mystified and misled the Agricultural Committee of the previous year, he would decline attending the committee on its reappointment. In the debate on 6 May he openly opposed the resolution on agriculture moved by Lord Londonderry (the leader of the House); immediately afterwards he offered his resignation as Commissioner of Woods and Forests, but it was not accepted. (See 'Biographical Memoir' prefixed to *The Speeches of the Rt. Hon. William Huskisson,* London, 1831, vol. I, pp. 84–5.)

[2] MS in British Museum.—*Letters to McCulloch,* XXXII.

therefore necessary that I should no longer delay telling you
that I was very much pleased with your lectures. I was glad
to find that the opinions which we both hold, were so ably
and clearly expressed, and cannot but anticipate from your
efforts their progress and general dissemination.

You go a little farther than I go in estimating the value of
commodities by the quantity of labour required to produce
them: you appear to admit of no exception or qualification
whatever, whereas I am always willing to allow that some of
the variations in the relative value of commodities may be
referred to causes distinct from the quantity of labour necessary to produce them. If 1000 bricks vary in relative value
to a certain quantity of muslin, produced by the aid of
valuable machinery, it may be owing to one of two causes:
more or less labour may be required to produce one of them;
or wages may have risen or fallen generally. With respect to
the first being a cause of variation we entirely agree, but you
do not appear to admit that although the same quantities of
labour shall be respectively employed on the bricks and the
muslin that their relative values may vary solely because the
value of labour rises or falls, and yet the fact appears to me
undeniable. To this second cause I do not attach near so
much importance as Mr. Malthus and others but I cannot
wholly shut my eyes to it.—

There is another passage in your lecture which I think
requires a slight correction; you say "Every produce may
be employed to satisfy the wants or to add to the enjoyment
of its possessor; *or it may be employed as capital and made to
reproduce a greater value than itself*".[1] It may be employed
as capital if it be a commodity that can be used in reproduc-
tion, or if it can be exchanged for such, but if you produced

[1] This sentence, altered to meet Ricardo's point, appears in McCul-loch's *Discourse on...Political Economy*, 1824, pp. 105–6.

wine and I produced fine cloth we could neither use them as capital, nor exchange them with each other for commodities which could be used as such.

I was much pleased with your leading article in the Scotsman, which reached me to-day, on the proofs of prosperity; and shall look with interest to the promised article on profits.[1] I have however one remark to make and that is on the observation that profits and wages may both be high. In what medium can they both be high? They may indeed be both paid by an abundance of the quantity of the commodity produced, but then the commodity will be of comparatively low value and profits will be high, if the proportion of the whole quantity produced paid for profits be great—if the proportion be small profits will be low and wages high.

I am glad that The Edinb. Police Bill is likely to be framed to your satisfaction—We should have made a good fight for you.

Truly y.^{rs}

D RICARDO

492. RICARDO TO TROWER [2]

London 25 March 1822

My Dear Trower

I should very much like to accept your kind invitation to pass a few days with you during the short vacation of Parliament, but it will not be in my power. I have various engagements which I am bound to fulfil, and which will

---

[1] 'Standard of National Prosperity', in the *Scotsman,* 16 March 1822; a high rate of profit is the proof of national prosperity. The promised 'Inquiry into the Circumstances which Determine the Rate of Profit' formed the leading article in the No. of 6 April 1822. Both articles, only slightly altered, are incorporated in *Edinburgh Review,* March 1824, Art. I, 'Standard of National Prosperity —Rise and Fall of Profits'.

[2] Addressed: 'Hutches Trower Esqr / Unsted Wood / Godalming'.
   MS at University College, London.—*Letters to Trower,* LVI.

render my absence from London very inconvenient. I very much regret being obliged to deny myself the pleasure which a visit to you would have given me.

I saw Mr. Mill yesterday and gave him your message. He requested me to say to you that his occupations at the India House will prevent him from being absent during the holidays. It is the period at which the election for Directors takes place, when there are frequent Court days which he is expected to attend. He desired to be kindly remembered to you.

I should be neglecting my duty if with my opinions of the Sinking Fund I did not do every thing in my power to get rid of it. Of what use can it be to diminish the debt in time of peace, if you leave in the hands of ministers a fund which experience shews will be used only for the purpose of ultimately further increasing the debt? While ministers have this fund virtually at their disposal they will on the slightest occasion be disposed for war. To keep them peaceable you must keep them poor.

The answer to every proposal for the adoption of good measures in the Agricultural Committee, is that the Agriculture of the country is in a state of unparalled distress, and that the Committee was appointed for the purpose of affording it relief. I had no idea of being able to do any good now, in the way of making better laws, but I hoped to lay the foundation of a better system in future. In that hope I shall probably be disappointed, for the regulations which you mention as too restrictive are protested against most vehemently by the country gentlemen, who form themselves into a compact body determined to yield no point which has the least semblance to diminished protection. We meet to day to hear the Report read, which was to be prepared by our chairman.[1]

[1] Lord Londonderry.

I was obliged to withdraw my motion for the return of 25 March 1822
Corn sold in Mark Lane, because I was waited on by the
officer to whom the order was directed to say that he had no
means of complying with it. I then moved for a return of
the corn imported into the Port of London, which has not
yet been laid on the table of the House—I will send it to you
when it is printed.[1] The return which the officer told me
could not be prepared has however been laid before [the][2]
Committee,[3] and if I can get a copy I will send it to you.

I know of no Poor Rate returns made to the House this
Session,[4] neither have I seen Mr. Chetwynd's Vagrant Bill.[5]
I will enquire for them at the Vote Office this day, and if you
do not receive them by the Post, you may conclude that they
are not yet in the hands of members.

Mrs. Ricardo unites with me in kind remembrances to
Mrs. Trower.

Ever Truly Y^{rs}
DAVID RICARDO

Mr. Chetwynd's bill has been this moment left at my house
—I send it by this day's post.

---

[1] 'Return of the Monthly Arrivals of Corn, (distinguishing British from foreign,) into the Port of London, for the years 1819, 1820, and 1821', ordered to be printed 17 April 1822. (*Parliamentary Papers*, 1822, vol. XXI (n. 203).)
[2] Covered by seal.
[3] The return is referred to in the Report of the Agricultural Committee of 1822 (which is dated 1 April) but is not given in full. There was published later, on the motion of Ricardo (see *Courier*, 2 May 1822), a somewhat different return under the title 'A Return of the Quantity of British Wheat, Barley and Oats, actually sold in Mark Lane for the last Ten Years.' (*Parliamentary Papers*, 1822, vol. XXI (n. 297).) This return is dated 6 May 1822 and signed by Geo. Levick, Inspector of Corn Returns. Cp. *Protection to Agriculture*, Appendix B, above, IV, 270–71.
[4] See below, p. 201.
[5] Presented in the House of Commons on 20 March 1822.

493. RICARDO TO HODGSON [1]

London 30 March 1822

Dear Sir

I am really very much concerned at being the cause of so much trouble to you. Your letter rec^d this morning makes me fear that I was wrong in not speaking more decidedly in the first instance, on the subject of the approaching vacancy in the representation for Liverpool.[2] Since I saw you I have consulted with a friend on the soundness of whose opinion I place great reliance, and his advice to me was to be contented with the position in which I was, and by no means to be induced by any ambitious views to aim at the representation of Liverpool.[3] This advice agrees with my own judgement, and I therefore again repeat, what I said hastily in my note of yesterday, that I relinquish altogether every idea of becoming a Candidate. I thank you very much for the interest you have taken in my favour, but let me request you to consider my answer as a final one, given after due deliberation. If you knew me better you would be satisfied that I was unfit both for the contest, and for the dignity you would confer on me. You would, in case of my success, have the responsibility cast upon you of having been in-

[1] MS in the possession of Lady Charnwood, to whom I am indebted for a transcript.

David Hodgson, a Quaker, partner in the house of Cropper, Benson & Co., merchants at Liverpool. On his evidence to the Agricultural Committee of 1821 see above, VIII, 370, n. 2 and *Cobbett's Weekly Register,* 29 Sept. 1821, p. 733.

[2] Canning, the sitting member for Liverpool, had been appointed Governor-General of India. Although he never took up that post, he retired from Liverpool in the autumn (having become Foreign Secretary) as it was too laborious a constituency; 'Huskisson was selected to succeed him as the only tory able to conciliate the Liverpool merchants, and after a hollow contest he was elected, 15 Feb. 1823' (*Dictionary of National Biography,* art. Huskisson).

[3] Cp. the similar advice given by Mill on another occasion, above, VII, 110.

strumental in giving to the town of Liverpool an inefficient   30 March 1822
representative.

With feelings of gratitude for your kind disposition toward me

I remain Dear Sir

Very faithfully Yours

DAVID RICARDO

D. Hodgson Esqr

494. RICARDO TO M^cCULLOCH [1]

London 19 April 1822

My Dear Sir

I requested Mr. Murray to send you an early copy of   19 April 1822
the Pamphlet which I have just published.[2] I hope you have received it. It is quite possible that you may differ with me about the precise remedy (and the time of applying it) for the present distress, but I think I can confidently rely on your sanction to all the principles which I have laid down. In fact they are the same as you have yourself over and over again most successfully advocated. Though now more feebly urged I am convinced that they cannot be brought before the public too often, and I have been particularly induced to submit them to their attention now as the sentiments which I have expressed in the House of Commons have been constantly misapprehended and misstated both in and out of Parliament.—

An application has been lately made to me to represent to you that Dr. Kelly would be pleased to have his cambist[3]

[1] MS in British Museum.—*Letters to McCulloch*, XXXIII.
[2] *On Protection to Agriculture.* Reviewed in the *Scotsman*, 27 April 1822.
[3] *The Universal Cambist, and Commercial Instructor; being a Full and Accurate Treatise on the Exchanges, Monies, Weights, and Measures, of all Trading Nations and their*

noticed by you in any article of yours in the Edin. Rev. In mentioning this I have done all that I think it right to do. You are best able to judge of the merits of the work, and of the propriety of noticing it.—

I remain my dear Sir with great esteem.

Y.^{rs} very truly

DAVID RICARDO

495. McCULLOCH TO RICARDO [1]

[*Reply to 486 & 491.—Answered by 497*]

Edinburgh 17 April 1822

My Dear Sir

I avail myself of the opportunity afforded by my friend Mr. Stewart Ingliss going to London to send you three of my Lectures—Mr. Ingliss attended my Prelections last winter, and naturally felt desirous to be introduced to a gentleman to whom the science he has been studying is under such infinite obligations—I hope you will excuse the liberty I have taken in offering to make him acquainted with you—You will find Mr. Ingliss to be a very agreeable man, he has seen a great deal of the world, and is much esteemed by his friends here—

The Lectures I have sent you are on the accumulation and employment of capital—I had some more written but the subjects were not of sufficient importance to allow me to trouble you with such illegible manuscripts—But when I get the Lectures on value, wages, profits, &c written I shall, if you do not interdict me, send them to you—Although I trust

---

Colonies; with an Account of their Banks, Public Funds, and Paper Currencies, by Patrick Kelly, LL.D., 2nd ed., revised, 2 vols., London, for the Author, 1821.
[1] Addressed: 'David Ricardo Esq M.P. / Upper Brook Street / London' and marked: 'Hand by Stewart Ingliss Esq'.—Received after writing letter 494.

MS in *R.P.—Letters of McCulloch to Ricardo,* XIV.

there is nothing you will consider erroneous in these Lectures,
yet I should not like you would estimate my Political
Economy by them only—In order to give any chance of
making the subject popular I must pass slightly over some
of the more difficult parts, and must dwell on those that are
more obvious and easily understood—I am also frequently
under the necessity of stating propositions with fewer conditions than I would do were I writing a book on the subject;
for, otherwise the general truth would not strike the mind of
the listener with sufficient force to excite his attention or to
make any durable impression—This is the reason why in
speaking of exchangeable value in the Lecture you had already
in your hands I did not like to encumber it with mentioning,
what would not have been understood, the modification of
the general principle occasioned by the different durabilities
of capital—This, however, is not a subject which I have
evaded; but on the contrary I have dwelt long upon it, and
have endeavoured as well as I could to make my pupils
comprehend it—

Accept my best thanks for your kindness in sending me
the book on Bullion and in procuring the accounts respecting
Ireland from Sir J. Newport—I have made considerable use
of these accounts in the forthcoming No of the Review[1]—
When you see Sir John I beg you will have the goodness to
mention how much I feel indebted to him for his attention—
Perhaps if he approves of what I have already done he may
be induced to send me some more statements of the same
kind—I should especially like to be possessed of all the

---

[1] *Edinburgh Review,* Feb. 1822
[No. 72, published late in April],
Art. VIII, 'Comparative Pro-
ductiveness of High and Low
Taxes'. Sir J. Newport's contri-
bution is no doubt a table on
p. 530 showing that the additional

taxation imposed on Ireland since
1807 had been accompanied by a
fall in the Revenue: the remainder
of the article is merely a slightly
expanded version of an article
under a similar title in the *Scotsman,* 1 Dec. 1821.

attainable information respecting Irish tithes—If I had a sufficient stock of raw materials I would endeavour to work them into a tangible and effective shape in the 73rd No of the Review[1]—Perhaps Mr. Hume could supply me with some facts[2]—If he does he may depend upon it I shall not throw them away—

I have written an article on the Corn Laws for the forthcoming Review[3]; and were it not that you will have the Review itself in a few days I would have sent you the sheets of it—I have done all that I could to render this article efficient; but perhaps the success has not corresponded to my exertions —Perhaps you will think I have exaggerated the pernicious effect of the corn laws; but I assure you, that if I have done this it was unintentional, my object was not to please any class of persons but to state distinctly what I conceived to be the exact truth respecting their operation—The Report of the Committee just published is disgraceful—it is discreditable not only to the House of Commons but to the country—it is in fact so miserably absurd as hardly to deserve to have its errors pointed out—

I have sent along with the Lectures a copy of a small Tract which I wrote with the intention of publishing in the Scotsman—I found, however, that it was too long; and that the million who read Newspapers would much rather have the space occupied by it filled with the accounts of murders, assassinations, and so forth—I only printed a dozen of copies of this Tract and it serves merely for the purpose of keeping as it were the main points in my view—The history of the different theories and opinions entertained respecting commerce has long been a favourite subject with me; and if I had

[1] June 1822, Art. III, 'Ireland'.
[2] Cp. above, p. 153.
[3] Feb. 1822, Art. VI, 'Agricul- tural Distress—Causes—Remedies'; a review of the Report of the Agricultural Committee.

got rid of some of my heavier tasks I should like to bestow
a little attention on it.[1]

Mr. Austin said to me that you had some thoughts of
visiting Scotland during this summer—I trust you will carry
them into effect—No stranger I am positive would be more
kindly received: and I really think were it nothing else that
you ought to come and see the country of Adam Smith—Say
came from France for this purpose, and has in this instance
set an example which I hope you will follow—

There is among the papers obtained in the Sentinel office
a letter from the Lord Advocate expressing *his approbation
of the paper*—This was just giving them a *carte blanche* to
libel and abuse everybody—If his Lordship be not severely
handled for this most improper conduct and for his partner-
ship in the Beacon he will not be treated as he deserves—[2]

Mr. Ingliss will bring back the Lectures—I remain with the
greatest respect and esteem

Yours most truly

J. R. M^cCULLOCH

Permit me to say how much I was gratified by what you
said respecting the Agricultural Report in the House of

[1] A short 'Sketch of the Progress
of Commercial Science in England
in the Seventeenth Century,
Part I' appeared in the *Scotsman*,
19 Jan. 1822, but in spite of the
announcement 'to be continued',
it had no sequel. No copy of the
tract has been traced: the whole of
it is probably embodied (as the
Scotsman article is) in the historical part of McCulloch's article
'Political Economy' in the *Supplement to the Encyclopaedia Britannica*.

[2] The Glasgow *Sentinel* had
succeeded the *Beacon* as the
channel of personal attacks on the
Scottish Whigs; but in the course
of a quarrel among its editors
a box of manuscripts had been
surrendered to one of the defamed
persons, and the disclosure of the
names of the writers and supporters
of the newspaper occasioned a
fatal duel and much litigation. (See
H. Cockburn, *Memorials of his
Time*, Edinburgh, 1856, pp. 392–9,
and J. G. Lockhart, *Life of Scott*,
Edinburgh, 1837, vol. v, p. 153.)

17 April 1822 Commons[1]—In the Article in the Review I have taken exactly the same view that you have taken of the effects of taxation, and have stated distinctly that it is impossible it can be the cause of the *peculiar* distress experienced by the agriculturists —Would it not be better to abolish the restriction at once? I incline to think that this would be preferable to a gradually diminishing rate of duties—

496. SAY TO RICARDO[2]
[*Reply to* 488]

Paris 1er Mai 1822

Mon cher Monsieur

1 May 1822   J'ai reçu votre lettre du 5 de mars. Les developemens pleins de justesse et de clarté qu'elle renferme, reduisant les questions à leurs termes les plus simples, ne seront pas inutiles aux progrès de l'Economie politique. Je me range à votre avis sur plusieurs points; mais je sollicite un nouveau jugement de votre part sur les suivans.

Vous me dites:

"In your last edition of the *Catéchisme* you say (page 2) that the riches of a person are in proportion to the value of the commodities which he possesses, and not in proportion

---

[1] On 3 April; see above, V, 148 ff.
[2] MS in *R.P.—Minor Papers*, pp. 194–7. A very different version, probably rewritten by Say for publication (cp. above, p. 31, n. 1), is given in *Mélanges*, pp. 131–6 and *Œuvres diverses*, pp. 426–9. In one of the passages added to the later version Say writes 'Savez-vous bien, mon cher monsieur, que votre lettre contient un aveu précieux que je regarde comme un hommage rendu à la vérité. C'est quand vous dites que *vous n'aimez pas à mettre en un bloc*

les frais de production, et que *vous avez besoin de savoir dans quelle proportion chacun d'eux donne de la valeur à un produit.* Il m'avait semblé que jusqu'ici vous n'accordiez ce privilège qu'au travail ou à l'industrie; et que vous le refusiez au fermage et à l'intérêt du capital. En parlant ainsi des différens *frais de production*, vous approuvez implicitement l'analyse et l'estimation que j'ai essayé d'en faire'. (*Mélanges*, pp. 134–5, *Œuvres diverses*, p. 428.)

of their quantity...but when your pupil calls upon you to explain what is the measure of the value of things, you answer that it is the quantity of all other things that the proprietor is enabled to command by their means, if he consent to exchange them.

"Now in this I think there is a contradiction; for we are told that riches are in proportion to value, and value in proportion to the quantity of things; therefore riches are in proportion to the quantity of things. And yet you say that riches are in proportion to value and *not* in proportion to the quantity of things."

La contradiction apparente que vous trouvez ici, Monsieur, vient de ce que vous ne faites point, comme moi, une différence entre la quantité de choses utiles *dont un homme peut jouir,* et la quantité de choses utiles *qui peuvent servir à faire une acquisition.* Suivant moi, cette derniere quantité de choses utiles compose seule la richesse dont l'Economie politique puisse s'occuper, parce que l'accroissement ou le decroissement de cette seule quantité, sont soumis à des lois qu'elle puisse assigner.

Ce n'est point le cas des choses utiles ou agréables qui ne peuvent servir à faire une acquisition, qui n'ont point de valeur échangeable. Un homme dont les terres sont assises sur une couche de pierres à bâtir commune à tout le canton, ou dont les terres sont traversées par une rivière qui traverse aussi la plupart des autres terrains, possède des pierres de taille et de l'eau, qui certainement sont des choses utiles et agréables, mais ces choses (que je suppose n'avoir dans le pays aucune valeur echangeable) ne sont point une partie de sa fortune; leur accroissement et leur décroissement, ne dépendent pas des lois de l'Economie politique, mais de lois physiques qui sont etudiées par ceux qui s'occupent de geologie et d'histoire naturelle.

Tout ce qui nous empecherait d'etre d'accord serait donc que vous voulussiez meler dans les considerations d'Economie politique aux *richesses sociales* (ou valeurs echangeables) les *richesses naturelles* (ou ces utilités qui ne sont le fruit d'aucuns services productifs et que Smith appelle *value in use*). Veuillez revoir ce que je dis de ces deux sortes de richesses page 201 de mon *Catéchisme* (2.ᵉ edition) et tome 2 page 500 de mon *Traité* (4.ᵉ édition).

Par une suite necessaire, je ne saurais separer l'idée de la richesse sociale, de l'idée d'un *possesseur,* et je vous avoue que je desapprouve toutes les définitions des richesses où l'on ne fait pas entrer l'idée d'un homme ou d'une autre communauté qui les possèdent, et d'un autre homme ou d'une autre communauté qui ne les possèdent pas et qui ont le desir de les acquerir, desir fondé sur leur utilité qui est par là suivant moi la premiere base de leur valeur echangeable. On serait injuste de me reprocher la longueur et la complication des définitions de richesses qui reposent sur toutes ces idées. Pour caracteriser une chose, il faut bien énoncer tous les caractères qui lui sont propres et qui la différencient d'une autre chose.

Vous me dites:

"Let us suppose that the same cause, namely an economical process, which lowers the value of gold one half, lowers at the same time, in the same degree, hats, shoes, etc. In this state of things, a pound of gold will command just as many hats, shoes, etc. as before...I ask is the man equally rich as before who has a pound of gold? You first answer *No* because he has not a commodity of equal value, etc."

Je vous demande bien pardon: je ne reponds pas *Non;* je reponds *Oui,* car, dans cette supposition, une livre d'or peut acheter la même quantité de produits et que la valeur echangeable de la livre d'or est en proportion de la quantité de choses qu'elle peut acheter. Mais en même tems je dis que les services productifs (qui forment nos revenus) ont doublé de valeur, puisque une pareille quantité de services productifs, peut obtenir une double quantité d'or, de chapeaux, de souliers, etc. Et comme le doublement de la valeur des services productifs (c'est à dire des services de l'industrie, des capitaux et des terres) double la valeur des fonds d'où ils proviennent (qui sont les facultés humaines, les capitaux, et les terres) j'en conclus que, dans votre supposition la nation est le double plus riche. Ses produits valent autant et leur quantité est double.

Il me semble que cette doctrine explique tous les phénomènes et qu'elle est conséquente au principe que la richesse que l'on possède, est en proportion de la quantité de choses que l'on peut acquerir par son moyen.

Je suis fort reconnaissant de l'accueil que la Societé Economico-politique a bien voulu me faire, et je lui temoigne ma gratitude dans une lettre que j'adresse à son secretaire Mr. Cowel, jun^r. Je soumets en même tems aux méditations de la Societé, deux ou trois questions dont la solution me semble importante.[1]

Notre nation, absorbée par les affaires, par les plaisirs, et par les querelles politiques, donne bien peu d'attention aux questions économiques. Dans une tres belle institution que nous avons, (le Conservatoire des Arts et Métiers) je dévelope deux fois par semaine les principes de l'Economie politique, dans des discours publics pour tout le monde: et, j'ai honte de le dire, près de la moitié de mon auditoire est composé d'etrangers, Anglais, polonais, russes, grecs,

---

[1] The letter to John Cowell is printed in Say's *Œuvres diverses*, pp. 438–9; the two questions, in *Political Economy Club, Minutes of Proceedings, 1821–1882*, p. 51.

espagnols, portugais, américains.[1] Le prince hereditaire de Dannemarc,[2] qui va partir pour Londres, ne pouvant suivre cet enseignement qui est fort etendu, m'a prié de l'initier en particulier aux principes de cette science, qu'il m'a paru saisir fort bien; ce qui est d'un bon augure pour les peuples qu'il est appelé à gouverner. J'espere que cela pourra influer sur le bon accueil qu'il trouvera sans doute en Angleterre. J'ai souvent enrichi mes leçons en l'entretenant de vos ouvrages.

Agréez, mon cher monsieur, les nouvelles assurances de ma haute consideration et de mon très sincère dévouement

J. B. SAY

Londres Mr David Ricardo
    membre de la Chambre des Communes.

497. RICARDO TO M^cCULLOCH[3]
[*Reply to 495*]

London 7 May 1822

My Dear Sir

I like your article on the Corn Laws in the Review very much.—I am glad to find that we so nearly agree, in all our views, respecting the pernicious influence of those laws. I am sure that they will ultimately be repealed;—the growing knowledge of the country will enable every one to see that freedom of trade in corn is of the greatest importance to its welfare.

I have read your lectures with great satisfaction. Your defence of manufactures against the attacks which are in-

---

[1] See André Liesse, *Un professeur d'Économie politique sous la Restauration—J.-B. Say au Conservatoire des Arts et Métiers,* Paris, Guillaumin, 1901 (ch. v, 'L'auditoire du cours d'économie industrielle').

[2] See letter 498.
[3] Addressed: 'J. R. M'Culloch Esqr / Buccleugh Place / Edinburgh'.
      MS in British Museum.—*Letters to McCulloch,* XXXIV.

cessantly directed against them, is excellent. I believe with you that our manufacturing population is as moral as the agricultural and certainly much better informed. Adam Smith's view on this subject is I think very defective.[1]—

I have looked for faults, and not for beauties, in your lectures—I have been able to find very few that appear to me to be such, and where I do find them, they are chiefly on points, on which a little difference of opinion exists between us. I have marked the passages in the papers, and you will be able very easily to refer to them.

1 You say "The demand for labour must increase as the capital of the country increases, and it must diminish as the capital diminishes." This is not absolutely true—I may build myself a workshop[2] or construct a steam engine with my savings—I should thereby increase my capital, but the year following I might employ no more labour.

2 "While she does this (augment her capital) she will always have a constantly increasing demand for labour, and will be constantly augmenting the produce of her land and labour, and of course also her people."

Remark. The same as the last.

3 "And the capitalist who can invest capital so as to yield a profit of 10 pcᵗ has it equally in his power to accumulate twice as fast as the capitalist who can only obtain 5 pcᵗ for his capital."

Remark. This is understated—he could do more than accumulate twice as fast. Out of two loaves I may save one, out of four I may save three.

4—Remark. He could not give employment to additional workmen.

---

[1] See *Wealth of Nations*, Bk. I, ch. x, pt. II; Cannan's ed., vol. I, pp. 128–9.

[2] 'workshop' replaces 'house'.

5—Remark. This may be misunderstood—less is not consumed—you acknowledge that all is consumed; but it is consumed by a different class, by the reproductive instead of the unproductive.—

6 "The interests of individuals is never opposed to the interests of the public."

In this I do not agree. In the case of machinery the interests of master and workmen are frequently opposed. Are the interests of landlords and those of the public always the same? I am sure you will not say so.

7 Remark. I deny that we should be able to employ the workmen displaced by the employment of machinery.

These are all the remarks I have to offer against any of the passages in your lectures; in favor of them I could make many, but that is unnecessary. They are very clear, and cannot fail to convince.—

Mr. Inglis dined with me on Saturday—he appears to be an intelligent agreeable man—I am sorry that my occupations will prevent me from seeing him so often as I could wish. I will return your papers by him.—

I am now going to the House to fight the best battle I can against the Country gentlemen.[1]—I am very badly supported, —even Bennet and Ellice give me little hopes of dividing with me.[2]

I have requested Sir J Newport and Mr. Hume to send you whatever information they may have respecting tithes—they promise to furnish me with some for you, and I shall not fail to remind them of their engagement.

I do not quite agree with you about reverting at once to a free trade in corn.—The price of corn is indeed low, but

---

[1] See above, V, 164 ff.
[2] Henry Grey Bennet, member for Shrewsbury, and Edward Ellice, member for Coventry: neither appears in the list of the minority who voted for Ricardo's Resolutions on 9 May.

land has not gone out of cultivation. It would I think be 7 May 1822 desirable that the process by which it should be made to go out should be very slow—you would otherwise make the situation of the farmer irretrievable—he would be ruined past redemption.—

Y^{rs} very truly
DAVID RICARDO

498. SAY TO RICARDO [1]

Mon cher Monsieur

Permettez-moi de vous adresser Monsieur Adler Secre- 8 May 1822 taire intime de Son Altesse Royale le prince hereditaire de Dannemarc[2] qui part pour visiter l'Angleterre. Ce Prince a desiré, non seulement de faire connaissance avec vos institutions, mais avec les hommes les plus éminens de votre pays; il devait donc desirer de vous voir, et je m'estime heureux de pouvoir vous mettre en relation avec lui en vous recommandant Mr. Adler, qui est lui-même un homme d'un merite distingué.

Vous ne trouverez pas le Prince, étranger au langage de notre science. Jaloux de faire le bonheur des peuples qu'il est appelé à gouverner, il a voulu chercher avec moi les sources de la prosperité des nations; et j'ai admiré tout à la fois sa noble perséverance, son excellent jugement et son extrême sagacité. Auprès de qui peut-il mieux s'informer de l'Economie de votre nation, des maux qui pèsent sur votre agriculture, de leurs causes, de leurs suites probables, de

[1] MS in *R.P.—Minor Papers,* p. 198.
[2] Succeeded to the throne in 1839 as Christian VIII (1786–1848). At this time being suspected of liberalism he lived in retirement and during the years 1819–22 travelled abroad. He arrived in London on 15 May (*Annual Register for 1822,* 'Chronicle', p. 87). Cp. above, p. 192.

l'etat de votre système monetaire et de votre commerce, en un mot de tout ce qu'un Prince, honnête homme, peut demander à un profond publiciste, qu'auprès de vous?

Agréez, Mon cher Monsieur, la nouvelle assurance de ma haute considération et de mon inaltérable dévouement.

J. B. SAY

Paris 8 mai 1822
Monsieur David Ricardo, membre du
Parlement d'Angleterre
à Londres

499. RICARDO TO TROWER [1]

London 20 May 1822

My Dear Trower

I will follow your advice and take care not to expose myself to the resentment of the Farmers when Parliament breaks up. If they knew their own interest well they would feel no resentment against me, because the measures which I have proposed [2] would make their trade a much more secure one than it can be under the operation of the present, or of the amended, law. I believe it will be a good time at the end of the Session to put in execution a project which I have long entertained, of making a short tour with my family on the Continent. I shall probably go as far as Switzerland, and after an absence of a couple of months seek my own retirement in Gloucestershire. My constant attendance in the House, and the little anxiety which the part I have taken on the Corn question naturally has excited makes a little rest and recreation necessary—I think I shall enjoy my journey, and shall improve my health by it.—

[1] MS at University College, London.—*Letters to Trower*, LVII.

[2] Ricardo's Resolutions on Foreign Corn, above, V, 158–9.

Mr. Huskisson and I did not exactly join our forces; he 20 May 1822
abandoned his resolutions in the Committee, and I adopted
those of them which laid down the correct principles, and
added to them my own practical measure, which I argued
was more consonant with his principles than the one which
he recommended. Lord Althorp proposed a permanent duty
of 20/- on the importation of Wheat, and a permanent drawback of 18/- on the exportation of Wheat, which was supported by Brougham. On what principle either the proposer
or supporter of such resolutions could proceed I know not,
nor have either of them ventured to expound it to the House.

You have no doubt seen Mr. Turner's Pamphlet[1]—he sent
it to me with a very kind note, hoping he said that it was
written in the fair spirit of criticism. On that score I have
nothing to complain of, but he has failed to convince me of
a single error in principle in the work which he attacks. Is it
not strange that a writer in the present day should say that
rent is a cause of high price and not the effect of it?

"The extra rents to the landlord are not the measure of
the whole loss sustained by the public in consequence of the
Corn law," says M'Culloch,[2] and to this doctrine you demur.
I apprehend he means to say that the loss to the country is
a real one. It must not be supposed that because the landlords get a high price, which is paid by the consumer, the
whole inconvenience to the country is an improper and
unjustifiable transfer of property—it is much more than this,
the landlord does not gain what the consumer loses—there

[1] *Considerations upon the Agriculture, Commerce, and Manufactures
of the British Empire; with Observations on the Practical Effect
of the Bill of the Right Hon.
Robert Peel, for the Resumption
of Cash Payments by the Bank of
England; and also upon the*
*Pamphlet lately published by David
Ricardo, Esq., entitled, Protection
to Agriculture.* By Samuel Turner,
F.R.S., London, Murray, 1822.
[2] *Edinburgh Review,* Feb. 1822,
Art. VI, 'Agricultural Distress—
Causes—Remedies', pp. 474–6
(in substance).

is a real diminution of production, and the real loss is to be measured by such diminution of production, without any regard to price or value.

I sent you a copy of Mr. Scarlett's bill[1]—that of Mr. Courtenay[2] is not yet printed.

Mrs. Ricardo and I were sorry not to see you on the last evening you were in London, but we acknowledge that your charge was too important to be neglected.

The South Sea Plan[3] has failed so I need say nothing on that point. We shall see what ministers will do to raise the £2,200,000 p^r ann^m.—

I wish you were in the House to give me support in attacking the fallacious arguments for monopolies and restricted trade which are daily brought forward. I do my best, but that is bad enough:—it is difficult to express oneself in terms sufficiently familiar to be understood by those who either understand nothing on these subjects, or who have imbibed prejudices to which they obstinately adhere. I am a very bad speaker, and am sorry to say I do not improve— I have not one good supporter; there are some who understand the subject but they are on the ministerial bench, and dare not always speak as they think.—

Very truly Y^{rs}

DAVID RICARDO

[1] To amend the Poor Laws.
[2] Relating to Gaols, Bridewells and Houses of Correction, presented in the House of Commons on 13 May 1822.
[3] The South Sea Company had at first been willing to take up the annuities to be issued for the Naval and Military Pensions but subsequently changed their mind. (See above, V, 160 and 191 and *Hansard,* N.S., VII, 784.)

500. RICARDO TO [COWELL] [1]

My Dear Sir

I have read Mr. Cowell's [2] paper with attention. It is 21 May 1822 ingenuous, but I think his remedy for Agricultural distress would not be so efficacious as he appears to imagine. He admits that the distress is not caused by taxation, but by a too abundant supply of produce, and he would relieve the farmer by diminishing the cost of production; which he un-doubtedly would do, by reducing those taxes which affect him as a producer. But what taxes do affect him as a pro-ducer? Tithes and Poor rates. Is it practicable to relieve him from these? I think not, but suppose it was, would not corn sink to a lower price in consequence of a remission of these taxes? What prevents a farmer or corn dealer from selling his corn below present prices? The certainty that present prices cannot compensate the future grower for the cost of pro-duction. He holds his corn with some confidence whilst he is assured that no corn can come into the market below a certain cost and remunerate the grower, but if the taxes were remitted on future production, the competition against him would be more alarming to his mind and I cannot have the least doubt he would be inclined to sell at a lower price. If the low price be caused by abundance there can be no remedy for it but increased demand or diminished supply. The farmer has a right to expect a diminished supply while the

[1] The MS was purchased by Messrs Maggs at Sotheby's sale of 28 April 1937, lot 647, described as 'The property of Mrs Herbert W. Verner'. The same property included letters from Byron to Master J. Cowell, at Eton College, and to Mr and Mrs Cowell, 1812–13.

The recipient is no doubt John Welsford Cowell (*ca.* 1795–1867) often referred to as John Cowell, jun., an original member and the secretary of the Political Eco-nomy Club, Agent of the Bank of England at Gloucester and Bristol, 1836–1845, author of several pamphlets on banking.

[2] Presumably John Cowell, sen., father of the preceding.

market price continues below the natural price, but reduce the future natural price by taking taxes off from the production of corn, and you encourage rather than discourage an abundant supply. Suppose 70/- p^r q^r to be the remunerating price, you would hold your wheat with confidence at the present price of 50/-, but reduce the remunerating price to 50/- and you would be less disposed to keep your corn out of the market. If I should be wrong in this view I ask what effect have these taxes on the price of corn? probably about 7/- p^r q^r and therefore this species of relief could not exceed that amount.

I may be told that there are other taxes from the repeal of which the farmer would get relief; I answer, there are, and by the repeal of such taxes, he as well as every other consumer would be relieved. The less he pays to the state the more he would have for himself, and the better could he meet his difficulties. To relieve him from such taxes would afford no inducement to produce more corn, because it would not make the production of corn relatively cheaper than the production of any other commodity. This is the essential difference between taking taxes off that affect the producer, and taking those off which affect consumers generally. In the first case you diminish the cost of production of one commodity relatively to the cost of all others; in the second case you leave them all in the same relation to each other.

I fear I have very imperfectly explained myself but I am so much engaged that I cannot even attempt to do it better. It is possible that I may have a bias on this subject—I am not however conscious of it.

Yours very truly
DAVID RICARDO

Tuesday even^g 21 May [1822] [1]
   Upper Brook Street

---

[1] Omitted in MS. Paper watermarked '1821'; 21 May was a Tuesday in 1822.

501. RICARDO TO TROWER [1]

My Dear Trower

I am told that nothing has been laid before the H of Commons in the present Session, respecting the Poor Rates. There is a committee sitting on Poor Rates Returns, but they have not yet made their Report.

9 June 1822

Mr. Mill is acquainted with the Editor of the Chronicle [2] —I have given your letter to him with a view to get it inserted in the above paper; he will speak to the Editor on the subject, but he has doubts whether so long a letter can be inserted, at the present time, when the Parliamentary proceedings engross so large a portion of the paper. [3]—I have read your letter, and agree with the greatest part of it. I am much flattered by the approbation you express of my plan of bullion payments. You estimate the coin in circulation previous to 1797 higher than I think it really was. The whole amount of circulation, at the present moment, both in London and the country, does not probably much exceed 32 millions, of which there are nearly 16 millions of Bank of England notes of 5 pounds and above, 7,500,000 of sovereigns, and nine millions of country Bank notes. If this be true there has been little or no falling off in the amount of Bank of England notes and coin together since 1819, but country Bank notes have diminished to the amount of 7,500,000£, and if we could get returns it would I think be found to be confined

[1] MS at University College, London.—*Letters to Trower*, LVIII.
[2] John Black, editor and manager of the *Morning Chronicle* since the death of James Perry in 1821; 'a particular friend of my father,' says J. S. Mill, 'imbued with many of his and Bentham's ideas, which he reproduced in his articles....Black was one of the most influential of the many channels through which my father's conversation and personal influence made his opinions tell on the world' (*Autobiography*, pp. 89–90).
[3] Trower's letter was not published.

chiefly to the Agricultural districts;—it is nevertheless a great reduction.

If paper money displaced 20 millions of notes the whole profit from the interest of 20 millions was not enjoyed by the Bank of England, the country Banks participated in the advantage.—By a return laid before the H of Commons more than 19 millions of sovereigns have been coined since 1817. During the period that the Bank so foolishly issued coin, when it was advantageous to export it, they got rid of 5 millions of sovereigns,[1] so that if these were all exported more than 14 millions of sovereigns must now be in the country. Besides this quantity of gold it is probable the Bank may have a tolerable supply of bullion, and perhaps also some guineas. How badly has this business been managed! We might safely, even with payments in coin, dispense with 3 millions of gold since we are to maintain the 1 and 2 £ circulation in the country.—

On tuesday, Mr. Western brings forward his motion respecting Mr. Peel's bill, I am very much interested in that discussion.[2]

Mrs. Ricardo unites with me in begging our kind remembrances to Mrs. Trower.

Y^{rs} very truly
DAVID RICARDO

London 9 June 1822

If your letter is inserted I will send you the paper.—

---

[1] In the months of April and September 1817. (See Tooke's *History of Prices,* vol. II, p. 51.)

[2] See above, V, 198.

502. RICARDO TO MARIA EDGEWORTH [1]
[*Answered by* 510]

My Dear Miss Edgeworth

You began your note[2] with a little flattery which im-   20 June 1822
mediately disposed me to pay the utmost attention to its
contents. I am however sorry to say that I cannot give you
an opinion on a point so speculative as that which you have
submitted to my consideration. On such a subject I should
have little regard for any one's opinion, and the advice which
I would venture to give you, is to judge for yourself of the
relative stability of the funds of the two countries, and to
consider also their relative prices. Having done so keep your
money in the French stocks or transfer it to the English as you
may think most expedient, but I would by no means recommend to you to speculate on distant and uncertain events, and
to be often transfering your money from one country to
another.

Whether in selling out your French stock at an advanced
price of 13 pc[t], and repurchasing 3 pc[t], you would get a
profit of some hundreds of pounds would of course depend
on the price at which you formerly sold your 3 pc[ts] compared
with that at which you would now repurchase them.

Although I can give no advice respecting the sale of your
French Stock, I am of opinion that you should not leave your
money in Mr. Delessert's hands when you have sold, unless
you are satisfied to remain for sometime without any interest.
To be sure that you shall obtain the same amount of 3 pc[ts] as
you possessed before, you ought to buy the 3 pc[t] at the same

---

[1] MS in the possession of Mrs. Harriet J. Butler.
[2] This note is wanting. Ricardo had presented her with a copy of *Protection to Agriculture,* 2nd ed., 1822. For this copy, inscribed 'Miss Edgeworth from the author with his kindest regards', see Catalogue 15 of H. Stevens, London, 1936, item 793.

20 June 1822   time as you sell the French 5 pc$^{ts}_{.}$. While your money is in
Mr. Delessert's hands both the English and French Stocks
may rise considerably, and you may have to make a great
sacrifice in purchasing either one or the other at a future
time.—

I will only add that I am a holder of French Stock, and at
present have no thought of parting with it. If it rose to 100—
I might probably be tempted to bring the money to this
country, and employ it in the purchase of land or on mortgage.—

Yours very truly

DAVID RICARDO

Upper Brook Street
20 June 1822

503. M^cCULLOCH TO RICARDO [1]
[*Answered by* 504]

Edinburgh 22 June 1822

My Dear Sir

22 June 1822   The conduct of the Lord Advocate in reference to the
Treasury press of this part of the Empire is, I understand,
to be discussed on Tuesday next in the House of Commons—
I am told on what I consider good authority, that the Advocate means to urge the example of the Scotsman as an apology
for the outrageous personalities of the papers patronised by
him—But supposing it to be true that the Scotsman had been
as personal as the John Bull or the Beacon, surely that is but
a very indifferent reason for the first law officer of the Crown
in Scotland, and whose duty it is to prosecute for libels,
becoming a partner in a manufactory of blackguardism—Still
however the prevalence of any habit is to a certain extent an
excuse for others indulging in it; and the Lord Advocate will

---

[1] MS in *R.P.*—*Letters of McCulloch to Ricardo*, XV.

22 June 1822

probably use the argumentum ad hominem so frequently resorted to in the House, and say "how can you, the gentlemen on the opposite side, accuse me of patronising a libellous paper when you are yourselves the patrons of one that is still more so"? As I am well acquainted with the Lord Advocate's *regard to truth,* I am almost certain that this or something like it will be said; and I assure you the idea that any Journal with which I am connected should be stigmatised as affording an example for indulging in attacks on private character is anything but agreeable—

Now as you have been a subscriber to the Scotsman for upwards of three years, you must be well able to say whether it really deserves the character which I believe the Lord Advocate and his friends will give of it—If you are of opinion that it does *not* deserve this character you will oblige me extremely by saying so in the House—Removed as you fortunately are from our petty broils and contentions, your opinion would have infinitely more weight with the country and also with the House than that of any of the other party members who are likely to speak on the question; and *I* would rather have your suffrage than that of half the House—

The only case in which the Scotsman could be said to be personal was that of Wilson now Professor of Moral Philosophy—But what had Wilson done? He was proved by evidence under his own hand to have written a most scandalous libel on the Editor of the Scotsman who had never even mentioned his name;[1] and it was also proved by the

[1] See in *Blackwood's Magazine* for Sept. 1819, p. 671 ff., 'Pilgrimage to the Kirk of Shotts', a jest on the Edinburgh Reformers, in the form of a letter from 'Hugh Mullion' to his brother 'Mordecai', accompanied by a cartoon. McCulloch is not mentioned by name, but referred to as the 'Galloway Stot' or the 'Scotsman'; he is described 'with those dull, heavy, leaden eyes, and that sallow cadaverous face', being overtaken by a fit of epilepsy while riding a recalcitrant mule, while one of those present

22 June 1822 same unquestionable evidence that Wilson had been in the habit of libelling, calumniating and traducing his most intimate friends—It was a disgrace to Government to send such a man to teach morals; and nothing too severe could be said in reprobation of such a scandalous proceeding—

I have been obliged to interrupt the writing of my Lectures in order to write a general article on Political Economy for the Supplement to the Encyclopaedia Brittannica—I was very averse to engage in this undertaking, but I could not get it avoided—I have not time to execute it as I could wish—

Mr. Buchannan the Editor of Smith has lately been engaged in an attempt to overthrow your system de fond en comble! You have little, however, to fear from his attacks—He is an extremely feeble antagonist—He writes well but he has no stuff at bottom—I reviewed some of his positions about demand and supply in a late Number of the Scotsman[1]—

exclaims, 'Pure fallow, is this him that wishes to mend the constitution? I'm sure nae burrugh's half sae rotten as his ain breast', etc. Another article in the same number of *Blackwood's*, p. 655 ff., 'Tickler on the Scotsman', attacks McCulloch's contributions to the *Edinburgh Review:* 'in days of yore, it was at least written by gentlemen. How can Mr. Jeffrey tolerate such an insult upon himself and his old associates, as a quarterly visit from so low a person as this Scotsman?' Cp. above, VIII, 204–5.
[1] The *Caledonian Mercury,* an Edinburgh newspaper published three times a week, of which David Buchanan was the editor, had criticised Ricardo's recent speeches on the agricultural distress in a leading article on 13 May 1822, and had followed this up on 25 May with lengthy 'Observations on Mr. Ricardo's Doctrine of the Principles which Regulate Prices', concluding that price depends exclusively on demand and supply. The *Scotsman* of 8 June replied with an article 'Cost of Production the Regulating Principle of Price'. The controversy was continued with two articles in the *Mercury* of 20 and 22 June, 'On Mr. Ricardo's Theory of Prices', and with further articles in the *Scotsman* of 27 June and in the *Mercury* of 6 July.

I was very well pleased with the result of Mr. Westerns 22 June 1822 motion—It is not easy to fathom Brougham—I should think he must have gone far to destroy all reliability on his knowledge of the principles of economic science[1]—

Have you seen Colonel Torrens of late? He has, for what cause I dont know, given up all correspondence with me— I am sorry for this but cannot help it—

I hope you have resolved to visit Edinburgh this summer— I am with great regard

Yours most truly
J. R. McCulloch

504. RICARDO TO M^cCULLOCH [2]
[Reply to 503]

London 26 June 1822

My Dear Sir

You will see by the Newspapers that there was a long 26 June 1822 debate in the House last night on the subject of the Lord Advocate's subscribing to the Beacon. In his (the Lord Advocate's) speech he did not mention the Scotsman, and therefore it was not necessary for me to say any thing in defence of the management of that paper. If he had accused it of dealing in personal abuse I should have vindicated it from that charge. The Lord Advocate had a bad cause, and the majority of 25 which divided against enquiry, will not clear him in the public opinion.—

I have only time to write these few lines.—

Y^{rs} very truly
DAVID RICARDO

---

[1] Brougham had spoken and voted for Western's motion of 11 June on the Resumption of Payments.

[2] Addressed: 'J. R. M'Culloch Esqr / Buccleugh Place / Edinburgh'.
MS in British Museum.—*Letters to McCulloch*, XXXV.

505. RICARDO TO MILL [1]

London 6th [2] July 1822

My Dear Sir

There is no chance I think of Parliament being prorogued so early as the middle of this month, but my family have become impatient to commence their journey, and I have consented to take my departure with them on friday next.[3] I receive your blessing with gratitude, and regret that it could not be given to me by yourself in person.

I will write to you as you request, but I much fear that all my observations in the form of a journal will be very uninteresting. I will try my hand in the mode you require, and shall then be better able to judge whether it will be wise and prudent to persevere.—

I hope you are enjoying yourself in the country.—I am glad that Mr. Holland succeeded in procuring for you admission to Mr. Hope's grounds. I doubt not you will become acquainted with Mr. Hope—I am sure he will make an effort to become acquainted with you if he knows who, and what you are.—

I shall fully expect to hear from you sometimes while I am abroad—a letter from you will be a great treat to me when I shall be among the mountains of Switzerland.—

Mrs. Ricardo and my girls desire to be most kindly remembered.

Y[rs] very truly

DAVID RICARDO.

Shall you be able to do any thing for John my servant?

---

[1] Addressed: 'James Mill Esq[r] / Dorking / Surry'. Franked by Ricardo 'July Eight' (replacing 'Six').

MS in Mill-Ricardo papers.
[2] Replaces '5th'.
[3] 12 July.

506. RICARDO TO MILL [1]

Coblentz 4 Augt 1822

My Dear Sir

I wrote a very long letter to you in the form of a daily   4 Aug. 1822
journal of our proceedings and movements, but it was so
inexpressibly dull and stupid, that although I did send it to
you I resolved not to plague you with any more like it.[2] As
it may be agreeable to me to know hereafter the names of the
places through which we pass, the time at which we did pass
through them, and some of the trifling occurrences with
which the remembrance of the places may be associated in
my mind, I have not wholly discontinued noting, in the
journal form, the events of each particular day, and as they
may have some little interest with Osman and Harriet, I continue to send them a sheet as soon as it is completely scribbled
over. To you however I will not be so troublesome but will
from time to time let you hear from me that you may be
able to trace our progress, and that you may be informed of
some of the feelings which are excited in our little party at
the view of so many novel objects. Our journey has hitherto
proceeded without disappointment or accident, over roads
with very few exceptions as good, and many of them much
better than we have in England. We approached Cologne,
from which place the beautiful scenery on the banks of the
Rhine commences, through Holland, and after we had quitted
the frontiers of that country at Nimeguen till we arrived at
Cologne, the roads were execrably bad, but this is the only
bad road over which we have hitherto travelled. In Holland
the roads are admirably good, they are mostly paved with
the small Dutch clinker, over which there is a thin layer of

---

[1] Addressed: 'James Mill Esqr /
East India House / London'.
   MS in Mill-Ricardo papers.

[2] That letter forms the first section
of the *Journal of a Tour on the
Continent* in Vol. X below.

sand, so that the carriages run upon it with the same facility with which they would do on our favorite walk in Kensington gardens. This improvement was made in King Louis Bonaparte's time, and it is not the only one for which the slow methodical Dutchman is indebted to the Revolution. I had not been in Holland for 30 years and I saw it again with pleasure—it is a very peculiar country: there is not a spot in it, which does not give you the idea of cleanliness and comfort. Their doors and window frames appear always newly painted, the glass is so clean; the stone posts, and iron chains suspended from them so much ornamented, the houses so universally good, that you cannot divest yourself of the idea of being amongst a wealthy and thriving people. The sight of their shipping in every place; their excellent rivers, and the immense internal trade which is carried on by means of their peculiarly constructed boats, never fails to give me pleasure. In short I find I have a great regard for the Dutch, and I think you as a political Economist would view them with an equal degree of favor. Although to my eyes the appearance of their houses, their harbours, their streets and their people conveyed no other impression than that of wealth and prosperity, I have heard from many individuals the most pathetic complaints of the decay of trade, and the approaching ruin of Holland. I have asked myself repeatedly whether the complainants, or I, were most likely to be mistaken, and I should have decided against myself did I not remember the instructive remark of Dr Smith, that during a long period, which he mentions, the English were always complaining of ruined trade and delapidated resources, and yet during that time they had made the most rapid advances in wealth and prosperity.[1] All countries I apprehend have this disposition,

[1] 'The annual produce of the land and labour of England, for example, is certainly much greater than it was, a little more than a

and they think themselves ruined if their progress is only checked, although it may be positively in an advancing state. In speaking however of the towns in Holland I must not forget those which lay in our way to them. I mean those in Flanders: Ghent, Brussells, Antwerp, and particularly the last, are very handsome towns. Through what a great number of fine towns you may pass in a few days: besides Lisle, and those I have mentioned, there is Rotterdam, The Hague, Leyden, Harlem, Amsterdam, Utrecht, Nimeguen. After seeing these it is enough to make one melancholy to enter the first Prussian town. Cleves, Gueldres, Neuss are very dull; Cologne is something better, and the one from which I am now writing the best of any which I have visited during this journey. The situation of Coblenz is beautiful. Since I was here last,[1] a bridge on boats has been built over the Rhine to Ehrenbrestein; there was formerly a Pont Volant. The fortifications of Ehrenbrestein, a place incredibly strong by nature, were destroyed by the French, but are now nearly formed again since the peace. They are to be stronger than ever. The material part is already accomplished, and they are now proceeding very slowly with them. The whole expence will be 13 millions of Prussian Dollars, or nearly 2 millions sterling. We have been all over the works—they are well worth seeing, but principally, according to my view, for the beautiful prospect which the high ground commands. The Mosselle forms a junction with the Rhine at the entrance of

century ago, at the restoration of Charles II. Though, at present, few people, I believe, doubt of this, yet during this period, five years have seldom passed away in which some book or pamphlet has not been published, written too with such abilities as to gain some authority with the public, and pretending to demonstrate that the wealth of the nation was fast declining, that the country was depopulated, agriculture neglected, manufactures decaying, and trade undone.' (*Wealth of Nations,* Bk. ii, ch. iii; Cannan's ed., vol. i, p. 326.)

[1] In 1817.

this town, and I am sure I know enough of your taste to say that you would be greatly pleased with the lovely country by which we are here surrounded. We have also been this morning to see a curious garden formed on the side of a high hill by an old eccentric Priest, who has a number of curiosities in his house. He very courteously came out into his garden to meet us, but we could very imperfectly converse as he could not speak French, nor English, though he could in a slight degree understand those who spoke in the former language. His garden commands a very extensive view of the fortifications; of the surrounding country; and of the town of Coblentz. I have no doubt that the old gentleman is very happy in his agreeable domain. We arrived here yesterday, and in the evening witnessed some of the festivities on account of the King of Prussia's birth day. A fire balloon was sent up from the square in which our Inn is placed, and it performed its part very well. It rose slowly, dwindled in appearance to a speck, and at last disappeared. We were pleased to see the good feeling which animated the adults towards the children. A cord was stretched around a circular place to give room to the operator to perform the office of filling the balloon, and the children were without exception allowed to occupy the front places, the men and women standing behind them. To-morrow we shall leave Coblentz for Mayence, next day we shall go to Frankfort, and after seeing Heidelberg, Carlsruhe, and Baden, shall, in a few days afterwards, proceed to Schaffhausen and Berne. If you write, which I hope you will, pray direct to me at Geneva. I am always afraid that our letters should follow rather than precede us. It is difficult while moving about so incessantly as we do, to fix accurately the time at which we shall arrive at each place.

I see very little of the people; when I say, I see little, I

mean I converse with very few. I do not know enough of
French to keep up a conversation in that language, but I do
very well when I can find any one who can *speak* French,
and *understand* English. I met one or two in Holland, amongst
those who were known to me slightly, who could do so, and
I had much pleasure in speaking to them. These gentlemen
had very little knowledge of Government, although they had
bestowed much attention on the subject. They spoke of the
rights of kings, as if Government could be legitimately
intended for any other purpose but the happiness of the
people. I wish I had brought a few copies of your article on
Government with me. I did however use the arguments with
which it supplied me to refute their theories. They had much
more sympathy with the King of Spain than with his long
misgoverned subjects.

Mrs. Ricardo is very much pleased with the life of a
traveller, under the favorable circumstances that she enjoys
that title. She has always been an admirer of every thing
foreign, and she is much pleased with the many novel things
which she every day meets with. The girls are also pleased,
and are very observant of the different costume of the
women, as we proceed from place to place. We had an
eccentric waiter at the Hague who afforded them a great deal
of amusement. He took an early opportunity of telling us
that he had travelled all over Europe, mentioning with great
precision each place that he had visited. I did not blame him
for this, it was a very pardonable piece of vanity; but nothing
could be mentioned, while he was waiting on us, which had
reference to *any* place, but we had some new history of his
travels. One complained of the money of Holland, he wished
we had seen the money of Poland, which was much worse.
Our courier said something to displease him, and he came
to make a formal complaint to me. He said he had travelled

far more than the Courier, and would not therefore be talked
to by him in the way in which he addressed him.—This man
was a great oddity.—You will be glad that I have got to the
end of my paper, but I must not conclude, without giving
you the kind regards and wishes of my fellow travellers. We
also desire to be kindly remembered to Mrs. Mill.

Ever truly Yours

DAVID RICARDO

507. RICARDO TO MILL [1]

Geneva 17th Sepr 1822

My Dear Sir

I arrived here on the 9th ins^t and had the pleasure of
receiving your letter,[2] which had been at the Post Office with
several others from my friends in England for some days.
I am glad that you were able to give me a good account of
yourself and of the benefit which you had derived from the
pure air which you had been some time before inhaling.
I trust that on my arrival in London I shall find you strong
and hearty, and no longer under the necessity of living the
life of seclusion which you did last winter. The news of
Lord Londonderry's death[3] reached me at an obscure place
on the Lake of Zurich, and I soon after learned from the
Newspapers all the particulars of his melancholy end. I, as
little as you, could have expected such an act from a man of
Lord Londonderry's apparent coldness and indifference, and
attribute it as you do to madness, but I cannot agree with
you that he had not great fatigue to undergo; on the contrary
I have often wondered how he and some other of the
ministers could sustain the burden imposed upon them, it

4 Aug. 1822

17 Sept. 1822

---

[1] Addressed: 'James Mill Esqr /
East India House / London'.
MS in Mill-Ricardo papers.

[2] Mill's letter is missing.

[3] He had killed himself on 12
August.

has often appeared to me to surpass what the human frame could endure. His place was not filled when the last accounts which we have received here by the public papers from England left that country—I think with you that it will be difficult to find another so expert as he was in cajoling the House of Commons. From what I have seen it does not appear improbable that Canning's destination will after all be changed; a few days will however give us correct information on this subject.[1]

On my arrival at Geneva you will easily suppose that I was not long in seeking out the residence of our friend Dumont. I found that during the summer he lived in the country, at a short distance from the town, and at a place very appropriately named for our friends residence, "Les Philosophes"; a name not recently given, but one which it had long before Mr. Dumont went to live there. I took the first opportunity of calling at his house but I learned there that he was at Copet and not expected home before the evening—I left my name and address, and the morning following had the pleasure of seeing Mr. Dumont enter our room at the Inn immediately after breakfast. It is impossible to tell you how friendly he was to us, he enquired concerning our stay and our intended route and when we told him we were going to Chamouny, and intended to return to Geneva he expressed a wish to get rid of an engagement which he had that he might be enabled to accompany us. He also fixed on a day for me to dine with him when I was to be introduced to many of the distinguished men of Geneva. He took me with him in his carriage, for he has a comfortable little Char with one horse, to Geneva, and shewed me whatever was worth seeing there. His first object was to get excused from his engagement, which he easily effected, and

---

[1] Cp. above, p. 182, n. 2.

the next morning we all set off together for Chamouny. This expedition took us four days, and as we were favored by the weather nothing was wanting to our enjoyment. Dumont was in every respect a great acquisition to us; he knew every step of the country and pointed our attention to the objects most worthy of notice. At Chamouny you know that you are at the foot of Mont Blanc and that several Glaciers which descend from that mountain are not only visible but actually reach the valley. One of these glaciers is called the Mer de Glace from its extent and its wave like appearance. To see the Mer de Glace in perfection you must ascend one of the ridges of Mont Blanc called Montanvert the summit of which is more than 5000 feet above the sea. This difficult task the girls and I determined to accomplish and Dumont did not for a moment hesitate about accompanying us. We set off at 6 oClock in a very fine morning on our mules and had to ascend for two hours and a half over a road so rough that I was astonished how the mules could make their way—they rather danced than walked up the hill; for the greatest part of the way their movements seemed a succession of leaps. The mule which carried Mr. Dumont was a strong one, but he is very heavy, and from the repeated stops which the mule made, it was evident he had a very hard task to perform. After two hours and a half of these ups and downs over fragments of rock we reached the summit, and were compensated for our trouble by a very fine view of the glacier and the surrounding rocks which require a very different pen from mine to be accurately described. To reach the summit of this mountain was the least of our difficulty, we had the descent to perform, and that without the aid of mules, over the road which I have described. Even mules are not trusted to go down this mountain with persons on their backs. Mr. Dumont I am sure felt the full difficulty of the task, but he bore all patiently and followed us without a murmur or complaint for 3 hours till we reached the bottom. We are none of us the worse for the fatigue we underwent and I believe Mr. Dumont felt greatly pleased at the result of this trial of his strength. You know that Mr. Dumont was always a chearful pleasant companion, full of anecdote and fond of conversation—he is not in the least altered but retains all his former vivacity and good spirits. I found him and many other persons at Geneva in a very despairing mood respecting public liberty—they are all loud in their complaints of the conduct of England as the great enemy of all liberal principles and as combining with the kings and emperors of the continent to enslave mankind. With respect to their opinions on Government I think them all a little too much inclined to aristocratical preponderance, at least such would be the effect of the measures they recommend. There may certainly be a great difference between England and this country and different forms may in consequence be necessary. In England we know that the Aristocracy have great influence over the people from the power which they possess of injuring them in some way or other,—it is denied that any such influence is possessed here though I find it difficult to believe. They expect too much from the lower and middling class of people, they should perform their [duty][1] at whatever price it may cost them, they say, and have no idea of taking securities that their duty and interest should as little as possible be opposed to each other. Their great fear is of the apathy of the people and of the little interest they feel in the choice of their representatives. They however unite in declaring that the Government here has improved and is improving. I collected most of the information which I have given you from the conversation which took place at the

[1] Omitted in MS.

Duke of Broglie's where I dined yesterday with Mr. Dumont. He is living at Copet the residence of Madame de Stael. Mr. Sismondi was there and our conversation turned entirely on Politics and Political Economy. Mr. Sismondi you know has many of Mr. Malthus opinions on the latter science which he advanced with great boldness, but I think with very little skill. He found it impossible to answer the objections made to his system by the Duke and myself and contented himself frequently with saying that they were answerable—he was sure altho' he could not at that moment reply to them.— I was quite charmed with Madame de Broglie. She appeared to me to conduct herself with such admirable propriety taking just so much part in the conversation as to give one the idea of its being interesting to her, at the same time that her remarks were pertinent and shewed she was tolerably familiar with such subject. Her gentlewomanly ease appeared to me admirable and I think her greatly entitled to my gratitude for making me feel so much at home in her company.—A few days ago I dined with Mons.ʳ La Rive where I met a Doctor Bruttini and his son, and Mr. Simond the author of travels in England, and of a Tour in Switzerland. The latter book I have read and was pleased to observe that he was the advocate for the anti malthusian doctrines of Political Economy. Mr. Simond was born at Lyons, lost his father and brother during the horrors of the Revolution, went to America at an early age where he long resided. He married a relation of Jeffreys but lost his wife. He is now again married to a Genevese lady, has become a citizen of the Republic and is probably settled here for life. He is an agreeable and an intelligent man, and I had great pleasure in conversing with him. Lausanne and this place abound with English—I was surprised to find at this Inn on my return from Chamouny Mr. Norman and Mr. Cowell—I was very glad to meet for they are both very pleasing, clever, and excellent men—they drank tea with me that night and the next day proceeded on their journey to Italy. They had been here a week or two ago and were then hospitably entertained by Mr. Dumont. I am sorry that Mr. Norman's health is but indifferent and that he has not very much improved it by his journey.

Before I received your letter I had determined to go into Italy. I shall not however proceed further than Florence. Give my kind regards to Ralph if you see him—he is a good fellow and is wise in knowing how to choose a judicious path to happiness. Remember me kindly to Mr. Tooke. I hope he is at work and that he will be prepared with the result of his labours when I see him in England. Mr. Dumont desires to be kindly mentioned to you—I gave him Mr. Bentham's message—he did not appear to plead guilty to the charges made against him.—This is the day that I am to dine with Dumont. The Duke whom I like very much, Sismondi, Simond, Prevost, La Rive, and perhaps Humboldt, the traveller, who is here for a day, will be of the party. A Mons.ʳ Rossi of whom Dumont speaks highly was to be there if he returned from a tour in time. I shall have much to tell you when we meet. To-morrow we quit Geneva. Mrs. Ricardo and the girls thank you for your remembrance of them and beg their kindest regards to you. With our united kind wishes to Mrs. Mill I remain

Very truly Yʳˢ

DAVID RICARDO

MARY sends her particular love to you.— [1]

---

[1] This line in Mrs. Ricardo's handwriting.

508. RICARDO TO MILL [1]

Bologna 10ᵗʰ Octʳ 1822

My Dear Friend

10 Oct. 1822   My last letter to you was dispatched from Geneva, on the day that I was engaged to dine with our friend Dumont. I met a very agreeable party at his house, and he gave us the best dinner I had seen at Geneva. Monsʳ Sismondi, Mr. Simond, The Duc de Broglie, Monsʳ De la Rive, Monsʳ Bellort, Monsʳ Prevost, young Romilly, and one other gentleman, whose name I forget, partook of our friend's hospitality. He appears to live very comfortably at his country seat, and to be very much respected by the circle in which he moves at Geneva. We quitted Geneva the morning following, and had a delightful journey to Sᵗ Maurice. We passed the rocks of Meillerie, which Rousseau has so beautifully described in his Nouvelle Heloise. Nothing can be more beautiful than the country as this place—we stopt the carriage, and we, young ones, devoted three fourths of an hour to the climbing of these rocks, from which we had a fine view of the lake, and of the various interesting spots which are on its borders, such as Chillon, Clarens, Ville-neuve, Vevay, Lausanne &cᵃ &cᵃ; the whole way to Mar-tigny is through the most beautiful and interesting country. The next day we proceeded to Martigny, and the day fol-lowing to the Convent at the summit of the Grand Sᵗ Bernard. This was a great undertaking with a lady of Mrs. Ricardo's weight, and the elements seemed to conspire to make the undertaking more difficult. We, however were not to be daunted by these obstacles, and with much exertion succeeded in our object of paying a visit to the good monks of Sᵗ Ber-nard;—they received us very kindly, lodged us tolerably

[1] Addressed: 'James Mill Esqʳ / East India House / London '.—MS in Mill-Ricardo papers.

comfortably, fed us as well as "un jour maigre" would allow them, and gave us their blessing at departing next morning. After this expedition we prepared to cross the Simplon, and in two days after our return to Martigny we found ourselves at the South side of the Alps at Domo D'Ossola. The weather was uncommonly favorable for this journey, and we were all filled with admiration of the grand road which has been made over the almost inaccessible spots through which it has been carried. Enough is not said by travellers of this excellent road;—it is perfect as a road independently of its situation, but when we consider the difficulties which nature opposed to its formation too much cannot be said in praise of those who projected and accomplished the work. On the Piedmontese side the traveller passes thro' some terrific and sublime valleys, overhung by rocks, which appear to threaten his destruction at every step, and just under him there rages a foaming torrent which hurries every thing before it. It is impossible to give any just description of the grandeur of this part of the road; it must be seen to be understood. No part of this long road exhibits any mark of neglect, on the contrary a great many persons are at work upon it to render it (if possible) more perfect than it is.

From Domo D'Ossola we proceeded to Baveno, on the Lago Magiore, which we crossed in our way to Como. From Como we went to Cadenobia, about the center of the lake, or rather of the 3 lakes, which join in this spot. We saw two or three palaces on the lake of Como among others that of the late Queen, which is falling into decay for want of an inhabitant. We stayed 3 or 4 days at Milan, and saw the chief objects worthy of notice in that town. The Cathedral alone is an object which would repay one for a long journey, but there are many other things well deserving of attention. Bonaparte has left traces of himself at Milan as well as in so many other places, but the grand gate at the end of the Simplon road is only half finished: he intended it as a memorial of his successes over the Austrians at Marengo and Ulm, and the history of those battles, in Alto relievo, in which he himself is of course the most prominent person, lies in the workshop and was quite ready to be put up. They say at Milan that the gate will be finished, but of course the stone which is to record the defeat of the Austrians will not be put up. We passed thro' Verona, at which place the congress was about to meet. We slept there two nights, and employed ourselves actively, as travellers should do, in seeing the curiosities of the place. From Verona we went to Venice, a curious and interesting town, in which a horse is not to be seen, and if there he would not find a street in which he could put his foot. Canals, alleys, and bridges, are the only means of communication in Venice. I find it very difficult to account for the want of streets—they could not indeed be made now, without destroying one half of this populous town, but why were they not made originally as they are in Holland? what could induce the first inhabitants to be contented with the miserable courts and alleys which deprive them of the benefits of a free circulation of air. There are some beautiful spots in Venice, and it abounds in grand and magnificent churches and palaces. It would be impossible to give a just idea of the treasures it possesses in buildings and pictures—I never saw finer pictures in my life. They are chiefly by Titian, Paul Veronese, Tintoretto, Palma &c^a. How much of the public property must have been devoted to the purpose of embellishing the town in the days of the prosperity and glory of Venice! We visited the dungeons in the palace, to which state prisoners were formerly condemned, but which are no longer in use at the present time,—they are dreadful places, and many a deed of blood has been performed in them. We

left Venice yesterday morning—slept last night at Ferrara,   10 Oct. 1822
and arrived here in the middle of this day. In our travels in
Italy we have found the people generally in employment,
and with the means of subsistence in tolerable abundance.
We have not met with any great number of beggars till we
came to this town, and here they swarm. I walked this
afternoon into one of the large churches with the girls, and
to my great surprise was addressed by a fat well dressed
priest, who I thought was about to give me some information
respecting the church, when I found to my great surprise that
he was telling me a piteous story which I could not understand, and was asking charity of me. I do not know whether
I was right or wrong, but I did not give him a single sous.

I have not met any one who can give me any interesting
information respecting these countries. I met Cowell and
Norman at Milan, they will go on to Florence and Rome.
Norman is very assiduous in procuring useful information,
and he will have a great deal to tell us when he gets home.
They have had some difficulty in getting the consent of the
Government at Milan to Mr. Norman's brother proceeding
with them into Italy, on account of some informality in his
passport. Mr. Cowell exerted all his powers of eloquence
and persuasion, and at last succeeded in getting the informality
rectified.

I have met in my travels two young Poles,[1] who have been
travelling for some time—they addressed me, and asked me
whether I was the author of a work on Political Economy.
I found they had been pupils of Say, were very fond of the
science, and one of them had hopes of becoming a professor
of it in the College at Warsaw they drank tea with me at
Milan—they told me that they had been in England for a short

[1] Kunatt and Rulikowski, on whom see below, Vol. X, *Journal of a
Tour on the Continent,* entry for 23 Sept. 1822.

time, and knew Mr. Lefevre—I hope they will be the means of disseminating correct opinions in their own country.—

Have you seen our friend Tooke lately? I hope he has been employed in writing during my absence: when you see him give my kind regards to him. I find it very difficult to get any very accurate information of the variation in the relative value of gold and silver in the places where I have been. M. Carli an intelligent Banker at Milan told me that the agio on Napoleons had been for a very long time 15 cents of a franc, but since the peace it had risen to 26, at this price of 26 he paid me the francs which I was entitled to demand of him, in Napoleons. Another banker to whom I applied would have furnished them at 28. Without knowing accurately the French mint proportions it is impossible to know what proportion this value of gold bears to the value of it in England.

I hope this letter will find you, and those with whom you are nearly connected, well and happy. I wish you could partake with me in the enjoyment of this delightful climate. The weather is heavenly fine; it is as warm as in July in England. We are revelling in the abundance of grapes which are very excellent, but we are too late for any other good fruit. I had some fine figs at Como, they were small but delicious. Since leaving Como I have not seen any. We have not met with any mulberries which I expected to see here in perfection. We propose being at Florence on sunday—we shall stay there several days and on quitting it I shall be gradually approaching towards home, which I shall be glad to reach. Mrs. Ricardo, Mary and Birtha desire to be most kindly remembered to you they also join me in best wishes to Mrs. Mill.

Ever truly Y^{rs}

DAVID RICARDO

509. RICARDO TO MILL [1]

My Dear Friend

Turin 3 Nov.ʳ 1822

A long time has elapsed since I last wrote to you but 3–4 Nov. 1822 you have often been present to my thoughts, and if I have not written it was because I did not think I had any thing interesting to communicate to you. You will remember that I have very little intercourse with any one out of the small circle of my own family, and therefore I could have little to say to you except I was to give you some account of the places through which I have passed, and the objects which are chiefly shewn to strangers in those places. To venture on this would be a foolish attempt, when I might refer you to so many publications in which you could obtain the most satisfactory information on such points. Till lately we have passed quietly from one town to another, generally finding good Inns and civil waiters, excellent roads, and all the facilities which are afforded to modern travellers, but after leaving Florence, or more properly, after leaving Pisa, in our way to Genoa, we met with almost every cross accident to which travellers can be exposed. The roads were rendered nearly impassable by the torrents of water which descended from the mountains, and the Inns were the most detestable hovels into which weary travellers could enter in search of a little wholesome food, and refreshing repose. A part of the way from Pisa to Genoa, till within this month, was by water, but a new road has been for sometime preparing, and it was thought to be in so forward a state as to justify the opening it for travellers. I had heard a great deal of this new road, and of the facilities which it afforded, and approached it with the most perfect confidence. As I got near to it I

[1] Addressed: 'James Mill Esqʳ / East India House / London'.—MS in Mill-Ricardo papers.

heard some whispers of its being a little difficult to pass for a
mile or two, and when close upon it I discovered that for
a mile or two, I was to substitute a post or two. For about
3 or 4 posts the road is the worst I ever travelled—we were
obliged to cross and recross torrents, and to go over rocky
ground which threatened destruction to the carriage at every
step. We were obliged for several stages to have 6 horses,
and for 2 out of the 3 or 4 abovementioned posts we were
constantly attended by a dozen men, to steady the carriage,
and prevent it from overturning. We walked a considerable
distance, but were obliged to go inside the carriage over the
torrents, and also over much of the rough road. Over one
of the torrents we were all carried, it was not thought safe
to cross it in any other way. After a day of great fatigue we
expected to get at a tolerably comfortable Inn, but we were
obliged to stay all night at a place such as I fancied only
existed in the imagination of a novel writer. The new road
has been commenced at both ends, and it is the centre of it
only which is in the state of desolation I have described,—
the part which is finished, and which goes over very steep
hills, is excellent, and would not suffer by a comparison with
the justly famous Simplon road. It is, I doubt not, the
intention of the Government to complete the whole on the
plan commenced, and if they are not impeded by the accumulation of water in the low ground, they will finally accomplish
a very desirable work. The present bad state of the road is
in some measure to be ascribed to a great fall of rain which
has lately taken place, and which carried away 3 stone bridges
in Genoa, and made the town inaccessible to a carriage, on
the side we entered it. We arrived at the suburbs after dark,
and had to walk 4 miles, often thro mud and water, to get to
a comfortable Inn. At Genoa our misfortunes ended, we got
into excellent quarters, and were very much pleased with the

town and harbour. We stayed there three days, and then left it for Turin. Turin is also a very good town;—it would very much please you, as you may walk almost all over the town under lofty arcades, which protect you alike from sun and rain. The palace of the King is magnificent, particularly on the inside; almost every room is lined with glass, or with gilded pannels, and I never was in a more extensive habitation.—The Kings of Sardinia have also provided themselves with a most magnificent burying place on the top of a very high hill, a few miles from Turin—it is the grandest place of the kind that I have ever seen.—To-morrow I shall leave Turin, and the following day I expect to be in France, on my way to Paris. I have not been further than Florence, for which you will probably blame me, and ask, why, when only four days from Rome, I did not go on to that city. If I had, you would then have probably asked why I did not go on to Naples. My answer to your first question is that to go to Rome would have detained me 3 or 4 weeks longer, and have forced me to travel at a time of the year the most unpleasant. To confess the truth too my curiosity is satisfied, and all my wishes incline towards home;—I have been out long enough, longer than I calculated upon, and if I had gone to Rome I should still have seen churches, pictures, and antiquities, of which I have seen enough to satisfy me. For the distance we have been we have seen a great deal of Italy, for from Milan we went to Verona, Venice, Bologna, Florence, Leghorn, Pisa and Genoa. Most of these towns are very good, but Venice, Florence, Pisa and Genoa are much superior to the rest. At Leghorn there is a superb burying ground, called the English burying ground, in which there are a great number of very handsome monuments erected to Englishmen who have died abroad and who have been buried in this ground. I accidentally stumbled on poor Horner's—it is a very handsome one, and there is a basso relievo very like him upon it. I wish he had lived; he was much superior to the general race of young politicians.

I have not seen a newspaper since I left Florence, so I know nothing of what is going on in England.—I hear that Corn is very cheap, and landlords in despair—I am surprised at the depression continuing so long. I suppose Cobbett is in high spirits;—does he continue his attacks on me? My brother tells me in a letter which I have just received from him, that Hume has been receiving great honours in his native country, I am glad to hear it, I thought his fame was rather sinking before I left England.

I hope Mr. Bentham is well—I saw a bust of Franklin in a Sculptor's shop at Leghorn, it struck me as being very like Mr. Bentham, and as I am a great admirer both of Franklin and Bentham, I thought I could not do better than buy it. It must be a bargain because it answers the object of two busts.[1] It led however to a piece of extravagance, for having Franklin, and seeing Washington staring me in the face, as if asking me if he also was not worthy of favor, I could do no less than acknowledge the justness of his claim, and accordingly bought him also—I hope to find them both in England on my arrival.

The last time I saw Mr. Cowell and Mr. Norman was at Milan, I saw them at the Opera there, the evening before I left the place. They gave us every reason to expect to see them again at Florence, but I neither met them there, nor heard any tidings of them. I began this letter at Turin, and have finished it at Susa, at the foot of Mont Cenis, which we

---

[1] Cp. the version given by the biographer of Bentham: 'His countenance so greatly resembled that of Benjamin Franklin that David Ricardo purchased the bust of the American, supposing it was intended for the English philosopher.' (*Autobiographical Recollections* of Sir John Bowring, 1877, pp. 338–9.)

propose crossing to-morrow. On friday I hope to be at Lyons, and on friday sen'night at Paris.

Pray remember me kindly to such of my friends as may ask after me, particularly to Mr. Tooke. Mrs. Ricardo and my girls join with [me][1] in kind wishes to Mrs. Mill and yourself—

Ever truly Y^{rs}

DAVID RICARDO

Susa 4th Nov^r

Lyons 8. Novr I have brought my letter with me to this town, where we arrived safe yesterday even^g—

510. MARIA EDGEWORTH TO RICARDO[2]
[*Reply to* 502.—*Answered by* 511]

Edgeworth's Town
July 9th 1822

You have settled my mind my dear Sir about my little monies in the French stocks—and I shall leave mine in company with yours there—in safer and better they cannot be— Thank you for taking the trouble to write so fully on the subject. You must allow me to set this down to the account of your kindness for me and not to the influence of what you call the *bit of flattery*—Since you acknowledge that you are fond of it I should be afraid to offer you a bit,—even the nicest, for it is only those who "say they hate all flattery who are then most easily flattered."

We are quietly settled at home again, and as happily engaged in our home occupations as if we had never seen the

---

[1] Not in MS.
[2] Addressed: 'D. Ricardo Esqre M.P. / Upper Brook St^t / London'. London postmark, 12 July.
    Received by Ricardo on his return from the Continent on 8 December.
    MS in *R.P.*—Extracts in *Economic Journal,* Sept. 1907, pp. 432–3.

visions of London glories—The home-habits and thoughts are so immediately resumed and join so perfectly the past with the present,—the day we left home with the day we returned—that the intervening months would seem to me but a dream, like Mahomets dream, when his head was dipped into the tub—, were it not for certain evidences of reality, which have left impressions too strong and too grateful ever to be effaced. Every, even the slightest circumstance, of our happy visit to Gatcomb park has the stamp of reality upon it—our drives in the delightful phaeton with the two Harriets—the two dear Harriets[1]!—and Mrs. Ricardo's fur tippet!—I feel it still—and all her kindness to me and mine—Then our most pleasant of all parties in London,—our breakfast parties at your house[2] and the conversations with you and Mr. Mill and M. de Broglie &c. All these we recollect with a sober certainty of having much that is really useful left in our minds as well as much that was agreeable and gratifying at the moment—

Now that I am three hundred miles from you I regret however that I did not make still better use of my time when I was with you—that I did not make more advantage of your kind readiness to explain and discuss and of that candid mild truly philosophic temper in discussion of which, tho' I call it philosophic, there are so few living or dead examples even among philosophers.—(Do you call this flattery—No—you feel it to be truth—) Among the number of questions I should wish to hear you discuss is one of *vital* consequence to this country—the question *for* and *against* the potatoe which has for some hundred years past been alternately cried up as the

[1] Maria Edgeworth's sister and Ricardo's daughter-in-law.
[2] 'Our delightful breakfasts at Mr. Ricardo's' are mentioned on 9 March 1822 in a letter of Maria Edgeworth from London. (*Life and Letters of Maria Edgeworth,* ed. by A. J. C. Hare, 1894, vol. II, p. 65.)

blessing and cried down as the bane of Ireland. In Berkeley's Querist (which by the by contains in the pressing style of interrogation as much deep thought in the subtle form of doubts as Socrates himself could have proposed had he lived in Ireland) there is this query

"Whether it is possible Ireland should be well improved while our beef is exported and our labourers live upon potatoes." [1]

In the article on Cottagers in the Encyclopedia Brit^a [2] the same question is ably discussed—But I do not feel that it is put at rest in my mind—At this moment when half Ireland is famishing apparently from the failure of one potatoe crop the arguments come home to the stomach I grant but when in another month new and good potatoes are in every creatures mouths, and the famishing bodies revive the case w^d alter and we should recollect the many years of plenty and independence the thousands of hardy bodies and merry souls which have (in smoke perhaps—but no matter—*if* happy) blessed the potatoe.

As to the objection of the potatoe's not being a store-able food M. L'Asteyrie [3] shows how, by an easy process, it can be made into storeable flour—I enclose a sample which he gave us in 1803—

As to potatoes facilitating the cottager's subdivision of property that is a weighty objection—

As to its encouraging the Irish peasantry in sloth—this does not appear to me a valid objection—It is only arguing from the abuse not the use—If he is at ease about this years food and has time to spare use the time but do not complain that it is not employed in another way of raising food.

---

[1] [Part I], Query 173.
[2] By McCulloch, see above, VII, 337.

[3] Comte de Lasteyrie-Dusaillant (1759–1849), a writer on agriculture.

As to all the Malthean objections to the potatoe,[1] do not all these apply to machinery to manufactures to all that tends to save time and labor and encrease the wealth of a country—

In fact you in England who do not live upon potatoes and who have gone through all the prosperity and adversity of manufactures are you better off—are you happier—I don't ask whether you are richer than we are in Ireland. Take an average of years—don't fix your eye upon this dreadful time of famine.

I wish my dear Sir that after your return from your intended excursion to France you would come to poor little Ireland and see and judge of it for yourself.—How happy we should be to have you at Edgeworths town. What does Mrs. Ricardo say? What does my dear Mary say? and Bertha? I am sure they would be glad to see Fanny and Harriet again—Pray think of it seriously before autumn comes and then you would easily arrange how to put the plan in execution. Mrs. Edgeworth and my brother earnestly pray you to think of it—

I take the liberty of enclosing to you a copy of a letter of Mr. Strickland to the Committee for the relief of the Irish poor, which Mrs. Strickland wishes to forward to her friend, and Walter Scotts friend Mr. Morritt. I have written the direction upon it—and leave it open for you to read if you have time or inclination. I must trouble you to put it into a cover—I could not venture a cover lest it should be overweight.

The poor in this county are not famishing—In this parish we have not had need of your generous English subscriptions.

In another frank by this post I enclose to you a letter for poor Mrs. Smith of Easton-Grey[2]—May I still say of Easton-

---

[1] See *Essay on Population,* 5th ed., 1817, vol. III, p. 238 ff.

[2] Thomas Smith, her husband, had died on 31 May.

9 July 1822

Grey?—I should be very much obliged to Mrs. Ricardo if she would write to tell me something of that poor lady whom we pity sincerely. I want to know whether she remains at Easton Grey—I hope so that she may be near your family whom she loves and who would be kind friends to her— I have requested her not to answer my letter—I know answering letters of condolence is dreadfully painful—But I am truly anxious to hear *of* her.

Give my love and Fanny's and Harriets to your Harriet and Mary. Assure Mrs. Ricardo of our grateful remembrance of all her hospitable and affectionate kindness—and if she does not know it let me tell her that she stands as high in our esteem as in our affection.

I am dear Sir

Your sincere friend

Maria Edgeworth

Mrs. Ricardo once asked me for some directions to tradespeople in Paris—Did I send or shall I send them—Can I be of any use by letters of introduction to some of our friends in Paris—Command me and you will see whether I shall obey with alacrity.

511. RICARDO TO MARIA EDGEWORTH [1]

[*Reply to 510.—Answered by 514*]

Bromesberrow Place Ledbury 13 Dec.[r] 1822

My Dear Miss Edgeworth

13 Dec. 1822

I am sure you will have concluded that I had left London before your letter reached me, when you found a

[1] Addressed: 'Miss Edgeworth / Edgeworth Town / Ireland', redirected: 'Blackcastle Navan'. Franked by Ricardo 'Ledbury December Fourteen 1822'.—MS in *R.P.*—Extracts in *Economic Journal*, Sept. 1907, pp. 433–5.

reasonable time had elapsed, and you had no answer to it. I therefore need not tell you that such was the fact, and that the first time I saw it was on sunday last[1] on my arrival from Dover at Brook Street.—I have seen a great deal more of the Continent than I expected when we parted in London. My companions and I journey'd on very comfortably together through Holland, by the Rhine, through Switzerland, till we arrived at Geneva, when a grand consultation took place whether we should return home or proceed into Italy.

If this question had been to be decided by ballot, or even by open voting, the result would not have been a moment doubtful, but as it depended on the fiat of an absolute monarch, some pleadings were necessary. At Geneva we received letters from all our dear children at home—they all conveyed good news—they told us that Mrs. Clutterbuck was safely in bed with a little girl, that she was going on well, and that all the rest were in perfect health. These facts were strongly urged, and the absolute monarch was graciously pleased to give directions to prepare for passing the Alps. Thanks to Bonaparte this passage was not a difficult task; we crossed the Simplon in the most beautiful weather, and visited successively the towns of Milan, Verona, Venice, Bologna, Florence, Leghorn, Pisa, Genoa and Turin. From the latter we crossed Mont Cenis, and made the best of our way to Paris. At Paris we stayed three weeks, and finished our excursion by a prosperous voyage across our narrow channel, immediately after the hurricane of thursday last would permit a vessel to put to sea. Our little party have returned in perfect health, and highly delighted with our tour. If we have a complaint to make it is that we had too few difficulties to combat with. We were not robbed nor be-

----

[1] 8 December.

nighted. The roads were almost uniformly good, and our carriage neither broke down, nor was it overturned. Landlords were civil to us—they gave us good beds and wholesome food, and their charges were by no means unreasonable. Notwithstanding this want of striking adventures, the recollection of our journey is a source of great pleasure to us, and we talk over the little incidents of it with a great deal of interest and animation. At Geneva I had the satisfaction of seeing our friend Dumont in good health;—as a proof of it, he accompanied us to Chamouny, and accomplished, *with us young ones,* the ascent of the Montanvert. I need not say that his society afforded us all much gratification, for you know what an agreeable companion he is. This was not the only pleasure which awaited me at Geneva and in its neighbourhood;—the Duke and Mad.^{me} de Broglie were at Coppet, and I went with Mr. Dumont to dine with them. I had never seen Mad.^{me} de Broglie before: I was delighted with her. I do not know whether you know it, but I am very shy, which I, sometimes, perhaps generally, hide under as bold an exterior as I can assume. All the painful feelings of shyness vanished after I had been five minutes in the company of the Duchess—she was so affable, so unaffected, and made me feel so much at my ease that I could scarcely believe I was in her company for the first time. The Duke was kind and agreeable as usual. Monsr Sismondi was of the party. He and I differ much in our views on subjects connected with Polit.^l Economy, and these differences were brought under discussion. I had a powerful ally in the Duke; the brunt of the battle fell on him and he defended our common principles with great judgement and ability. Madame sat by as umpire, and if she did not determine in favor of either of the contending parties, she at least kept us within the rules of order and fair play. Although I think that Mr. Sismondi has taken an erroneous view on these questions, I am fully sensible of his great talents and pleasing manners—it gave me great pleasure to meet him a second time at a dinner given to us by Mr. Dumont the day before I quitted Geneva. At Paris I again had the satisfaction of seeing Mons.[r] and Mad.[me] de Broglie with the Baron de Stael—they all reached that city after I had arrived there. I did not fail to pay my respects at Paris to Mons.[r] Delessert and his brother; from both gentlemen I received many acts of kindness; they were always willing to give me or procure for me every information I required respecting commercial and financial subjects. At Mons. B. Delesserts I had the pleasure of sitting next to Mad.[me] Gautier[1] at dinner, who besides her other claims to my good will added that of calling you her friend.

You will think that I have devoted a sufficient portion of my letter to an account of my travels,—I will now attend to the topics touched upon in your letter. And first, upon the subject of French stock. You will have observed that there have been great variations in the price, accordingly as the opinions in favor of peace or of war have prevailed. Peace appears now to be probable: if it should not be disturbed, all alarm respecting the goodness of our security will for the present cease. I retain a favorable opinion of the soundness of the resources of France, and at the present depressed price of stock I have not any intention of selling mine, but if the price should rise to 95 I shall be disposed to sell about half of what I have. My reasons for doing so are, first, that I bought at a much lower price, and secondly because the measures pursued by the French Government are such as I think will at no distant time produce internal disorder, if they do not disturb the relations of peace with foreign countries. I am

[1] Sister of Benjamin Delessert.

pretty confident however that the funds will survive, let whatever changes that may take place.

I am pleased to hear that though you have all fallen again into the regular course of your former habits and pursuits, you yet retain a pleasing recollection of your journey to England; above all am I pleased that the recollection of me and mine is associated in all your minds with agreeable reflections. This is such acceptable intelligence to me that I readily give it credit, notwithstanding that your letter confirms me in my former suspicion of your wishing to give pleasure to your friends by placing their good qualities in the most prominent and agreeable light.

I do not know that I have given the question *for* and *against* the potatoe that degree of attentive consideration to entitle me to speak with confidence upon it. It is probable, I think, that, as in most other contested opinions, the parties on both sides have been guilty of exaggeration. I confess I have always inclined to that view which regards it as an evil that the population of a country should be chiefly fed and supported on potatoes. But my objection rests almost wholly on the fact which we have so often witnessed of the crop being uncertain and liable to peculiar accidents. We cannot, I think, doubt, that the situation of mankind would be much happier if we could depend with as much certainty on a given quantity of capital and labour producing a certain quantity of food, as we can depend upon the same quantity of capital and labour producing a certain quantity of manufactured goods. It is evident that in the latter case we can calculate upon results almost with absolute certainty; in the other case we must always be exposed to the uncertainty of the seasons, which will render the crop fluctuating. If it be granted that certainty, with respect to the production of quantity of food, be desirable, it follows that of all the different qualities of food on which mankind can be sustained, provided it be not too difficult to obtain it, that quality is most desirable for their general consumption, on the production of which we can rely with the most certainty. In comparing wheat and potatoes I apprehend the former approaches much nearer to the desired end than the other, and for that reason I give it the decided preference. The argument, that the failure of the potatoe crop is only occasional, and that at all other times there will be in the world a much greater number of happy and contented beings, appears to me defective. Judging by my own feelings, if, for five, six, or seven years of easy competency, with respect to food, I had to endure one year of famine, and to witness the sufferings of my family and friends for that one dreadful year, I would rather that I had never been born;—no happiness, (and it is happiness of no extraordinary kind of which we are speaking) can compensate perpetual hunger, and all the evils in its train, for one year, much less can it compensate for the dreadful suffering of starvation, if that should be the consequence. Answer this objection and I am for the potatoe. You say, that the potatoe is a storeable food, and you would, I conclude, infer from that fact, that provision might be made in years of plenty for the occasional years of scarcity. There can be no doubt if it be a storeable food, and if the preparation of it for store were not expensive, so that the price should not be greatly enhanced to the consumer in the years of deficient crop, great progress would be made in the defence of the potatoe, but we must be satisfied as to this fact; and then I should still require some proof that there were among you some of those patient, plodding, calculating merchants who would be contented to enter into a speculation on a prospect of its success in four, five, or ten years. Give me these securities and I will fight with you till death in favor of the potatoe, for my motto, after Mr. Bentham, is "the greatest happiness to the greatest number."

As to the objection of potatoes facilitating the cottagers subdivision of property, we might have said the same of wheat in former ages. While potatoes continued very cheap it would have that tendency, but I do not know why potatoes might not become in time as dear as wheat, for let it be always remembered that it is not quantity that regulates price, but facility or difficulty of production. If the people of all countries lived on potatoes, I can conceive the world to be many times its present amount of population; potatoes to be increased 50 or 100 times in quantity; and yet to be doubled, tripled, or quadrupled in value. Sloth and rags are no more the concomitants of potatoes, than of wheat. With the one we might have an industrious, happy people, equally as with the other, only 3 times (perhaps) more numerous. Good government does not depend on the food of the people, and I have great doubts whether the population of Ireland would have been wiser or happier if they had never lived on any other food but wheat, provided the crop of wheat had been subject to the same vicissitudes from seasons that potatoes are liable to. It is quite certain it would never have been so numerous.

I agree with you as to many of the Malthean objections to the potatoes being unfounded they might equally apply to machinery in manufactures;—in fact Malthus himself does so apply them.[1]

I think we are not only richer but happier in England than in Ireland, and for the reasons I have before given, we are never so near actual famine as you are; what can you put in the scale against this dreadful evil? I should be glad to accept your summons and go to Ireland to judge for myself, I thank

[1] See Malthus's *Principles,* above, II, 352–7.

you for the tempting offers you make me, so does Mrs. Ricardo, so does Mary, and so also does Birtha, but it is for the present out of the question, we shall however hope some day to pay you a visit at Edgeworth Town. We thank Mrs. Edgeworth and your brother for the encouragement they are pleased to give to it.

I am writing to you from the house of my son, and I am requested by him and Harriet, by Mrs. Ricardo, and by Mary and Birtha, to give their kind regards to you, Miss Fanny, and Miss Harriet. When I have such a message I always feel a difficulty how to word the sentence so as to include myself amongst those who are sending the kind regards, but though I may be unskilful, my young cousins must not do me the injustice to suppose that I forget [them.] [1] To prevent all possibility of their coming to so erroneous [a concl]usion, I do now assure them of my continued reg[ards] and I beg them to preserve me in their kind remembrance.—

Ever my dear Miss Edgeworth

Your sincere friend

DAVID RICARDO

I have not sent till this day the letter you inclosed to me, to Mr. Morritt.

I have not seen Mrs. Smith yet, but I have heard from her —she is in tolerable health, and is behaving under her misfortunes like a good and wise woman.

---

[1] MS torn here and below.

512. RICARDO TO TROWER [1]

Bromesberrow Place Ledbury
14 Dec.[r] 1822

My Dear Trower

Your letter of the 11th July[2] did not reach me till sunday last, on which day I arrived in Brook Street from Dover. I left London for the Continent very early on the 12th July, and proceeded by the Steam Packet from the Tower-Stairs to Calais: this voyage was performed in about 13 or 14 hours. I was accompanied in my tour by Mrs. Ricardo, my two youngest daughters, Miss Lancey (the governess) Mrs. Ricardo's female servant, and a courier. As I could not comply with your request contained in the letter of the 11th, mentioned above, to give you an account of the journey I intended to make, I will, now that it is over, lay before you the route we followed. From Calais we went to the principal towns in the Netherlands; then to Holland, where we visited Rotterdam, The Hague, Amsterdam, Sardam, Utrecht, &c. &c. From Holland we followed, in an opposite direction, the course of the Rhine, and saw all the beautiful country on the banks of that noble river. We halted for a day or two at Coblentz and Frankfort. From Frankfort we went to Heidelberg, Carlsruhe, Baden, &c. &c., and entered Switzerland at Bale. From Bale our course was to Schaffhausen, Zurich, Wallenstadt, Zug, Art, Lucerne, Meyringhen, Interlachen, Grindlewald, Lauterbrun, Berne, Lausanne, Geneva, and Chamouny. From Chamouny we returned to Geneva, and from thence went to M[r]. S[t]. Bernard, Martigny, Bryg, and then across the Simplon, to Como. From Como we proceeded to Milan, Verona, Venice, Bologna, and

---

[1] Addressed: 'Hutches Trower Esq[r] / Unsted Wood / Godalming / Surry', and franked 'Ledbury December Fifteen'.

MS at University College, London.—*Letters to Trower*, LIX.
[2] Trower's letter is missing.

Florence. Florence was the extreme point of my tour. We then went to Leghorn, Pisa, Genoa and Turin. From Turin we crossed Mount Cenis, made the best of our way, through Lyons, to Paris. At Paris I stayed 3 weeks, arrived in London on the 8th of this month, and here on the 12th. I have given you a hasty sketch of the countries through which we have passed and shall only add that we met with scarcely any difficulty worth mentioning; were all very much pleased with the beauties of nature and of art which we have seen; and have been uniformly in good health.

At Geneva I was most hospitably received by my old friend Dumont, who is universally esteemed and respected by his countrymen—he accompanied us to Chamouny, and was adventurous enough to go up the Montanvert with me and my girls. At Coppet, which is near Geneva, I found the Duke de Broglie, whose acquaintance I had had the pleasure of making last autumn in London.[1] I do not know whether I ever mentioned him to you—he is married to Madme de Stael's daughter. He and the Baron de Stael, his brother in law, paid rather a long visit in England, and employed their time in seeing every thing worthy of notice. They are both clever men, but the Duke is particularly so. Political Economy is his favorite study, and I am happy to say that he is one of the best defenders of those principles which I think the correct ones I ever met with. I knew this before

---

[1] In his memoirs, the Duc de Bro- glie places his first meeting with Ricardo in March–April 1822. He was then in London, and he received a note from Miss Edge- worth, 'elle ne m'invitait pas, elle me sommait de me trouver le lendemain à deux heures chez M. Ricardo, où j'étais attendu'. Malthus was of the party and they had a long discussion: 'il va sans dire, pour ceux qui me con- naissent tant soit peu, que j'étais, de tous points, avec M. Ricardo'. Although he adds, 'j'aurai occa- sion de revenir sur mes rapports avec M. Ricardo', no more is to be found in the published memoirs; see *Souvenirs 1785–1870 du feu Duc de Broglie*, Paris, 1886, vol. II, pp. 236–7. Cp. above, p. 230.

I went abroad, but at Coppet I had an opportunity of hearing
him to great advantage, for on the day that I dined with him
there, M Sismondi, who has published a work on Political
Economy, and whose views are quite opposed to mine, was
on a visit at the Duke's house. M. Sismondi advanced his
peculiar opinions, which were combated by the Duke and
me—but the difficult part of the contest fell chiefly on the
Duke, who defended our common principles so well that it
appeared to me Monsr Sismondi had no chance with him.
Mons. S. indeed once or twice confessed he could not answer
the points objected to him, but he would never agree that
they could not be answered. Mr. Dumont, and Mad.^{me} de
Broglie, sat by as umpires, but they only interfered to see
fair play. Mad.^{me} is a very pleasing lady—she on this occasion
as well as on a subsequent one, for I met them again at Paris,
left a very pleasing impression of herself on my mind.
Notwithstanding my difference with Mons. Sismondi, on the
doctrines of Political Economy, I am a great admirer of his
talents, and I was very favorably impressed by his manners—
I did not expect from what I had seen of his controversial
writings to find him so candid and agreeable. M. Sismondi's[1]
takes enlarged views, and is sincerely desirous of establishing
principles which he conceives to be[2] most conducive to the
happiness of mankind. He holds that the great cause of the
misery of the bulk of the people in all countries[3] is the
unequal distribution of property, which tends to brutalize
and degrade the lower classes. The way to elevate man, to
prevent him from making inconsiderate marriages, is to give
him property, and an interest in the general welfare;—thus
far we should pretty well agree, but when he contends that
the abundance of production caused by machinery, and by

[1] 'views' is del. here.
[2] Replaces 'which are'.
[3] 'in all countries' is ins.

other means, is the cause of the unequal distribution of property, and that the end he has in view cannot be accomplished while this abundant production continues, he, I think, entirely misconceives the subject, and does not succeed in shewing the connection of his premises with his conclusion.[1]

At Paris I saw M. Say several times, but never found him much inclined to talk on the points of difference between us. I believe M. Say finds it difficult to converse on these subjects; his ideas do not flow in a sufficiently rapid course for conversation.[2] Speaking to the Duke de Broglie of M Say he observed that he did not appear to him to have the least notion of the doctrines of the New School,—that his notes in the French translation of my book shewed clearly that he did not know what the subject in dispute was. In France very little is understood about Political Economy, altho' they have some good writers on that subject. M. Garnier, the translator of Adam Smith, had completed an additional volume of notes for a new edition of Smith's work when he

---

[1] Sismondi gives some account of his discussion with Ricardo at Geneva in an article 'Sur la balance des consommations avec les productions', in *Revue Encyclopédique*, May 1824, p. 266: 'M. Ricardo, dont la mort récente a profondement affligé non pas seulement sa famille et ses amis, mais tous ceux qu'il a éclairés par ses lumières, tous ceux qu'il a échauffés par ses nobles sentimens, s'arrêta quelques jours à Genève dans les dernières années de sa vie. Nous discutâmes ensemble, à deux ou trois reprises, cette question fondamentale sur laquelle nous étions en opposition. Il apporta à son examen l'urbanité, la bonne foi, l'amour de la verité qui le dis-

tinguaient, et une clarté à laquelle ses disciples eux-mêmes ne se seraient pas attendus, accoutumés qu'ils étaient aux efforts d'abstraction qu'il exigeait d'eux dans le cabinet'. (The article was reprinted in Sismondi's *Nouveaux principes d'économie politique*, 2nd ed., Paris, 1827, vol. II, p. 408 ff.; cp. his *Études sur l'économie politique*, Paris, 1837, vol. I, p. 81 ff.)

[2] Say wrote of himself: 'Je n'ai presque jamais été content de ma conversation. Ma seconde pensée est en général meilleure que la première, et malheureusement c'est toujours celle-ci qui se produit dans la conversation.' (*Œuvres Diverses*, p. xv.) Cp. above, VI, 161.

died. This new edition has just been published,[1] and I had

an opportunity while in Paris, of seeing the additional volume, and of reading the lengthened remarks which he makes on my opinions. M Garnier is in every instance opposed to me when I attack his favorite author, but I am sure that the observations of the D de Broglie on Mr. Say's knowledge of my principles are equally applicable to M. Garnier. M. Say's brother, Louis Say, has written a thick volume of criticism on Adam Smith's, Malthus', his brother's, and my doctrines;—he quarrels with all our opinions, but shews pretty evidently that he knows very little about them.[2] M. Ganilh, a deputy, has also made remarks on my work, but I have not seen them—the Duke gave me no encouragement to read them.[3] At Geneva the 1st number of a review has been lately published, with the names of the writers of the different articles signed to them. There is an article, on two houses being better than one, by M. Rossi—another on law, by Dumont, one on Polit. Econ., by Sismondi, and several others. The Duke de Broglie told me that he had half promised to write an article on my book—if he does, I shall be eager to see it.[4] Besides the gentlemen I have mentioned

---

[1] In 6 vols.—Germain Garnier had died in 1821.

[2] *Considérations sur l'industrie et la législation, sous le rapport de leur influence sur la richesse des états, et examen critique des principaux ouvrages qui ont paru sur l'économie politique,* par Louis Say (de Nantes), Paris, Aillaud, 1822.

[3] Ch. Ganilh, *Des systèmes d'économie politique, de la valeur comparative de leur doctrines, et de celle qui parait la plus favorable aux progrès de la richesse. Seconde édition, Avec de nombreuses additions relatives aux controverses récentes de MM. Malthus, Buchanan, Ricardo, sur les points les plus importants de l'économie politique,* 2 vols., Paris, Treuttel et Würtz, 1821.

[4] *Annales de législation et d'économie politique,* No. 1, Nov. 1822. Rossi on 'Assemblée législative —Division en deux chambres'; Sismondi reviews John Barton's pamphlets on labour; Dumont 'Des présomptions anté-judiciaires'. After a second number the *Annales* were discontinued and the Duc de Broglie's article never appeared.

I met some very clever men, but had too little time to improve my very slight acquaintance with them.

In all the countries through which I travelled the people appeared to be enjoying ease and plenty. Provisions are everywhere uncommonly cheap, and nothing prevents those fine countries from making a most rapid progress in wealth and population, but the unsettled state of the governments. Nobody seems to think that the present order of things will continue long on its present footing, which damps all enter-prise and speculation that requires a few years to reap the fruits from them.

When I go to town I will make some inquiry after your papers,[1] I ought to have done it before I left England, but my time was so taken up that I never thought of it.—I wish you had expanded the subject into a pamphlet—it is not too late now, and I hope you will undertake it.

We shall I suppose have an active session of Parliament;— the continued distress of the agricultural class will make the country gentlemen clamorous for some measures to relieve them. They do not see that no relief can be afforded them, but at the expence of the other classes of the community— they must either withhold a part of the dividend of the stock-holder, or pay a fewer number of pounds than that which they have contracted to pay, to their mortgagees and other creditors. I do not wonder that a depreciation of the currency is a popular measure with landed gentlemen for it at once enables them to effect these two darling objects. Many of them conscientiously believe that there would be no injustice in it, and here I am at issue with them. In this county they are very favorable to an income tax, because, they say, it would reach the Stockholder, as if the stockholder was now exempted from his just share of the taxes. They talk of calling

[1] Probably Trower's letter on currency, cp. above, p. 201.

a county meeting at Hereford, where some such measure is to be recommended as a fit object for a petition to Parliament —if I am here I shall attend it, and shall be induced perhaps to try to prove the insufficiency of the proposed remedy.[1]

I have not yet read O'Meara's book[2]—I do not wonder at its having been read with great interest.

I hope Mrs. Trower and your family are well, pray make Mrs. Ricardo's and my kind regards to her——

Ever My dear Trower

Y.^{rs} truly

DAVID RICARDO

513. RICARDO TO MALTHUS[3]

Bromesberrow Place
Ledbury 16 Decr 1822

My Dear Malthus

A long time has elapsed since there has been any communication between us, and I take an early opportunity after my arrival in England to address a few lines to you, principally with a view of hearing some account of yourself and family, from your own pen.

I have been actively employed since we last met, for not only have I wandered about Switzerland, but I have been as far as Florence. In my way to Florence I deviated from the direct road to see Venice, and on my return from it I did the same thing in order to visit Genoa. Our journey has been an uncommonly prosperous one, for we have all enjoyed perfect health, and have met with few or no difficulties. My

---

[1] Cp. below, p. 266.
[2] *Napoleon in Exile; or A Voice from St. Helena. The Opinions and Reflections of Napoleon on the most important events of his Life and Government, in his own words,* by B. E. O'Meara, London, Simpkin and Marshall, 1822.
[3] MS at Albury.—*Letters to Malthus,* LXXXII.

companions as well as myself have very much enjoyed this tour.

When I was at Geneva I saw a good deal of our friend Dumont, who accompanied us to Chamouny, and returned with us to Geneva. At Coppet I met M. Sismondi. He, the Duke de Broglie, and I, had a long conversation on the points of difference between us,—the Duke took my side, but after a long battle we each of us, I believe, remained in the same opinion that we commenced the discussion in. M. Sismondi has left a pleasing impression on my mind. Mad^{me} de Broglie had a great deal of patience and forbearance—She is I think a very agreeable lady.

I stayed in Paris 3 weeks just previous to my return to England. M de Broglie and the Baron de Stael arrived there after me—I had the pleasure of seeing them 2 or 3 times. I was very much pleased with Mons. Gallois,[1] who made me acquainted with M. Destutt Tracy, a very agreeable old gentleman, whose works I had read with pleasure.[2] I do not entirely agree with him in his Political Economy,—he is one of Say's school:—there are nevertheless some points of difference between them. I saw Say several times, but our conversation did not turn much on subjects connected with Political Economy—he never led to those subjects, and I always fancied that he did not much like to talk upon them. His brother Louis Say has published a thick volume of re- marks upon Adam Smith's, his brother's, Your and my opinions. He is not satisfied with any of us. His principal object is to shew that wealth consists in the abundance of enjoyable commodities,—he accuses us all of wishing to heap up what we call valuable commodities, without any

[1] J.-A. G. Gallois (*ca.* 1755–1828), French politician and publicist, and a friend of Bentham.   [2] See above, I, 284–5.

regard to quantity, about which only the Polit. Economist should be anxious. I do not believe that any of us will plead guilty to this charge. I feel fully assured that I do not merit it should be made against me.

Mon.ʳ Garnier is dead, but previous to his death he had prepared an additional volume of notes for a new edition of his translation of the "Wealth of Nations," and which has lately been published. I had an opportunity of looking it over, and naturally turned to those places where he criticizes me. He has bestowed a good deal of space on his remarks upon my work, but they do appear to me quite irrelevant. Neither he nor M. Say have succeeded in at all understanding what my opinions are. Your name often occurs in this last volume—I believe he differed from you also, but I had not time to read the whole of his book.—

I hope you have been very industrious in my absence and that we shall soon see the new edition of your last work.[1] I am anxious to know how you deal with the difficult question of value—I shall read you with great interest and attention.—

I am sorry to find the agricultural distress continue—I was in hopes that it would have subsided before this time. I suppose we shall hear much on this subject next session of Parliament and that I shall be a mark for all the country gentlemen. There is not an opinion I have given on this subject which I desire to recall—I only regret that my adversaries do not do me justice, and that they put sentiments in my mouth which I never uttered. Dr. Copplestone in his article in the Quarterly Review[2] charges me with maintaining the absurd doctrine that the price of gold bullion is a sure test of the value of bullion and currency. A Mr. Paget has

[1] *Principles of Political Economy,* ed. 2, not published till 1836.

[2] April 1822, Art. XI, 'State of the Currency', pp. 243–4 and 249.

addressed a (printed) letter to me[1] in which I am accused of
holding the same opinion, and every body knows how
pertinaciously Cobbet persists in saying that I have always
done so.[2] I must fight my cause as well as I can, I know it
is an honest one (in spite of Mr. Western's insinuations[3]) and
if it be also founded in truth, and on correct views, justice
will be finally done to me.—

I arrived in London the beginning of last week,—I saw
Tooke for a few minutes, and was glad to hear from him that
he had been writing, and was nearly ready for the press.[4]
I have a very good opinion of his judgment, and of the
soundness of his views—he will, I think, from his practical
knowledge, throw much light on the question of the influence of an over supply or of an increased demand, without
a corresponding supply, on price.

I am now on a visit to my son. On the 27th I shall go to
Gatcomb for a week. From the 3^{d} to the 17 Jany I shall be
with Mrs. Austin at Bradley, Wottonunderedge; and from
the 17th to the 2^{d} feb^{y} with Mrs. Clutterbuck, Widcomb,
Bath. Where shall you pass your holidays? Is there any
probability of my seeing you at Bath? I should be glad to
meet you there.—

I read in the papers with much concern of the renewal of

[1] Thomas Paget, *A Letter addressed to David Ricardo, Esq.
M.P. on the True Principle of
Estimating the Extent of the Late
Depreciation in the Currency; and
on the Effects of Mr. Peel's Bill
for the Resumption of Cash Payments by the Bank,* London, for
the Author, 1822.
[2] See above, p. 123, n. 1; also
Cobbett's Weekly Register, 9 Nov.
1822, p. 338.
[3] See above, V, 526. Western's

Second Address to the Landowners
had been published while Ricardo
was on the Continent.
[4] Thomas Tooke, *Thoughts and
Details on the High and Low Prices
of the Last Thirty Years, Part I,
On the Alterations in the Currency,*
London, Murray, 1823 (Preface
dated January 1823). Parts II,
III and IV, which complete
the work, were published as
a separate volume in June 1823.

disturbances amongst the young men at the College[1]—I know how distressing to you such insubordination is, and greatly regretted that you should have been again exposed to it:—I hope that order was quickly restored.—

I saw Mr. Whishaw in London for a few minutes—I am not without hopes of seeing him at Mrs. Smith's at Easton Grey where I mean to pass 2 nights on my way to Bradley.—

Pray give Mrs. Ricardo's and my kind regards to Mrs. Malthus and believe me ever

Truly Yours

DAVID RICARDO

514. MARIA EDGEWORTH TO RICARDO [2]
[*Reply to 511.—Answered by 515*]

Black Castle

Navan—

Dec.ʳ 28ᵗʰ 1822

Welcome dear Sir most welcome you and your family back to England—I feel as if I had warm friends nearer to me—and though you cannot come now, I feel assured that at some future time you and yours will be in the midst of us at Edgeworths town—by the time we have done quarrelling about decking K Williams statue with orange ribbons, and by the time we throw no more bottles or rattles at our Lord Lieutenants—

How kind you were to take the trouble of writing me so

---

[1] The students had blown open with gunpowder the College gate and smashed the windows of the houses of the Professors (*The Times*, 19 Oct. 1822).

[2] Addressed: 'David Ricardo Esqʳᵉ MP / Gatcomb-Park / Glou- cester / England', redirected: 'A Austin Esq / Wottonunderedge / Gloucestershire'.

MS in *R.P.*—Extracts in *Economic Journal*, Sept. 1907, pp. 435–8.

long a letter—You who have so much to do—The result of your travels was delightful to me—and thank you for sparing me the pictures palaces, houses and churches (S.ᵗ Peters to boot) of which all commonplace travellers have given me an indigestion—not likely to be cured by Eustace—I wish I were in the midst of you for an hour or two to hear you talking over the *little incidents*—Even in Humboldt *the personal narrative* is always what interests me most.

The potato cause rests between us now I think on *a single point*—By the by it is only with those who argue well, *candidly,* and for *truth's sake,* that an argument can readily be brought to a single point.

☞ (Please to observe that as I take a good half of this compliment to my own dear self you need not be squeamish, but swallow the other half quietly and without making as many wry faces at it as an Irish woman at a fair makes when offered a glass of whiskey—Head averted—outstretched hand rejecting—"*Oh phoo!—Paw!—I never* touch it— How could you think!...nasty stuff!...*I!* of all people!— Never!—

"*But—see Judy—I sweeten the glass for you*"—replies the experienced tempter sipping his sweet half.—"Why *then!*" replies the lady and down goes the other half in pure politeness)

To return to the potato-cause—too near allied perhaps to the whiskey-evil. You handsomely promise that you would join me in defence of this root of plenty if I could prove to you that it has the essential advantage which other things equal sh.ᵈ as you justly observe decide the choice of a nations food viz—*Security*—*security* that the supply will be constant—or as I should add that the deficiency if it occur in the food chosen can with the greatest probability be supplied from other sources.—

I add this because it does not appear to me essential that the nation should confine itself to one species of food tho' *that* may be its staple supply—

Then I come to your *required 1st quality of storeability.* You see I set formally to work at the argument as your own dear Bentham or Mill would do.

I did send you in my last letter or will send you in my next a sample of potato flour, which was made by M. L'Asteyrie at Paris in the year 1803, which he gave to me and I have kept ever since—You will see that it is good—therefore you must admit that potato flour can be stored—and will be good at the end of 20 years.—

Then comes to be considered next the practicability of storing potatoes in this country upon a large scale and the cost of so doing—And here for the present I must pause in this part of the argument—I must wait till I have further information—I have written to Paris to M. L'Asteyrie to ask whether his process for storing potato flour has been carried on to any extent—and at what expense—Then I will inquire *how* or *if* it could be carried on in this country.

In the mean time I have this morning put some questions on the comparative advantages of corn and potatoes and I will give you the result in the answers of a clear headed man who has had much experience in farming land and in living among the lower classes of the people here so as to know their habits

1st Q^y—Do you think that there is more chance one year with another that a wheat crop should fail or a potato crop?

Answer—More chance of the wheat crop failing—and more chance that oats sh^d fail than potatoes—I reckon potatoes the most secure and profitable crop—

Q^y—If you had to feed this neighborhood, for ten

years to come and all depended on you, would you depend
on potatoes or corn

Answer Potatoes certainly—

Q^y—Are potatoes—corn and oats likely to fail the same
season, or from the same causes or on different seasons
and from different causes

Answer On different seasons and from different causes—

Q^y—Why?—

Answer—Because it is the *blast* which injures the wheat
and *that* does not touch the potato—It is the *frost* which
injures the potato and that does not touch the wheat or oats
—Damp which injures wheat and does not injure potatoes
is frequent in Ireland—

But suppose my Dr Sir that potatoes failed altogether
the corn being safe you would have a supply of food—Since
corn being a storeable commodity you might have as much
stored as you please or as calculation of chances showed to
be necessary—So that even if potatoes be not storeable we
have all that is required if we cultivate a certain proportion
of both potatoes and corn—

Corn must be cultivated otherwise there could not be
straw to supply manure for the potatoes—It is therefore only
necessary to settle the proportion between the two—

The distress which arose last year in Ireland it has been
asserted arose from the *general* failure of the potatoe crop.
But it could not have arisen from that cause for this plain
reason the failure was not general—Potatoes were plentiful
and good in many parts of this country though bad in others
—The distress as far as I have been able to learn arose partly
from want of communication and information between the
places where there was plenty and places where there was
scarcity—and partly from want of money. Where there was
sufficient information there was plenty of food appeared both

potatoes and corn, but there was actual want of money to
purchase this food or there was a want of exchangeable value
or commodities among the lower classes—All the money
they had went for rent and did not fully pay the rent—Remember I am now merely stating facts—

Where the potatoes *did* fail this, as I am informed arose
in great measure from the improvidence of the people who
did not plant them in time—

I admit that these habits of improvidence are to be taken
into account against the general security of the potatoe-crop
as national food—But though you may take it into account
you must only account it as an evil that should be remedied
not as a decisive argument against a positive good—You
would surely as a legislator seek for the cure of a moral evil
that admits of remedy instead of giving up in indolent
despair a good which is only rendered insecure by the bad
habits which you ought to reform.

From pretty extensive information which I have collected
I learn that potatoes are not only the most profitable crop but
that the proportion of profit is considerable.

In this County of Meath several farmers have after paying
rent and all expenses of manure labor &c one fourth clear
profit on their potatoes.

There is a difference of profit in favor of potatoes over
wheat of £3 per acre at an average—the wheat selling at 40s.
a barrel (*a barrel* being in this part of Ireland 20 stone—14 lbs.
weight to the stone—

Potatoes selling on an average at 5 shillings a barrel or 3d.
a stone—

This year the potato crop in *this* county being abundant
potatoes are selling in the market at $1\frac{1}{2}d.$ a stone—Wheat at
present selling from 18 to 23 shillings per barrel.

Now I am tired and so are you tired of me I am sure—

I must drop down at once from the affairs of the nation to my own paltry concerns.—Will you be so kind to advise me where I should place £300 which I want to place so as *of course* to have as high interest as is consistent with *security*— I sh^d wish to place it so that I might without diminution of the principal take up that principal in the course of a year or two—shall I buy into

> French 5 per Cents
>
> English 3 per Cents
>
> or   Spanish—I do-not-know-what-per Cents?

With affectionate remembrances and true esteem for Mrs. Ricardo and love to Mary and Birtha and to Harriet if she be with you I am

> Dear Sir
>
> Your grateful and much attached friend
>
> MARIA EDGEWORTH

Neither Fanny or Harriet are with me else their love w^d accompany mine—

I shall be at this place 3 weeks longer therefore if you should feel the good spirit move you to write to me within that time direct to me

> Black Castle
>
> Navan.

I am with a dear Aunt Ruxton—my fathers only surviving sister—very like him—76 years old and with as warm a heart and lively faculties as a woman of twenty—I am well and happy—Tell me that you are the same—A merry Christmas and a happy new year to you—I am old fashioned enough to wish my friends these good things

All well at home—I heard from them yesterday

515. RICARDO TO MARIA EDGEWORTH [1]
[*Reply to 514*]

Wottonunderedge
11 Jan.ʸ 1823

My Dear Miss Edgeworth

I hope that your venerable aunt Ruxton will long con- 11 Jan. 1823 tinue to enjoy life, and that you may, in many future visits to her, find no decay of the good feelings and lively faculties, which must now be a source of so much gratification to you.

I thank you much for your entertaining story. I was not so squeamish as Judy, but swallowed my portion of the agreeable draught you had mixed up for us, without affecting to make a wry face,—it went down very pleasantly.

On the subject of the potatoe, we are so far agreed that we both think security for a due supply of the principal food of the people of the first importance; but you add that if the supply of the principal food is not constant, you would be satisfied with a fair probability of the deficiency being supplied from other sources. So would I, but here you raise another important question, namely, whether there is any fair probability of a substitute being provided in case of a failure of the potatoe crop, when potatoes are the chief food of a people? The impossibility of providing any substitute is the stronghold of those who are enemies to the potatoe. They say, and say justly, 1ˢᵗ, that it is not to be supposed that any much greater quantity of grain will be provided than what is necessary for the average demand, and that if the demand should increase, in the degree in which it would do, if the bulk of the people, living before on potatoes, required all at once a large portion of corn, there could be no supply adequate to it, and consequently the price would rise enor-

---

[1] MS (in Ricardo's hand) in *R.P.*—Extracts in *Economic Journal*, Sept. 1907, pp. 438–41.

mously. 2dly, Supposing the first objection unfounded, and an adequate supply of corn procurable at its ordinary price, the people could not afford to buy it, and would be starving in the midst of plenty. As wages, in a potatoe country, would be regulated with reference to the average value of that root, the people would have no means, when the potatoe crop failed, of buying the dearer food. These objections appear to me conclusive against any dependence on substitutes, and therefore we are bound to consider what security we have for the regular supply of the potatoe itself, or of the storeable flour of potatoes of former years of plenty, to come in aid of a deficient crop. Before I say any thing on this question I wish to observe that the chief objection which the adversaries to the potatoe make against it, as the principal food of the people, is equally applicable to grain, which they think should be the principal food.

When the crop of grain fails, they say the people can have recourse to cheaper substitutes, such as potatoes. They can never make dear food a substitute for a cheap one, but they may make cheap food a substitute for a dear one. This argument would be just if at all times a supply of the cheap food could be obtained, but in a country where wheat constitutes the chief food of the people, no supply of potatoes ever is grown which can be adequate to feed the people if the crop of wheat fails. No more potatoes are grown than what are usually required in addition to the average crop of wheat. How then can potatoes be substituted for wheat? From whence are they to come? There is no limit to the rise in the price of potatoes which would take place under the circumstances supposed. In fact we should not substitute a cheap for a dear food, for this food which was ordinarily cheap would become as dear as wheat.

If it be said that when potatoes constitute the chief food

of a people, we might, by a failing crop, be deprived of $\frac{3}{4}$ of our usual supply, and that when wheat constitutes such chief food, we are never deprived of more than one fourth by a failing crop, I observe that this may be a good reason for preferring the wheat, because it is a more secure crop, and this brings us to the main question the comparative security afforded by the two species of food.

We will first consider the quality of storeability of the potatoe flour, for I like the formal method, after the manner of Bentham and Mill, whose example you have so well followed.

1. That Potatoe flour will keep for the requisite time appears to be proved by tolerably good evidence: for the present I will assume the proof to be satisfactory.

2. The next point is the cost of preparing and storing potatoe flour. If the cost be great it will come under one of the two objections usually and I think successfully made against substitutes, namely that we must never attempt in the case of a bad crop to substitute a dear for a cheap food. Potatoe flour might in such case be a good[1] provision against a failing crop of wheat but not against a failing crop of potatoes.

3. The next and most important point is the comparative hazard of a failure in the crops of wheat and potatoes. The answers to your questions given by the gentleman to whom you referred them, and in whose opinion you have confidence are very satisfactory and if confirmed by men of experience in the practical details, would remove all my objections to the potatoe, provided that the two following questions should be answered as satisfactorily. Q. What is the proportional difference of an average and a deficient crop of potatoes? The same question as to wheat. I fear, from the effects which I

---

[1] 'substitute' is del. here.

have observed of a failing crop of potatoes in Ireland, and a failing crop of wheat in this country that the answers would not be satisfactory for the potatoe. The gentleman to whom you referred your questions you say is a farmer, and I observe in his first answer he says "I reckon potatoes the most secure and profitable crop" Now this answer is a little suspicious. What is "secure and *profitable*" in the estimation of a farmer is not so in the estimation of a legislator. A short crop with a high price, its never failing attendant when general, is what a farmer wants—it is always most profitable to him and most secure in his sense of the word, but the legislator would commit a great error if he were guided by the same rule: He is to secure an abundant supply of food for the people and is to care nothing about profitable crops to the farmer.

It would never be necessary or profitable, I should suppose, to cultivate corn merely for the purpose of getting straw for manure. If straw be necessary, a large quantity will always be obtained from that portion of wheat, barley, and oats, raised for the higher and middling classes of the people. We should have a large quantity of these altho' the great bulk of the people should be always fed on potatoes.

What you state respecting the want of money to purchase food among the lower classes last year is precisely the evil which will accompany every failure of the potatoe crop in Ireland. No food is so generally cheap as potatoes,—if they fail what can they buy? Mr. Western and others asked in the last Session of Parliament how the distressed state of agriculture could proceed from abundance when there was an actual famine in Ireland? Nothing can be more satisfactorily explained,—wages regulated by potatoes will never be adequate to purchase wheat under any probable abundance of that grain.

Whether any part of the late failure of the potatoe crop proceeded from the improvidence of the people in not planting in time, is of no importance to the present question, for the same improvidence might and probably would exist if they depended on wheat for their sustenance. You will give me credit for wishing to have all the moral evils of society cured that are curable—I know of none which I am more anxious to see removed than the improvidence of the lower classes. In your country this improvidence is the great bar to the happiness of the people, I know of no country in which it is not. To provide a remedy for it appears to exceed the talents and skill of the legislator, for under the head of improvidence I class the early and inconsiderate marriages of which Malthus has so well treated. When once the labouring classes know how to regulate their own affairs, and understand and foresee the circumstances which are to procure them happiness, or plunge them in misery, we shall be very near atchieving all the good within our reach. It cannot be doubted that good laws and good government will do a great deal for us,—laws which shall afford prompt protection to person and property, which shall visit with immediate punishment the acts which they forbid, and which shall give the greatest encouragement to the acquiring of information amongst all classes of the people. But where am I running to? I am a great way from the potatoe question, I shall only revert to it to say once more that all my objections against the unbounded use of "this root of plenty" would vanish if we had an equal security against the failure of the crop that we have in regard to wheat.

I wish I could give you advice worth having respecting the investment of your £300. I can only say that if your case were mine I would rather buy French 5 pc^t than English 3 pc^t In buying either you will of course be subject to a loss of principal, for they may both fall considerably in price. I would not buy Spanish stock notwithstanding the tempting cheapness of price. If you know any banker or merchant of reputation that would take your money at 4 pc.^{t} I should recommend that mode of disposing of it. You may buy India Bonds but I dare say they bear a high premium. Exchequer bills pay little interest, and are rather troublesome, for they become due, and must be renewed if they are not paid off.

We are all (6 of us) staying with my daughter Mrs. Austin, and are as happy as the kindest people and the possession of every comfort can make us. We passed a delightful fortnight with my son and Harriet they are not with us here. On friday next we go for a fortnight to, not the least beloved of our beloved children, Mrs. Clutterbuck, after that I shall be prepared to meet all the charges and vituperation of the landed gentlemen against me, who are strangely infatuated as to the causes of the distress which they are suffering—

Mrs. Ricardo and the rest of the inmates of this house desire to be most kindly remembered to you.

We passed 2 days with our excellent friend Mrs. Smith— we had not been at her house since its late agreeable master was laid in the grave—we missed (and lamented the loss of) our poor friend every moment that we passed at Easton Grey. Our visit was a melancholy one, yet it had in it much to sooth and interest us. Mrs. Smith was never in such full possession of

[The end of the page, with the signature, is cut off.]

516. RICARDO TO MILL [1]

Wottonunderedge 14 Jan 1823

My Dear Sir

Immediately after seeing you in London I proceeded, 14 Jan. 1823
as I told you I should, to Bromesberrow Place, where I
passed a fortnight in the most agreeable manner possible.
Every mark of kindness and affection was lavished on me
by the kind master and mistress.—I had a room to myself to
pass my mornings in, I had none of the cares which annoy
me at home, of master, and enjoyed a pure air and a beautiful
country. What more can a man desire? I found Mrs. Osman
in very poor spirits. During our absence abroad she had
lost her mother and had not yet recovered the shock
which that sudden event had occasioned. Our presence
was of great service to her—she by degrees recovered her
spirits and we had the satisfaction of leaving her much
better.

From Bromesberrow we went to Gatcomb for 5 days but
they were the most unpleasant of any that I ever passed in
that spot. The house was cold and dismantled and I was
incessantly employed during the time I was there in paying
bills, settling accounts and talking to tenants. I was rejoiced
when this necessary but irksome business was at an end; it
was the more heavy from having been long neglected: I had
not been at Gatcomb before for nearly a twelvemonth. We
were all I believe glad to turn our backs on this our favorite
residence although the next place we were going to could
not fail to give us many painful feelings: it was to Easton
Grey the residence of Mrs. Smith. Every thing there recalled
to our recollection the benevolence, the chearfulness, and the
excellent social qualities of its late master. We found Mrs.

---

[1] MS in Mill-Ricardo papers.

14 Jan. 1823 Smith in good health, living quite alone in her large house, and seldom seeing any of her neighbours. The first sight of us reminded her strongly of the loss she had sustained, but she soon recovered herself. If I had to point out an example of a woman's conducting herself with great propriety and good sense under a heavy misfortune, it would be Mrs. Smith. She feels, and feels strongly the loss of her excellent husband but does all she can to get over these feelings and to make the best use in her power of the resources that are left to her. She finds consolation in books and business, for she attends to the details of a farm which used to afford amusement and employment to Mr. Smith. We stayed with Mrs. Smith 2 nights and quitted her with feelings of increased goodwill and affection.

Our next visit was to a very different house, from the house of mourning, which Mrs. Smith's might in some respects be called, we went to one in which mirth, and good humor, appear to have taken up their abode, I mean Bradley, the residence of Mrs. Austin, where we now are. The chearfulness of Mrs. Austin is delightful, and seems to communicate itself to every thing around her. She is one of those happy and I cannot help adding wise beings who repels all melancholy and desponding feelings and ever views the affairs of life under the most chearing aspect—she courts chearfulness, and it seems to come at her call. Her husband is in much better health than he was, and they have 4 lovely children. Our visit here will end on friday, when we shall go for a fortnight to Mrs. Clutterbuck's. This little journey to the houses of my married children, has, and will be, very agreeable to me—it is delightful to see them all happy, and all deserving of being so.

Yesterday I believe the Political Economy Club met,— I conclude so from a passage in a letter which I received from

14 Jan. 1823

Malthus,[1] otherwise I should have expected that the meeting had been on the monday preceding, for I always thought that our day was the first monday in the month.

If the next meeting should be on the 2^{d} monday in february pray let me know, as it will induce me to stay at Widcomb 2 days longer. I wish to be present at the next meeting, and shall be in town on Saturday the 1st if it be the first monday in the month—I shall not come till monday the 3^{d} if it be the 2^{d}.[2]

Mr. Coke and Mr. Wodehouse must be very much mortified at the success of Cobbett at their Norfolk meeting. I confess I am astonished at it. It reflects no great honour on the assembly to pass such resolutions, and will be used as an argument by Anti-reformers against the extension of the suffrage. If any of the speakers at the meeting had exposed the dishonesty of the objects for which the petition asked I do not believe they would have been adopted. Every body seems afraid of Cobbett.[3]

I have been looking over the debates in Parliament on former occasions when Agricultural distress was the subject of them. In Western's and Brougham's speeches in 1816 I find opinions totally at variance with those which they now maintain. From Western's I have made some curious extracts. This subject of distress will be often brought under discussion, I suppose, next session and such men as Western, Atwood, and Lethbridge will think they have cause for triumph over me—I feel confident they have none and if they

[1] Malthus's letter is missing.
[2] The Club met on 3 February and Ricardo was present. (*Political Economy Club, Minutes of Proceedings, 1821–1881*, p. 56.)
[3] The meeting at Norwich on 5 January which was to be addressed by the two members for the county was taken over by Cobbett and in the uproar adopted his petition for the cancellation of debt. (See *Coke of Norfolk and his Friends*, by A. M. W. Stirling, London, 1912, pp. 481–4.)

14 Jan. 1823 do not misrepresent what I have said, which they and others invariably do, nothing will be found to have occurred to overturn any of the principles for which I have contended.—

I hope Tooke is making great progress with his book— he is a very useful and able ally.

Mrs. Ricardo and the rest of your friends here desire to be kindly remembered to you.

Ever

Y.^{rs} truly

DAVID RICARDO

James Mill Esqre

517. RICARDO TO TROWER [1]

Wedcomb House, Bath
30 Jany 1823

My Dear Trower

30 Jan. 1823 Before Parliament meets it will be wise in me to discharge my debt to you, and to assure you that I felt great gratification at the receipt of your letter.[2] It was very kind of you to write to me so soon after the receipt of mine. I was very desirous of hearing from you, and am glad to find that you are well, and as usual in the road of improvement, storing your mind with useful knowledge.

In my last I told you I intended to go to the Hereford meeting, but I could not be at it on account of the late period to which it was postponed. Cobbett as usual asserted false-hoods respecting my opinions; and the landed gentlemen being strongly inclined to confiscate a part of the property of the fundholder sought to cover their projects with a shew of justice—they of course will magnify the effects of Mr. Peel's

[1] Addressed: 'Hutches Trower Esqr / Unsted Wood / Godalming'.　MS at University College, London.—*Letters to Trower*, LX.
[2] Trower's letter is missing.

bill, and will admit no other cause for their distress but the 30 Jan. 1823 augmented value of the currency.[1] I am rather singularly circumstanced—agreeing as I do with the reformers, on the subject of parliamentary reform, I can not agree with them that taxation and bad government has been the cause of our present difficulties: I believe that under the best possible government, and without taxes, we might have been involved in similar troubles. Still less can I support the doctrines of the new converts to reform, who attribute our distress to every cause but the right one, and who not being governed by principle will quit the cause of reform the moment that the times mend. I on the contrary am a reformer on principle, and whether we get rid of our difficulties or continue to struggle under them shall advocate a reform of the house of commons, because I think it would very materially contribute to good government and to the happiness of the people. I am sorry that you do not agree with me on this subject,—the objection you make, that reformers are not agreed in what they want, is not I think a weighty one,—all real reformers

---

[1] The meeting at Hereford, on 17 Jan. 1823, had been called to consider a petition to Parliament for the relief of 'the unparalleled and daily increasing distress of the agricultural interest of the country'. Cobbett was present and said: 'It was Mr. Ricardo who had persuaded the ministers that the landlords and tenants were doing so well—it was he who repeated the old Scotch doctrine of Adam Smith, that all taxes fell on the consumer; this doctrine might be very well as applied in several instances to persons in trade, but not so to real property. The error was in laying down the proposition at all in an extensive way, for it nowhere universally applied....

Ministers, proceeding on this false foundation, were resolved not to alter the currency —not to make bank-notes a legal tender'. Another speaker, the Rev. Mr Smithies, 'agreed that much of the existing evil might be traced to the calculating economy of Mr. Ricardo, and the cold-blooded sophistry of Mr. Peregrine Courtenay; and also that, in its consequences, an adherence to the system would transfer their estates to the Jew-jobbers of Change-alley.' The petition adopted prayed for an investigation into the variations of the currency with reference to the adjustment of debts. (*The Times*, 20 Jan. 1823.)

are agreed on the principle: they want a house of commons which shall speak the sentiments of the people, and are willing to agree to any details which shall not interfere with that important principle. Lord Folkestone has become a staunch reformer, and more nearly agrees with the views which I think correct than any man in the H of Commons, Burdett and Hobhouse not excepted.[1] You will soon have an opportunity of giving your opinion on this interesting question at the County meeting of Surry—I hope you will speak there— I know beforehand that I shall applaud every thing you shall say on Agricultural distress, but I shall condemn your opinions on Reform.[2] Strange that you should like a House of Commons which represents only the interests of a very small fraction of the people!

Thinking as you do that much service would be done to the science of Political Economy by an examination at some length of the different systems advocated by Malthus and me, why do you not undertake it? I cannot help thinking that you have already prepared the materials for such a work, because you have given a great deal of consideration to the subject and are in the habit of making notes and remarks on every book which greatly interests you. You ought to let us have such a work from your pen. Without half the pretensions which you have to offer, I boldly ventured, and as I have had no reason to repent it why are you not encouraged to follow my example?

The die appears to be cast, and war will immediately recommence in Europe. One would have thought it impossible that France would have exposed herself to so much risk, as a war with Spain, against principles of freedom, must involve

---

[1] Lord Folkestone (1779–1869), M.P. for Salisbury, afterwards third Earl of Radnor.

[2] The meeting took place on 10 Feb. 1823. Trower did not speak.

her in. I hope her defeat will follow, and that the consequences of this rash step may be the establishing of *real* representative Governments all over Europe. I wish to approve of the conduct of our ministers, and as far as it is yet known it appears to have been firm and judicious. I hope we shall keep out of the contest, but it will be a difficult task to do so if the war should be of long duration.

You have I conclude read the pamphlet in defence of Government.[1] Many of the points are well put, but how miserably the question of the Sinking fund is handled. A tolerably good case may be made out in favor of the Sinking fund, but the author of this pamphlet has taken up untenable ground, and is constantly contradicting himself, and exposing his ignorance. What sort of a Chancellor of the Exchequer will Robinson make? He is a good tempered man, a tolerable political economist, and well inclined to liberal principles of trade, but he is a very timid man. He will never I fear dare to act on enlarged views of policy, but will like his predecessors be always for conciliating particular interests. I did not like what he and Lord Liverpool said lately at a dinner in the city given by the Shipping interest—I am sure they did not speak their real sentiments.[2] I am surprised that

---

[1] *Administration of the Affairs of Great Britain, Ireland, and their Dependencies, at the Commencement of the Year 1823. Stated and Explained under the Heads of Finance, National Resources, Foreign Relations, Colonies, Trade, and Domestic Administration,* [Anon.] London, Hatchard, 1823. Cp. above, V, 250.

[2] At the Anniversary Dinner of the Ship-owners' Society, 12 Dec. 1822, Lord Liverpool said: 'We owe our security to our navy, and we owe our navy to that system of navigation laws under which our country has so long acted with so much advantage to her best interest'; it was in the application of those laws, and 'not by the adoption of fanciful and impracticable theories', that England could find her security. Robinson, still President of the Board of Trade, 'was deeply impressed by the truth of the opinions just expressed by his noble friend'. (*The Times,* 13 Dec. 1822.)

Huskisson was not appointed to the office of Chancellor of the Exchequer, every body expected that he would be Van's successor.[1]

There has been a talk, I believe nothing more, amongst ministers about restoring the two standards, but I am assured all thoughts of it are relinquished.—Lord Liverpool is very decidedly against it. I am sorry to hear that Huskisson is not much disinclined to it. I have lately seen a letter from Lord Grenville on this subject to one of his friends, in which he expresses himself strongly and ably in favor of the single standard. His Lordship's opinions on the subject of the currency appear to me to be very sound. Lord Lansdowne I have been informed is inclined to the two standards—Baring I suspect is the ringleader in this conspiracy.—

I leave Bath on Saturday next—I hope I shall soon see you in London.

Pray give Mrs. Ricardos and my kind remembrances to Mrs. Trower and believe me My dear Trower

Y^{rs} truly

DAVID RICARDO

---

[1] Huskisson had been appointed President of the Board of Trade and Treasurer of the Navy in succession to Robinson; but he did not obtain a seat in the Cabinet till the autumn of 1823. 'Canning wanted Huskisson for his Chancellor of the Exchequer, and he was so far right that Huskisson has no competitor for that situation; but although Lord Liverpool values Huskisson's talents very highly, bringing him into the cabinet was out of the question. The *louche* origin of Huskisson, the reports afloat as to the early part of his life, and his admirable pamphlet on the bullion question in 1812 [should be 1810], which the monied men of the City will never forgive him, are insuperable obstacles to his promotion to a seat in the cabinet' (J. L. Mallet's MS Diary, entry of 16 Jan. 1823, when the changes in the Administration were about to take place. On the alleged Jacobinism of Huskisson in his youth, see the 'Biographical Memoir' [by E. Leeves] prefixed to his *Speeches*, 1831, vol. 1, p. 9 ff.).

518. MᶜCULLOCH TO RICARDO [1]
[*Answered by* 520]

Edinburgh 21ˢᵗ March 1823

My Dear Sir

I was extremely gratified on perceiving you had returned
from the Continent, where I had been told you meant to
reside for the winter. In this case I confess my gratification
did not arise entirely from disinterested motives: I was
certainly well pleased that you should be in the H of Commons to support the cause of sound principle and policy; but
I was better pleased with the prospect it gave me of seeing you
in the end of April or the beggining of May when I mean to
make a short trip to London where I have never hitherto been.

I hope you will be satisfied with what I have been dooing
since I had the pleasure of hearing from you—I took a private
opportunity to send you a little while ago a separate copy
of a general article on Political Economy I have written for
the Supplement—Being much occupied at the time with the
composition of my Lectures, I did not get so much pains
and consideration bestowed on it as I could have wished; but
I think that in some respects I have set the subject in rather
a new point of view, and that it may be of some use—If it
be fortunate enough to meet with your approval I shall be
satisfied—But if there be, and I am sure there must, points
on which your opinions differ from those I have expressed,
I beg you will have the goodness to state them, that I may
reconsider them—

Mr. Blakes pamphlet[2] has astounded me—I thought that
the question of depreciation had been one of the *res judicata*

---

[1] Addressed: 'David Ricardo Esq
M.P. / Upper Brook Street / London'.
   MS in *R.P.—Letters of MᶜCulloch to Ricardo,* XVI.

[2] William Blake, *Observations on
the Effects produced by the Expenditure of Government during the
Restriction of Cash Payments,*
London, Murray, 1823.

of Political Economy—one of the few points about which there neither was nor could be a controversy—I agree with Mr. Blake that the first effect of a sudden expenditure on the part of government is to depress the exchange and to cause an export of bullion, provided bullion be at the time the most profitable article of export—But why did the exchange become unfavourable with America and those countries in which we had no extraordinary expenditure? Besides is it not quite visionary to suppose that any expenditure on the part of government could raise the value of bullion in this country for six or seven years without occasioning its importation? Mr. B says (p 8) that when the exchange fell to 10 per cent the transmitting of bullion to the Continent would gain a profit of 8 per cent by selling the bills drawn against it; but they would have done the same with any other species of produce; and there is hardly any whose price would have been so suddenly raised in the home market by exportation as bullion—Much of what Mr. B says about the effect of war expenditure seems also to be very ill-founded. But in judging of questions of exchange I always entertain a very great distrust of my own powers, being totally ignorant of all practical details on the subject; and for this reason I should esteem it as a most particular favour if you could find time to give me a few remarks on Mr. Blakes pamphlet—If his views are just they ought to be still more widely disseminated; but if, as I believe you will think, they are false, their fallacy ought to be exposed—

I finish my Lectures tomorrow—I have had sixty students, which I consider good encouragement indeed—I believe they have been pretty well pleased[1]—

---

[1] '*Course of Political Economy.*— Mr. M'Culloch will commence his Course of Public Lectures on Political Economy, in the Clyde Street Hall, on Tuesday, the 14th. of January, at three o'clock. The Lectures will be continued on alternate days; and will be con-

I have written an article for the forthcoming Review on East and West India Sugars which I hope you will approve— It appears to me to be a very important question.[1] I am with the greatest respect and esteem

My Dear Sir

Ever truly yours

J. R. M^cCULLOCH

519. MARIA EDGEWORTH TO RICARDO [2]

Extract of a Letter from Paris

"Comte Lasterye assures me that his process for drying, keeping, and storing Potatoe flour has succeeded and been carried to great extent—that it may be preserved in casks, in bins, in jars, or piled in Store-rooms with fewer precautions and at less expence than common wheaten flour because it is neither liable to fermentation nor to be destroyed by vermin—That he has some by him, perfectly sound and good, which he prepared in the early part of the Revolution"

Edgeworths Town
March 22^d 1823

My dear Sir,

Above in invisible ink is the answer which I have at last received to my inquiries respecting the storing of potato flour—But probably Mr. Robinson[3] and many others will not leave you leisure now to think of potato flour.

We follow with ardent and intense interest all the debates in the houses of parliament in which you take a part—and all those on which the fate of this country depend.

---

cluded early in April.—Mr. M'-Culloch's Private Class for Conversations and Exercises on the Subjects treated in the Lectures will commence nearly at the same time.—Buccleugh Place, 14th. Dec. 1822.' (Advt. in the *Scotsman*, 14 Dec. 1822.)
[1] *Edinburgh Review*, Feb. 1823, Art. X; McCulloch supported the proposal to equalise the English import duties on East and West India sugars, which discriminated in favour of West India. See Ricardo's speech on the question, 22 May 1823, above, V, 297 ff.
[2] MS in *R.P.*—The opening quotation is written in pale ink not in Miss Edgeworth's handwriting.
[3] The new Chancellor of the Exchequer.

I am glad you were in the main pleased with Mr. Robin-
sons opening speech[1]—I thought it the clearest and ablest
finance speech I ever read.

Look at the trial of the Dublin rioters[2]—reported by Green
—published by Milliken in Dublin—of course to be had
from Hanlet or any Dublin bookseller—Those who heard
the speeches of Plunket North and Bushe assure me that
there never was a more correct report—

If you could find time I wish you w^{d} look into the
"Memoires sur le dixhuitieme siecle et sur la revolution
Francaise". Memoires "de l'Abbe Morellet"[3]—

There are many sensible observations in this book on the
freedom of commerce—on the forming the constituent
assembly—and on the causes of the French revolution—
Very interesting now when we shall probably go over much
of the same work in Spain and probably in another revolution
in France.

Bentham and Mill will not agree with Morellet that the
right of the people of any nation to legislate or to share in
legislating depends on possessing property in land.

I dare not take up more of your time—Accept the united
esteem and affection of your 3 friends and cousins—and keep
continually in your head your good intention of coming to
visit Ireland.—

Love to all your family
Believe me Affec^{y} your friend
MARIA EDGEWORTH

[1] On 21 February.
[2] The trial of Dublin Orange-
men for riot, which ended in their
acquittal.
[3] *Mémoires de l'abbé Morellet, de*
l'Académie française, sur le dix-
huitième siècle et sur la Révolution;
précédés de l'éloge de l'abbé
Morellet, par M. Lémontey, Paris,
Ladvocat, 1821, 2 vols.

520. RICARDO TO McCULLOCH [1]
[*Reply to 518*]

London 25 March 1823

My Dear Sir

I had just finished reading your essay "Political   25 March 1823
Economy" for the Supplement to the Encyclopedia [2] when
I received your letter. If you had written two days later our
letters would have crossed on the road for I should not have
lost any time in expressing to you the pleasure which I felt
in the perusal of your excellent article. Besides a valuable
historical sketch, you have given so clear an exposition of all
the important principles of the science that you have left
nothing for me to wish for. The objections which have been
made to the doctrines concerning Value, Rent, Profit, Wages,
Demand, and Markets have been perspicuously and fairly
pointed out, and most satisfactorily answered. My only
regret is that the Essay is not published independently of the
work in which it will appear: it will I fear not meet with so
numerous a class of reader in the Supplement as its merits
would ensure if it were a separate publication. [3]

I am happy to find by your letter that you are about to
visit London—I have long desired to know you personally,
and to express by word of mouth to you the esteem and
respect which I entertain for you. I quite agree in opinion
with you about Mr. Blake's publication. He shewed it to me
before he printed it, and I used the privelege of a friend in
freely giving him my sentiments upon it: he was kind enough
to give to my remarks the most attentive consideration, but
he at last came to the conclusion that he had taken a correct

[1] Addressed: 'J. R McCulloch
Esq[r] / Edinburgh'.
MS in British Museum.—*Letters
to McCulloch*, XXXVI.
[2] Vol. VI, pp. 216–78.

[3] McCulloch reprinted the article,
with some additions, as *The
Principles of Political Economy*,
Edinburgh, 1825.

view of the subject. Mr. Blake appears to me to agree with those whose opinions he attacks without being himself aware of it. He agrees with them that paper money should agree with the standard whatever variations in value that standard may undergo:—he agrees that in our case the restriction bill which he says ought never to have been enacted, prevented that equalization of value:—he agrees that if the ministers had had to raise loans from 1800 to 1815, and there had been no restriction bill, they would have raised sums, much less in nominal amount, than what they actually did raise, and consequently for those loans we should now have had a much less nominal sum to pay for the dividends on such loans. In what then does Mr. Blake differ from us? In the meaning of the word depreciation, and as to the fact whether the difference between gold and paper was owing to a rise in gold, or a fall in paper. In both these points he appears to me to be wrong: depreciation as applied to money must be understood to mean relative lowness as compared with the standard, and nothing else, and therefore money may be depreciated although it should rise in absolute value. As to the second point whether in point of fact gold really rose or paper really fell, there is no criterion by which this can be positively ascertained but all the appearances are against Mr. Blake. If money continued of the same value whilst gold rose, why did commodities rise also? Mr. Blake's solution is most un-satisfactory—he attributes it to an increased Government expenditure. I should deny that an increased Gov.^{t} expenditure could raise for any length of time the prices of those commodities even for which Govern.^{t} has a demand, but it is impossible to attribute to it the prices of all other things for which Gov.^{t} has no demand. When £120 of the money in England is worth only £100 of the money of Hamburgh or of France all having been before of the same value it is

impossible I think to deny either that Hamburgh and French
money have risen or English money fallen. Mr. Blake denies
both propositions. The case you put of America is unanswerable. You need not I assure you have the l[east]
distrust of your judgment respecting exchanges, because
you are unacquainted with the practical details on the subject,
the theory, as you know, is very simple, and practice is in
strict conformity with it.

I am glad to hear that your lectures have been successful—
you are doing a great deal of good in the world—I wish I was
as usefully employed, but my powers of writing or speaking
are very limited. There have been several good pamphlets
on the East and West India sugar question—these pamphlets
shew how much way the good doctrines are making.¹ I have
no doubt you will give us a good article on the subject.—
I have at different times seen some good papers from your
pen in the Scotsman—It gives me the greatest satisfaction
that we so exactly agree on all the great questions respecting
commerce and Political Economy.—

I am with great esteem
Truly Y^{rs}
DAVID RICARDO

521. RICARDO TO GOLDSMID²

Upper Brook Street
4 April 1823

My Dear Sir

The approbation which you express of the sentiments
which I endeavoured to deliver to the House, a few evenings

¹ Lists of such pamphlets are given by McCulloch in *Edinburgh Review*, Feb. 1823, Art. X, and in *Literature of Political Economy*, p. 93.

² MS in the possession of Lt.-Col. O. E. d'Avigdor Goldsmid. I am indebted to Miss D. Jessel for a transcript.—A freely edited version was published in *Memoir of*

ago, in favour of religious liberty,[1] gives me great satisfaction. It appears to me a disgrace to the age we live in, that a part of the inhabitants of this country are still suffering under disabilities imposed upon them in a less enlightened time. The Jews have most reason to complain, for they are frequently reproached for the dishonesty, which is[2] the natural effect of the political degradation in which they are kept. I cannot help thinking that the time is approaching when these ill-founded prejudices against men, on account of their religious opinions, will disappear, and I should be happy if I in any way should be a humble instrument in accelerating their fall.

I carry my principles of toleration very far;—I do not know how, or why any line should be drawn, and am prepared to maintain that we have no more justifiable ground for shutting the mouth of the Atheist than that of any other man. I am sure it will be shut, for no man will persevere in avowing opinions which bring on him the hatred and ill will of a great majority of his fellow men.

With best wishes

I remain

Very truly Yours

DAVID RICARDO

Sir Francis Henry Goldsmid, London, Kegan Paul, 1879, pp. 91–2, but omitted from the 2nd ed., 'revised and enlarged', 1882; reprinted in *Letters to Trower,* LXI. A more accurate reprint from the MS in 'Selections from Sir I. L. Goldsmid's Correspondence and other Papers relating to the History of the Admission of the Jews of England to Parliament', in *Transactions of the Jewish Historical Society of England,* vol. III (1903), pp. 130–1.

The recipient of the letter was Isaac Lyon Goldsmid (1778–1859) the champion of the emancipation of the Jews, partner of Mocatta and Goldsmid, bullion brokers.

[1] On 26 March; above, V, 277 ff.

[2] In *Memoir of Sir F. H. Goldsmid* this is changed into 'reproached with following callings which are'.

522. RICARDO TO MILL [1]

Upper Brook Street
12 April 1823

My dear Mill

My poor sister[2] was very anxious to have my brother
to attend her in her confinement, and as she had much
exceeded the time she reckoned on, he was obliged to remain
much longer than he expected in London. His stay here had
very much affected his health, and the unfortunate result of
his attendance has nearly overpowered him. He is so very
unwell that I think it right to accompany him to Brighton—
we shall go there this day—I think of returning in the middle
of next week.—My sister had very nearly died during her
last confinement, which made her so anxious to have my
brother now, who had attended her when she had her first
two children, but was too ill to do the same last year. She
has left 4 children the eldest of which was only 3 last January.
I am sure that my brother did every thing for her that skill
and affection could prompt—he is persuaded so himself, yet
he feels most acutely the afflicting termination of his anxiety.
I hope the quiet and good air of Brighton will speedily
restore him to the state in which he was in before.—

Mrs. Osman has been agitated by the late occurrence, and
does not get on as I could wish—her pulse was very high
all day yesterday.

I spoke to Mr. Bankes[3] concerning Mr. Peacock's[4] admission to the library of the British Museum;—his name

---

[1] Addressed: 'James Mill Esq! / 1
Queen Square / Westminster /
London'. Franked by Ricardo:
'Brighton April Thirteen 1823'.
   MS in Mill-Ricardo papers.
[2] Esther Wilkinson, died 10 April
1823.

[3] Henry Bankes, M.P. for Corfe
Castle, one of the trustees of the
British Museum.
[4] Thomas Love Peacock, the
novelist, was Mill's colleague as
Assistant Examiner at the East
India House.

will be entered, and he has only to shew himself at the Museum, after monday next, to be admitted.

I thank you for your article on Prison Discipline[1]— I shall take it with me to Brighton.—

I rejoice at your promotion.—I hope your determination respecting John may prove to have been a good one.[2]

Ever Y^{rs}

DAVID RICARDO

Brighton, Sunday

I very foolishly put this letter in my pocket, and brought it here instead of sending it to you from Brook Street

523. RICARDO TO MALTHUS[3]

London 29 Apr! 1823

My Dear Malthus

After the most attentive consideration which I can give to your book,[4] I cannot agree with you in considering labour, in the sense in which you use it,[5] as a good measure of value. Neither can I discover, exactly, what connexion the constant labour necessary to produce the wages and profits on a commodity, has with its value. If it be a good measure for one commodity, it must be for all commodities, and as well as valuing wheat by the constant quantity of labour necessary

---

[1] In *Supplement to the Encyclopaedia Britannica.*
[2] Mill had been promoted First Assistant Examiner of India Correspondence. At the same time he had decided against sending John to Cambridge and had obtained for him an appointment in the Examiner's office. (Bain, *James Mill,* p. 207; J. S. Mill, *Autobiography,* p. 81.)

[3] MS at Albury.—*Letters to Malthus,* LXXXIII.
[4] *The Measure of Value Stated and Illustrated with an Application of it to the Alterations in the Value of the English Currency since 1790,* London, Murray, 1823.
[5] Viz. 'the labour which commodities will command'; *Measure of Value,* page v.

to produce the particular quantity given to the workman, 29 April 1823
together with the profit of the farmer on that particular
quantity, I might value cloth or any other thing by the same
rule.

I know indeed that I might make out a table precisely such
as yours,[1] in which the only alteration would be the word
cloth, instead of the word wheat, and you would probably
then ask me whether your principle were not of universal
application. I should answer that it contains in it that radical
objection, which you make, against the proposed measure of
your opponents. You may, if you please, arbitrarily select
labour as a measure of value, and explain all the science of
Political Economy by it, in the same way as any other man
might select gold, or any other commodity, but you can no
more connect it with a principle, or shew its invariability,
than he could. Let me suppose that cloth could not be made

[1] The following is a portion of Malthus's 'Table illustrating the invariable
Value of Labour and its Results':

1.	2.	3.	4.	5.	6.	7.	8.	9.
Quarters of Corn produced by Ten Men, or varying Fertility of the Soil.	Yearly Corn Wages to each Labourer, determined by the Demand and Supply.	Advances in Corn Wages, or variable Produce commanding the Labour of Ten Men.	Rate of Profits under the foregoing Circumstances.	Quantity of Labour required to produce the Wages of Ten Men under the foregoing Circumstances.	Quantity of Profits on the Advances of Labour.	Invariable Value of the Wages of a given Number of Men.	Value of 100 Quarters of Corn under the varying Circumstances supposed.	Value of the Product of the Labour of Ten Men under the Circumstances supposed.
150 qrs.	12 qrs.	120 qrs.	25 pr.Ct.	8	2	10	8.33	12.5
150	13	130	15.38	8.66	1.34	10	7.7	11.53
150	10	100	50	6.6	3.4	10	10	15
140	12	120	16.66	8.6	1.4	10	7.14	11.6
140	11	110	27.2	7.85	2.15	10	9.09	12.7
130	12	120	8.3	9.23	0.77	10	8.33	10.8
130	10	100	30	7.7	2.3	10	10	13

(*Measure of Value*, p. 38)

in less than two years, the first line of my table must be altered, and the figures would stand in the following order

$$150 \quad 100 \quad 25 \text{ pc}^{\text{t}} \quad 7\tfrac{1}{2} \quad 2\tfrac{1}{2} \quad 10 \quad 10 \quad 15.$$

They would do so because 10 pieces of cloth, would, with the accumulation of profit for 2 years, be of the same value as a commodity, the result of the same quantity of labour, which could be produced in 2 years.—I do not know how you will treat this objection but in my opinion it is fatal to your whole theory.[1]

I have the same objection to your measure which I have always professed—you chuse a variable measure for an invariable standard. Who can say that a plague which should take off half our people would not alter the value of labour? We might indeed agree to transfer the variation to the commodities, and to say that they had fallen and not that labour had risen, but I can see no advantage in the change.

We might again discover modes by which the necessaries of the labourer might be produced with uncommon facility and in consequence of the stimulus which the good situation of the labourers might give to population, the rewards of labour, in necessaries, might be no higher than before: would it be right in this case, in which nothing had really altered but necessaries and labour, to say that they only had remained steadily at the same value, and because a given quantity of corn, or of labour could exchange only for (perhaps) $\tfrac{3}{4}$ of the former quantity of linen, cloth, or money to declare that it was the linen, cloth, or money which had risen in value not labour and corn which had fallen?—

Two countries are equally skilful and industrious, but in one the people live on the cheap food of potatoes, in the other

---

[1] The objection is more fully stated in letter 529.

on the dearer food, wheat. You will allow that profits will be higher in the one country than the other. You will allow too that money may be nearly of the same value in both, if we chuse any thing else as a measure of value but labour. You will further agree that there might be an extensive trade between such countries. If a man sent a pipe of wine from the potatoe country, which cost £100, and which might be sold at £110 in the wheat country, you would say that the wine was at a higher value in the country from which it was exported, merely because, in that country, it could command more labour. You would say this altho' the wine would not only exchange for more money, but for more of every other commodity in the wheat country.—I contend that this is a novelty which cannot be considered an improvement—it would confound all our usual notions, and would impose upon us the necessity of learning a new language. All mankind would say that wine was dearer in the wheat than in the potatoe country, and that labour was of less value in the latter.

In page 31 there is a long passage on the reason for chusing labour as a standard with which I am not satisfied. A piece of cloth is 120 yards in length and is to be divided between A and B, it is obvious that in proportion as much is given to A less will be given to B, and vice versa. This will be true altho' the value of the whole 120 yards be £100, £50 or £5. Is it not then a begging of the question to assume the constant value because the quantity is constant, and because it is always to be divided between 2 persons.

Allowing you your premises, I see very few instances in which I can quarrel with your conclusions. I agree with all you say concerning the glut of commodities; allow to you your measure and it is impossible to differ in the result.

29 April 1823   I hope soon to see you. I have hardly been able to find time to write this letter, I am so busily engaged.—I am serving on a committee.[1]

Ever Y.^{rs}

DAVID RICARDO

524. RICARDO TO M^cCULLOCH [2]
[*Answered by* 526]

London 3 May 1823

My Dear Sir

3 May 1823   I expected ere this to see you in England; I hope nothing has occurred to prevent you from putting your good intention into execution, as I fully depend on the meeting which I have so long desired.

I presented the petition you sent me, and advocated its prayer with the best reasons I could offer, but neither the House nor the Reporters paid much attention to me. This is now of no importance, as the prayer of this, and of similar petitions, has been granted by Government.[3]

I have read your observations[4] on Mr. Blake's pamphlet, and think that there are some contradictions which you charge upon him of which he is not guilty. First, with respect to the currency, the only change in Mr. Blake's opinion, since he wrote his former pamphlet,[5] is that he formerly thought the difference between gold and paper, as it existed during the war, was owing to paper falling, while

---

[1] The Select Committee on the powers of the Commissioners of Sewers in the Metropolis; it was appointed on 25 Feb. 1823 and its Report is dated 10 July 1823.
[2] MS in British Museum.—*Letters to McCulloch*, XXXVII.
[3] See below, p. 291, n. 2.

[4] A very long review of Blake's *Observations on...Expenditure* in the *Scotsman*, 12 April 1823.
[5] *Observations on the Principles which regulate the Course of Exchange; and on the present Depreciated State of the Currency.* London, Lloyd, 1810.

gold remained fixed, he now thinks gold rose and paper 3 May 1823 remained fixed. In support of that opinion Mr. Blake is obliged to contend that gold rose in value in this country from which it was exported, and fell in value, or remained fixed, in the countries to which it went. This is the opinion which you attack, and I quite agree with you that Mr. Blake is wrong, but you have not understood Mr. Blake's argument, and suppose him to support principles which he would be the first to condemn. In this dispute Mr. Blake and you attach a different meaning to the word value. If we measure the value of gold by foreign[1] commodities which are the objects of commerce between 2 countries,[2] it is clear that gold could not in such a measure be exported from a country where it was dear to one where it was cheap. If wine was the measure, gold could never be paid for wine but when wine was dearer in the country which imported it, which is another way of saying that gold was cheaper in that country. But in France where wine is made, wine may fall in value, and at the same time the expences of conveyance may be increased. Under these circumstances England may not import more wine from France, and if France has to pay England a subsidy not having any thing but gold and wine (we will suppose) to export, she is obliged to pay gold. In all the commodities of France which are bulky, and which she cannot export, gold will rise in France, and in England all commodities will rise. The exchange will only deviate from par enough to cover the expences of the transmission of gold, but if we measure the value of gold by the goods of France in France, and by the goods of England in England,[3] gold will come from a country where it rises in value to another where it is

[1] 'foreign' is ins.
[2] This is McCulloch's measure of the value of gold, which he applies to both countries.
[3] This is Blake's measure.

falling in value. If under these circumstances France should keep up the same quantity of money as before, by means of a paper circulation, no commodity would fall or rise in France, except gold, which would rise, and the exchanges would deviate more from par than by the amount of the expences of transmitting gold, because the bill would not be paid for in gold, but in paper, which has been prevented from equalizing itself with the value of gold. This is Mr. Blake's argument and it must be admitted that the case is possible, but I think there is very little probability of its occurring.

There is a great deal of ambiguity in the use which Mr. Blake makes of the word value, he appears to me to have no common standard by which to measure it generally, but has a particular standard for each particular country. I made this objection to him, and also objected to the use which he made of the word depreciation, which induced him to give me the explanation contained in the inclosed[1] paper.

From what I have said you will see that Mr. Blake's fault is rather that of refining too much, and that he cannot with any justice be said to have[2] become the patron and apologist of theories whose fallacy he has himself demonstrated. His conclusions are the same as ours—he is for adhering inflexibly to a standard, and his book may rather be considered as an enquiry into the causes of the alteration in the value of the standard, than an enquiry into the causes of the alteration in the currency.

I cannot understand what Mr. Blake means by an imaginary currency of invariable value,[3] or why when he speaks of the

---

[1] 'inclosed' replaces 'following'.
—The enclosure is wanting.
[2] The remainder of this sentence is a quotation from the *Scotsman's* review of Blake.

[3] Blake does not seem to use this expression in *Observations on... Expenditure*, 1823.

value of commodities in different countries he measures value by such different standards. In favor of Mr. Blake I should contend against you that it is possible for gold to go from a country where it is increasing in value on account of the peculiar obstacles to the exportation of other things, but though I admit the possibility I agree with you in thinking that Mr. Blake has failed to make out that such was our case during the war, and that all the difference between gold and paper was owing to a rise in the value of gold. Mr. Blake's arguments respecting the effects of a war expenditure are still more objectionable,[1] I cannot say one word in defence of this theory.

Have you seen Mr. Malthus book on the measure of value? His arguments appear to me fallacious from beginning to end—he would have done much better to rest his defence of the standard he has chosen upon the old arguments in its favor, which I think unsatisfactory, but those which he now uses are delusive and are scarcely to be understood.—

Believe me ever most truly Y^{rs}

DAVID RICARDO

---

[1] Blake's conclusion is, 'that the expenditure and consumption occasioned by the war have been the chief causes of the increased production during its continuance, and of the distress that has prevailed since its termination.' (*ib.* p. 120.)

525. RICARDO TO GROTE [1]

[May], 1823.

My dear Sir,—

May 1823   [...] I shall see Mr. Maberly[2] to-day, and will, if convenient to him, fix on the Friday following.[3]

I am sure I need not say to you that your observations on my conduct in Parliament respecting the two important questions which have lately been under discussion,[4] have given me great pleasure. The approbation of such as you is the only reward which I expect for doing my duty, and amply recompenses me for my poor exertions for the public good.

Believe me ever, my dear Sir,

Very truly yours,

DAVID RICARDO.

P.S.—I have seen Mr. Maberly; he agrees to Friday the 16th.

[1] Incomplete. From *The Personal Life of George Grote,* by Mrs. Grote, London, Murray, 1873, pp. 42–3. Mrs. Grote gives the date as 'March, 1823', which however disagrees with the postscript, for in 1823 the 16th was a Friday only in May. Cp. also the following extract from a letter of Mrs. Grote to G. W. Norman, dated 30 May 1823: 'We had two very pleasant little dinners in "Threddle" [the Grotes' house in Threadneedle Street, over the banking house] last week. Mr. Ricardo was of the first, together with Messrs. Mill and Maberly. We lauded Mr. R. for his two speeches on Reform and free discussion, and backed his courage to persevere in delivering similar sentiments on future opportunities. We breakfasted there some days afterwards (which I agreed to do rather than dine). It happened to be the morning of the Westminster dinner [23 May 1823; see above, V, 484] and George "prompted" him upon most of the topics which he put forward at the dinner. Place says at least fifty people, additional, went, on purpose to hear Ricardo speak.' (From *Posthumous Papers,* edited by Mrs. Grote, 'for private circulation', London, 1874, pp. 24–5.)

[2] Probably William Leader Maberly (1798–1885), radical M.P. for Northampton, one of the original members of the Political Economy Club.

[3] 'To dine with Mr. and Mrs. George Grote', notes Mrs. Grote.

[4] See Ricardo's speeches in Parliament on freedom of the press, 26 March, and on parliamentary reform, 24 April 1823.

526. M^cCULLOCH TO RICARDO [1]
[Reply to 524]

Edinburgh 11 May 1823

My Dear Sir

I am greatly indebted to you for your letter of the   11 May 1823
3rd inst. I shall certainly profit much by the observations
you have made on my article on Mr. Blakes pamphlet—I fully
agree in all that you say as to the possibility of a case occurring
in which, owing to the difficulties in the way of the conveyance of other commodities, gold might be sent from a
country where it was dear to one where it was cheap, and
I regret that I did not state this in the article in the Scotsman—
But then to be of any use to Mr. Blake he must make out that
this possible case, was actually realised for a period of six
years; and this not in reference to one only but to all descriptions of commodities we had to export, which would certainly
be a very wild supposition—Though I believe it would have
been as well not to have said it, still I cannot help thinking
that I had pretty good grounds for affirming that Mr. Blake
has become the apologist of theories he had formerly condemned—All the more intelligent opponents of the doctrines
in the Bullion Report held the very opinions that Mr. B now
holds—They said the value of gold has risen, but the value
of paper has remained constant; and in contending that gold
had risen they used almost the same arguments that Mr. B
now uses—But Mr. B was then of an opposite opinion—Gold
he then said is constant, it is the paper which has sunk—Has
he not then contradicted himself?—Is he not become the
apologist of theories he had formerly impugned? He may
now, as before, disapprove of the Restriction in 1797; but he
certainly ascribes very different effects to that measure now
from what he did in 1810—

---

[1] MS in *R.P.*—*Letters of McCulloch to Ricardo*, XVII.

I have read Mr. Malthus pamphlet—Though he should gain no other palm, he must be allowed praise for having rendered himself so very unintelligible—I have not had time sufficiently to reflect on the subject; but it occurs to me that human labour must have different values in different countries and at different periods, according to the dearness or cheapness of the maintenance of the labourers, or of the machines which labour, and according to their different degrees of skill &c— But suppose that the skill of the labourers continues invariable, and that they are now fed on wheaten bread and beef, and that ten years hence they are fed on potatoes exclusively: In the latter case a given quantity of commodities will certainly command a much greater quantity of labour than in the former case, and yet, it appears to me that, the exchangeable value of any given quantity of the commodities produced at the two periods would be equal—An equal quantity of cloth, corn, or any other commodity is produced at the two periods, and by an equal quantity of labour—The one must, therefore, be exactly equivalent to the other; and the only difference will be that the profits of stock have increased proportionally to the fall of wages. If there be no fallacy in this case it shews conclusively that the labour which commodities will command is not a measure of their exchangeable value or any thing like it—I trust, however, that you will have the goodness to give me your opinion at some length on this pamphlet—I cannot say how much I have been advantaged by your notes on Mr. Malthus former work—

It was my intention to have left this for London a fortnight since; but as my evil genius would have it, I was seized with a sore throat, a disease which has been very general here, a day or two before I intended setting off—I have now got rid of the sore throat, and though I am still affected

by a very bad cough, I propose sailing for London on   11 May 1823
Wednesday[1]—

Mr. Stuart requests me to offer you his thanks for the
trouble you took in presenting the Petition about the stones[2]—
The repeal of the duty is a great object to Mr. Stuart—he has
one of the best quarries in the kingdom—It was formerly
nearly worthless; now it is expected to bring some thousand
pounds a year—Excuse me for encroaching so much on your
valuable time; and believe me to be with great esteem

Ever truly yours

J. R. McCulloch

527. TROWER TO RICARDO[3]

[*Answered by* 533]

Unsted Wood. May 25. 1823

My Dear Ricardo

Your last kind letter[4] was forwarded to me at my   25 May 1823
Mother's at Clapton, with whom we have been passing some
time. Whilst there, we made occasional morning excursions
to London, and I was in hope, upon some one of those visits,
to have found my way to Upper Brook Street. But, unfortunately, I was then upon the invalid list; and was thereby
necessarily much circumscribed in my operations. Since my
return home I have found my health considerably improved,
and hope, ere long, to be restored to my accustomed
feelings.—

---

[1] 14 May.
[2] On 17 April 1823 'Mr. Ricardo
presented a Petition from Fife, for
a remission of the Duties on
Stone, carried coastwise.' On
29 April, when other petitions on
the same subject were presented,
the Chancellor of the Ex-
chequer declared that 'it was his
intention to move the Repeal.'
(Reports in the *Morning Chronicle;* the matter is not mentioned
in *Hansard.*)
[3] MS in *R.P.*
[4] Ricardo's letter (dated 24 April;
see below, p. 316) is wanting.

I read with interest the exposition of your opinions upon the subject of *Reform;*[1] and find, that you are as great a radical as ever. You know, that I am inimical to all *sweeping systems* of reform; but I, at the same time, admit, nay more *insist* upon the necessity of such alteration in the *practise* of our constitution, as time and circumstances have rendered necessary. The course of events is progressive. Time waits for no man—and a long lapse of years may and must produce such alterations in the habits, opinions, and circumstances of a people as to render some changes in their constitution *necessary,* in order to preserve that sympathy between a people and their institutions without which there can be neither happiness, nor security—But here I would stop. Limit the changes to the *necessity,* and make these changes gradually.—

Well, what say you to Malthus's Measure of Value. I am most impatient to hear! I have, as yet, merely run it over very cursorily, in order to see the sort of view he proposed to take of the subject; and therefore am not, at present, prepared to say much about it. But, I think there must be some fallacy in his reasoning—The points, that I doubt about are 1st the reasoning by which he endeavours to prove the "*constant value of labor,*" and 2^{d} the mode in which he proposes to account "for *the difference in the value of money in different Countries*"—

Again his doctrine with respect to the effect of *profits* on the value of produce appears to me to be erroneous. Is not the fall of profits a *consequence* of the fall in the value of produce; and not a fall of value the *consequence* of a fall of profits.

I do not venture to give any decided opinion at present as I really have run over his book so hastily, that I am not

---

[1] In the House of Commons, on 24 April; see above, V, 283 ff.

qualified to pronounce upon it. I am glad he has taken an important principle *singly,* as it can more easily be investigated—I think too he ties *you* down much more closely than he is justified in doing to *labor* as the sole measure of value— You have distinctly stated over and over again, that *profit* is an important item in the value of all commodities—

He refers several times to a work of Mr. Torrens on the production of Wealth, is it worth reading?

I am glad to see he has abandoned his mean measure of *Corn and Labor.* No doubt he is a very candid man, and has truth alone for his object. The whole tendency of this tract appears to be to confirm the doctrine, in his former work, that the principle of *supply and demand,* and *not the cost of production* is the general regulator of exchangeable value.—

What he says of Blake's notion is very just—"it has an air of contradiction not removed by shewing, that the main cause of high prices was a great demand."[1]—Nobody denies, that the effect which Mr. Blake attributes to an unfavorable exchange would operate *for a time,* but to make out his case he must shew that it operated *permanently.*—The last part of Blake's book[2] is very good. He treats the landlords as they deserve—Malthus too has given them a good hit or two, and the effects of both together will, I think, operate beneficially on the public mind. Surely Mr. Weston will abandon his motion.[3]—I hope Corn wont get higher, but I fear it will. A short supply, with no present prospect of future abundance—

I thank You for the account you sent me of the number of dividends in the funds—I fully expected the numbers would have been greater. What say You to our Spanish

---

[1] *The Measure of Value,* p. 72.
[2] See above, p. 271, n. 2.
[3] On Western's motion see above, V, 309.

speculation? Where is the national feeling in Spain? I think matters will be accommodated at Madrid—

By the by I wish you would enquire among some of your Spanish friends if any Talavera Wheat could be now got from Spain. I have sown it for some years, and with great success. But in course of time it *deteriorates,* and I should be very glad if I could get a fresh sample from Spain.—A small quantity would suffice.—

What say You to Quentin Durward—I have been very much amused with it. It differs considerably from some of his latter performances, and is better than many of them. At last he has given us a hero, for whom we can feel a warm interest. The character of Louis and the Duke are capital—

But I must have done—Pray make our kind remembrances to Mrs. Ricardo and your family and believe me yours ever

most truly

HUTCHES TROWER.

528. RICARDO TO MARIA EDGEWORTH [1]

London 26 May 1823

My Dear Miss Edgeworth

Your letter,[2] which I received a few days ago, was a very kind one, and if I did not feel that I really had very good excuses to offer for not having written to you long ago, I should have felt reproved by your forbearance. You are a good and merciful judge, and from the commencement of our acquaintance have been inclined to interpret favorably every action of mine—I stand in great need of your indulgence, and pray you to continue on all occasions to extend it to me.

[1] MS (in Ricardo's hand) in *R.P.* —Extract in *Economic Journal,* Sept. 1907, p. 438.   [2] Maria Edgeworth's letter is wanting.

Your journey to Scotland has commenced under happy auspices as far as weather is concerned, and I have no doubt that the formidable 27th, on which day you are to cross the water, will be got over with little inconvenience. I have often suffered from sea sickness, and greatly commiserate those who are obliged to endure it.

Cousin Fanny was a kind hearted girl in insisting on giving up her place to her sister Sophy,[1]—she will be sure to have her reward,—a kind act is never done without its being accompanied with gratification which more than repays for the sacrifice which it may require. I trust you, Harriett, and Sophy, are deriving the greatest possible degree of pleasure from your excursion, and that you will have a great intellectual treat in your visit to Sir W. Scott. I shall be very glad to have an account from yourself of this interesting visit.[2]—

I admire alike the great unknown of the North, and the great known of other places, and think myself fortunate in having got into a situation which gives me an opportunity of witnessing the display of talents, and ingenuity, of the highest description in others, and which I can never hope to emulate. My pretensions are of the humblest kind, and I feel assured I owe every thing I enjoy to the forbearance and indulgence of those about me.—

Your restless nation gives us a great deal of trouble in Parliament. The best amongst us do not know how to manage you, nor what course to take to give you the blessings of peace, order, and good government. You have been so long subjected to misrule as hardly to be in a fit state to be reclaimed by common means. Coercion and severity have

[1] Maria Edgeworth was going to Scotland with her half-sisters Harriet and Sophy.

[2] For her account, in a letter to Mrs. Ruxton, 8 June 1823, see *Life and Letters of Maria Edgeworth*, 1894, vol. II, p. 95 ff.

proved of little use, and I hope the system of indulgence, kindness, and conciliation will now be tried. If that system will not succeed I hope we shall get rid of you altogether;— we could do very well without you,—you are a great expence to us, and prevent us from making any great improvements in our own government, as all our time is taken up in attending to yours.—

You enquire after my family,—here follows a brief sketch of our domestic history. Mrs. Ricardo is not very well,— she is very subject to low spirits, and at the present moment does not regard the world and its affairs in so favorable a light as I could wish. Mrs. Osman Ricardo has been with us since Feb^y, and during great part of the time has been indisposed—she is now quite well though not so strong as before her illness.—Mr. and Mrs. Austin and their children have been our visitors for some time—the children are not very well, but Mrs. Austin is not only in good health but in excellent spirits. We all find her a chearful and delightful companion;—if she were not my own child I should be lavish in her praise. Mrs. Clutterbuck has not been in London this winter;—she has had much to bear in consequence of the alarming illness, first of her husband, then of her child. If she too were not my child I would tell you how admirably she behaved under her trials, as it is, I shall only say that they are at an end, and that she is now enjoying health, peace, and happiness in her new residence, to which she has lately removed. They have a delightful place[1] near Chippenham, not many miles from Bowood.—Mary and Birtha and Osman, and Mortimer are quite well, and thus ends the family history.—No, unhappily it does not end here.

About six or seven weeks ago we had to deplore the death of a young and very amiable sister of mine,[2] whom I believe

---

[1] Hardenhuish Park, in Wiltshire.   [2] Esther, died 10 April 1823.

you did not see when you were in London. She was married to a nephew of Mrs. Ricardo, Mr. Wilkinson. I saw her the day before her death in good health and in as good spirits as the prospect of her immediate confinement would allow her to be. The next day she gave birth to her fourth child and 3 hours after expired. This sad event has plunged a very large family into the greatest affliction. She was very dear to all her brothers and sisters.

26 May 1823

[The remainder is wanting.]

529. RICARDO TO MALTHUS [1]

London 28 May 1823

My Dear Malthus

I will, to the best of my power, state my objections to your arguments respecting the measure of value. You have yourself stated, as an objection to my views on this subject, that a commodity produced with labour and capital united, cannot be a measure of value for any other commodities than such as are produced precisely under the same circumstances, and in this I have agreed that you are substantially correct. If all commodities were produced in one day, and by labour only, without the assistance of capital, they would vary in proportion as the quantity of labour employed on their production increased or diminished. If the same quantity of labour was constantly employed on the production of money, money would be an accurate measure of absolute value, and if shrimps, or nuts, or any other thing rose or fell in such money, it would only be because more or less labour was employed in procuring them. Under such circumstances every commodity which was the produce of a day's labour would naturally command a day's labour, and therefore the

28 May 1823

---

[1] MS (in Ricardo's hand) at Albury.—*Letters to Malthus*, LXXXIV.

value of a commodity would be in proportion to the quantity of labour which it would command. But though such a money would measure accurately the value of every commodity produced under circumstances exactly similar, it would not be an accurate measure of the value of other commodities produced[1] with a large quantity of capital, employed for a length of time. In the case just supposed a quantity of shrimps, would be as accurate a measure of value, as a quantity of money produced by the same quantity of labour, but when capital is employed, and cloth is the product of labour and capital, you justly say, that cloth is not a correct measure of the value of shrimps and of silver, picked up by labour alone, on the sea shore, and yet, with singular inconsistency, as I cannot help thinking, you contend that the shrimps and the silver, picked up by labour alone on the sea shore, are accurate measures of the value of cloth. If you are right, then must cloth be also an accurate measure of value, because the thing measured must be as good a measure as the thing with which you measure. When I say that £4 and a quarter of wheat are of the same value, I can measure other values by the quarter of wheat as well as by the £4. – You say "It is conceded that when labor alone is concerned in the production of commodities, and there is no question of time, both the absolute and exchangeable values of such commodities may be accurately measured by the quantity of labour employed upon them"[2] Nothing can I think be more correct, and it is perfectly accordant with what I have been saying. Your mistake appears to me to be this, you shew us that under certain conditions a certain commodity would be a measure of absolute value, and then you apply it to cases where the conditions are not complied with, and suppose it

[1] 'either' is del. here.
[2] This and the following quotations are from a missing letter of Malthus.

to be a measure of absolute value in those cases also. You appear to me too to deceive yourself when you think you prove your proposition, because your proof only amounts to this, that your measure is a good measure of exchangeable value, but not of absolute value. You say. "If the accumulated and immediate labour worked up in a commodity be of any assumed value, £100, for instance, and the profits of the value of £20, including the compound profits upon the labour worked up in the materials, the whole will be of the value of £120. Of this value $\frac{1}{6}$ only belongs to profits, the rest or $\frac{5}{6}$ may be considered as the product of pure labour." This is quite true, whether we value the commodity by the quantity of labour actually employed upon it, by the quantity which it will command when brought to market, or by the quantity of money, or any other commodity, for which it is exchanged, $\frac{5}{6}$, in all cases, will belong to the workmen, and $\frac{1}{6}$ to the master. "Consequently the value of $\frac{5}{6}$ of the produce is determined by the quantity of labour employed on the whole; and the value of the whole produce by the quantity of labour employed upon it, with the addition of $\frac{1}{6}$ of that quantity." This is really saying no more than that when profits are one sixth of the value of the whole commodity (in which no rent enters) the other $\frac{5}{6}$ go to reward the labourers, and that the portion so going to the labourers may itself be resolved into labour and profits in the same proportions of 5 and 1. Five men produce 6 pieces of cloth of which 5 are paid to them, the men; if profits fall one half the men will receive $5\frac{1}{2}$ pieces, and then you say the cloth is of less value; but in what medium? in labour you answer. You appear to me to advance a proposition that cloth is of less value when it will exchange for less labour, and to prove it by shewing the fact, merely, that it actually does exchange for less labour.

You say "But when labour is concerned, it follows from

what has been conceded, that the value of the produce is determined by the quantity of labour employed upon it." By value here you mean absolute value, and then you immediately apply this measure of absolute value, which is only conceded in a particular case, to a general proposition, and say "consequently" consequently on what? on this particular case; "consequently the *value* of $\frac{5}{6}$ of the produce is determined by the quantity of labour employed on the whole" that is to say "consequently the quantity of labour which $\frac{5}{6}$ of the produce will command is determined by the quantity of labour employed on the whole" the same is true, in the same sense, of $\frac{5}{6}, \frac{5}{7}, \frac{5}{8}, \frac{5}{9}$ or of any other proportions in which the whole may be divided. My only object has been to shew, and if I am not mistaken I have succeeded in shewing, that a measure of value which is only allowed to be accurate in a particular case where no capital is employed, is arbitrarily applied by you to cases where capital and time necessarily enter into the consideration.—

I fear I have been guilty of many repetitions. I shall not regret it however if I have made myself understood.

[The remainder is wanting.]

530. RICARDO TO McCULLOCH [1]
[Answered by 541]

London 8 July 1823

My Dear Sir

I hope you have reached your home in safety, and that you found all your friends in good health. I trust that you will not omit coming to us again next spring—we shall all be delighted to see you and shall be prepared to learn with

[1] Addressed: 'J. R. M'Culloch Esqr / Buccleugh Place / Edinburgh'.   MS in British Museum.—*Letters to McCulloch,* XXXVIII.

docility all the good principles which you are to teach us.
You have already done much for the good cause, and I have
little doubt that you are destined to do much more.—We
must endeavor to get some of the grown gentlemen in the
House of Commons to attend your lectures, and to perfect
themselves in the science for which there appears to be a
growing taste.[1]

I shall leave London for Gatcomb on monday next, I will
thank you to give directions to the Newsman to send the
Scotsman to me there.

My principal object in writing to you is to enclose the
papers with which Mr. Tooke has furnished me respecting
the Exchange with America—I hope you may find them
useful for the object which you have in view.[2]—

I am writing to you from a Comm͞ee room in the H of
Commons and have only time to assure you that I am and
ever shall be

Y^{rs} truly

DAVID RICARDO

[McCulloch had been on a six weeks' visit to London, during which
time he had many discussions with Ricardo and his circle. (On this
see below, p. 312.) A facetious account of one of these meetings is
given by Mrs. Grote in a letter of 22 June 1823 to G. W. Norman:
'Before I see you again...we shall be consigned over to the intermin-
able controversy about the "measure of value." The last discussion I
heard on this most fertile subject was between Messrs. Ricardo, Mill,
Grote, and McCulloch (of Edinburgh), in the "Threddle" [the Grotes'
house in Threadneedle Street], and after about one and a half hour's
laborious exertion (which, however, was not profitless), it was resolved
to postpone any further argumentation *sine die,* Mr. McCulloch closing

[1] McCulloch came to London after Ricardo's death, and from April to June 1824 gave the first course of the Ricardo Memorial Lectures; many Members of Parliament attended, according to the reports which were regularly published in the *Globe & Traveller* newspaper. Cp. below, p. 391, n. 1.

[2] For the refutation of Blake (cp. below, p. 345).

the debate with, "Wall, I think the *quastion* must be *soobjacted* to a more *sevear anallasis* before we shall arrive at a definitive conclusion."' (From George Grote's *Posthumous Papers,* edited by Mrs. Grote, 'for private circulation,' London, 1874, p. 25.) See also the following letter, hitherto unpublished, which was written when McCulloch was about to return to Edinburgh.

BLAKE TO M^cCULLOCH¹

My Dear Sir,

30 June 1823

I cannot help suspecting from the conversations that we have had that some points of my pamphlet have escaped your observation I have therefore sent you a copy which I solicit you to accept and I have marked many of the passages to which I had occasion to refer during our discussions. You will see that if I have erred I have erred deliberately and I have not done so through ignorance of the doctrines which you and Mr Ricardo advocate. I regret very much that our amicable disputes are put an end to for the present and I hope they may be renewed when you visit us next Spring we must take care not to fall into the situation of the two brothers in the times of James 2nd a Catholic and Protestant who disputed till each converted the other. I have examined the data you furnished to Malthus for Kircudbright² and I find you are quite right as to wages having doubled—this is a "nodus" for both sides—And as you seemed to find that depreciation accounted for all difficulties and placed you upon velvet I beg to offer you a velvet pillow for your voyage. I observe that during the period from 1783 to 1800 *when there was no depreciation* wages rose from 25 to 30 ℔ cent—consequently accordingly to the received Theory Profits must have fallen from 25 to 30 ℔ cent—yet it is generally admitted (the rate of interest proves it) that profits rose. Pray reconcile this to yourself and to yours very sincerely

W^M. BLAKE]

Portland Place
June 30th 1823

¹ Addressed: 'J. R. McCulloch Esq. / 35, Frith Street'.
MS in the Overstone Library of the University of Reading (inserted in McCulloch's copy of Blake's *Observations on...Expenditure,* 1823).

² See the table of wages in Kircudbright from 1760 to 1822, in Malthus's *Measure of Value,* 1823, p. 75; cp. *ib.* p. 76, n. and Malthus's letters to Napier, in *Economic Journal,* 1897, pp. 268–9.

531. RICARDO TO MALTHUS [1]
[*Answered by* 532]

London 13 July 1823

My Dear Malthus

M Culloch and I did not settle the question of value 13 July 1823 before we parted,—it is too difficult a one to settle in a conversation.—I heard every thing he had to urge in favor of his view, and promised, during my holiday, to bestow a good deal of consideration on it.

He means exactly what you say:—he does not contend that commodities exchange for each other according to the quantity of labour actually worked up in them, but he constitutes a commodity the general measure, by which he estimates the value of all others. A pipe of wine kept for 3 years has no more labour worked up in it than a pipe of wine kept for a day, but he says the additional value on account of time must be estimated by the accumulations which a like amount of capital actively employed in the support of labour would make in the same time. An oak tree which has been growing for 200 years has very little labour actually worked up in it, but its value is to be estimated by the accumulated capital which the original labour employed would give in the same time. He and you in fact differ as to your original measure. I think he could not give any other good reason for chusing a medium which requires labour and capital to produce it, rather than one which requires labour only, excepting that commodities in general require the combination of the two, and that a measure, to have any claim to be even an approximation to an accurate one, should itself be produced under circumstances somewhat similar to the commodities which it is to measure. If all things required precisely the same quantities [2] of capital and labour, and for the

---

[1] MS at Albury.—*Letters to Malthus*, LXXXV.   [2] In MS 'quanties'.

same length of time, to produce them, any one of them would
be an accurate measure of the rest; but this is not the case;
the conditions admit of infinite variety, and therefore which-
ever we chuse it can only be an approximation to truth, and
we are bound to give good reasons for preferring it.

I should indeed be wanting in candour if I refused to
admit that my money measure would not measure the
quantity of labour worked up in commodities. I have admitted it over and over again. I am also ready to admit that
your money measure will measure exactly the quantity of
labour and profits together of which commodities are composed, but so will my money measure. Neither of them will
measure the quantity of labour alone worked up in commodities, but they will both measure the quantity of labour
and profits together of which commodities are composed.
Suppose gold always to require the same quantity of labour,
for one year, before it can be brought to market, will you say
that all variations in wages and profits may not be estimated
in this medium? You would indeed say that many of those
variations would be ascribable to the variations in the value
of the medium, and not to any alteration in the value of the
thing measured, because you do not think that it is any proof
of invariability in a commodity that it requires always the
same quantity of labour, and the same duration[1] of time to
produce it. If I allow the justice of your objection, I am at
liberty to apply the same to your medium. The same quantity
of labour applied for a day will always produce the same
given quantity of gold, gold is therefore an invariable measure you say. I find this gold vary in relation to another
commodity which always requires the same quantity of
labour and capital to produce it, you say it is never the gold
but it is always the commodity which varies, and when you

[1] 'duration' replaces 'quantity'.

are asked why, you answer because labour never varies. Double the quantity of labour in a country, or diminish it one half, always leaving the funds which are to employ it at precisely the same amount, and you tell us notwithstanding the condition of the labourer is in the one case a very distressed one, in the other a very prosperous one—that the value of his labour has not varied. I cannot subscribe to the justness of this language. The question is whether you are right not whether I am wrong.

Suppose that a man in India could pick up in a day precisely the same quantity of gold as in England, and that all trade in provisions were forbid between the two countries. The small quantity of rice and clothing in India which are necessary for the support of a labourer would be of precisely the same value as the quantity of wheat and clothing necessary for a labourer in England. But this would not long continue. All manufactured commodities would be of a high comparative money value in India, and consequently we should export manufactured commodities, and import gold;[1] the reward of a labourer in England would come to be a much larger quantity of gold than he could actually pick up here. No gold would be then obtained in England but by means of importation. Under these circumstances you would say that money was of a low value in England and you would be correct if all men[2] agreed to constitute labour the measure of value; but in this they do not agree, and as we should find that at the very moment that gold was low, relatively to labour, in England, it was high relatively to manufactured commodities of every description, with which in fact gold would be purchased from India, if we took these commodities for the measure we should be bound to say that gold was cheap in England and dear in India. You must remember

---

[1] 'consequently' is del. here.   [2] 'all men' replaces 'we'.

that the point in dispute is whether labour be the correct measure of value, you must not then take the fact for granted, and then offer it as a proof of your correct conclusion.—

We leave London for Gatcomb early to-morrow morning. Next week we expect to have my sister[1] and her family with us—we shall have one bed disengaged if you and Mrs. Malthus will come over to us.—I am sorry I cannot ask all your party.

Ever truly Y^{rs}

DAVID RICARDO

532. MALTHUS TO RICARDO [2]
[*Reply to* 531.—*Answered by* 536]

[St. Catherine's, Bath, *ca.* 21 July 1823][3]

My dear Ricardo,

I am much obliged to you for your letter, and am glad to find that you are engaged to give the subject of value a good deal of consideration during your holidays. Under these circumstances you will not probably consider as an interruption any remarks which may have a tendency, however slight, to throw light on the general question.

I cannot agree with you in thinking it essential to a good measure of value that it should be produced under circumstances similar to the commodities which it is to measure. In the case in question, it appears to me that if the rate of profits be allowed to affect the value of commodities, that is, if as you have elsewhere stated, the value of a commodity is composed of labour and profits, it is impossible that a commodity which consists partly of capital employed for a

---

[1] Hannah Samuda; cp. below, p. 327.

[2] MS in Mill-Ricardo papers.

[3] The date is conjectured only approximately. Cp. the concluding paragraph.

certain period can ever properly measure the variations in the natural and absolute values of commodities, arising from the variations of profits. Supposing cloth and gold for instance to be produced under the same circumstances, that is with the same quantity of labour and capital employed for the same time, and profits to fall from 20 to 10 per cent, it is quite obvious that your money measure, or the gold, would not express the quantity of labour and profits worked up in the cloth. A considerable change would have taken place in this quantity which would not in the slightest degree be ma[t]ched by your measure, though it would be accurately estimated by mine.

The whole therefore seems to depend upon the question, whether the natural and absolute values of commodities in the place and at the time in which they are produced, are, or are not, composed of the accumulated and immediate labour worked up in them with the profits upon that labour for the time that it has been employed. And that they *must* be so composed, seems to follow necessarily and unavoidably from the general concession that where labour is concerned without capital or time, the natural and absolute values of commodities will be determined by the quantity of labour employed on them. Because, if in any place the commodities produced without capital have their natural and absolute values determined by the labour worked up in them, the other commodities produced with capital and time, and the same quantity of labour, must exceed the former commodities in *natural and absolute value* exactly by the profits for the time the advances have been made, and these profits can only be reckoned in labour because the advances consist only of labour. But if the natural and absolute values of commodities must be determined by labour and profits, whenever time is concerned, and if further it clearly appears that the labour which a commodity will command must be precisely the same as the labour worked up in it with the addition of the profits, it follows incontestably that a given quantity of labour must always be of the same natural and absolute value, that is, if we estimate its value in the same way as we estimate the value of all other commodities, a given quantity of labour will always be composed of the same quantity of labour and profits united.

I quite agree with you that I have no right to choose a particular object for my measure and to estimate every thing by it, unless I can shew its *peculiar and preeminent* fitness for the purpose. But this, it appears to me, I have done to those who with the requisite preliminary knowledge, will impartially give due attention to the subject. Indeed I think I have done it in the short statement just made, to which I own, after all that I have heard since my pamphlet has been published, I am quite unable to anticipate a valid objection.

The general concession that the value of commodities is determined by the *quantity* of labour employed upon them, when time is not concerned, is the foundation on which I rest. This foundation once allowed, puts an end at once to all idea of *arbitrary* selection in taking labour as a measure. The other steps follow as strictly as any proposition in Euclid. The proof which may be said almost to be of the class called intuitive is in reality complete without the table or the parts immediately connected with it. These parts merely supply a further confirmation of the truth by answering the following question. How comes it about that labour should remain of the same value in the progress of society, when it is known that it must require more labour to produce it? And the answer to this question is, that as profits depend upon the *proportion* of the whole produce which goes to labour, it must necessarily happen that the increase of value occasioned by the additional quantity of labour will be exactly counterbalanced by the diminution in the amount of profits, leaving the value of the labour the same.

I own it appears to me rather odd that you and Maculloch should particularly object to my doctrine on account of its making the same quantity of labour of the same value while the condition of the labourer is very different, when according to your own doctrines the value of labour in America is actually *lower* than the value of labour in the Netherlands. I however expressed myself without sufficient care, when I intimated that if any number of labourers were imported or exported the value of labour would remain the same. This will only be true after the supply comes to be affected by the increased or diminished number of labourers. If the corn obtained by 20 men be divided among ten, then the value of the wages of 10 men will be much less than the quantity of labour employed to produce them with the addition of profits, and vice versa. The truth of my proposition requires as I have elsewhere[1] stated (p. 30.) that the wages of the labourers who produce the wages to be advanced should be the same as the wages advanced; which will always be the case except in very violent and unnatural changes, and would be the case in the instances supposed after the first year.

The only difficulty in the doctrine, as it appears to me, arises from the different efficiency of labour in different countries and at different periods. It is certainly true that upon the principle of demand and supply which is the foundation of all value, the commodities of different countries do not exchange with each other according to their natural and absolute values in each country. They must be affected both by the greater abundance arising from greater efficiency, and

[1] *The Measure of Value.*

by the influence of the practical measure of value chosen by the commercial world. The distribution of the precious metals which goes so far in regulating the rate at which commodities practically exchange with each other, is greatly though not wholly influenced by the different efficiency of labour. It may be said indeed to be wholly influenced by it, if we add—(efficiency) in the purchase of the precious metals.

But all these influences are fully taken into consideration in the following propositions. The *natural and absolute value* of every commodity in the country and at the time at which it is produced is determined by the labour and profits required to produce it in that place and at that time. And the exchangeable values of all commodities, whenever an exchange can be effected, either in distant countries or in different parts of the same country are universally determined by their natural and absolute values multiplied into the excess of the value of money in one place above the other,—on the supposition of the value of money being estimated by the quantity of labour and profits necessary to purchase it at each place; and I own I do not see how we can estimate the value of money at any particular place or time in any other way, with any approach towards correctness. I cannot help considering these two propositions respecting natural and exchangeable value as very simple and useful. Of course when the value of money is the same, the natural value will also be the exchangeable value.

You are quite right in what you say about India. No mode of procuring the precious metals can ever maintain them of the same value in different countries. And it is for this very reason that I would on no account substitute *money* for *labour.*

I fear I must have dreadfully tired you. We leave St Catharines for Town on friday next. I must be at the College on monday.[1] We are much obliged to you for your kind invitation, but as usual towards the end of a vacation we are hurried, and are unable to accept it.

Mrs M joins in kind regards to Mrs Ricardo.

Ever truly Y^{rs}

T R Malthus.

P.S. At different periods in the same country as no exchange can be effected, we can only refer to natural and absolute value; and then estimate the relative value of money, not with a view to an exchange, but to the different power of money at each period in reference to commodities which have not changed in natural value.

533. RICARDO TO TROWER [2]
[Reply to 527.—Answered by 547]

Gatcomb Park
24 July 1823

My Dear Trower

The latter part of my residence in London was so taken up by parliamentary business that I had not really time to write to you. Besides the regular attendance which I always give to the House I was obliged to be every day on some committee, which, altogether, entirely occupied my time; but now that I am once more settled in my peaceable retreat in the country, I remember my debt to you, and hasten to discharge it.

I regret that I did not see you oftener in London during my six months campaign, particularly as you give me no

---

[1] 28 July. Term began on 1 August.

[2] Addressed: 'Hutches Trower Esqr / Unsted Wood / Godalming', and franked by Ricardo 'July Twenty five'.

MS at University College, London.—*Letters to Trower*, LXII.

N.B. Letter 535 was written later on the same day.

hope of a visit here. I know you are usefully employed as a country gentleman;—equitably settling differences between your poorer neighbours, and arresting as far as you can the diffusion of erroneous principles amongst your richer ones, yet I would wish to see you more in London, for that is the place in which we meet a succession of clever men in all branches of knowledge, and in which we gain instruction by the active opposition which all our speculations whether right or wrong encounter. If you had been there lately you would have met Mr. MCulloch of Edinburgh, the writer of many able articles in the Edinburgh Review, and in the Encyclopedia, on Political Economy. Mr. MCulloch is an agreeable, well-informed man, a sincere lover and seeker of truth, and I think you would have been pleased with him. He had a great deal of discussion with Blake but did not succeed in weaning him from his newly published opinions.[1] With Malthus, as you know, he greatly differs, and their conferences have not been attended with the effect of reconciling them to each other's views. He attended the last meeting of our Political Economy Club and the result of our discussions on that day convinced him, as we all had been long before convinced, that the progress of the science is very much impeded by the contrary ideas which men attach to the word value.[2] When Malthus speaks of a rise or fall in the value of a commodity he is estimating it in the particular measure of value which he himself recommends; MCulloch, Mill and I are thinking of quite a different measure. Torrens and Warburton again have their particular view of a proper measure; and therefore until we can agree as to some common measure by which to estimate the variations in the value of the com-

[1] See Blake's letter, above, p. 302.
[2] At the meeting on 2 June 1823, one of the questions discussed was 'Can there be an increase of Riches without an increase of Value?' proposed by N. W. Senior. (*Political Economy Club, Minutes of Proceedings, 1821–1882*, p. 59.)

modities of which we speak, altho' it be not, as it appears impossible any can be, an accurate measure of value, we cannot understand each other. To this task several good understandings are I hope at this time devoted, for all appear to acknowledge the necessity of adopting some general measure. I know MCulloch's attention is turned to the subject[1] and I expect much from his accuracy and precision.— Malthus is I know quite full of the subject but then his views run in a particular direction from which nothing can make him swerve.—As for myself I mean also to turn my thoughts to the subject, but I fear I cannot arrive at any sounder conclusions than the acknowledgedly imperfect ones which I have already published.

In one of the Committees, which I have lately attended, we were directed by the House to enquire into the cause of the want of employment of the poor in Ireland, and into the best means of remedying the evil which all agree exists.[2] It is a favorite plan, with many, for Government to lend capital to Ireland, in order that the people may be employed. Against such a scheme I have the most decided objections, which I never fail to urge. If the greater part of the Irish members could have their way, we should not only grant a vast number of charitable loans but we should encourage all sorts of manufactures by bounties and premiums. Amongst other schemes we have listened with great attention to Mr. Owen, who assures us that if we give him 8 millions of money he will make Ireland now and for ever happy. The Irish appear to me to differ from the rest of the inhabitants of the United

[1] He intended to write the article 'Value' for the *Supplement to the Encyclopaedia Britannica;* see below, p. 334.

[2] The Committee was appointed on 20 June 1823 (Ricardo being added to it on 23 June) and reported on 16 July 1823. (See 'Report from the Select Committee on the Employment of the Poor in Ireland', with Minutes of Evidence, *Parliamentary Papers,* 1823, vol. VI.)

Kingdom, and not to take a commonly enlightened view of
their own interest. They have no idea of waiting patiently
for the profitable result of a well considered speculation. An
English landlord knows that it is not his interest to make his
tenant a beggar by exacting the very hardest terms from him
if he had the power of dictating the rent, not so the Irish
landlords—they not only do not see the benefits which
would result to themselves from encouraging a spirit of
industry and accumulation in their tenants, but appear to
consider the people as beings of a different race who are
habituated to all species of oppression:—they will for the
sake of a little present rent, divide and subdivide their farms
till they receive from each tenant the merest trifle of rent,
altho' the aggregate is considerable.—They consider as
nothing the severe[1] means to which they are obliged to resort
to collect these rents, nor to the individual suffering which it
occasions. Ireland is an oppressed country—not oppressed
by England, but by the aristocracy which rules with a rod
of Iron within it; England could redress many of her wrongs
but stands itself in awe of the faction which governs.

What say you to Agriculture and its prospects? Is the
distress over? Shall we have a short crop? If we have will
the ports be opened? If the ports be opened how will the
future prospects of landlords and tenants be affected by it?
These are interesting topics. You have no doubt seen Tooke's
publications[2]—they are I think very clever. What is your
opinion of that theory of his on which he lays so much stress:
the continuance, for a succession of years, alternately, of good
and bad seasons. Out of twenty successive years he contends
you will frequently find only 2 or 3 good crops, and then
perhaps for the same number of years only 2 or 3 bad ones.
He makes the scientific part of the subject very difficult, for

---

[1] Replaces 'painful'.   [2] See above, p. 250, n. 4.

he will not allow you to reason with a view to practice from an observation of the produce for 10 years; according to him you must look to the a[vera]ge[1] result of a period of from 30 to 50 years.

The country about me is looking beautiful, but it is n[ot] possible to enjoy it amidst the incessant rain which at present prevails; a great quantity of hay will be spoiled.

Will the war in Spain soon be at an end to be renewed at some future opportunity by the friends of liberty there, with greater effect, or will they yet offer so much resistance to the French, as to prolong the contest, and have a chance of ultimately prevailing over their formidable enemy? I fear their case is for the present hopeless, but I trust might will not long continue to subdue right.

Mrs. Ricardo unites with me in kind remembrances to Mrs. Trower.

Ever Yours
DAVID RICARDO

534. TROWER TO RICARDO [2]
[*Answered by* 535]

Unsted Wood. July 20. 1823

My Dear Ricardo

It is a trite saying but a true one, that "hope deferred sickens the heart." And, *I* have been hoping, for a long time past, week after week, and day after day, that I should have the pleasure of hearing from *You*. My last letter was written to You, as far back as the month of May last, and, in our ordinary course of correspondence, the month of June would not have grown old before my eyes had been gladdened by the sight of your hand writing. But, alas! a *whole season* has

24 July 1823

20 July 1823

---

[1] MS torn here and below.

[2] The cover is wanting: it was addressed to Ricardo in London and forwarded to Gatcomb (see Ricardo's reply).—MS in *R.P.* —*Minor Papers*, pp. 218–20.

20 July 1823 passed away since I have had the pleasure of hearing from You; for your last letter is dated *24 April!!!*[1]

I know, that your constant and close attention to your parliamentary duties, leaves You but little leisure during the Sessions; but of that little I have hitherto enjoyed a portion, and cannot rest content in the loss of my accustomed privilege—As however the Sessions are now closed, and You are the master of your time again, I trust that You will make amends for your long silence, and write off your arrears.

In looking back upon the proceedings of Parliament, during the last Sessions, I think it impossible not to feel gratified, upon the whole, at the course of their proceedings.—

It is obvious, that a more enlightened spirit, a spirit better suited to the temper of the times, has influenced their decisions, than has been evinced on former occasions.— Ireland has claimed a large share of your attention, and distressing as the state of that unhappy country is, and incapable of receiving any immediate amendment, yet, it is obvious, that the measures adopted by parliament with regard to Ireland, must eventually produce considerable benefit: the seeds of a more enlightened and just policy have been sown, and must in due course of time, produce their proper fruits.—

A similar spirit has dictated the measures adopted with regard to the commercial and domestick affairs of this Country. A new course of proceedings has been marked out; much has been done, still more has been promised; and the spirit in which this promise has been made, affords a sufficient security for its future performance.—

The absurd and mischievous shackles with which commerce has been so long fettered, have in many instances been broken; and in spite of remaining prejudices must ere long be entirely removed. Many sanguinary and unjust laws,

[1] This letter of Ricardo is missing.

which have long stained our statute book, have been blotted out, and a sincere determination has been evinced to improve our criminal code. Other important measures have been under the consideration of the legislature; and members of parliament, may, I think, return to their constituents, with a consciencious pride, that they have been administering to the happiness and prosperity of their Country.—

In the mean time the actual prosperity of the Country has been making rapid strides, and upon the whole, I think it is not too much to assert, that we have weathered all our difficulties; and that nothing but a continuance of peace, and common sense in our rulers, are necessary to insure the continued prosperity of the Country.—

I do not expect any considerable variation in the prices of corn; my hope is they will remain where they now are— These prices are adequate to remunerate the cultivators of all such land as ought to remain in cultivation. The ensuing crop cannot be large; if the weather is favorable it will not be deficient.—

I want to know what You think of Malthus' Measure of Value.—

Mrs. Trower desires to join with me in kind remembrances to Mrs. Ricardo and family and I remain My Dear Ricardo
Yrs very truly
HUTCHES TROWER.

535. RICARDO TO TROWER [1]
[*Reply to* 534.—*Answered by* 547]

24[th][2] July 1823

My Dear Trower

Just as I was about sending my letter to the Post yours of the 20.th was delivered to me, it came with a weekly dispatch and parcel by the coach from my house in London. I am glad that I wrote before I received it, as you will see I had you in my recollection.

You have answered some of my questions respecting the approaching crop—I quite agree with you that a price neither too high nor too low is what we now want, but can we long have it with the present corn law? I think not, and must use my best efforts to get it amended.

We are deserving of some of the praise you bestow on us for a more liberal spirit than heretofore in Parliament. We shall I hope go on from Session to Session getting rid of some of the absurd regulations which fetter commerce till all shackles are removed. Huskisson behaved very well after I left London in refusing to have any thing to do with the Lords' amended bill respecting the magistrates interference with wages in Spitalfields—the bill was quite spoiled, there was nothing left in it worth retaining.[3]

You ask me what I think of Malthus "measure of value" I have in some degree answered your question in my letter, for I have told you that a good measure of value is among the things of which we know little. Malthus's is objectionable because his measure is not invariable which a measure of value should be.

---

[1] Presumably enclosed in Letter 533, of the same date.
MS at University College, London.—*Letters to Trower,* LXIII.

[2] Replaces '25th'.
[3] Cp. above, V, 309.

Suppose an epidemic disorder were to carry off one fourth of our people labour would rise as compared with all commodities—Malthus would call this a fall in the value of commodities, whereas nothing would have altered except the supply of labour. Malthus objects to my measure of value, and justly, because it is not itself produced under the very same circumstances as the commodities whose value it is to measure. "Your money" he says "is produced with certain portions of fixed and circulating capital, and with it you would measure the variations of commodities produced with other and very different proportions of fixed and circulating capital." Does he not fall into the same error?—his money is produced with labour alone and he makes it a measure of the value of commodities produced under all the varieties of mixed proportions of capital and labour. In a country where the people feed on rice or potatoes a great deal of labour may be commanded with a small proportion of the whole produce of labour, instead of saying as the fact would appear to be that labour was cheap in those countries and dear in England we should be bound to say commodities were dear in those countries and cheap in England although their money price was the same. Surely this cannot be right.

Ever Y.^{rs}

D R

536. RICARDO TO MALTHUS [1]
[*Reply to 532.—Answered by* 540]

[Gatcomb Park, 3 Aug. 1823]

My Dear Malthus

3 Aug. 1823   The value of almost[2] all commodities is made up of labour and profits, but in chusing a measure of value it is not necessary that it should possess the property of determining what proportion of the value of the commodity measured belongs to wages, and what proportion belongs to profits. You make it a reproach on my proposed measure that it will not do this, and prefer your own because it will. Now as I do not think this quality essential to a measure of value, I shall not defend mine for not possessing this quality. This consideration appears to me wholly foreign to the question under discussion.

We agree I believe that nothing can be a measure of value which does not itself possess value. We agree too I believe that a measure of value to be a good one should itself be invariable, and further that in selecting one thing as a measure of value rather than another we are bound to shew some good reason for such selection, for if a good reason be not given the choice is altogether arbitrary. Now the measure proposed by you has value and therefore not to be objected against on account of any deficiency of that quality, but I do not think it is invariable and by the concession which you make in your last letter you appear to give up your measure,

---

[1] Addressed: 'The Revd T. R. Malthus / East India College / Hertford'. Franked by Ricardo 'Minchinhampton August Three 1823'.

MS at Albury (as printed in the text).—*Letters to Malthus*, LXXXVI. A draft, with cover addressed and franked, and dated inside 'Gatcomb Park 2 Augt 1823', which was enclosed by Ricardo to McCulloch, is in British Museum, Add. MSS 34,545, fols. 97–100; it was printed in *Letters to McCulloch*, XL. The draft contains a few variants and corrections.

[2] 'almost' is ins. in draft.

for you say that "you expressed yourself without sufficient care, when you intimated that if any number of labourers were imported or exported the value of labour would remain the same" This is a large concession indeed, and I think entirely subverts your measure, because if it be true of labourers exported or imported, it must be true also of labourers born or dying in the country. If by poor laws imprudent marriages are encouraged, and population becomes excessive the effect on the value of labour will be precisely the same as if labourers had been imported, and if an epidemic disorder break out, and many labourers die, it will be the same as if they were exported. Nay more, if the people be well educated, and be taught caution and foresight with regard to the increase of their numbers who shall say that the effect on the value of labour will not be the same as an exportation of labourers? You have I think been imprudent, which is much at variance with your usual practice, in conceding this point;—you allow us to enter into your fortress and spike all your guns. You add, indeed, "this will only be true after the supply comes to be affected by the increased or diminished number of labourers." When will the supply not be affected by the increased or diminished number? What follows will not assist you, for you say "If the corn obtained by 20 men be divided among ten, then the value of the wages of 10 men will be less than the quantity of labour employed to produce them with the addition of profits and vice versa" What profits? they might have been 50 pc^t, and may from the circumstance mentioned be reduced to 5 pc^t. You speak of profits in this place as if they were a fixed amount, and forget that they fall when wages rise. Besides I will not admit the extravagant supposition that the corn obtained by the labour of 20 men is bestowed as wages on 10 men, but I will suppose that the corn obtained by 20 men had been sufficient to command the labour of 30 men but that owing to a diminished supply of labour this same quantity of corn, obtained by the same number of men, is bestowed as wages on 22 men. In this case I ask you whether corn has fallen in value in the proportion of 30 to 22? If you say yes, then you do not admit that labour may rise in value in consequence of exporting labourers, and if you say no, there is an end of your measure, because you then acknowledge that commodities do not vary according to the quantity of labour they can command. I do not see how you are to extricate yourself from this dilemma. I cannot discover what the value of the precious metals, in different countries, can have to do with this question. A piece of cloth or a piece of muslin can command more labour in India than in England; on this we are agreed, but we are not agreed in our explanation of this fact. You say the piece of cloth, or muslin, is more valuable in India than in England and your proof is that it can command more labour in India. You would say so altho' both cloth and muslin were exported from India to England, from the country where they are dear to the country where they are cheap. I, on the contrary, say that it is not the cloth and muslin which are dear in India and cheap in England but it is labour which is cheap in India and dear in England, and that cloth and muslin would come to England from India altho' there were no such commodities as gold and silver on the face of the earth. I say further that you are bound to admit this by the concession which you have made, for you must admit that labour might be rendered cheap as effectually in England by prevailing on English labourers to be satisfied with the moderate remuneration of food paid in India as by the importation of labourers, and if you do not admit it I beg to ask why you refuse to do so;—I beg you to point out the distinction between a supply of labourers from abroad with a consequently reduced remuneration of food, and a supply of labourers from the principle of population and a consequent reduction in the remuneration paid in food. Can you be said to have given a good reason for the selection which you have made of a measure of value when it will not bear close examination. You have repeatedly said that a commodity on which a quantity of labour has been bestowed will always exchange for a like quantity, together with an additional quantity which will constitute the profits on the advances. Now this I consider to be your main proposition, and on its truth must depend, according to your own view, the correctness of your measure. Is it true then that every commodity exchanges for two quantities of labour, one equal to the quantity actually worked up in it, another equal to the quantity which the profits will command? I say it is not. This year corn is cheap, and I must give a certain quantity of it to procure the labour of ten men to be worked up in the commodity which I manufacture, but next year when I take my commodity to market, corn is dear and wages high, and therefore to procure a certain quantity of labour I must give more of my finished commodity than I should have given if corn had been plenty and wages low. If corn had been cheap and wages low, my profits would have been high, as it is they are low. I want to know, in these two cases whether the commodity does really exchange for the two specific quantities of labour mentioned above; you answer my question by saying that you always make a reserve of the first quantity, and all above it you call profits. But I contend that labour of one value has been expended on the commodity, and when it comes to market it is exchanged for labour of another value, and that is the sole reason why the balance, over and above the labour expended on it, is small. Why is it small but because the value of labour is high. No such thing, you say, labour never varies, and yet you cannot but confess that if corn had been abundant and if wages had remained the same[1], the manufactured commodity would have exchanged for a great deal more labour. You say "How comes it about that labour should remain of the same value in the progress of society, when it is known that it must require more labour to produce it"? you must mean "to produce the remuneration paid for it" and you add "the answer to this question is that as profits depend upon the *proportion* of the whole produce which goes to labour, it must necessarily happen that the increase of value occasioned by the additional quantity of labour will be exactly counterbalanced by the diminution in the amount of profits, leaving the value of labour the same." I confess I cannot understand this answer. We are enquiring about the meaning which should be attached to the words "increase of value" "diminution of value". You tell me that increase of value means an increased power of commanding labour: I deny that this definition is a correct one, because I deny the invariability of the standard measure you have chosen, and to prove its invariability you speak of the proportions in which the whole produce is divided, and that if wages have more profits have less; all which is true, but what connection do you prove between this proposition and the invariability in your measure of value? In your answer you use the words "increase of value"; that is to explain the meaning of the words required to be understood, by the use of the words themselves. You mistake M Culloch's and my objection to your doctrine if you suppose it to be on account of its making the same quantity of labour of the same value, while the condition of the labourer is very different; we do not object to it on that account, because as you justly observe our own

---

[1] Draft inserts here 'in corn', but the final copy omits it.

3 Aug. 1823

doctrines require the same admission, but we object to your saying, that from whatever cause it may arise that the labourers condition is deteriorated, he is always receiving the same value as wages. When *our* labourers are badly off, altho' (we say) they have wages of the same value, profits must necessarily be very low; according to you wages would be of the same value whether profits were 2 pc.^{t} or 50 pc.^{t}

I think I have shewn you that your long letter was acceptable by doing that which is really a difficult task to me, writing a longer one myself. I am however only labouring in my vocation, and trying to understand the most difficult question in Political Economy. All I have hitherto done is to convince myself more and more of the extreme difficulty of finding an unobjectionable measure of value. As far as I have yet been able to reflect upon M Culloch's and Mill's suggestion[1] I am not satisfied with it. They make the best defence for my measure but they do not really get rid of all the objections. I believe however that tho' not without fault it is the best.

I am sorry you could not spare a few days for a visit to us, if you will come to Gatcomb before we go to town I shall be very glad to see you.

I have been writing a few pages in favor of my project of a National Bank, with a view to prove that the nation would lose nothing in profits by abolishing the Bank of England, and that the sole effect of the change would be

---

[1] They proposed to consider 'the labour of a man and the labour of a machine' as 'exactly the same' (below, p. 369); this change of definition met in their view the objections to the quantity of labour worked up in a commodity as a measure of value. For this theory, see McCulloch's letter 546, his *Principles of Political Economy*, 1825, pp. 102–3 and the 2nd ed. of Mill's *Elements of Political Economy*, 1824, pp. 95–9.

3 Aug. 1823 to transfer a part of the profits of the Bank to the national treasury.

Mrs. Ricardo unites with me in kind regards to Mrs. Malthus. Y^{rs} ever

DAVID RICARDO

537. RICARDO TO MILL [1]
[Answered by 539]

Gatcomb Park
7th Augt 1823

My Dear Sir

7 Aug. 1823 As no letter has yet reached me from you, I suppose I must be the first to commence our correspondence. I charge you however to give me an early reply, as the interval for letter writing is short before you will appear in person at Gatcomb. You have been lately so feasting your eyes with beautiful country, that I do not expect ours will make much impression upon you,—yet you will see something to admire in our walks, which were projected during your last visit, and which are now in a very improved state. Our plantations too have made great progress, and to my eyes, which have not been contemplating the beauty of Dorking and Leatherhead, our woods, water and groves appear delightful. We have had the common lot of being deluged with rain yet we have not been without intervals of fine weather, and one advantage has attended the wet, our grass looks green and luxuriant, and our cattle contented and happy. I do not know whether you are aware of the great care Mrs. Ricardo has taken, to appropriate the middle pond, before our house, for her gold and silver fish. That they might be unmolested by intruders of the sealy tribe the pond was emptied before they were put into it, and a number of men were employed

[1] Addressed: 'James Mill Esqr / East India House / London'.—MS in Mill-Ricardo papers.

for about 6 weeks, 2 or [3][1] years ago, to clear it of all the 7 Aug. 1823 mud which had collected in it.

These were not the only precautions taken, for the water, with which it was fed from the upper pond, not only passed through a grating, but a plate of iron was made with innumerable small holes thro' which the water was also obliged to pass, that no stray fish might enjoy the luxury of associating with the gold and silver fry. Before Mrs. Ricardo introduced her favourites to their new abode, she observed in the glass globes, in which a few of them had a temporary residence, 3 fish which were of a lighter hue than the gold fish, but she had admitted 2 of them into the pond with the rest before she shewed either of them to us. After the two were in their comfortable quarters, she shewed us the third, when we unanimously decided it was a perch. There was however no remedy for the error that had been committed, and the two perch have been at free quarters ever since. A few days ago one of these perch shewed himself, as Mrs. Ricardo thought, to her view, and she persuaded herself that a little expert angling might enable her to get rid of these unwelcome intruders. In the upper pond Mr. Samuda[2] had in vain tried all the resources of his art to catch fish, but not one would bite, yet he was the champion fixed upon to wage war with the two intruders. He commenced his work at a moderate early hour, and prepared himself with a good stock of patience to wait the result—but he had scarcely thrown in his hook before a perch was safely landed on the bank. Again he threw it in and after another minute appeared a second perch. It was hardly necessary to try any further but it was thought prudent to throw in the hook once more, a third perch was caught, and so he went on till he caught 50. He commenced hostilities again the next morning and caught 40 more, since

[1] Omitted in MS.   [2] Ricardo's brother-in-law.

which he has made other attacks, with success, though not with as great as before. Mrs. Ricardo is quite in despair and knows not what to do to protect the young gold and silver fish against these rapacious intruders.

There is a great difference of opinion among us as to the source from whence our misfortunes spring. Mrs. Ricardo, in this instance, seems to have embraced Mr. Malthus's theory of population, and stoutly contends that all the perch which have been caught, and all which remain in the pond, are the progeny of the original pair. Others think that in spite of the precautions taken some spawn, or young fish, has found its way from the upper pond. We beg of you to bring with you a good theory on the subject, and above all to ascertain whether the perch is a deadly enemy to young gold fish.—

We have seen most of our neighbours since we have been here—they have most of them imposed upon themselves the irksome duty of paying us a morning visit, for the omission of which I would have given them my licence. They are kind hearted people and I must not repine at the trifling sacrifices required of me. We miss very much our poor friend Smith; with his company we were always pleased. Our girls and boys have all been with us;—on one occasion they were all here at the same time. Mrs. Clutterbuck now lives within 18 miles of Gatcomb, which will give us great facilities for seeing her often.

I must not omit to mention the schools to you—they are going on well—Both of them are always full, and many boys and girls are waiting for vacancies to be admitted. The boys and girls in the upper classes read, write, spell and cipher very well, and many are constantly leaving the school after having become tolerable proficients in these branches of learning. Considering the little attention which I can pay to the school from my occasional absence from it, the master had done very well. I cannot help flattering myself that I am performing a real service to this place by supporting these institutions.

I have devoted a few days to the writing of a short tract to prove the practicability of the Government becoming the sole issuers of paper money. I feel fully assured that Commissioners might be appointed on such a plan, to manage the whole concern, that ministers would have much less influence over them, to make them swerve from their duty, than what they have possessed, and have indeed exercised over the B^k of Eng^d.

Malthus has written to me 2 long letters[1] in defence of his measure of value. His arguments are not very cogent; indeed I am often puzzled to find any connection between the premises and conclusions of his propositions. It would be a real service to the science of Political Economy to shew what the real difficulties are in the way of finding any accurate measure of value. We can at last only come to an approximation of a correct measure of value, and that must be the best which is itself the least liable to variation. I believe we have hit upon the best, but something more should be said to prove it such. I wish I could perform that task, but a more able pen must undertake it.

Remember that we shall expect you early in September, and shall hope to see as many of your family as you can bring with you. Mrs. Ricardo has already expressed her wish of seeing Mrs. Mill, I hope it is unnecessary for me to say my wish coincides with hers, and that if she come we will endeavor to make her visit agreeable to her. Mrs. Ricardo and my girls desire their kind regards

Ever Y^{rs}

DAVID RICARDO

[1] Letter 532 and an earlier one which is missing.

538. RICARDO TO MᶜCULLOCH [1]

[Answered by 541]

Gatcomb Park 8 Augᵗ 1823

My Dear Sir

  Mr. Wigram, the chairman of the East India company, has at length sent me the paper respecting the sales of tea, which I enclose. I hope it will answer the purpose for which you required it. [2]

  The difficult subject of value has engaged my thoughts but without my being able satisfactorily to find my way out of the labyrinth. I have received 2 long letters from Malthus on the subject, and as it may assist you to know the pours and contres of Malthus's doctrine I enclose his last letter and my answer. [3] Return them by the post, but take care your parcel is not over weight when you have read them. I am in no hurry for the answer as it is a copy. [4] I wish also you would send me your own views on this subject in writing. In your article on Polit. Econ. in the Encyclopedia, you do not, I think, do quite justice to the argument of our opponents. I cannot get over the difficulty of the wine which is kept in a cellar for 3 or 4 years, or that of the oak tree, which perhaps originally had not 2/ expended on it in the way

---

[1] Addressed: 'J. R. MCulloch Esqʳ / Buccleugh Place / Edinburgh'.
 MS in British Museum.—*Letters to MᶜCulloch,* XXXIX.
[2] Enclosure wanting. MᶜCulloch was preparing an article on 'East India Company's Monopoly—Price of Tea', for the *Edinburgh Review,* Jan. 1824 (Art. VIII). It is no doubt Wigram's paper that he describes on p. 459: 'We have now in our possession an *official* account commencing with the first sale in 1820, and ending with the second sale in 1823, containing a statement of the various descriptions of tea sold by the East India Company at their quarterly sales, the prices at which the teas were put up, the prices at which they were actually sold, the total quantities sold, and the quantities refused by the dealers, at the Company's upset prices.'
[3] Letters 532 and 536.
[4] See above, p. 320, n. 1.

of labour, and yet comes to be worth £100. There is no 8 Aug. 1823
difficulty in estimating all these in a measure of value such
as ours, but the difficulty is in shewing why we fix on that
measure, and in proving it to be, what a measure of value
must be, itself invariable.

I have written a short essay on the Plan of a National
Bank,[1] in which I have endeavored to shew that no one
would be injured by such an establishment, but the Bank
of England and the other issuers of paper money in the
country who have no claim whatever to a profit which may
be compared to that which is derived from the seignorage of
money.

I have been expecting a letter from you every day. I hope
I shall soon hear from you. The ladies of my family desire
to be kindly remembered to you,—my daughter Mary in
particular who is obliged to you for your efforts to make her
understand Political Economy—she is grateful for your able
article on that subject which is safely arrived.[2]

Ever Y^{rs}

D RICARDO

539. MILL TO RICARDO [3]
[Reply to 537.—Answered by 548]

My dear Friend East India House 8th August 1823

It was set down in my minds calendar to write to you 8 Aug. 1823
this very day, and forestall your letter. I remained at Dorking

---

[1] Published posthumously in 1824.
[2] Perhaps the *Encyclopaedia Britannica* article, see above, p. 275.
[3] Addressed: 'David Ricardo Esq. M.P. / Gatcomb Park / Minchinhampton / Glostershire'.

MS in *R.P.*—Printed in *Minor Papers*, pp. 206–9 and 229. The

cover, which bears the postcript on one side and the address on the other, has been there regarded as an independent letter from John Stuart Mill, owing to its being sealed with the initials 'JSM' (cp. below, p. 390, n. 1); the handwriting, however, is undoubtedly

till wednesday morning, and deferred writing till I should get to town, and be more able to speak with precision about my Gatcomb movements.

I must first tell you, that I have been at work, and, I think, to good purpose, at Dorking. Last year I did something considerable towards the exposition of all the phenomena classed under the title of *Thought.*[1] I have pursued the subject, during the last few weeks; and all the phenomena called intellectual, (still leaving the moral) have undergone investigation. You know my opinion was, that they might all be expounded upon the principles of Hartley, and might be satisfactorily shewn to be nothing but sensations, and the ideas, the copies of these sensations, combined in groups by association. I think I have now made this satisfactory exposition; that I have not left one point doubtful, or likely to be disputed but by those who lie under the dominion of previous associations, and are not capable of the degree of attention which is necessary to break their fetters. After explaining, in an elementary manner, the phenomena of sensation, and the representations of sensations, the ideas, and also the laws of association, and the artifice of naming, I proceed to apply these elements, and examine how far they go in accounting for all the complicated phenomena, included under the titles, Imagination, Memory, Belief, Judgement, Ratiocination, Abstraction, and so on. No body has seen the papers but John, whose mind however is perfectly ripe to judge of them: and to him the expositions appear to be easy of comprehension, and perfectly satisfactory. I doubt

that of James Mill and the post-mark on the cover (8 Aug. 1823) agrees with the date of the letter.
[1] During the summer of 1822, the first holiday which he spent at Dorking, Mill had begun writing his *Analysis of the Human Mind;* he worked at it during his vacations at Dorking for eight years and published it in 1829. (See J. S. Mill, *Autobiography,* pp. 68–9.)

not that they will appear equally so to you. I confess that the evidence has turned out to be shorter, more simple, and conclusive, by far, than I had dared to anticipate. I should like to have your opinion of it; and if I can get it copied, so that you would be able to read it, I will send it to you. The whole is within a very narrow compass; and it will need to be a good deal dilated, and made familiar by illustrations, in writing it afresh for the public. In its present shape, the analysis is given in the naked state in which it presented itself to me, as I advanced step by step.—I mean to go on, next, to the exposition of the *Will,* and the different phenomena commonly classed under it, the desires, passions, &.c., called the "active Powers of the mind", by the Scotch and other philosophers. This will be easy; and when this is done, the whole of what we call mind will be explained. I shall then look upon myself as having rendered no small service to the cause of light. I got so full of my subject, that I could not tear myself away from Dorking. There was, however, another reason. For as it is necessary that McCulloch[1] and I should so arrange our matters, that one of us shall always be here; and as business came on which rendered it impossible for him to go away at the time which had been originally settled between him and me, that so I might have the half of my holidays now, and the other half to go to Gatcomb with, the latter half of September; I lost nothing by staying at Dorking: for now the time of my getting to Gatcomb will be necessarily postponed for some weeks beyond the time when I hoped I could be with you, and as my stay will also be shortened I shall make my run down to you by my single self. I shall have an ostensible week for you, which I shall make all but two; for I can come off by the night coach on a wednesday evening; and I can be with you all the evening

[1] William McCulloch: Mill was now next to him in the office.

of the next tuesday week. I regret that I shall not see your country in all its beauty; but I come to enjoy yourselves, my own dear friends; and I shall be happy in spite of all the rest. My wife prays me to say every thing to Mrs. Ricardo expressive of her sense of her kindness, in her wishes to see her and girls. With respect to her, however, she hardly proposes to wean her little one[1] so soon; and would not be easy at leaving her in the hands of those she has at Dorking. We must look forward to a future time. I beg my own kind regards, and all my gratitude to Mrs. Ricardo. A propos of gratitude, tell her that the turtle came in admirable order, and was a high treat to some friends we had with us from London, who celebrated her health in a bumper. Tell the young ladies not to forget me, nor to let absence deprive me of one jot of their affections: for I cannot consent to lose an atom. Mine, they may be assured, will stand the trial of time.

I am happy to hear that you have been employed upon your proposed Tract: and have no doubt of your proving the merits of your plan.[2] Poor Malthus, and his Measure of Value! I am more and more satisfied that your account of the matter, which both McCulloch and myself have adopted, is the true exposition; and that it wants nothing but to be somewhat better expressed than any of us has yet done it, to satisfy every body, except Malthus and Torrens. McCulloch gave me hopes that he would write an article Value in the Suppl. on purpose.[3] He also told me that you were to reconsider the subject with your pen in your hand. Why should you despair of putting what you conceive clearly down upon paper clearly? Why despair of doing any thing?

[1] Mary, the Mills' eighth child, born in 1822.
[2] The Plan for a National Bank.
[3] No article 'Value' appeared in the *Supplement to the Encyclopaedia Britannica.*

Where is that able pen you talk of? I shall try mine upon the subject one of these days. Some one of us three must do it—or it will not be done. Let us all try, and we can adopt the best.

I have been reading the correspondence of Voltaire and D'Alembert, the two last Volumes, in the large collection of Voltaires works. I think it would interest you much. It contains some of the most interesting points of the history of literature at that time in France; one of the most interesting of all the portions of that history—also much information on the state of the human mind, and the instruments by which it was worked upon both for good and for evil—in short I recommend it strongly to your perusal. You will be much entertained, and somewhat edified, by running over a good deal of the works of Voltaire. For elegance and wit, they are almost always delightful; and frequently admirable in tendency.—

Whatever you do, let the consideration of the grand cause be always uppermost. The real principles of good government have you alone, among public men, who thoroughly understand them. You alone therefore can be their real champion.

Ever yours

J. MILL

I must say a word about the poor fishes. I think the error was in not making the pond for the gold and silver darlings, higher up than all the rest. For the spawn of these cormorant fish is so very small that it will make its way through almost any thing through which water will go. The stronger fish, which will be sure to devour the spawn of the weaker, will prevent the favourites from multiplying, I should fear; though they may not consume the grown ones. They all devour the young of one another. What sport for Mr. Samuda! How happy!

540. MALTHUS TO RICARDO [1]
[*Reply to 536.—Answered by* 542]

E I Coll August 11th 1823

My dear Ricardo,

I am much obliged to you for your letter, and for shewing me that I had made a rash and unnecessary concession. I was deceived at the time I wrote to you by the strong case occurring to me of the food obtained by 20 men being divided amongst 10, owing to a great mortality or exportation of labourers. I did not then see that instead of profits there would, for that year, be a very great loss, and instead of any thing to be added on account of profits, there would be a great subtraction to be made from the labour employed in procuring the food, which would make the thing answer completely even on so extravagant a supposition. You were however inclined to draw much too large inferences from my concession than it would have warranted, if I had adhered to it. In fact it only supposed an exception in the case of a very violent and sudden change occurring in the interval between the time of the production of the food of the labourer, and the time of its being paid as wages, which would very rarely be so much as a year, and the effect of which would be quite at an end after that time had expired. The concession therefore would not apply either to any natural increase of population, or any retardation in the rate of it from prudence. But in reality I find that there is no occasion for any concession.

I do not find fault with your measure because it does not determine what proportion of the value of a commodity

---

[1] Addressed: 'D. Ricardo Esqr M.P. / Gatcomb Park / Minchinhampton / Gloucestershire.' MS in British Museum, Add. 34,545, fols. 102–5.—*Letters to McCulloch*, XLII. The letter was sent to McCulloch (see below, p. 353, n. 2) and retained by him.

belongs to wages and what to profits. I do not consider my measure as determining this, although it is always equal to the two united; but I find fault with it, because it varies with the varying profits of other commodities and therefore cannot possibly measure with any tolerable accuracy these variations.

You say you cannot discover what the value of the precious metals in different countries can have to do with this question. This surprises me I own a good deal. You who have proposed a measure of value formed of the precious metals obtained in a particular way, appear to me to be imperatively bound to furnish your readers with the means of distinguishing between a high price of labour while money remains of the same value, and a high price occasioned by a low value of money. Would you *really* say that cloth and muslin were not dear in India where they cost four or five times as much labour as in England, and that the prodigious difference in the exchangeable value of the products of the same quantity of labour, were exclusively occasioned by the *naturally low value* of labour in India, although perhaps according to your own mode of estimating, it might not be easy to shew that labour was of lower value in India than in America. Indeed I believe that profits are higher in America, and therefore the value of labour in India ought to be lower. And though it may be true that the same sort of exchanges might take place, if there were no precious metals, yet we could form very little notion of what the rate of these exchanges would be, without a reference to actual facts, and these facts shew that this rate is most powerfully influenced by the proportion which money bears to labour in the places where the commodities are produced. As a political Economist are you not bound to shew whether this prodigious difference in the money price of labour in America and India is occasioned by the dif-

ference in the quantity of labour required to produce the
wages in each country, or by a difference in the value of
money; and further is it not to be expected that you should
shew how to estimate the value of money in different
countries?

You deny that every commodity exchanges for two
quantities of labour, one equal to the quantity actually
worked up in it, another equal to the quantity which the
profits will command, yet it does not appear that the case you
produce (though unusual as it involves a sudden change in
the value of money) goes any way towards supporting your
objection. You say, in substance, that having paid common
wages one year, if corn becomes dear the next, and wages rise,
the commodities will not command the quantity of labour
stated in my proposition; but surely it will, if we estimate
profits by the difference between the quantity of accumulated
and immediate labour advanced to produce a commodity and
the labour which it is worth when sold: and I would submit
to you whether this is not a much more *natural* and *correct*
mode of estimating profits, than even in money the value of
which may have changed in that short interval. What sort of
profits are those which when a man continues to employ the
same quantity of labour in his business may leave him absolutely nothing to live upon. Let us suppose him to have
employed ten labourers at 10£ a piece, and to sell his commodity for 110£, he will appear to have gained 10 per cent;
but it will be obviously only a nominal not a real gain if he is
obliged to pay 110£ for the same quantity of labour next year.
Should this price of labour continue he must necessarily give
up his business unless the money price of his commodity
rises. This shews the absolute necessity of measuring value
and profits in labour, not in money, whenever there is the
least suspicion that money may have altered in value. But if

we measure profits by the difference between the labour advanced and the labour which the commodity will command,
and (excluding the variable article money) I would ask how
we can estimate profits but upon the actual advances, which
are acknowledged to be accumulated and immediate labour,
then it appears to me to follow as clear as the sun, that if
value as you say in the beginning of your letter is made up of
labour and profits, the variable wages which command the
same quantity of labour must be of the same value, *because*
they will always have cost in their production the same
quantity of labour, with the addition of the profits upon that
labour. Your doctrine is that the value of wages rises when
more labour is employed on their production. I quite agree
with you that as far as that part of their value which resolves
itself into the labour advanced is concerned, they *do increase*
in value; but you have fallen into the important error of considering their value as made up of labour alone instead of
being made up of labour and profits, as you justly say is the
case with almost all commodities. But as the wages of labour
like other commodities are unquestionably made up of
labour and profits; I am utterly at a loss to conceive what
view you are taking of the subject, when you say that you
dont understand the connection between the invariability of
labour as a measure of value, and my proposition which
shews that as the positive value of the labour worked up in
the wages of a given number of men increases, the positive
value of the profits (the other component part of their whole
value) diminishes exactly in the same degree. If these two
propositions can properly be considered as having no connection with each other, I must have quite lost myself on
these subjects, and can hardly hope to shew their connection
by anything which I can say further. I will however just add,
that they appear to me to have the same kind of connection

as your proposition respecting the constant value of commodities produced in the same way as the precious metals,
and a fall in the value of profits in the same degree as a rise
in the money price of the same quantity of labour. In this
case, which in a manner goes through your book, you make
the fall of profits prevent that rise in the value of the commodity which would otherwise take place from what you
state to be a rise in the value of the same quantity of labour.
Allowing the premises I should allow that the connection was
complete and satisfactory, and that such commodity would
remain of the same value. Then why I would ask is there no
connection between the constant value of the wages of the
same quantity of labour, and that fall in the value of profits
which prevents the rise which would otherwise take place in
the wages of the same number of men from the increase in the
quantity of labour required to produce them?

You observe "Can you be said to have given a good
reason for the selection which you have made of a measure of
value, when it will not bear close examination" You have no
doubt the fullest right to find fault with all my reasons; and
I can honestly assure you that the more strictly you examine
them the more you will please me; but I don't think that I
fairly lay open to the charge which you elsewhere seem to
make of defining an increase of value to be an increased
power of commanding labour, without giving reasons for it.
The invariability of the value of labour is indeed my *conclusion*, but by no means the definition with which I set out. And
this *conclusion* appears to me to follow in the strictest manner
from the concessions which you and other Political Economists have made, and are indeed generally acknowledged.
I own to you that after paying the greatest attention to all
you have said I consider this conclusion as quite safe from
you. If it be vulnerable at all, it must be from weapons which

apply equally to your system and mine, and which deny the existence of absolute value; but this would unquestionably confuse one of the most important distinctions in political economy, and would be taking up a position which after all appears to me to be by no means tenable.

It is no doubt true that demand and supply are the real foundation of all exchangeable value, and that the *only* reason why labour is a correct measure of this value when nothing else is concerned, is that the supplies from the same kind and quantity of labour would on an average be in the same proportion to the demand for them; but if the labour in different countries or in different periods of the same country were very different in physical force, the products of the same number of days of these different kinds of labour would not be in the same proportion to the demand and would not therefore exchange with each other. But still it might without impropriety be said, that the products obtained by a person who worked only six hours a day would be scarcer and dearer in reference to the natural wants and numbers of the society than the products obtained by persons who worked 12 hours a day and that therefore it would be more proper to say that the products in the first case are dearer, than that labour is cheaper. Practically all the circumstances of this kind are taken into consideration in the two propositions I stated in my last letter, to which I do not now see any exceptions.

I am glad you are writing. I should like much to pay you a visit at Gatcomb, but fear I shall have no opportunity.

Kind regards

Ever truly y^{rs}

T R MALTHUS

541. MᶜCULLOCH TO RICARDO [1]
[Reply to 530 & 538.—Answered by 543 & 544]

Edinburgh 11ᵗʰ Augt 1823

My Dear Sir

    I am greatly obliged to you for the paper containing an account of the E.I. Cos sales of tea; and for the communication of Mr Malthus letter to you and your answer—I enclose the former but I have used your permission to retain the latter for a few days that I may the better profit by what appears to me to be one of the most acute and able articles that has ever come from your pen—It ought to convince Mr Malthus though I suppose it will not.

    After I came home Jeffrey pressed me to write an article on the Navigation laws, and I have since been so incessantly occupied with Taxation, that I have never been able to resume the consideration of the grand subject of value. Still, however, were it not for the doubts which you entertain I should myself have none respecting the proposition that it is by the *quantity of labour* only that all exchangeable value is to be estimated. I do not exclude all reference to time; but I refer to it only in order to assist me in discovering the quantities of labour which have been actually expended on or are worked up in the commodities whose value is to be measured. I need not say to you that time of itself produces no effect whatever; it only affords space for really efficient agents [2] to produce effects. But whether these agents be men, or the processes which nature herself carries on in the production of commodities seems to me to be wholly immaterial provided it require *equal capitals to set them in*

---

[1] Addressed: 'David Ricardo Esq / M.P. / Gatcomb Park / Minchinhampton / Gloucestershire'.

MS in Mill-Ricardo papers.
[2] 'agents' replaces 'causes'.

motion. If you give men wages, they only give you back an
equivalent for these wages, and for the period of their
advance, just as natural agents do when you employ them:—
that is, to give an example, when you give them a fluid, or
a capital in the shape of a fluid, to turn it into wine. There is
no more to be taken into account in the one case than in the
other. In both cases you employ certain capitals, that is
certain quantities of labour to produce certain effects; and
if the capitals be equal and the times in which the effects have
been produced be different, it is at once a proof that more
labour has been required to produce the one effect than the
other, and an exponent of that greater quantity. The circumstance of workmen being independent would not affect this
result. They can only be regarded as machines worth a
certain quantity of capital or labour; and their produce is to
be valued by the quantity of that labour expended on it.
I may be deluding and deceiving myself; but I confess I can
discover no fallacy in this reasoning. If it requires a capital
of £1000 to set the muscles of the masons in motion who
build me a house; and if it also requires £1000 to set fermentation, purification, and all the other processes in motion
which produce me a cask of wine, is it not plain that both
the house and the wine cost the same quantity of labour if
they are produced in the same time? and is it not also plain
that if it requires different times to produce them it can only
be because different quantities of labour are wrought up in
them? The truth is that natural agents are quite as expensive
as men. To get any thing possessed of value from them you
must always give them capital or accumulated labour to work
upon; and to get anything valuable from labourers you must
do just the same thing.

   I can see no difficulty in the case of the tree. Suppose that
a machine which cost only 2/ had been invented 100 years

ago; that this machine was indestructible and cost no repairs, and that it had been all the while employed in the production of a commodity which was only finished today. This commodity might perhaps be worth £100 or £200; but whatever value it may be possessed of, it must have derived it entirely from the continued agency of the machine, or from the quantity of labour expended in its production. Now this is just the case of the tree. The capital employed in its production was small; but the length of time that this capital has been employed has rendered its produce the result of a great quantity of labour, and has, therefore, made it highly valuable.

There is a radical and essential difference between the circumstances which determine the exchangeable value of commodities, and a measure of that value, which I am afraid is not always kept sufficiently in view. If you are to measure value, you must measure it by the agency of some one commodity or other possessed of value, and not as Mr Malthus proposes by referring to the agent employed to give value; and as the circumstances under which every commodity is produced must always be liable to vary none can be an invariable measure, though some are certainly much less variable than others and may, therefore, be used as approximations. It is evident I think that there neither is nor can be any real and invariable standard of value; and if so it must be very idle to seek for that which can never be found. The real inquiry is to ascertain what are the circumstances which determine the exchangeable value of commodities at any given period—and these I think are all clearly reducible to one—the comparative quantities of labour bestowed on their production. If we establish this proposition we shall make the subject as plain as it ever can be made, and will at once put to rest the objections of Malthus, Torrens and so forth;

but if we fail in this the subject will always be encumbered with difficulties. Whenever I have time I shall apply myself to the consideration of this subject; and I am fully satisfied that it must be my own fault if I do not make it clear that precisely the same quantities of labour have been expended on one thousand pounds worth of wine, cloth, and timber.

I am extremely glad to learn that you have written your Essay on a National Bank, and I shall be most anxious to see it. I will use the liberty to send you the proofs of the more difficult parts of my article on Taxation—they will recal Kensington garden to your recollection.

The paper you sent me from Mr Tooke is completely conclusive on the subject of Mr Blake's pamphlet; it shews him to be equally at variance with fact as with principle. Accept my grateful thanks for all your kindness; and with kindest regards to Mrs and Miss Ricardo believe me to be with the greatest respect and esteem

Ever faithfully yours
J. R. M^cCULLOCH

542. RICARDO TO MALTHUS [1]
[Reply to 540.—Answered by 545]

Gatcomb Park, Minchinhampton
15 Augt 1823

My Dear Malthus

It is a prudent step in you to withdraw your concession for I am sure that your theory could not stand with it.

[1] Addressed: 'The Revd T. R. Malthus / East India College / Hertford'.
   MS at Albury (as printed in the text).—*Letters to Malthus*, LXXXVII. A draft, which Ricardo sent to McCulloch, is in British Museum, Add. MSS 34,545, fols. 106–9; it was printed in *Letters to McCulloch*, XLIII. Some of the variants and corrections of the draft are here given in the footnotes.

margin notes: 11 Aug. 1823; 15 Aug. 1823

You find fault with my measure of value, you say, be-cause it varies with the varying profits of other commodities. This is I acknowledge an imperfection in it when used to measure other commodities in which there enters more or less of profits than enters into my measure,[1] but you do not appear to see that against your measure the same objection holds good, for your measure contains no profits at all, and therefore never can be an accurate measure of value for commodities which do contain profits.

If I had no other argument to offer against your measure this which I am going to mention *when used to you* would be fatal to it. You say that my measure cannot measure com-modities produced by labour alone. Granted; but if it be true how can your measure measure commodities produced with labour and profits united? You might just as well say that 3 times 2 are 6, and that twice 3 are not 6,—or that a foot measure was a good measure for a yard, but a yard was not a good measure for a foot. If your measure will measure my commodity accurately, mine must do the same by yours. These are identical propositions and I confess I see no answer that can be made to me.

The fact really is that no accurate measure of absolute value can be found. No one doubts the desirableness of having one, but all we can ever hope to get is one tolerably well calculated to measure the greatest number of commodi-ties, and therefore I should have no hesitation in admitting your measure to be the best, under all circumstances, if you could shew that the greater number of commodities were produced by labour alone without the intervention of capital. On the other hand if a greater number of commodities are produced under the circumstances which I suppose to attend

---

[1] Draft reads 'in which there does not enter so much, or more, of profits, than my measure itself contains;'.

the production of the commodity which I chuse for my measure, then mine would be the best measure. You will understand that in either case I suppose a degree of arbitrariness in the selection, and I only contend that it would be best employed in selecting mine.

When you say that my great mistake is in considering commodities made up of labour alone, and not of labour and profits I think the error is yours, not mine, for that is precisely what you do[,] you measure commodities, by labour alone, which have both labour and profits in them. You surely will not say that my money, produced by labour and[1] capital, and by which I propose to measure other things, omits profits. Yours does; what profits are there in shrimps, or in gold picked up by daily labour, on account of the labourer, on the sea shore?[2] How much more justly then might this accusation be brought against you?

You object to me that I am inconsistent in wishing to leave the consideration of the value of money here and in India out of the question when speaking of the value of labour and of commodities in this country and in India. I, you say, to leave out the consideration of the value of the precious metals who have proposed a measure formed of them! There is nothing inconsistent in this. In examining your proposition which rejects my measure and adopts another, I must try it by your doctrines, and not by mine which you reject. A conclusion founded on my premises might be a just one, but if you dispute my premises and substitute others the conclusion may no longer be the same, and in examining your doctrines I must attend only to the conclusions to which your premises would lead me. You ask "would you really say that cloth and muslin were not dear

[1] In draft 'profits' is del. here.
[2] In draft this sentence replaces 'Yours does, and you do not deny it.'

in India where they cost four or five times as much labour as in England"? You know I would not, because I estimate value by the quantity of labour worked up in a commodity, but by the cost in labour of cloth and muslin in India[1] you do not mean the quantity of labour actually employed on their production, but the quantity which the finished commodity can command in exchange. The difference between us is this, you say a commodity is dear because it will command a great quantity of labour, I say it is only dear when a great quantity has been bestowed on its production. In India a commodity may be produced with 20 days labour and may command 30 days labour. In England it may be produced by 25 days labour and command only 29. According to you this commodity is dearer in India, according to me it is dearer in England.

Now here is my objection against your measure as a general measure of value, that notwithstanding more labour may be bestowed on a commodity it may fall in value[2] estimated in your measure—it may exchange for a less quantity of labour. This is impossible when you apply your measure legitimately to those objects only which it is calculated to measure. Would it be possible for example to apply more labour to the production of shrimps, or to pick up grains of gold on the sea shore, and yet to sell those commodities for less labour than before? certainly not, but it would be quite

---

[1] In draft he had first written, in place of the beginning of this sentence: 'You know I would not because I estimate value by quantity of labour, but if I adopt your measure I may say so because it is possible that though cloth and muslin may cost more labour in India it may also command more and things are dear'. Here he broke off, and replaced this by 'You know I would not because I estimate value by quantity of labour, but in doing so I do not therefore adopt your measure and your meaning because by the cost in labour of cloth and muslin in India'. Finally he revised as in the text. (*N.B.* The reading of the deleted passages is uncertain.)

[2] The remainder of this sentence is ins. in draft.

possible to bestow more labour on the making of a piece of cloth, and yet for cloth to exchange for a less quantity of labour than before. This is another argument in my mind conclusive against the expediency of adopting your measure.

I repeat once more that the same trade precisely would go on between India and Europe, as far as regards commodities, if no such thing as money made of gold and silver existed in the world. All commodities would in that case as well as now command a much larger quantity of labour in India than in England, and if we wanted to know how much more, either of those commodities as well as money, would enable us to ascertain. The same thing which makes money of a low value in England makes many other commodities of a low value there, and the Political Economist in accounting for the low value of one accounts at the same time for the low value of the others. I do not object to accounting for the low value of gold in particular countries, but I say it is not material to an enquiry into a general measure of value, particularly if it be itself objected to as forming any element in that measure.

Suppose a farmer to have a certain quantity of cattle and implements and a hundred quarters of wheat; that he expends this wheat in supporting a certain quantity of labour, and that the result is 110 q^{rs} of wheat and an increase of $\frac{1}{10}$ also in his cattle and implements, would not his profits be 10 pc^{t} whatever might be the price of labour the following year? If the 110 q^{rs} could command no more labour than the 100 q^{rs} could command before, he would, according to you, have made no profits; and you are right if we admit that yours is a correct measure of value,—he would have a profit in kind but no profit in value. If wheat was the[1] measure of value, he would have a profit in kind, and the same profit in value. If money was the correct measure of value, and he

---

[1] Draft contains in addition 'general'.

commenced with £100, he would have 10 pc.ᵗ profit if the value of his produce was £110. All these results leave the question of a measure of value undecided, and prove nothing but the convenience, in your estimation, of adopting one in preference to another. The labourer, however, who lived by his labour, would find it difficult to be persuaded that his labour was of the same value at two periods, in one of which he had abundance of food and clothing, and in another he was absolutely starving for want. What he might think would certainly not affect the philosophy of the question, but it would be at least as good a reason against the measure you propose as that of the farmer in favor of it, when he found that he had no profits because he had no greater command of labour, although he might have more corn or more money. You call every increase of value nominal which is not an increase in the measure you propose;—I do not object to your doing so, but those who do not agree with you in the propriety of adopting this measure may argue very consistently in saying they are possessed of more value when they have £110 than when they had £100, although the larger sum may not when it is realised command so much labour as the smaller sum did before, because they not only admit but contend that labour may rise and fall in value, and therefore in respect to labour he may be poorer although he possesses a greater value.

I have said that the value of most commodities is made up of labour and profits: If this be so, you observe, "it is as clear as the sun that the variable wages which command the same quantity of labour must be of the same value, *because* they will always cost in their production the same quantity of labour with the addition of the profits upon that labour." I confess that I cannot see the connection of this conclusion with the premises. Whether you divide a commodity in 8,

7, or 6 divisions it will always be divided into two portions, variable portions, but always 2. If the division be in 8 the portions may be 6 and 2, 5 and 3, 4 and 4, 7 and one. If 7 they may be 6 and 1, 5 and two, 4 and 3, and so on. Now this is my admission. What we want to know is what the number of[1] those divisions are, or what the value of the commodity is, whether 8, 7 or 6? And have I come a bit nearer to this knowledge by admitting that whatever the value[2] may be it will be divided between two persons? Whatever you give to the labourer is made up of labour and profits, and therefore the value of labour is constant! This is your proposition. To me it wants every quality of clearness. I find that at one time I give a man 10 bushels of wheat for the same quantity of his labour for which at another time I give him 8 bushels: Wheat according to you falls in the proportion of 10 to 8: I ask, why? and your answer is because "as the positive value of the labour worked up in the wages increases, the positive value of the profits (the other component part of their whole value) diminishes exactly in the same degree." Now does this positive value refer to the same quantity of wheat? certainly not, but to two different quantities, to 10 bushels at one time to 8 at another. You add "if these two propositions" (namely the one I have just mentioned, and the invariability of labour as a measure of value) "can properly be considered as having no connection with each other I must have quite lost myself on these subjects, and can hardly hope to shew the connection by any thing which I can say further["]. I hope you do not suspect me of shutting my eyes against conviction, but if this proposition is so very clear as it is to you, I cannot account for my want of power to understand it. I still think that the invariability of your measure is the

---

[1] 'the number of' is ins. in draft. [2] 'or the divisions' is del. here in draft.

definition with which you set out, and not the *conclusion* to which you arrive by any legitimate argument. My complaint against you is that you claim to have given us an accurate measure of value, and I object to your claim, not that I have succeeded and you have failed, but that we have both failed—that there is not and cannot be an accurate measure of value, and that the most that any man can do is to find[1] out a measure of value applicable in a great many cases and not very far deviating from accuracy in many others. This is all I have pretended to do, or now pretend to have done, and if you advanced no higher claims I would be more humble, but I cannot allow that you have succeeded in the great object you aimed at. In answering you I am really using those weapons by which alone you say you can be defeated, and which are I confess equally applicable to your measure and to mine, I mean the argument of the non-existence of any measure of absolute value. There is no such thing,—your measure as well as mine will measure variations arising from more or less labour being required to produce commodities, but the difficulty is respecting the varying proportions which go to labour and profits. The alteration in these proportions alters the relative value of things in the degree that[2] more or less of labour or profit enter into them, and for these variations there has never been, and I think never will be any perfect measure of value.

I have lost no time in answering your letter, for I am just now warm in the subject, and cannot do better than disburthen myself on paper.

Ever my dear Malthus
Truly Y.rs
DAVID RICARDO

[1] In draft 'to find' replaces 'to say that he has found'. [2] In draft 'the degree that' replaces 'proportion as'.

543. RICARDO TO M^cCULLOCH [1]
[*Reply to* 541]

My Dear Sir

As you express some interest in the discussion going on   15 Aug. 1823
between Malthus and myself I send you 2 more letters. [2]
Return them at your convenience. I will write shortly in
answer to your observations on value.—

Truly Y^{rs}

D RICARDO

Gatcomb Park 15 Aug 1823

[The following unfinished draft of a letter to McCulloch was
probably written on 15 Aug. 1823,[3] but on that day Ricardo confined
himself to sending to McCulloch the above short letter with its
enclosures; a full reply went only with letter 544 of 21 August which
includes most, though not all, the arguments contained in this draft.
Hitherto unpublished; MS in Mill-Ricardo papers.]

My Dear Sir

I sent you a few days ago[4] a letter which Mr. Malthus wrote   15 Aug. 1823
to me, in answer to one which I had written to him, and my reply
to it, by which you will be able to judge of the controversy
between him and me respecting the merits of the measure of value
which he proposes. I find by your letter[5] that you adhere to the
proposition that value is to be estimated by quantities of labour,
but I cannot help thinking, that, even according to your statement, that language is not quite accurate. The continued agency
of a machine worth only 2/ may, after a very long period, produce
a commodity worth £100, but surely strictly speaking there is no
more labour in the commodity than what was originally bestowed
on the two shilling machine. We all acknowledge that 2/, with

---

[1] Addressed: 'J. R. MCulloch,
Esqr / Buccleugh Place / Edinburgh'.
    MS in British Museum.—*Letters
to McCulloch*, XLI.
[2] Letter 540 and a draft of letter
542, which were enclosed, re-

mained in McCulloch's possession.
[3] After receiving McCulloch's
letter of 11 August and before
sending him the *second* pair of
Malthus letters on 15 August.
[4] On 8 August, by letter 538.
[5] Letter 541.

its annual accumulations, at a compound rate of interest or profit, will at last yield £100,[1] and perhaps there would be no difficulty in shewing that a commodity so produced is not therefore precluded from being accurately measured by a commodity which has an equal capital employed on it in the support of labour. But the real difficulty is this: here are two commodities both produced by labour and by labour only; one has been produced and brought to market in one day, the other in 365 days. One is worth a pound but the other is worth much more than £365. If profits are 5 pc⸍, it is worth £383. 5–; if 10 pc⸍ £401. 10– which of these shall be our measure of value? If we chuse the former, which is Mr Malthus' measure, and suppose the gold from which his money is made to be picked up by daily labour on the sea shore, the relative price of a commodity produced by the same quantity of labour, in one year, when profits are 5 pc⸍, will be as I have just said £383. 5. Let every thing remain the same, except profits, which shall rise to 10 pc⸍, and the commodity immediately rises to £401. 10. But if we chuse a commodity for our measure, gold for example which we will suppose cannot be brought to market in less than a year although it has precisely the same quantity of labour in it as Mr Malthus's gold[2] then though a commodity produced in a day may be still worth £1, and the gold produced in a year 383 times and a quarter that value, yet when profits rise to 10 pc⸍ gold does not alter in value and still is not 383 times and a quarter times the value of the commodity produced by daily labour, nor yet 401 times and a half.

[1] The following is written as an alternative over the remainder of this sentence and the next three sentences: 'and should yield that sum to preserve an equality of profits but we question the accuracy of calling that by the name of labour which is really accumulated capital without labour. The tree which originally cost 2/- for labour and becomes worth £100 does not really owe its value wholly to labour. You may say that the best commodity by which to measure trees and all other commodities is one in which labour principally or exclusively enters—that is another question, but I ask whether we must not acknowledge that there are many exceptions to the proposition that commodities are valuable in proportion as labour enters into them and therefore never vary but on account of a greater or smaller quantity of labour being required to produce them.'

[2] The last fifteen words are ins.

15 Aug. 1823

A commodity produced in two years with the same quantity of labour that another is produced in one is more valuable than the commodity produced in one, and a commodity produced with the labour of one man for 52 weeks is more valuable than a commodity produced by the labour of 52 men for one week. I know how you explain this you say you estimate the value of the commodity not by the quantity actually worked up in the commodity but by the capital which employs it, and therefore if equal capitals are employed you have a right to say equal quantities of labour are employed, and a capital employed for two years though of precisely the same amount as one employed for one year may be said to employ more labour than a capital employed for one, but this is adopting Torrens view and saying that commodities are valuable in proportion to the capitals employed upon them and not in proportion to the actual labour employed. And there are great difficulties to get over even if we admitted this language. You and I are both manufacturers, you produce your commodity in two years I mine in one—we employ equal capitals. Suppose your commodity to be two and a $\frac{1}{4}$ times the value of mine and that nothing occurs to interfere with the facility or difficulty of producing either commodity but that labour rises and profits fall. If your commodity is the measure of value mine will rise, if mine is yours will fall. The two commodities change in relative value and yours is no longer two and a quarter times the value of mine. Can it be said that the proportions of capital we employ are in any way altered? or the proportion of labour? certainly not, nothing has altered but the rate of distribution between employer and employed and this affects us differently— profits have fallen and there is a larger proportion of profits in your commodity than in mine—this and this only is the reason why they alter in relative value. Now if you said "of all commodities I know, or can conceive, one, in which labour enters for a certain time, and which always requires the same quantity of labour to be bestowed upon it, is the best measure of value["], that I should understand, but it is quite a different proposition from the one which you actually maintain. But then you must not say that it is a perfect or an accurate measure of value for if you did [1]

---

[1] 'not' is ins. here by an obvious mistake.

Malthus might retort on you as I do on him and ask you how your measure could be an accurate measure for his shrimps, if his shrimps were not also an accurate measure for yours when he withdrew, from his shrimps, the only cause of variation which you acknowledge.[1] The fact is there is not any measure of absolute[2] value which can in any degree be deemed an accurate one. When we measure the length of a piece of linen it is one simple element only we measure—the length of the linen nor of the measure is not liable to alter with the weight or with any other of the properties either of the linen or of its measure[3]— not so with its value—value is made up of two elements, wages and profits, and therefore can be measured accurately only by a commodity (having value) in which these elements are[4] mixed up in precisely the same proportions as in the linen itself. To speak rigidly what is fit to measure one commodity is fit to measure but few others, but if we are not in want of this great nicety we shall make the nearest approximation to a correct measure of value by chusing a commodity for our measure which is produced under circumstances with respect to time nearly approaching to those under which the greatest number of commodities are produced, (for it is time only which makes any difference in the proportions in which profits and wages enter into the value of different commodities)[5] and which shall itself be invariable as far as[6] variations may be caused by variable quantities of labour being employed on its production.

You estimate value by the quantity of labour bestowed on the agent of production and not by the quantity bestowed on the thing produced—this I repeat is Torrens mode of estimating value for it is in fact saying that commodities are valuable according to the value of the[7] capital employed on production and

[1] The following is written as an alternative over the last sentence: 'allowing however that your proposition was that which I have first mentioned you would be bound to admit that it was an arbitrary selection and was not an accurate measure of general value.'

[2] 'absolute' is ins.

[3] This clause originally read: 'the length does not alter with its weight or with any other of its properties'. It was imperfectly revised.

[4] 'and must always be' was ins. and then del.

[5] This clause is ins.

[6] The rest of the sentence replaces 'the employment of labour upon it is concerned.'

[7] 'agent' is del. here.

the time for which it is employed. This is however a very different thing from saying that commodities are valuable according to the quantity of labour worked up in them. But what means have you of ascertaining the equal value of these agents? If all men employed the same agents of production they might be compared, their proportional quantities would indicate their proportional values,[1] but one man employs wine of last year as a capital, which he proposes to sell with a year's profit at the end of this,—another employs food and clothing for the same period,—the relative[2] values of food and clothing and of wine just made alter[3] on account perhaps of a demand for labour, which unequally affects the value of these commodities. These then are no longer equal capitals, but what has made them unequal? not any thing connected with the quantity of labour necessary to produce them, for that is just the same as before. They both command less labour than before, but in unequal degrees. Shall we estimate their value by this power over labour? we then adopt Malthus measure. Though one has fallen 10 pc! more than the other estimated in labour, it has fallen only 5 pc! more estimated in some other thing, and there may be some perhaps in which one has not varied at all. How are we to measure these differences and say which of all these commodities is to be the measure by which all shall be referred, and which shall be itself declared to be invariable. What are the circumstances which are to give it this character of invariability. This is the test to which I would bring all your speculations, and if you propose a commodity as a measure of value I should ask you to tell me on what grounds you advanced the pretensions of its being itself an invariable commodity, and if you made no such pretensions for it I should then ask what circumstances would in your opinion make it such?]

---

[1] The last eight words are ins.
[2] 'relative' is ins.

[3] 'and alter fundamentally' is del. here.

544. RICARDO TO M^cCULLOCH [1]
[*Reply to 541.—Answered by 546*]

Gatcomb Park 21 Augt 1823

My Dear Sir

You will have received two more letters which have passed between Mr. Malthus and me on the subject of his measure of value, and which I sent to you a few days ago. I fear that you will not agree with either of us, but will still contend for the mathematical accuracy of the measure which you and I both prefer. I do not see the great difference you mention between the circumstances which determine the exchangeable value of commodities, and the medium of that value. I agree with you that if you are to measure value you must measure it by the agency of some one commodity or other possessed of value,—that is what Mr. Malthus and we all propose to do, and the only difference between us is respecting the circumstances which are to determine the value,—the invariable value, of the commodity which we chuse for our measure. Is it not clear then that as soon as we are in possession of the knowledge of the circumstances which determine the value of commodities, we are enabled to say what is necessary to give us an invariable measure of value? We all acknowledge too, that 2/, with its annual accumulations, at a compound rate of profit, will at last yield £100, and should do so to preserve the equality of profits, but I question the propriety of calling these accumulated profits by the name of labour, and of saying that the

---

[1] Addressed: 'J. R. MCulloch Esqr / Buccleugh Place / Edinburgh'.

MS in British Museum.—*Letters to McCulloch*, XLIV.

A rough draft of a portion of this letter, written on the back of an old cover addressed to Ricardo, is in *R.P.* It was published in *Minor Papers*, p. 224, and is printed below, p. 359, n. 1.

A copy in Ricardo's hand, sent to Malthus and returned by him (see opening of letter 545), is in Mill-Ricardo papers.

An earlier version of this letter is printed as an appendix to letter 543.

21 Aug. 1823

commodity so worth a hundred pounds was valuable in proportion to the quantity of labour bestowed upon it. The tree which originally cost 2/- for labour and becomes in after-time of the value of £100, has never strictly more than 2/ worth of labour employed on it.

A commodity, produced by the labour of one man in 52 weeks, is, and ought to be, more valuable than another produced by 52 men in one week. Yes, you say, because a capital employed for the 52 weeks gives more employment to labour than the capital employed for one, but there are in fact only equivalent quantities of labour in these 2 commodities. You explain this by saying that you estimate the labour bestowed on a commodity by the labour bestowed on the capital or agent by which the commodity is produced. This I think is Torrens mode of estimating value, for it is in fact saying that commodities are valuable according to the value of the capital employed on their production, and the time for which it is so employed. This is a different thing from saying that commodities are valuable according to the quantity of labour worked up in them. I do not however agree with either proposition, and I would ask what means you have of ascertaining the equal value of capitals? You say, "if it requires a capital of £1000 to set the muscles of the mason in motion who builds me a house, and if it also requires £1000 to set fermentation, purification and all the other processes in motion which produce me a cask of wine, is it not plain that both the house and the cask of wine cost the same quantity of labour, if they are produced in the same time? and is it not also plain that if it requires different times to produce them it can only be because different quantities of labour are wrought up in them?["]¹ This does not appear

¹ Ricardo's draft (see above, p. 358, n. 1) begins with this quotation and goes on: 'In this passage you assume ['two things' is del. here] that these equal quantities of capital

to me so plain. You assume that these equal quantities of capital now worth £1000 each will always be of equal value, but nothing is more probable than that one shall become more valuable than the other. These capitals are not the same in kind—what will employ one set of workmen, is not precisely the same as will employ another set, and if they themselves are produced in unequal times they are subject to the same fluctuations as other commodities. Till you have fixed the criterion by which we are to ascertain value, you can say nothing of equal capitals, for what is equal to day may be unequal in a year.[1] The question is, What are the circumstances which are necessary to give invariability to any commodity, for that ought to be the character of our measure. This is the test to which all measures of value must be brought, and to which I must submit any measure you may propose. If you said "Of all commodities I know, that one in which labour enters for a certain time, and which always requires the same quantity of labour, is the best measure of value", I should agree with you, but you must not propose it as one

now worth £1000 each, will always be equal to each other and will always command the same quantity of labour, but nothing is more probable than that one shall become more valuable than the other, it may become so in various ways—it would be more valuable than the other if while it commanded the same quantity of labour as before the other commanded less, or if they both commanded less, but the other a great deal less—or it might command more labour while the other commanded the same quantity— or both might command more but their power of doing so might increase unequally. You must define then what you mean by equal capitals, for the means of ascertaining their equality or variation of value is the very thing in dispute. If the value of the capitals depended upon the labour expended on them there would be little difficulty in the question, but this is denied, and I think with success.

'You say ["]in both cases you employ certain capitals, that is certain quantities of labour to produce certain effects". Here you speak of capital and labour as the same thing, and it is this part of your proposition which requires explanation.' Here the draft ends.

[1] Copy to Malthus reads 'unequal next year'.

against which no objection can be reasonably made, for if you did, Malthus might retort on you the argument I use to him,[1] and say if your commodity is a good measure for my shrimps, or for my gold picked up by daily labour on the sea shore, why is not my measure, (shrimps, or gold so picked up) a good measure for yours? To me it appears that we have a choice only amongst imperfect measures, and that we cannot have a perfect one, for there is no such thing in nature. When we measure the length of a piece of linen we measure length only, and we measure it by a commodity which has length that is invariable, but value is compounded of two elements wages and profit[2] mixed up in all imaginable proportions; it is in vain, therefore, to attempt to measure[3] accurately, unless your measure agrees precisely in the proportions of wages and profits with the commodity measured. A commodity which has wages in it alone, and no profits, and this is Malthus's measure, is not an accurate measure for commodities which have both labour and profits in them. All we can do is to make the best choice amongst confessedly imperfect measures, and I should have no hesitation in chusing[4] Malthus's if the number of commodities produced by labour alone were the most numerous, but as the contrary is the fact, as the great mass of commodities is produced by the union of labour and capital for a certain length of time, I have nothing to amend in the choice I have made; I consider it a mean; Malthus's is at one extreme of the scale, old oak trees are at the other. In one there is nothing but labour, in the other there is nothing but accumulations of capital from profits with scarcely any labour whatever, and therefore they are both unfit measures of value. I have not come to this

---

[1] See above, p. 346.
[2] Copy to Malthus 'of two elements of wages and profits'.

[3] Copy to Malthus has here in addition 'value'.
[4] Copy to Malthus 'selecting'.

conclusion without a great deal of reflection but I am quite open to conviction if you have any thing powerful to urge in favor of your view. Suppose wine and cloth to be both made in a year, with the same quantity of capital, and that a pipe of wine newly made and a certain quantity of cloth are each worth £50. Suppose profits to be 50 pc^t p^r Ann$^m_.$ a pipe of wine kept one year after it is made will be worth 75£, kept two years it will be worth £112. 10—but the piece of cloth will always be worth £50. Now if profits fall to 5 pc^t cloth and wine just made will be the same as before, each of the value of £50—but wine kept one year will be worth £52 10, and if kept two years it will be worth £55 2. 3 The value of the capitals employed is precisely the same, the quantity of labour employed is also the same, and while the time is the same the value of the finished commodity is also the same. When we see commodities thus vary on account of an alteration in profits, would it be right to assert that there was no other cause of variation but the greater or less quantity of labour necessary to produce them. Practically commodities vary very little on account of an alteration of profits, because profits, generally, vary very inconsiderably; but we are not less bound on that account to acknowledge that if profits did vary so would commodities.

I never had any doubt of Mr. Blake's being wrong; I am glad that the papers I sent you from Mr. Tooke were useful in shewing how the fact really was respecting the exchange with America.—

I shall be anxious to see your article on Taxation. Let me hear from you soon.

Very truly Yours

David Ricardo

545. MALTHUS TO RICARDO [1]
[Reply to 542.—Answered by 550]

E I Coll August 25th 1823

My dear Ricardo,

I am very much obliged to you for giving me your whole view on the subject of value by sending me your letter to M'Culloch.[2] I am a good deal engaged just at this moment, or should have answered your previous letter,[3] but I cannot return your letter to M'Culloch which I have read with great attention without a few words on its contents. I most fully agree with you in your remarks on his view of the subject. It does certainly appear to be a most unjustifiable and useless mode of applying the term, *labour worked up in a commodity* to the increase of value occasioned by the time it is necessary to keep it before it is brought to market; but I see no impropriety in saying with Adam Smith and myself that labour will *measure* not only that part of the whole value of the commodity which resolves itself into labour, but also that which resolves itself into profits. I of course quite agree with you in saying that the great mass of commodities is not produced by labour alone, but by the union of labour and capital; and consequently if I thought that my measure would not measure the profits of capital I would give it up without a moments hesitation; but it appears to me after the maturest consideration of all the objections which have been made to me, that it will measure both the quantity and the rate of profits accurately, and therefore will measure the value of an oak tree as well as of shrimps. You allow distinctly that my measure will measure the value of shrimps or of gold picked up on the sea shore. Now let us suppose for a moment that

[1] Addressed: 'D. Ricardo Esqr M.P. / Gatcomb Park / Minchinhampton / Gloucestershire.'

MS in Mill-Ricardo papers.
[2] Letter 544.
[3] Letter 542.

25 Aug. 1823

this gold which before was considered as being brought to market immediately must now be kept for a year before it is exchanged, and that profits were ten per cent, would not the exact difference between the value of the shrimps obtained by ten days labour and of the gold obtained by ten days, be ascertained by adding ten per cent to the labour employed upon the gold; and will not the gold in that case command 11 days labour, while the shrimps command ten, that is, will not the relative quantities of labour which they will command exactly measure the amount of the additional value given to the gold by the element of profits. Moreover if the natural and absolute condition of the supply of the shrimps were the employment of ten days labour, is it not correct to say that the natural and absolute value of the shrimps is measured by ten days labour; and in the same manner, as the gold in the case supposed could not be supplied without the addition of a value of ten per cent to the value of the labour employed, must it not be equally correct to say that the natural and absolute value of the gold in this case is measured by the eleven days labour. Apply this principle to the case of the cloth and wine which you have mentioned in the latter part of your letter, or to the case of the oak tree, and you will find it answer in every instance, whatever may be the variations of profits, or the length of time required to bring the commodity to market, while in all these cases of great variations or great length of time, your measure according to your own concessions would be greatly inaccurate.

You very justly say that as soon as we are in possession of the knowledge of the circumstances which determine the value of commodities we are enabled to say what is necessary to give us an invariable measure of value. Now what can determine the natural and absolute value of commodities, but the natural and absolute conditions of their supply.

Neither the advance of a certain quantity of corn nor even 25 Aug. 1823 of a certain quantity of money will secure this supply unless they will command the requisite quantity of labour. Labour is the real advance in kind and the profits may be correctly estimated upon the advances whatever they may be. Consequently it appears to me that the circumstances which determine the natural value of commodities must be the quantity of labour advanced, accumulated and immediate, with the profits upon such labour for the time that it has been employed; and if the quantity of labour so obtained be on an average the same as the quantity of labour which they will command, we are at once furnished with a ready measure of the *circumstances which determine the value of commodities,* or in other words an invariable measure of their value.

I cannot in the least degree enter into your view of the subject when you intimate, both in your letter to me and M'Culloch, that if my measure is a good measure for yours, yours must necessarily be as good a measure for mine. This appears to me the same thing as saying that if a foot will measure the variable height of a man, the variable height of a man will measure a foot. I say that my measure of a days labour, will measure the value of the variable quantity and value of cloth produced by a certain manufactory in a day; but surely the variable value of cloth will not measure the days labour. Supposing my measure to be invariable and yours not, mine would measure the variations of yours. Supposing your measure to be invariable, and mine not, yours would measure the variations of mine, but it is absolutely impossible that a variable measure can measure an invariable one. Thinking my measure an invariable one, I am [of]¹ opinion that it will shew the variations of yours occa-

¹ Omitted in MS.

sioned by the varying rate of profits, and that when you suppose the value of labour to rise, it is really only a fall in the value of money; because when we refer to the circumstances which determine the value of commodities, we shall find that money must have fallen in value, on account of the profits required to produce it having fallen, while the labour has remained the same. When you say that the value of wages necessarily rises as poorer land is taken into cultivation, you consider the value of wages as if it were composed of the element of labour alone, and not of labour and profits.

I am interrupted and can say no more without losing the post.

Ever truly Yours
T Rob^T Malthus.

546. McCULLOCH TO RICARDO [1]
[Reply to 544]

Edinburgh 24 Augt 1823

My Dear Sir

In so far as you differ in opinion with me on the vexata questio of value, I think the difference principally hinges on the interpretation we are to give to the word profit—Whether is the additional value we get back in exchange for a capital we have employed in production a compensation for time, or for our forbearance in not having consumed the capital immediately, or is it a positive additional value resulting from the employment of the capital and not dependent on time? If we agree in our answers to this question I think we

---

[1] Addressed: 'David Ricardo Esq M.P. / Gatcomb Park / Minchinhampton / Gloucestershire'. Edinburgh postmark, 25 Aug. 1823.

MS in *R.P.*—The greater part of this letter was incorporated, with slight changes, in the leading article of the *Scotsman,* 21 Feb. 1824, under the title 'Principles which determine the Exchangeable Value of Commodities and the Rate of Profit'.

shall agree in our opinions on value—Now, I think that
profit is not a compensation for time, but a positive additional value; and I think so for the reason that if I keep a cask
of wine a twelvemonth in which an effect is to be produced
I shall get a profit; whereas were I to keep a cask which had
already arrived at maturity and in which no effect was to be
produced for a hundred years I should get no profit whatever
—Suppose I have two capitals one a thousand pounds worth
of wine, and the other nine hundred pounds worth of leather
and £100 of money; if I throw the one into a cellar and give
the other to a shoemaker at the end of a year I should have
an equivalent value perhaps £1100 worth of wine and £1100
worth of shoes—Now, if the increased value of my capitals
be the effect of the change that has been operating on them,
and that it is so is certain from the fact that if I had either got
back the leather and money or the wine in the state they were
at the commencement of the year they would not have been
worth one farthing more, am I not entitled to say that this
increased value has been given to them by the operation of
agents which it cost equal capitals to set in motion and
furnish with materials whereon to exert themselves, and that
consequently both shoes and wine are the result of equal
quantities of labour? I admit that I should be wholly unable
to measure the increased value given to the leather or the
wine by a consideration of the effect produced; but the
essential point is to know that this increased value is not a
compensation for time but the result of a change operated
by agents which it has cost equal quantities of labour or
capital to set in motion—If I am right in this position I think
I shall have made a pretty decisive step towards the establishment of the principle for which I am contending: and
to shew that I am not right, you must shew that profits
are a compensation for time, and not the value of the

work performed by an agent set in motion by capital or labour—

Now with respect to the measure of profits—If I employ capitals in the building of houses, in the manufacture of cloth, or in commerce, I should be equally at a loss how to estimate the increased value or profit I am to get from them as if I had employed them in the production of wine—All that I should know was that the increased value, whatever it might be, was the result of labour: but to get a measure of that increased value I should be obliged to refer to agriculture—This is a branch of industry which *must* be carried on; and if the value of the various outgoings of the farmer be, as they always may be, reduced into corn, he is able by comparing these with his harvest to learn the precise additional value or profit that he obtains—It is by this profit that the profit of every other business will be regulated; and when 100 quarters employed on the worst land yields 110 quarters I shall know that £100 employed for an equal period in the production of wine will yield £110—My theory, therefore, is shortly this:—Profits are not a compensation for time but the value of an effect or operation; to produce this effect you must employ capital or labour, the effect being necessarily always equal when equally powerful agents, that is, equal capitals, are employed: and to measure the value of this effect or operation we are to refer for a standard to that branch of industry which must always be carried on, and whose profits can be determined by actual measurement—

You will observe how well this theory harmonises with your theory of profits; and this agreement is no slight presumption in its favour—

What you say about a piece of cloth and a pipe of wine seems to me to involve a fallacy—The piece of cloth is made, but the wine is *not* made—If the wine were made no effect would be produced by keeping it, and it would just as much as the cloth preserve the same value whatever might be the fluctuation of profits—

Neither does your objections, originating in the fluctuations to which capitals are liable, apply to my theory—If I were seeking a standard to measure values at distant periods they would apply and would be decisive; but this is no part of my object—I am only endeavouring to ascertain the circumstances which determine the comparative values of the commodities in the same market—The question agitated between you and Malthus is totally different—it is, what are the circumstances necessary to give invariability of value to any commodity?—This is a question which I believe is quite insoluble, but at any rate it does not come within the scope of my inquiries—I leave it to be settled by my masters— Before entering on this transcendental part of Pol Economy I must be more sure than I am at present of the elements; and before I attempt to get a measure of the value of cloth and wine in the reign of Augustus and George IV, I must obtain a measure of their value in the same market—

My opinions and those of Torrens differ materially— Torrens does not consider the labour of a man and the labour of a machine, or of the coals that are put on a fire in the same point of view: Now, whether right or wrong I consider them as exactly the same; and it is because I so consider them that I reckon it improper to make the distinction that he has done between immediate labour and the labour of capital—

I shall write you shortly on some points connected with Taxation, but I am sure you will be well pleased that I now close this long letter—I am with the greatest respect and esteem

Yours ever sincerely

J. R. M^cCULLOCH

547. TROWER TO RICARDO [1]
[*Reply to 533 & 535.—Answered by 549*]

Unsted Wood. August 26. 1823

My Dear Ricardo

26 Aug. 1823   After your long silence your late dispatch was particularly acceptable.—I well know how devoted your mind is, during the Sessions of parliament, to publick affairs, and what little leisure these leave You for the ordinary pursuits of life. I rejoice to see You so useful a member of parliament; and that your activity intelligence and tallents are so constantly employed for the publick good.—There is no pursuit, in which the mind can be engaged, more honorable or interesting; none more gratifying; and those are fortunate, who enjoy the means and the qualifications, which it requires.—

My attention has lately been drawn off, by a variety of circumstances, from the subject of political economy, I have not therefore yet seen Mr. Tooke's latter pamphlets; nor have I yet satisfied my mind on Malthus's last tract. This question of *measure of value* is a famous bone for the economists to pick; nor do I see how the matter is likely to be settled. If every measure be faulty, then the only course to be followed is to adopt that which is *least* so, and this is no easy question to determine. As to the term *Value,* I confess it does appear to me, that there is but one sense in which it can with propriety be employed; and that is in *relation* to the object for which it is to be *exchanged.* It is used to signify how much of one thing is worth or can procure so much of another thing. The determining the *measure* of this exchangeable value is a more difficult matter. To my mind *you* have

---

[1] Addressed: 'To / David Ricardo   MS in   *R.P.—Minor Papers,*
Esqr / M.P. / Gatcomb Park / Min-   pp. 220–23.
chinhampton'.

satisfactorily proved, that the *cost* of commodities is that measure. But, then comes the question what is to be included under the term *cost*. The *cost* of a commodity, no doubt, includes those expences, without which it cannot be produced. No commodity can be produced without *Labor,* and it is therefore said, that *Labor* is the necessary cost, the universal measure of value. But, *Labor itself* has its necessary *costs,* without which it cannot be produced; And these *costs* consist of a certain portion of the *necessaries of life,* and this portion is *constantly changing.* And, again, these *necessaries* cannot be obtained without *labor,* which is *their cost.* So that *Labor* is the *cost* of *necessaries,* and *necessaries* are the *cost* of *Labor!* And here is the difficulty—How are you to determine between them. If the earth had not brought forth its fruits, *spontaneously,* man could not have existed—Therefore *necessaries* had the *precedence* of Labor; but, if man had not stretched out his hand to gather these fruits, had he not thus appropriated them to himself, by his *Labor,* they would have been of no avail. Still, however, it may, perhaps, be doubted whether in the strictest, *earliest,* and simplest sense, it may not with truth be stated, that Labor is *not* an inevitable condition of the production[1] of necessaries, *as their cost;* whereas it can never be said, that *necessaries* are not the inevitable condition of the production of *Labor, as its cost.* Labor could not exist without necessaries. Necessaries may and do exist without Labor.—

I will not pursue these reflections further; into which I have been led inadvertently—I rejoiced to find by your letter, that so many choice spirits are engaged in the investigation of these interesting inquiries, and cannot doubt, that the result will prove satisfactory to the cause of science and of truth.—

[1] Replaces 'existence'.

I grieve at the continuance of this rainy weather. If it last much longer its effects will be very mischievous, and disappoint the sanguine expectations I had entertained of the gradual and steady improvement of agricultural affairs. But, in all these matters, which do not depend upon ourselves, my maxim is, that "*whatever is, is right.*"

The Spanish struggle is nearly over; and I rejoice in thinking that is. The grand object, to which I admit no other to be equal, is the *preservation of the peace of Europe*—And *this,* the course which events has taken, is likely to strengthen. Besides, the new spanish constitution is detestable; the people divided, and not yet ripe for the measures, the reformists are desirous of adopting. What do you think of the prospects of the holders of Spanish Stock? have You still got yours? I have mine.

How is the harvest in your neighborhood. I am glad You were upon the Irish Committee.[1] The interests of that Country are the most important subject, that can engage the attention of parliament. I still think, as I have long thought, that the most important measure would be to devise some means of preventing the subdivision of land into small tenements. How far consistently with the rights of private property, such an arrangement could be accomplished is, I am aware, a difficult question—But, the object in view is of great moment, and would justify a strong measure. Whether the imposition of any tax upon the proprietor of lands so leased, or the holding out of an encouragement to those who took farms beyond a certain quantity of land; or in what other way the object might be accomplished, I am not prepared to say; and am most ready, besides, to acknowledge the mischiefs of proceeding upon erroneous principles for the purpose of obtaining some supposed temporary advantage. I regret

[1] See above, p. 313, n. 2.

exceedingly that we are so far apart; and that difficulties of time and space are thus opposed in the way of our meeting. I feel a great desire to become acquainted with your residence and to take a peep at the beautiful Country that surrounds You. Besides, although letters are a most delightful resource to those who are necessarily separated by circumstances, yet this very intercourse begets the desire of a more easy and intimate interchange of sentiments, in which subjects, opinions which can be merely touched upon in letters may be pursued without limit, and expressed without reserve.—

Adieu My Dear Ricardo, pray remember Mrs. Trower and myself very kindly to Mrs. Ricardo and your family and believe me yours very sincerely—

HUTCHES TROWER

26 Aug. 1823

548. RICARDO TO MILL [1]
[*Reply to* 539]

Gatcomb Park 30 Augt 1823

My Dear Friend

Your last letter ought to have been noticed sooner, but I am always more pleased at receiving letters than in writing them, and in hearing what is passing in the minds and in the neighbourhoods of my friends, than in relating the less interesting matter that is passing in my own.

I am very much disappointed at the intelligence you give me that your visit here is to be a short one. Not only have you delayed it much beyond the time stipulated, but it is to be most unreasonably shortened. Mr. MCulloch and you have managed this matter very badly, and I cannot yet help hoping that you will, before you leave London, speak to your good natured chairman,[2] and arrange with him for a

30 Aug. 1823

---

[1] MS in Mill-Ricardo papers.　　[2] William Wigram; cp. p. 330.

longer absence from London than you now project. We should have been glad to have seen some of your children with you, and beg you now to bring any of them if you find it convenient. We regret that Mrs. Mill cannot on this occasion accompany you.

Since you have spent part of your holiday at Dorking, which ought to have been spent here, I am rejoiced to know that you have employed it profitably, and have actually got upon paper all that has been long floating in your mind on the difficult subject of Thought, Sensation, Association &c.ᵃ. I shall be greatly indebted to you if you make all these matters clear to me, for hitherto though I have occasionally paid a little attention to them, I have never been sure that I have accurately understood what the authors whose works I have read have wished to express. I believe the subject to be very difficult, but if any one can place it in a clear point of view, I am sure it is you. I long very much to see what you have done, and to profit by your labours.

It is singular that you and I should have selected the same book to read just at the same moment,—I was in the course of reading the correspondence between Voltaire and D'Alembert when I received your letter. Their letters have very much interested me, and nothing surprises me more than the fire and activity of Voltaire's mind, when borne down by age and infirmities. On the whole I think D'Alembert the best reasoner, and the most consistent man. His reproof to Voltaire for complying with some absurd religious ceremony, which every body knew Voltaire contemned and laughed at, is very well done; though I think he himself is not free from the imputation of useless and unnecessary hypocrisy on these matters, witness his remark on Bayle in the Encyclopedie which Voltaire notices. Voltaire's conduct in the affairs of Calas, Sirven, and De la Barre, was intrepid and manly, and entitles him to the gratitude and respect of all lovers of justice. The account of Voltaire's last visit to Paris and of his death which followed soon after as given by Grimm, and which is to be seen in the Review of his work in the Edinburgh,[1] is very interesting.

A great number of letters have passed between Malthus and me on the subject of "value". I have also had a couple from MCulloch on the same subject, but hitherto we have not much advanced the question. We proposed our measure, not as a perfect one, for we acknowledged its imperfections, but as the nearest approximation to a perfect one, and I still think that no better can be proposed, but Malthus tells us that his is perfect in every respect. He has always said, and says now, that if all commodities were produced under the same circumstances as our measure, it would be a perfect one, and he acknowledges it is a good measure for commodities now produced under the same circumstances. If this be true these commodities ought to vary exactly in the same degree, whether we use his measure or ours. Do they do so? certainly not; either then he must say that there may be two perfect measures of value which nevertheless measure un- equally, or he must give up one of them.

The grand cause, good government, is always present to my mind, but I hope it will have a better champion in the House of Commons. In every argument with my friends I do what I can to maintain the cause of truth, as far as I can see it, and frequently flatter myself that I am successful. I am quite sure that the good cause is advancing, though at a very moderate step, and all we can hope to do in our time is to help it a little forward.

My brother Moses has been with me some time, and will I hope not have quitted me when you come. He is in very

[1] *Edinburgh Review,* July 1813, Art. I, pp. 272–4.

30 Aug. 1823 good health and in excellent spirits. When in this state he is a most agreeable companion, for he is always ready to join in any pursuit. He is very deservedly a great favorite in this house.

Mrs. Ricardo and my girls are sensibly alive to all the kind expressions which you use in regard to them,—they confidently rely on retaining your favorable disposition, there is no chance of theirs towards you undergoing any change.

Mrs. Austin has been with us for a few days with her children, while her husband has been on a little jaunt of pleasure to Plymouth. We have all had great pleasure from this visit and it would have been without alloy if she had not had the misfortune of breaking a needle in her hand, one half of which went into it. She suffers a little pain, but cannot use her hand—I hope it will not be attended with any serious inconvenience to her.—

We have had two or three days, with scarcely any rain, which gives me hopes that we may be enabled to get the corn on the land safe into our barns—they say the harvest is a good one. I am very much surprised that the late weather had no greater effect on the markets.—

Ever truly Yours

DAVID RICARDO

549. RICARDO TO TROWER [1]
[Reply to 547.—Answered by 551]

Gatcomb Park
31 Aug! 1823

My Dear Trower

31 Aug. 1823   To make up for my former omissions I lose no time in replying to your last kind letter, and I am the more induced

---

[1] Addressed: 'Hutches   Trower   MS at University College, London.—*Letters to Trower*, LXIV.
Esqr / Unsted Wood / Godalming'.
Franked by Ricardo: 'August
Thirty one 1823'.

to do so, from a hope I entertain that you may not find it inconvenient to pay me a visit here in Gloucestershire. You say in your letter that you feel a great desire to become acquainted with my residence, and to take a peep at the beautiful country that surrounds me. Let me ask you then what hinders you from doing so? Travelling is now so easy all over England that it is no undertaking to go from your house to mine, and I beg seriously to call upon you to do it. I have some temptation too to offer you. I know you are pleased with Mill's company and although you do not quite agree in opinion with him, I am certain that you derive both pleasure and instruction from his conversation. Mill is coming to me in the middle of the next month (September), and you cannot do better than come at the same time—we shall all enjoy ourselves together—we shall walk and ride, we will converse on politics, on Political Economy, and on Moral Philosophy, and neither of us will be the worse for the exercise of our colloquial powers. I entreat you to take this matter into your serious consideration, and to assure Mrs. Trower that we will take great care of you if she will join us in promoting this little scheme.

Several letters have passed between Malthus and me on the subject of value, and one or two between MCulloch and me. We none of us exactly agree. MCulloch says he is not in search of a measure of value, his only object is to know what it is which regulates the relative value of commodities one to another, and that, he insists, is the quantity of labour necessary to produce them. But MCulloch uses the word labour in a sense somewhat different to Political Economists in general, and does not appear to me to see that if we were in possession of the knowledge of the law which regulates the exchangeable value of commodities, we should be only one step from the discovery of a measure of absolute value.

Malthus avows that he is in search of a measure of absolute value, he does more, he contends that he has found it, and that it is the value of daily labour which is the only permanent and unalterable measure of value. The reasons indeed by which he supports this opinion are far from satisfactory to me they seem so little convincing that I am sure he has not aided us in the search for this important measure.

I will mention only one contradiction as it seems to me of his. He says that my measure would be a perfect one if all commodities were produced under the same circumstances as my proposed measure, and that it is a perfect one for commodities so produced. Should not then my measure be as applicable to this description of commodities as his? and should not the commodities so particularised vary equally in his measure as in mine? they do not, therefore either my measure or his is not a correct one, or equally good measures will give different results.

The rain has given us a little respite here for two or three days, and we live in hopes that we shall be able to house the harvest from our fields.—The crop is said to be a good one. It is quite wonderful to me that corn has continued at so steady a price with the prospect which we have lately had. Can any thing more strongly prove that the supply in the country must have been very abundant than that corn should have risen no higher with so dismal a prospect as has lately been p[resen]ted[1] to us. Your maxim of "whatever is, is right" i[s in other] words [sayi]ng that what is inevitable must be patiently borne.

The preservation of the peace of Europe is a grand object, yet I cannot help regretting that the Spanish cause has not been better supported by the Spaniards themselves. If the French had been driven out of Spain, I do not see why the

---

[1] MS torn here and below.

peace of Europe w.^d have been disturbed. Other powers might indeed have joined in the attack, and the war would have probably ended as soon as the contest between liberty and despotism had been decided. I fear that Despotism will reign triumphantly for a time in consequence of the result of the present contest. I have sold my Spanish stock, I got for it rather a better price than that at which I purchased it.

I suppose that you continue to plant and improve at Unsted Wood and that you are now seeing in full beauty the effects of your former efforts in the same line. I forget whether your land is of a very good description, its being so or not makes a great difference in the progress of trees. I am living in a country where the soil is very poor. Beech flourishes with us, and larch and fir get on very well. I scarcely saw the place last year and therefore see the improvement of my small plantations more marked now than at any former period. As for improvements I attempt very few and am very much disposed to be satisfied with things as they are—Mrs. Ricardo on the contrary would always like to have a dozen men active in her employment, for the mere purpose of altering and improving.

Mrs. Ricardo and my family join with me in kind remembrances to Mrs. Trower.

Ever My Dear Trower
Truly Y.^rs
DAVID RICARDO

550. RICARDO TO MALTHUS [1]
[*Reply to* 545]

Gatcomb Park
31 Aug.ᵗ 1823

My Dear Malthus

I have only a few words more to say on the subject of value, and I have done. You cannot avail yourself of the argument that a foot may measure the variable height of a man, altho' the variable height of a man cannot truly measure the foot, because you have agreed that under certain circumstances the man's height is not variable, and it is to those circumstances that I always refer. You say of my measure, and say truly, that if all commodities were produced under the same circumstances of time &c.ᵃ as itself, it would be a perfect measure; and you say further that it is now a perfect measure for all commodities produced under such circumstances. If then under certain circumstances mine is a perfect measure, and yours is always a perfect one, under those circumstances certain commodities ought to vary in these two measures just in the same degree. Do they so? certainly not; then one of the measures must be imperfect. If they are both perfect mine ought to measure yours as well as yours mine.

There is no "impropriety in your saying with Adam Smith [2] that labour will measure not only that part of the whole value of the commodity which resolves itself into labour, but also that which resolves itself into profit," because it is the fact. But is not this true also of any variable measure you could fix on. Is it not true of Iron, Copper,

---

[1] Addressed: 'The Revᵈ T. R. Malthus / East India College / Hertford'. Franked by Ricardo 'September One 1823'.
    MS at Albury.—*Letters to Malthus,* LXXXVIII.

An earlier draft in Mill-Ricardo papers.
[2] *Wealth of Nations,* Bk. 1, ch. vi; Cannan's ed., vol. 1, p. 52.

31 Aug. 1823

lead, cloth, corn &c.ª &c.ª? The question is about an invariable measure of value, and your proof of invariability is that
it will measure profits as well as labour, which every variable
measure will also do.

I have acknowledged that my measure is inaccurate, you
say; I have so; but not because it would not do every thing
which you assert yours will do, but because I am not secure
of its invariability[1]. Shrimps are worth £10 in my money—
it becomes necessary, we will suppose, in order to improve
the shrimps to keep them one year, when profits are 10 pc.ᵗ,
shrimps at the end of that time will be worth £11. They have
gained a value of £1. Now where is the difference whether
you value them in labour and say that at the first period they
are worth 10 days labour and subsequently 11, or say that
at the first period they are worth 10£ and subsequently 11?

I am not sure that your language is accurate when you say
that "labour is the real advance in kind and [the][2] profits may
be correctly estimated upon the advances whatever they may
be." A Farmer's capital consists of raw produce, and his real
advances in kind are raw produce[3]. His advances are worth
and can command a certain quantity of labour undoubtedly,
and his profits are nothing unless the produce he obtains will
command more if he estimates both advances and profits in
labour, but so it is in any other commodity in which he may
value his advances and returns. Does it signify whether it
be labour or any other thing, provided there be no reason to
suspect that it has altered in value? I know that you will say
that provided his produce is sure to[4] command a certain
quantity of labour he is sure of being able to reproduce, not
so if he estimates in any other thing, because that thing and

---

[1] 'to which I say yours is still more subject' is del. here.
[2] Omitted in MS.
[3] Draft has here in addition: ', which he expects to have re-turned to him with a profit'.
[4] In draft 'can' instead of 'is sure to'.

31 Aug. 1823 labour may have undergone a great relative alteration. But may not the real alteration be in the value of labour, and if he act on the presumption of its remaining at its then rate may he not be wofully mistaken, and be a loser instead of a gainer? Your argument always supposes labour to be of an uniform value, and if we yielded that point to you there would be no question between us. A manufacturer who uniformly used no other measure of value than that which you recommend would be as infallibly liable to great disappointments as he is now exposed to in the vulgar variable medium in which he is accustomed to estimate value.

And now my dear Malthus I have done. Like other disputants after much discussion we each retain our own opinions. These discussions however never influence our friendship; I should not like you more than I do if you agreed in opinion with me.

Pray give Mrs. Ricardo's and my kind regards to Mrs. Malthus

Y^{rs} truly

DAVID RICARDO

551. TROWER TO RICARDO [1]
[*Reply to* 549.—*Answered by* 553]

Unsted Wood. Septr 3. 1823.

My Dear Ricardo

3 Sept. 1823 Many thanks for your kind letter—You have placed a temptation in my way, which I find it very difficult to withstand; and which I should not feel quite satisfied with myself if I *did*. It would not be a very gracious return for your kind invitation; nor would it evince any great desire for the pleasure I shall have in visiting you.—I will, therefore accept your agreeable offer of passing a few days with You

[1] MS in *R.P.*

at Gatcomb—I am afraid, however, I cannot contrive to be 3 Sept. 1823
with You exactly at the times You mention—No doubt,
I should rejoice in an opportunity of meeting Mr. Mill, of
whom I think very highly, and whose company and conversation are edifying and agreeable to me.—

But, unfortunately, my engagements are such, that I should
not be able to be with you before the end of the Month, say
the 30th.—

Next week I am going into Sussex, first, to pass a few days
with my Brother John at Muntham, and then to go to Newick
Park to my Brother in Law Mr. Slater.—On our return from
Sussex we have a short visit to pay in this neighborhood. So
that I should not be able to go hence to London before the
29th and to start for Gatcomb the following day.—

If this period should be perfectly convenient to you have
the goodness to suggest by what publick conveyance I had
better travel; whence it sets out, and at what hour; and where
I shall be deposited. I prefer travelling by *day* rather than
by *night;* if there is an option in the case, and no strong
arguments in favor of the Mail—I like to sleep when I am
in bed, and to be awake when I am up; with full power to
exercise those windows of the soul, which are the light and
the life of our existence.—

I am looking over Malthus' Measure of Value again, and
I confess I find it difficult to know what he would be at. To
my poor capacity he is very obscure; and I think inconsistent.

To me it appears, that whatever is the measure of absolute
value will be the measure of exchangeable value. Labor
originally was that measure; or, more properly speaking, the
necessaries which labor requires; but now to these must be
added the expences and profit on capital or in other words
the *costs of production.* I think the subject is rendered more
obscure by confounding with immediate labor, what is called

accumulated labor, but which in fact is capital—It is most important, that these two ideas should be kept distinct; because labor and capital, are, if I may so express myself, in constant opposition to each other. The employment and the rewards of labor depending upon the amount of capital. How Malthus can satisfy himself of the unalterable value of labor, I cant conceive, to me it is a compleat puzzle. Nor can I subscribe to some of his doctrines with respect to profit. He appears to forget, that it is the residue, *the surplus* after all expences are paid. These expences must have a constant influence upon the rate of profit, yet I dont see how the rate of profit is to influence these expences. And yet he talks of the fall of value *on account* of the fall in profits.—

I have often thought, that a useful view of the subject might be taken by excluding profit from the costs of production, and by exhibiting it in its true light, as the *surplus produce*—

In point of fact, it may be truly said, that the payment of profits is not a *necessary condition* of production—Production, to *a limited* extent, would, and does take place without it. The production necessary to a man's support does not require profit, nor does it always obtain it. There may be no surplus produce; there may be just sufficient to support the labor during the process of production, and no more. But, of this sufficient for the present as I am happy in thinking, that, ere long, I shall enjoy the opportunity of entering with more fredom into these and other topicks—

Mrs. Trower begs to join with me in kind regards to Mrs. Ricardo yourself and family and I remain

Yrs very truly—

HUTCHES TROWER

552. RICARDO TO MILL [1]

Gatcomb Park
5 Sepr 1823

My Dear Friend

John's paper [2] does not quite remove our difficulty. He acknowledges that "profits are only the wages of a particular kind of labour". Commodities vary then with the wages of this kind of labour—or rather they vary in proportion as the wages of the two kinds of labour affect them. If so, they do not vary in proportion to the quantity of labour employed on them, but in proportion to the wages paid for such labour. Commodities being made up of wages and profits, they vary in the degree that varying wages and profits may affect them.

It is true that the profits received by a man who keeps wine for a great number of years is no more than equivalent to what another man receives under another form, and immediately. We all agree with respect to the facts, but it is impossible to say that the value of commodities is proportioned to the quantity of labour employed upon them. A pipe of wine is double the value of a piece of cloth! and let me grant that it is so because double the quantity of labour is expended on it. No alteration takes place in the quantity of labour employed on either commodity, and yet wine rises to be as $2\frac{1}{10}$ to the cloth. Nothing has occurred but an alteration in the wages of the two species of labour. Com-

[1] Addressed: 'J. Mill Esqr / East India House / London'. Franked by Ricardo: 'Minchinhampton September Five 1823'. London postmark, 6 Sept. 1823.
 MS in Mill-Ricardo papers.
 On the same day (5 September) Ricardo was struck with his fatal illness (see the following letters).
[2] This paper has not been found.

It is a curious coincidence that the *Morning Chronicle* of the same date as this letter contains an unsigned article by John Stuart Mill on the Measure of Value (cp. the list of his writings mentioned above, IV, 7, n. 1); this, however, is a review of Malthus's pamphlet and does not contain the points discussed by Ricardo in the letter.

modities alter then in relative value not on account only of an alteration in the quantity of labour expended on them but also on account of the variation in the wages given for these two species of labour. Malthus supposes a man to pick up a certain number of grains of gold in a day, and no change to take place in the produce obtained by his labour, but that he always picks up the same quantity precisely. I suppose the same number of grains of gold to be produced in a year by the two species of labour. If we value the wine and the cloth in these two equal quantities of money before and after the variation of wages and profits they will appear to have varied in very different degrees. In which ought we to value them? Malthus says in his, because his is an invariable measure of value, always having the same quantity of labour employed on it. I say in mine, because mine also has always the same quantity of labour bestowed on it. In his measure there enters no profit, in mine there does.

Does not John mean that a commodity produced by the labour of one man for twelve months is of equal value with a commodity produced by the labour of 12 men in one month? If that is his meaning, he is in an error; the commodity produced in the twelve month will be the most valuable and the degree in which it will be so will depend on the rate of profits,—it would be more if profits were 10 pc^t than when they fell to 5 pc^t. With which shall we measure all things, with the commodity produced in 12 months or in one month, with the commodity produced in 5 years or that produced in one day? Say which you give the preference to, and why. I am persuaded that the selection must be arbitrary,—that they are all imperfect measures, and yet there are good reasons why amongst them one should be selected and why that one should be the commodity produced in a year.

My principal objection against John is that he proposes to prove that commodities are valuable in proportion to the quantity of labour expended on them, and then proves that capital is another name for labour; profit a name for the wages of that labour; and therefore commodities are valuable in proportion to *wages* of all descriptions *paid* for the production of them. Is not this to say that the value of commodities depends upon the value of wages and profits? If he said so he would say what is true, but the proposition is a different one from that which he first advances.

The four salmon, caught with a net, which has cost one days labour, will exchange for more than 2 deer, for the same reason that the labour of one man for twelve months is worth more than the labour of twelve men for one month; and eight salmon caught with a net made in a day, and which will last 2 days, are worth more than three deer; and therefore "capital enters into value otherwise than labour in a particular form and is paid at a different rate with immediate labor". I do not know whether I have made myself understood. John does not allow for profits increasing at a compound rate. The profits for 5 years are more than 5 times the profits of one, and the profits of one year more than 52 times the profits for one week, and it is this which makes a great part of the difficulty. Beg him to consider this and to let me know if I am wrong in my critique on his paper. I have been thinking a good deal on this subject lately but without much improvement—I see the same difficulties as before and am more confirmed than ever that strictly speaking there is not in nature any correct measure of value nor can any ingenuity suggest one, for what constitutes a correct measure for some things is a reason why it cannot be a correct one for others.—

Y^{rs} ever

DAVID RICARDO

553. A. AUSTIN TO TROWER [1]
[*Reply to 551*]

Gatcomb Park 6 Sept[r] 1823

My Dear Sir,

6 Sept. 1823   I am grieved to tell you that Mr. Ricardo is at this moment confined to his bed by an Illness originating from cold in the ear. The Ladies have been in constant attendance at his bedside for the last 2 days it has therefore devolved on me to write to you.

There is at present every appearance that a day or two will restore our Friend to health and that he will be able to enjoy your society on the 30th Inst. when he hopes to have the pleasure of seeing you here.

Should he contrary to all our expectations have a relapse you shall hear again. The information I have been able to obtain about the stage coaches is that there is one daily to Stroud (5 miles from here) and one 3 times a week to Minchin Hampton (one mile from here), the latter travels by night.

I am
My Dear Sir
Yours very truly
ANTH[Y] AUSTIN.

544. A. AUSTIN TO TROWER [2]

My Dear Sir

12 Sept. 1823   To correspond with you, one of my earliest friends would be a pleasing occupation if the nature of the com-

---

[1] Addressed: 'H. Trower Esq[re] / Unsted Wood / Godalming'.
  MS at University College, London.—*Letters to Trower*, LXV.
  The writer was Ricardo's son-in-law.

[2] Addressed: 'H. Trower Esq[re] / Unsted Wood / near Godalming', and redirected: 'J H Slater Esq[r] / Newick Park / Uckfield'.
  MS at University College, London.—*Letters to Trower*, LXVI.

munication I am unfortunately called upon to make had not converted it into a painful task—one which I should most unwilling have undertaken if any one of the Gatcomb family had been capable of performing it but the most unexpected death of our much esteemed, (I may say universally esteemed) friend Mr D. Ricardo has been too great a shock to be easily overcome. You will I dare say be anxious to hear the cause of this misfortune I will therefore just state the outline of the case. The cold in the ear produced a gathering attended with the most acute pain and so great a degree of consequent inflammation that the bone was injured and the injury communicated to the brain and caused a formation of matter there.

It is some satisfaction to know that every thing which the very best medical and surgical skill, and the most unremitted and affectionate attention could do was done to alleviate his sufferings and preserve his life, a life valuable not only to his own family and relations but to his country also. I will not attempt to describe to you the feelings of those who witnessed the event—you may conceive and I doubt not will sympathise with them. I am

My Dear Sir,

Yours most truly

ANTH^Y AUSTIN.

Bradley
    near Wottonunderedge, Septr 12. 1823.

This melancholy event happened yesterday at about noon and I returned home with Mrs. Austin in the evening I am in hopes that Mrs. A.'s bodily health has not suffered very materially from her constant attendance on her Poor Father. To time we must leave the cure of her mental sufferings

555. MILL TO MᶜCULLOCH [1]

East India House 19ᵗʰ Sept: 1823

My Dear Sir

You and I need not tell to one another how much we grieve on this deplorable occasion. With an estimate of his value in the cause of mankind, which to most men would appear to be mere extravagance, I have the recollection of a dozen years of the most delightful intercourse, during the greater part of which time he had hardly a thought or a purpose, respecting either public, or his private affairs, in which I was not his confidant and adviser.

My chief purpose in writing is the relief I shall find in communicating with the man who of all the men in the world estimated my lamented friend most exactly as I did; and also, in case you should not have received the particulars of his illness from any other quarter to give you a few details which will be interesting to you.

The malady commenced with a pain in the ear, which resembled a common ear-ache, and which they treated as the effect of some little cold. He suffered somewhat on the sunday night,[2] but had little pain remaining after he got up the next day; and the same symptoms were repeated for several nights and days. Towards the end of the week the suffering increased, and became dreadful, when the strongest applications were deemed necessary. On the saturday night the imposthume broke, and the pain abated: but so much was he reduced, and the whole frame affected, that they continued in considerable alarm. On tuesday morning however, he

---

[1] Addressed: '—MᶜCulloch Esq. / Scotsman Newspaper Office / Edinburgh' and marked 'private'. Seal 'JSM', cp. above, p. 331, n. 3. MS in British Museum.—

Printed in A. Bain, *James Mill,* 1882, pp. 209–11; and *Letters to MᶜCulloch,* XLV.

[2] 31 August.

seemed decidedly better, and Mrs. Ricardo wrote to me,
describing what had happened, and urging me to make a
run down to Gatcomb, as likely to help in cheering
the dear sufferer, and accelerating his convalescence. This
letter I received on the wednesday morning; and on the
friday morning I received a few lines from poor Mary,
written at twelve oclock on thursday, and stating that
they were all assembled in the adjoining room, waiting
every moment for the dissolution of her beloved father.
The pain in the head had returned, and after a period of
unspeakable agony, pressure on the brain ensued, which
produced first delirium, and then stupor, which continued
till death.

I have had several communications from the family since;
one from Mr. Moses Ricardo yesterday. Their sufferings
you who know how he was loved and how he was valued
can easily conceive. Of Mrs. Ricardo he says, that "though
she is looking shockingly, she does not complain, and
bears her loss with resignation and fortitude." The health
of those who are younger is less likely to be seriously
invaded.

There is a point which I must mention, though I shall
probably have to write to you about it more at length hereafter. Some of us have been talking of the desirableness of
some appropriate testimony of respect for his memory: and
the foundation of a lectureship of political economy, to be
marked by his name, has suggested itself. The thing will be
seriously considered, and you shall hear.[1]

I have only room to add, that as you and I are his two and
only two genuine disciples, his memory must be a bond of

---

[1] A fund was raised to support a Ricardo Lectureship on Political Economy for ten years; McCulloch was chosen as the lecturer. (See Bain, *James Mill*, p. 214.)

connection between us. In your friendship I look for a compensation for the loss of his.

Most truly Yours

J. Mill

Excuse me for addressing this to the Scotsman Newspaper Office—as I know not but there may be another of your name in Edin., and am anxious that this letter should certainly reach you.

INDEX OF CORRESPONDENTS
IN VOLUMES VI – IX
1810–1823

* denotes letters not previously published

Gatton Park
31 Aug. 1823

F

My Dear Malthus

I have only a few words more to say on

the subject of value, and I have done. You cannot avoid yourself
of the argument that a foot may measure the variable height of
a man, altho' the variable height of a man cannot truly measure
the foot, because you have agreed that under certain circumstances
the measure being it is not variable, and it is to those circumstances
that I always refer. You say of my measure, a very truly. that

that labour will measure not only that part of the whole value of the commodity which resolves itself into labour, but also that which resolves itself into profit, because it is — the fact that is not the true also of any divisible measure you will fix on, I do not know to am Copper, lead, cloth, corn exist?? The question is about an invariable measure of value, your proof of invariability is that it will measure profits as well as labour, which every variable measure will also do.

I have acknowledged that any measure is invariable you may — I have to, but not because it would not do every thing which you — you that you will do, but because I am not sure of its invariability, ~~————————————~~ however are worth £10 in any way in it becomes necessary we will support, in order to improve the 'things', perhaps to keep them one year when profits are safe', perhaps at the end of that time will be worth £11. They have gained a value of £1. Now where is the difference whether you value them in labour and say that at the first period they are worth 10 they, labour & consequently 11, a say that at the first period they are worth 10 £ subsequently 11 ?

I am not sure that your language is accurate when you say that "labour" is the real advance in kind & profits may be wrongly estimated upon the advance whatever they may be to Farmers reputed amounts of raw produce, & in real advances in kind are raw produce. The advances are worth & in raw produce

a certain quantity of his own land entirely, & his profits are nothing unless the producer be obtain will command more if he is traded with advance, & perhaps in labour, but is it in in any other commodity in which he may wish he advance & return. Does it signify whether it be labour or any other things provided there be no reason to suspect that it has altered in value? I know you will say that provided his purchase is sure to command a certain quantity of labour he is sure of being able to reproduce, but is it he is traded in in any other thing, because that thing a labour may have undergone a great relative alteration. But may not the real alteration be in the value of labour, and if he not on the presumption of its ever recurring at its then will may he not be wofully mistaken, & be a loser instead of a gainer? Your arguments always suppose labour to be of an uniform value, and if we yielded that point to you there would be no

& we know between us, A manufacturer may
other measure of value than that which you recommend were
to be infallibly liable to greater disagreements as he is now
exposed to in the various remote medium on which he is
accustomed to estimate value.

And now my dear Brother I have done; Like other
disputants often would disagree we each retain our own
opinions. These discussions however never influence our
friendship; I should not like your more than I do if you
agreed in opinion with me.

Pray give Mrs. Ricardo & my kind regard to Mr. Matthew

Y.rs truly
David Ricardo

Manufactured in England Dec 1823

The Rev.d Mr T. R. Malthus

East India College

Hertford

David Ricardo

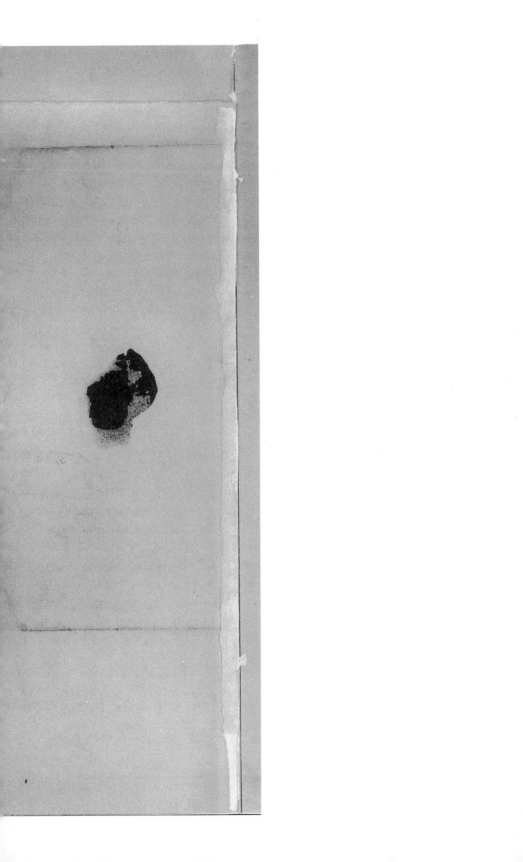